Susan McEwen McIntosh

Oxmoor House, Inc.
Birmingham

Book Division of Southern Progress Corporation
P.O. Box 2463, Birmingham, Alabama 35201

Southern Living ® Cooking Light

Library of Congress Catalog Number: 83-60431
ISBN: 0-8487-0545-9

Manufactured in the United States of America
Second Printing 1984

Southern Living ®

Foods Editor: Jean Wickstrom Liles
Senior Foods Photographer: Charles E. Walton IV
Photo Stylist: Beverly J. Morrow
Test Kitchens Staff: Lynn Lloyd (Director), Diane Hogan, Debby Maugans, Nancy Nevins, Connie Shedd, Peggy Smith, and Fran Tyler

Oxmoor House, Inc.

Manager, Editorial Projects: Ann H. Harvey
Production Manager: Jerry R. Higdon
Production Editor: Joan E. Denman
Foods Editor: Katherine M. Eakin
Copy Editor: Melinda E. West
Editorial Assistant: Karen P. Traccarella

Designer: Faith Nance
Illustrator: Robin Nance

Cover: *Treat your family or special guests to a satisfying main course of Marinated Beef Kabobs with Rice, Broccoli with Horseradish Sauce, and Cheesy Italian Salad. Even with Glazed Strawberry Dessert, calories stay under 600 for the entire meal (menu begins on page 70).*

Page i: *Swiss Cheese Sauce (page 203), Yogurt-Herb Sauce (page 203), and Basic Cheese Sauce (page 203) can transform a simple vegetable into an elegant side dish. Yogurt-Herb Sauce is especially good with steamed asparagus.*

Page ii: *The different shapes and colors of vegetables give Chinese Beef Stir-Fry its visual appeal. Serve this nutritious entrée with rice. Begin the meal with Oriental Spinach Soup and end with Gingered Fruit and Light Almond Cookies for dessert (menu begins on page 61.)*

Back Cover: *Use fresh or unsweetened canned fruit to keep calories low. Clockwise from front: Poached Pears with Pineapple Sauce (page 122), Fresh Fruit with Honey Cream (page 120), Light Raspberry Mousse (page 126), lemon sherbet with Mandarin Sauce (page 200), and Peach-Yogurt Shake (page 101).*

CONTENTS

AUTHOR'S NOTE

Readers of *Southern Living* magazine came up with the idea. They asked for recipes low in fat and calories. Letters from across the South poured in requesting delicious, sensible recipes that would make a low-calorie diet tolerable, and even enjoyable. As a result, in January 1982, "Cooking Light" appeared in the pages of *Southern Living* magazine. And every month since then, "Cooking Light" has delighted calorie-conscious cooks with a variety of delectable, nutritious recipes and menus.

The result? You have it in your hands. Because of the popularity of "Cooking Light" in the magazine, we now offer you the *Cooking Light* cookbook from *Southern Living* — a comprehensive reduced-calorie cookbook filled with over 500 easy-to-follow, great tasting recipes.

In the following pages you'll find everything from appetizers to salads, breads, and desserts — recipes that you expect to eat on a diet plus those recipes that you do not. Who would have thought that a dieter could have pizza? But this and every other recipe have been carefully tested in one of the *Southern Living* kitchens and calculated for calories by a registered dietitian.

The intent of this cookbook is to show you that nutritious, low-calorie eating can be enjoyable. We suggest a healthier way of preparing food that can (and should) be followed not just for a month or two in an effort to lose a few pounds, but for a lifetime. We want to help you reach your ideal body weight and stay there.

Along with the 500 delicious, reduced-calorie recipes, we offer information on how you can trim away calories in your own recipes. We've included suggestions on what to look for in the grocery store and how to use herbs and spices in place of the usual higher calorie seasonings.

You may know how to prepare reduced-calorie recipes, but if you can't put the recipes together into a menu plan, your work is all in vain. That's why we've included menus for breakfast, lunch, and dinner — some casual and some perfect for entertaining. There's a whole section on reduced-calorie meals for the microwave that will help you save time as well as calories.

Because it's often difficult to cook for two without leftovers, we have included several recipes and menus scaled down for only two servings. Follow our ingredient amounts, and you'll have just enough for you and your dieting partner.

For further guidance, we offer a weekly menu plan for 1200 calories a day and one for 1600 calories a day. And since we want *Cooking Light* to be your comprehensive, reduced-calorie cooking and eating guide, we've included a chart with information on the calorie, protein, fat, carbohydrate, and sodium content to be found in the most common foods and ingredients.

Read on — and enjoy your new adventure into cooking and eating light!

Susan M. McIntosh
Registered Dietitian

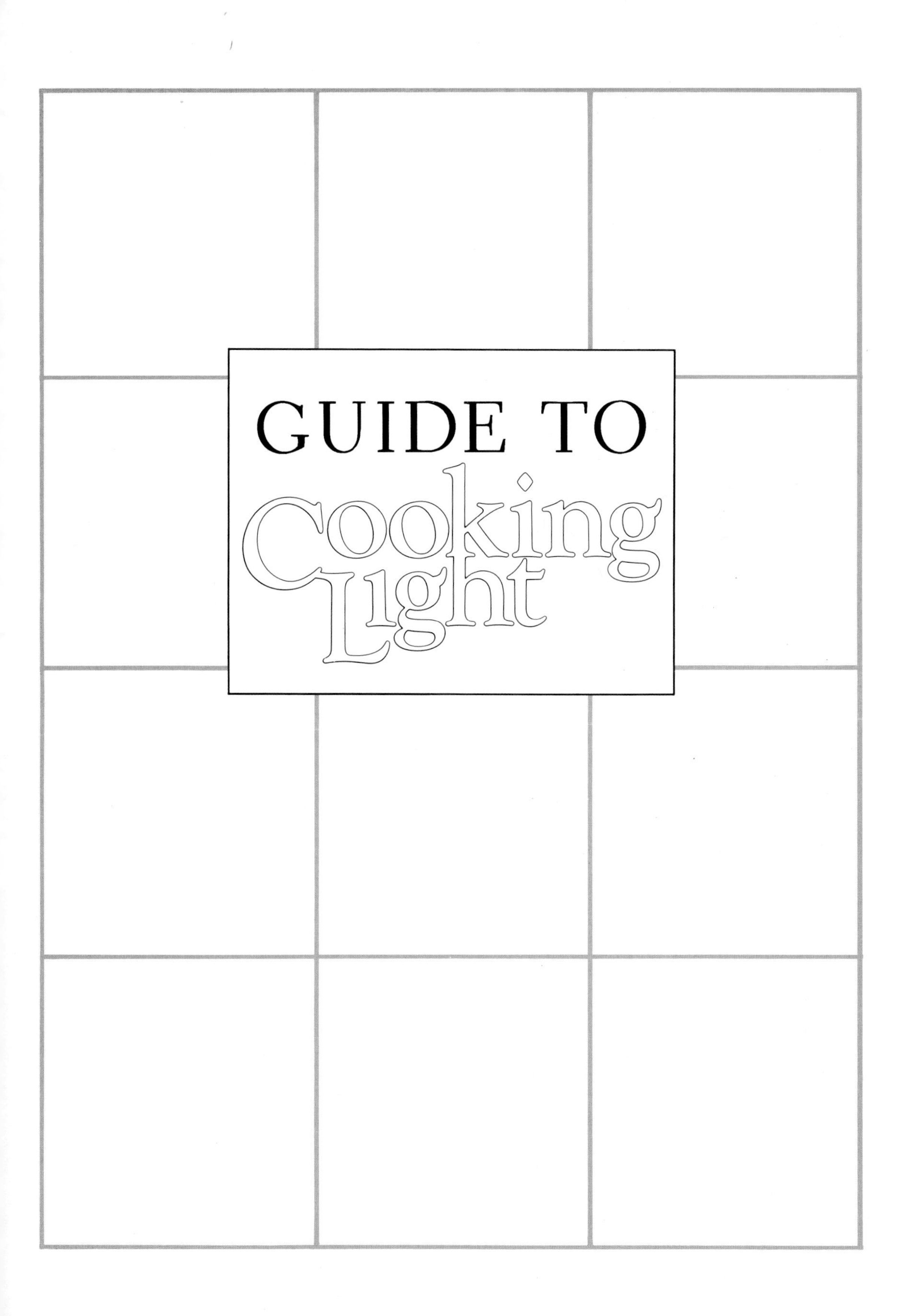
GUIDE TO
Cooking
Light

WHY COOK LIGHT?

We all like to look good, and in today's society "looking good" often implies being the right weight. What we eat, how much we exercise, and our body make-up all affect how we look. So for most of us, "looking good" is one of the best reasons for *Cooking Light*.

But if that's not reason enough, nutrition experts have told us that we need to control what we eat in order to live longer, healthier lives. Based on years of research, many scientists and registered dietitians have made recommendations about specific eating habits.

These recommendations have been incorporated into our recipes and menu plans. Here are the recommendations and an explanation of what they actually mean.

VARIETY OF FOODS

The human body needs over 50 different nutrients to grow and function — these nutrients include protein, fat, carbohydrates, vitamins, minerals, and water. While most foods contain more than one nutrient, no individual food contains all nutrients. To assure yourself of a balanced diet, it's important to **Eat A Variety Of Foods** daily from each of the five basic food groups:

- fruit and vegetables
- breads and cereals
- fish, poultry, meat, eggs, and legumes
- milk, cheese, and other dairy products
- fats and oils

Some popular fad diets recommend limiting the foods you eat to only three or four of these groups. However, when a dieter leaves off one or more of the groups, he lessens his chances of taking in all of the nutrients his body needs to function properly.

IDEAL BODY WEIGHT

Most of us feel better when we're not overweight. What's more, individuals at their ideal weight have a better chance of staying healthy. People who are overweight are more likely to develop high blood pressure, diabetes, and increased fat in the blood, and they have an increased risk of heart attack and stroke. The second recommendation is to **Reach And Maintain An Ideal Body Weight**.

If you've suddenly gone from a size 12 to a size 14 or can look in the mirror and see bulges that weren't there last year, you probably need to lose weight. Perhaps you have not noticed a weight gain until your doctor brings it to your attention. Whatever the case, the time to get started losing excess weight is now.

A general guide for determining a woman's ideal body weight is to allow 100 pounds for the first 5 feet of height plus 5 pounds for every inch over 5 feet. Therefore, the estimated ideal weight for a woman 5 feet 4 inches tall is 120 pounds.

The ideal body weight for a man is 106 pounds for the first 5 feet of height plus 6 pounds for every inch over 5 feet. A man measuring 5 feet 10 inches tall should weigh about 166 pounds.

These formulas are for men and women with average body frames. Subtract 10 percent from the above ideal body weight for men and women with small body frames, and add 10 percent to the ideal body weight for individuals with large body frames.

If you're excessively overweight or have other health problems, check with your doctor before beginning a weight-loss program.

FAT

Americans on the average eat too much fat. Dietary fat includes butter, margarine, vegetable oil, shortening, and the marbling in meat. Since fat is so high in calories, too much fat in the diet may result in excess weight gain. Nutritionists recommend that we **Cut Back On Dietary Fat** in an effort to reach and maintain ideal body weight.

Much of the fat we eat is from animal sources (meat, eggs, cheese, butter, and whole milk) which contain saturated fat and cholesterol. Some researchers think that eating foods high in saturated fat and cholesterol may increase levels of cholesterol in the blood, and that high levels of blood cholesterol will increase the risk of heart disease. Since there is still conflicting evidence on this subject, definite recommendations on cholesterol and saturated fat intake are varied.

STARCH AND FIBER

Nutritionists recommend that we **Eat Starchy, High-Fiber Foods Often**. Starchy foods such as potatoes, bread, and rice are sources of complex carbohydrates, some protein, and many of the vitamins and minerals which the body needs to function properly.

Most starchy foods are high in fiber, the part of food which cannot be easily digested by the body. A certain amount of fiber or roughage is needed in the diet to help prevent constipation. In addition, starchy, high-fiber foods help to control the appetite because they fill you up quickly.

Starchy, high-fiber foods are valuable to dieters and non-dieters alike. The high-calorie butter, sauces, and spreads often added to these foods during preparation or at the table are the extras which should be avoided.

SUGAR

Sugar, like starchy foods, is a source of carbohydrate. But unlike potatoes and rice, sugar provides only calories — no vitamins, minerals, fiber, or protein.

Eating too many foods high in sugar can lead to weight gain. Experts estimate that the average American eats over 100 pounds of sugar and other sweeteners a year. This includes the sugar added to coffee and tea, as well as the sugars and syrups in candies, soft drinks, ice cream, and breakfast cereals.

The fourth recommendation is that we **Avoid Too Much Sugar.** Cutting back on the amount of sugar sprinkled on food and limiting the intake of processed and convenience food items containing sugar are important steps in cutting calories.

SODIUM

If you've been told that you have hypertension (high blood pressure), consuming less sodium will help you keep your blood pressure under control. Even if your blood pressure is normal, you should **Avoid Too Much Sodium** in the diet.

Small amounts of sodium are required for each of us, but research has shown that in excess, sodium is a major factor in the development of high blood pressure, heart attack, stroke, and kidney disease.

ALCOHOL

Alcohol, like sugar, contributes little to our diets other than calories — and alcohol calories do add up quickly. Alcohol in moderation does not seem to be a threat to health, but heavy drinking can be a serious problem.

A person who drinks excessively often loses his appetite for other food. Vitamin and mineral deficiencies may result because of poor diet and because alcohol decreases the body's ability to absorb nutrients.

The recommendation, then, is **If You Drink Alcohol, Do So In Moderation.**

NUTRITION BASICS

The focus of *Cooking Light* is on the food we eat. Therefore, it is important to understand the composition of food and why some foods make better choices for our diets than other foods.

CALORIES

One of the most commonly used words in a dieter's vocabulary is "calorie." A calorie is a measure of energy (the capacity to do work) supplied by food. The body needs calories to live — for body functions such as breathing, heartbeat, and nutrient metabolism, and for physical activity such as running, swimming, or just talking.

When you take in more calories from food than your body burns for energy, the extra calories are stored as fat. A total of 3500 extra calories will result in one pound of body fat.

The only way to lose that extra body fat is to eat fewer calories than your body needs for energy or to burn extra calories by increasing your level of activity.

You can see that you'll have to cut your caloric intake by 500 calories a day, or burn up 500 extra calories in physical activity, to lose one pound of body fat in a week.

(7 days x 500 calories per day =
3500 calories = 1 pound of body fat)

All foods contain calories — some more than others. The number of calories a food contains depends on the amounts of water, carbohydrate, protein, fat, and alcohol present in the food. Water contains no calories; carbohydrate and protein each contain 4 calories per gram (or 112 calories per ounce); fat contains 9 calories per gram (252 calories per ounce); and alcohol contains 7 calories per gram (196 calories per ounce).

Foods high in fat such as whipping cream or a heavily marbled steak contain a relatively large number of calories; foods low in fat but with a high percentage of water such as cucumbers and tomatoes are lower in calories.

PROTEIN

Everyone needs protein to build, maintain, and repair body tissue. Protein makes up insulin, which regulates blood sugar; hemoglobin, which transports oxygen in the blood; and enzymes which help to digest food. Protein is also required for the formation of disease-fighting antibodies.

Protein can be burned as energy at a rate of 4 calories per gram. If the body does not receive enough calories from fat or carbohydrate, it will look to protein as an energy source, even at the expense of other important body-building activities.

Most of us eat much more protein than is needed for building, maintaining, and repairing body tissue. Experts recommend that the average adult man consume about 56 grams of protein per day and the average woman about 44 grams per day.

It may surprise you to learn that if you include 3 ounces cooked chicken, 1 cup milk, 2 slices whole wheat bread, and 1 tablespoon peanut butter in a day's meal plan, you will have eaten about 46 grams of protein. When you consider that many people eat meat at least twice a day plus other foods such as rice, spinach, and beans which supply additional protein, it is easy to see that we consume far more protein than our bodies need.

Any excess protein eaten will be used by the body as fuel for energy or stored as body fat. Therefore, you can gain weight from eating too much protein just as you can from eating too much fat and carbohydrate.

Protein is made up of 22 amino acids, eight of which are considered essential (cannot be manufactured within the body). The body can produce any of the remaining non-essential amino acids not present in the food we eat. All eight essential amino acids must be present for protein to perform its work adequately. Therefore, it's important to include foods which can provide sufficient amounts of the eight essential amino acids at each meal. Animal products (fish, poultry, meat, eggs, milk, and cheese) are called "complete proteins" since they contain all eight essential amino acids needed by the body.

By contrast, the proteins in vegetables such as dried beans and peas, seeds, and grains are considered "incomplete" since they contain only some of the essential amino acids.

In order for vegetable protein to equal the quality of animal protein, it is important to combine two or more vegetable proteins at one meal. If one vegetable contains the amino acid lacking in the second vegetable, the protein quality of the second vegetable is improved, and vice versa. Vegetable proteins complement each other when they are combined to improve total protein quality. Milk and milk products may also be used to complement vegetable proteins. Complementary proteins must be eaten at the same time for maximum benefit.

Some common examples of complementary proteins include:

- Macaroni and cheese (grain and milk)
- Red beans and rice (legume and grain)
- Peanut butter sandwich and milk (legume, grain, and milk)
- Dried beans or peas and cornbread (legume and grain)
- Sunflower seeds, walnuts, and peanuts (seeds, nuts, and legumes)

If a vegetarian avoids proteins from animal sources, even eggs, milk, and cheese, he may risk becoming deficient in vitamin B_{12}, a vitamin necessary for normal functioning of cells in the stomach and nervous system. Therefore, it is recommended that strict vegetarians take vitamin B_{12} supplements.

CARBOHYDRATES

Carbohydrates are a major source of energy and an essential part of a nutritious meal plan. Carbohydrates may be classified as complex carbohydrates (starches) or simple carbohydrates (sugars). Both types provide energy at the rate of 4 calories per gram.

Complex carbohydrates are present in whole grain breads and cereals, legumes, and vegetables. Foods containing complex carbohydrates are good for you because they're rich in vitamins, minerals, and fiber.

Simple carbohydrates are found in fruit, some vegetables, dairy products, and the refined and processed sugars we add to food. The naturally occurring sugars found in fruit, vegetables, and milk are simple carbohydrates which should be included in a nutritious meal. Along with the carbohydrate, these foods provide vitamins, minerals, and fiber.

Refined and processed sugars are simple carbohydrates which provide calories and almost no other nutrients to the body. These simple carbohydrates should be limited in the diet. Regular sugar, maple syrup, molasses, honey, and corn syrup are common examples. You will recognize these as the extras which are added to beverages, cereals, breads, and other foods to sweeten the taste.

Sucrose, lactose, fructose, glucose, sorbitol, and maltose are examples of hidden simple carbohydrates and are found in many processed foods. If you see one of these ingredients listed on a food label, you will know that a simple carbohydrate providing almost nothing but extra calories has been added.

Many diet books emphasize that foods rich in carbohydrates should be avoided when dieting. When a person goes on a very low-carbohydrate diet, several pounds of weight may be lost almost immediately. This weight loss is largely due to the loss of water from the body and not from the loss of body fat. When the dieter starts eating carbohydrate foods again, the body tissues will reabsorb much of the water which was lost and the body weight will probably increase.

FAT

Fat, like carbohydrate and protein, is another essential nutrient — even when dieting. However, dieters do need to watch the amount of fat they eat since fat is so concentrated in calories. Ounce for ounce, fat supplies over twice as many calories as either protein or carbohydrate.

Even though high in calories, fat is necessary for the transportation and absorption of valuable fat-soluble vitamins (A,D,E, and K) within the body. Fat tends to delay the onset of hunger since it remains in the stomach longer than carbohydrate and protein. Fat alone provides the essential fatty acids which are necessary to life.

While too much stored body fat is unhealthy, the body does need some body fat to act as an insulator in controlling body temperature. Body fat also is used to provide a protective layer around the vital organs.

Fat in food can be visible (as in butter, margarine, lard, shortening, salad oil, and mayonnaise) or invisible (as in egg yolks, whole milk, steak marbling, and most nuts). Whether obvious or hidden, fat is a concentrated source of calories.

Cholesterol is a fatty-substance present in foods of animal origin. It is manufactured within the body by almost all body tissues and is needed by the body to form hormones and cell membranes.

Several scientific studies have suggested that high levels of blood cholesterol are associated with an increased risk of heart disease. Therefore, most nutritionists recommend that people who have high blood cholesterol levels should avoid excess cholesterol in their diets.

Three types of fatty acids are present in the food we eat: saturated, monounsaturated, and polyunsaturated. Some studies have shown that saturated fats tend to increase blood cholesterol and that polyunsaturated fats tend to decrease blood cholesterol.

Saturated fats are usually solid at room temperature and are found primarily in animal products such as meat fat, poultry, whole milk, cheese, butter, and lard. In addition, saturated fat is found in coconut oil (an ingredient in most synthetic coffee creamers), palm oil, cocoa butter (found in chocolate), and the hydrogenated vegetable margarines.

Polyunsaturated fats are usually liquid at room temperature and are found in foods of plant origin. Safflower, sunflower, corn, sesame, soybean, and cottonseed oil contain mostly polyunsaturated fatty acids and are recommended for cooking.

Monounsaturated fats are present in large amount in avocados, olive and peanut oil, and in most nuts. Monounsaturated fats appear to have no influence on blood cholesterol.

Although saturated, monounsaturated, and polyunsaturated fats probably have different effects on blood cholesterol, they are equal in calories — each supplies 9 calories per gram.

VITAMINS AND MINERALS

Unlike protein, carbohydrate, and fat, vitamins and minerals supply no calories. However, they do work with protein, carbohydrate, and fat in making the body's energy and body-building systems work properly.

For most individuals, meal plans based on a variety of foods from the basic five food groups will supply sufficient amounts of vitamins and minerals. Therefore, vitamin and mineral supplements are usually unnecessary.

Vitamins are divided into two classes: water-soluble (vitamin C and the B vitamins) and fat-soluble (vitamins A, D, E, and K). Since the body rids itself of unused water-soluble vitamins daily, these vitamins should be supplied daily to maintain an adequate supply.

Fat-soluble vitamins are transported by fats and are stored within the body. On days that the body does not receive an adequate supply of the fat-soluble vitamins, it can use the stored vitamins.

The body needs vitamin C (ascorbic acid), found in citrus fruit and some vegetables such as broccoli, for tissue growth and repair and for formation of healthy gums, teeth, and bones.

Thiamine (a B vitamin) is required for normal digestion, nerve functioning, and carbohydrate metabolism. Some food sources of thiamine include whole grain and enriched breads and cereals, legumes, pork, and liver.

Normal nutrient metabolism requires a regular intake of riboflavin and niacin, two other B vitamins. The major food sources of riboflavin are dairy products, liver, dark green leafy vegetables, and whole grain and enriched breads and cereals. Niacin is provided by liver, poultry, fish, meats, legumes, and whole grain and enriched breads and cereals.

The body needs vitamin A for normal vision and for growth and maintenance of skin tissue. Yellow and dark green vegetables, liver, whole milk, and eggs contain vitamin A.

Calcium and iron are two minerals which are often found lacking in the average American's diet. Calcium's major role is in the building and maintenance of bones and teeth. The most important dietary sources are milk and milk products.

The critical role of iron is in the manufacture of healthy red blood cells and in the transportation of oxygen throughout the body. Liver, lean meat, dark green leafy vegetables, egg yolk, dried beans, shellfish, some enriched breads and cereals, and dried fruit are food sources of iron. Insufficient amounts of iron in the diet can cause a condition known as iron-deficiency anemia.

Sodium is a mineral which is used by the body to maintain fluid balance within the cells. But the average American consumes far more sodium than the body needs, with most of the excess taken in as table salt (1 teaspoon of table salt contains about 2000 milligrams sodium).

Sodium is present naturally in many foods and is a component in many food additives. Under normal conditions, most people can get all the sodium needed without adding salt to food. Too much sodium in the diet is thought to increase blood pressure, and high blood pressure is a major risk factor in the development of heart disease. Therefore, most nutritionists advise limiting the intake of sodium to about 3000 milligrams per day. One of the easiest ways to cut back on sodium is to decrease the salt added during cooking and at the table.

Food labels reveal hidden sources of salt and sodium. Monosodium glutamate, baking powder, baking soda, and some chemical preservatives contain sodium.

Most natural and processed cheeses are high in sodium, as are canned fish, bacon, ham, sausage, and luncheon meats. Sauces, such as soy, Worcestershire, chili, tartar, catsup, and mustard, also contain sodium.

While fresh vegetables contain little sodium, salt is generally added to frozen vegetables which are packaged in a sauce and most canned vegetables. High-sodium seasonings commonly used with vegetables include bouillon cubes and granules, bacon drippings, salt pork, and regular butter and margarine.

Fresh, frozen, and canned fruit and fruit juice are all low in sodium. Rice and pasta are also low-sodium foods unless a sauce or seasoning that contains salt is added. Regular hot cereals, such as grits and oats, contain almost no sodium, but instant varieties usually contain sodium.

Salt is added to most white and whole grain breads for flavor and for a tender, smooth texture. If your doctor has placed you on a strict low-sodium diet, you may have to look for salt-free bread or make your own.

The sodium count is almost always high in convenience and snack foods. Try to avoid most frozen and canned main dishes, such as pot pies and pizza; canned and dehydrated soups; and salty snacks, such as salted nuts, potato chips, crackers, and salted popcorn. Some of these products may be purchased in a low-sodium version. Low-sodium soups and bouillon cubes and salt-free nuts and potato chips are all available in the market.

WHAT ABOUT EXERCISE?

No diet or health program would be complete without an exercise plan. Exercise helps improve self-esteem and body tone and facilitates weight loss by burning up extra calories. Once you've reached your desired body weight, exercise helps keep unwanted pounds from returning.

Don't worry if you experience an increase in appetite during the first few weeks of a new exercise program; it's a normal occurrence. Research has shown that after about six weeks of moderate exercise your appetite should return to normal and that continued moderate exercise should help you to keep your appetite under control.

Exercise can be classified as anaerobic or aerobic. Anaerobic exercise, such as calisthenics, tennis, the 100-yard dash, bowling, and weight-training, requires only short bursts of energy. Anaerobic exercise does help to burn some calories and to develop muscle tone. However, it does not increase the cardio-vascular endurance.

Aerobic exercise requires a sustained supply of energy throughout the activity. Brisk walking, jogging, swimming, skating, dancing, cycling, rope jumping, and rowing are all forms of aerobic exercise. Each of these aerobic exercises burns calories at a high rate, increases cardio-vascular endurance, helps relieve tension, and tends to reduce high blood pressure.

One of the most practical aerobic exercises is brisk walking because it requires no special skills, training, or equipment other than a good pair of walking shoes. A person weighing 140 pounds can burn up about 180 calories by walking briskly two miles in 30 minutes. If that individual walked two brisk miles four times a week (eating and drinking no more than usual), he would be about 10 pounds lighter after 12 months.

The American College of Sports Medicine recommends that people exercise aerobically 15 to 60 minutes a day, three to five days a week. Check with your doctor before beginning a strenuous exercise program. Your doctor can help you decide what type of program is best for you.

Whatever activity you choose, remember that the more vigorously you exercise, the greater the number of calories burned. If you become breathless while exercising, you are over-exerting yourself. Slow down.

Be sure and take time to warm up and stretch your muscles before and after each exercise session. Don't try to do too much the first day. Moderation is important. It is better to exercise at a slower pace for a longer period of time than to go too fast and then stop.

In addition to engaging in a regular exercise program, you can burn up extra calories by adding movement in your daily activities. Take the stairs instead of the elevator; when shopping or working, park your car at the far end of the parking lot so that you'll have to walk farther to the building. At home, push the vacuum cleaner vigorously.

Don't get discouraged if it takes a while to get in shape. Remember that you grew out of shape over a period of months or even years. Begin a new exercise program slowly and gradually increase your pace.

Proper diet combined with regular aerobic exercise appears to be the most effective method for achieving weight loss and maintaining ideal body weight.

COOKING THE LIGHT WAY

As you look through the recipes in *Cooking Light*, you'll see how we've used several techniques to trim away sugar, fat, and calories. Once you've become familiar with a few of the techniques used in *Cooking Light*, you'll find it easy to trim away unwanted calories from your own recipes, too. Instead of boiling or frying vegetables and meats "as Grandmother used to do," get rid of excess fat (and calories) and save valuable vitamins and minerals by poaching, steaming, sautéing, stir-frying, grilling, or broiling.

POACHING

Fish does not have to be fried to be tasty. In fact, during the frying process, fish acts as a sponge, soaking up the high-calorie shortening or oil. Try poaching fish in a flavorful mixture of lemon and wine for a dish which is tender, moist, and low in calories.

Fish is poached by cooking it in a small amount of simmering liquid, such as wine or stock. The fish poacher or skillet is covered so that steam won't escape; the steam keeps the fish moist.

Combine white wine or lemon juice with water and herbs for poaching chicken. Be careful not to leave chicken or fish in the simmering liquid too long because overcooking will make the poached food dry.

Poach pears in red wine, fruit juice, and cinnamon or cloves. Try poaching other fruit such as apples and peaches as well.

Eggs are probably the most commonly poached food. Eggs are usually poached in water, but they may also be poached in milk or tomato juice for a change.

STEAMING

Why cook vegetables in a pan of boiling water until they're mushy and limp? Vegetables are more nutritious and have better color, flavor, and texture when steamed until crisp-tender. Since the vegetables do not stand in water during steaming, fewer water-soluble vitamins are lost than when vegetables are boiled.

To steam vegetables arrange the vegetables in a steaming rack. Place the rack in a pan with a small amount of boiling water, and cover with a tight-fitting lid. Make sure that the boiling water does not touch the vegetables and that the water continues to boil during the complete cooking time.

Add flavor without extra calories to steamed vegetables by placing fresh herbs and spices in the water. The vegetables absorb the flavor of the herbs and spices as they cook.

SAUTÉING AND STIR-FRYING

Sautéing and stir-frying are both light methods of cooking when the amount of oil or margarine is kept to a minimum. By using nonstick cookware or a regular skillet coated with vegetable cooking spray, vegetables and meat can be cooked quickly — often with little or no additional fat added.

A small amount of oil is recommended for sautéing some foods such as green pepper and celery which dry out if cooked with cooking spray alone. Other foods, such as mushrooms, onion, meat, fish, and poultry, release some liquid as they cook and can be sautéed in a nonstick skillet without oil or in a skillet coated with vegetable cooking spray.

Vegetables should be thinly sliced for sautéing and stir-frying. Meat, fish, and poultry should be cut into small, even pieces. Shake, toss, or stir the food to insure even browning.

GRILLING AND BROILING

When grilled over hot coals or broiled on a rack in the oven, meat, fish, and poultry lose extra calories as natural fat drips away. Remove as much fat as possible before cooking by skinning chicken and by trimming all visible fat from meat. Coat the broiler or grill rack with vegetable cooking spray to prevent the food from sticking.

Wine, vinegar, and lemon juice tenderize meat and are good ingredients for low-calorie marinades. Since lean meats, fish, and poultry tend to dry out during grilling or broiling, we recommend frequent basting with a low-calorie marinade or unsweetened fruit juice to keep the food moist.

OTHER COOKING LIGHT TECHNIQUES

You might think that food cooked without the usual fattening and salty seasonings tastes bland. Our recipes, however, show you how to liven up your meats, vegetables, salads, and desserts with herbs and spices.

Herbs and spices invite experimentation. As you learn more about their different characteristics, you'll begin to feel comfortable using them in your own recipes to replace fat and salt. (See the Herb and Spice Chart for suggestions.)

Use finely chopped fresh herbs when possible. Dried whole herbs are usually the next best choice since they maintain their strength longer than the commercially ground form. Just remember to use three times more fresh herbs in your recipe than you use of the more potent dried form.

The major role of herbs is to enhance food's natural flavor, but many also add visual interest to food. Use chopped fresh parsley or chives in pale-colored foods such as rice and potatoes. Sprinkle chicken, fish, and egg dishes with paprika before serving. When food looks attractive, mealtime will be more satisfying to dieters and non-dieters alike.

Wine is another ingredient used in several of our light recipes. The alcohol evaporates during cooking, leaving behind flavor and few calories. Feel free to experiment with a variety of table wines. However, avoid cooking wine if you're watching your sodium intake since cooking wine usually contains salt.

White wine is especially tasty with poultry, seafood, and egg dishes, while the stronger red wines are best with beef, pork, and lamb. Use wine as a marinade for less tender cuts of meat since it is an excellent meat tenderizer.

Unsweetened fruit juice is used as a sweetener in many of our reduced-calorie dessert recipes. Fruit juice does contain calories, but it also provides vitamins and minerals.

Vanilla extract, a popular flavoring for sweets, helps make up for decreased amounts of sugar in low-calorie desserts. A few drops will give a pleasant flavor to unsweetened hot tea. Almond extract added to low-sugar fruit desserts helps to bring out the fruit's natural sweetness without adding extra calories.

When preparing meat dishes, cut back on calories by draining the browned meat in a colander. To soak up even more fat, pat the meat dry with a paper towel.

Try chilling homemade broth so that the fat will rise to the top; after the fat hardens, just lift it off. What's left is a delicious, fat-free broth to use in soups, stews, and even for cooking vegetables.

Follow instructions carefully when preparing our light recipes. Some of the procedures may take a few extra minutes, but the calories you save will be worth the extra time.

After planning, shopping for, and preparing a light recipe, remember to divide the final product evenly into the number of servings specified on the recipe; otherwise, the calorie calculations will be incorrect.

MENU PLANNING

A key factor in any weight-loss program or in establishing healthy eating patterns is to create daily nutritious meal plans. The following are tips on planning lighter meals that will help you lose those unwanted pounds or just keep your weight where it is.

A lighter way of eating may require several changes for you. In the beginning, you may want to keep a diary of the foods you eat each day. By recording all meals and snacks, you'll become more aware of when you eat and why. If you snack more often when you're bored, try to plan activities (other than food-related) to fill your time.

Plan menus for a week at a time to better assure yourself of a balanced intake of nutrients. By knowing what you've planned for the entire day and week, you'll be less likely to stray from your diet.

Plan meals around your own schedule. It's best not to save up for one big meal a day; if you're too hungry when mealtime arrives, you may forget your good intentions and overeat. Look at each day as a whole, and plan meals and snacks so that you consume the total recommended amounts of calories and nutrients.

FOODS TO INCLUDE

Since no one food contains all the nutrients for a balanced diet, variety is a necessity. Some food should be eaten from each of several food groups daily.

Fruit and Vegetables: Fruit and vegetables should be included frequently on low-calorie menus. They're generally high in vitamins, minerals, and fiber, contain little if any fat, no cholesterol, and are relatively low in calories. The exceptions are olives and avocados, both of which are high in fat and calories.

Citrus fruit such as oranges and grapefruit, melons, strawberries, green pepper, potatoes, cabbage, and broccoli are all excellent sources of ascorbic acid (vitamin C). Include at least one vitamin C-rich food daily. Deep yellow and dark green vegetables, such as sweet potatoes, acorn squash, carrots, and spinach, as well as tomatoes, apricots, and cantaloupe provide large amounts of vitamin A. You should try to include a vitamin A-rich food in your diet at least every other day.

A balanced diet includes four servings from the fruit and vegetable group daily. One serving of this food group equals 1/2 cup sliced or cooked fruit or fruit juice, 1 small apple, 1/2 grapefruit, 1 medium orange, 1/2 cup cooked vegetable, or 1 small baked potato.

When you have a choice, eat bulkier, higher fiber food such as an apple instead of apple juice. Since the apple takes longer to eat, it may be more satisfying. In addition, the apple contains more fiber and will help to fill you up.

Breads and Cereals: A lack of understanding about the contributions which breads and cereals make to the diet has caused many people to omit these foods when trying to lose weight. Breads, cereals, pasta, and rice are rich in complex carbohydrates and, if whole grain, are high in fiber. Nutrients found in enriched or whole grain breads and cereals include thiamine, riboflavin, niacin, and iron.

You should include four servings from the bread and cereal group each day. One serving equals 1 slice whole grain or enriched bread, 1 ounce ready-to-eat cereal, or 1/2 cup cooked cereal, rice, or pasta.

Protein Foods: Protein foods include fish, poultry, meat, legumes, eggs, cheese, milk, and nuts. These foods are rich sources of protein, iron, thiamine, niacin, riboflavin, and phosphorus. Eggs and liver are valuable sources of iron and vitamin A, but they are also high in cholesterol.

We've already discussed that dried beans and peas are excellent sources of protein and fiber. Remember to plan a combination of complementary foods to obtain a high quality protein.

Include two servings of the protein group daily, choosing from a variety of sources. One serving of this group equals 2 to 3 ounces of lean, cooked fish, poultry, or meat, 2 eggs, or 1 cup cooked dried beans or peas.

Dairy Products: Milk and milk products are the main sources of calcium in diets. These dairy products also contribute riboflavin, protein, and vitamin B_{12}. Whole milk and fortified low-fat and skim milk provide vitamins A and D. Other foods included in this group are milk, buttermilk, yogurt, cheese, cottage cheese, ice milk, instant nonfat dry milk powder, and evaporated milk.

Be sure to choose products made from skim or low-fat milk, such as low-fat cottage cheese, low-fat yogurt, evaporated skim milk, and buttermilk. When fortified with vitamins A and D, skim milk products contain all the essential vitamins, minerals, and protein found in whole milk products but without the extra calories from the fat.

Servings recommended per day range from two for an adult, three for children up to 12 years of age, and four for teenagers. One serving of this group equals 1 cup milk, 1 cup yogurt, 1-1/2 ounces hard cheese, 2 ounces process cheese food, 1-1/2 cups ice milk, or 2 cups cottage cheese. Although these amounts provide equal amounts of calcium, calories per serving are not always the same.

Miscellaneous Foods: The final food group includes fats, alcohol, and sweets (including soft drinks, jams, jellies, honey, cakes, pies, and sweet breads) — extras that should be enjoyed only occasionally and only in small amounts. Fats, alcohol, and sweets provide almost nothing in the diet but calories. There are no recommendations for amounts to eat daily. You should concentrate on foods from the other four food groups instead and keep the fats, sweets, and alcohol as low as possible.

GROCERY SHOPPING

Choosing the right ingredients at the grocery store is very important in preparing nutritious, lighter meals. As you walk down the aisles, choose reduced-calorie mayonnaise instead of regular; ground chuck instead of hamburger; skim milk instead of whole; plain low-fat yogurt instead of sweetened, fruit-flavored yogurt; and fresh broccoli instead of broccoli packaged in a rich cheese sauce.

Learn to judge food labels carefully and take advantage of the increasing number of products with nutrient information on the label. Nutrition labels indicate the number of calories and the amount of protein, carbohydrate, and fat in a serving of the product. They also give an indication of major vitamins and minerals present in the product.

If there is no nutrition label, read the ingredient list. By law, the manufacturer must list ingredients in order of quantity. If the first ingredient listed is sugar, assume that the product contains more sugar than any other ingredient and is probably high in calories.

Combine lean pieces of chicken and low-calorie vegetables for a light, but satisfying, entrée of Chicken-Vegetable Crêpes (page 176). Calorie count for a serving of two filled crêpes is only 309.

WEEKLY MENU PLANS

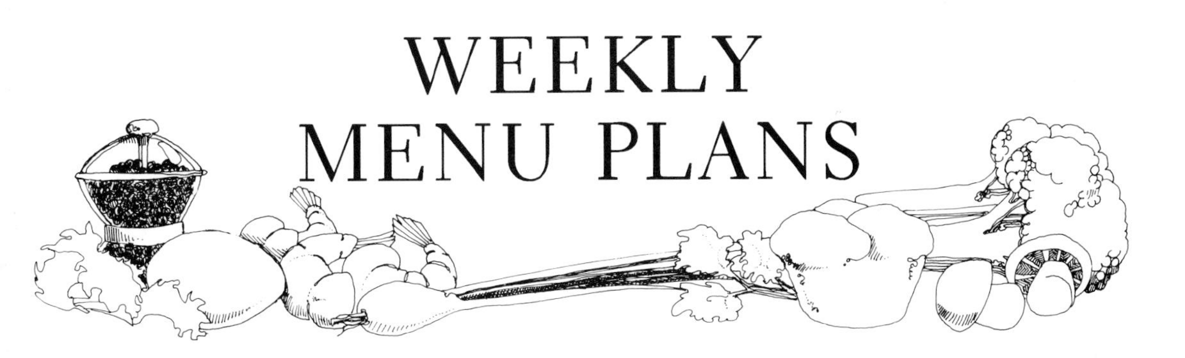

Now that you've become familiar with the basics of menu planning, it's time to incorporate these ideas into your own daily eating pattern. First of all, set realistic goals for yourself since it's impractical, and unsafe, to limit calories too much.

Try not to lose more than 1 to 2 pounds a week. Nutritionists recommend a daily calorie intake of not less than 1200 calories for women and not less than 1600 calories for men. If your calorie intake is any less, it's unlikely that you'll get the nutrients you need.

Following are two weekly menu plans, one for 1200 calories a day and one for 1600 calories a day. Use these menu plans as guides in establishing your new eating habits. Don't feel limited to the menus printed here, but modify them to suit your preferences.

We've suggested several *Cooking Light* recipes (indicated by asterisks) throughout the two plans; refer to the Index for the page numbers of these recipes. Feel free to personalize your menus by substituting other *Cooking Light* recipes for those listed. Choose a recipe of approximately equal caloric value to keep total calories for the day within your limits.

If a food listed in the plan is out of season, use the Calorie/Nutrient Chart to substitute a similar food that contains about the same number of calories. For instance, instead of 1 cup of cantaloupe (48 calories), eat ½ banana (51 calories) or ½ cup unsweetened fruit cocktail (46 calories).

Skim milk or fruit juice is listed as a beverage in some menus. If a beverage suggestion is not given, we recommend a beverage which provides few, if any, calories. Water is an excellent choice. You may also drink unsweetened tea (calorie-free) or coffee (2 calories per cup), but remember that both contain caffeine and should be consumed only in moderation.

If you're cooking for two or more dieters who need a different number of calories daily, these plans can be easily modified. Simply adjust the 1200 calorie plan to 1600 calories by increasing serving sizes or adding extra food items that total 400 calories. For instance, a person could get an additional 401 calories by eating 1 slice of whole wheat bread (68 calories), 1 medium apple (96 calories), 1 cup of skim milk (88 calories), 1 medium baked potato (103 calories), and 1 cup of tomato juice (46 calories).

Both the 1200 and 1600 calorie menu plans were designed to meet the Recommended Dietary Allowances (RDA) for adults over 19 years of age for protein, calcium, phosphorous, iron, potassium, vitamin A, thiamine, riboflavin, niacin, and vitamin C. The RDA are estimated levels of essential nutrients which will meet the needs of a majority of healthy persons in the United States; the Recommended Dietary Allowances do include a safety factor to allow for individual differences.

The flavor of cinnamon makes Spiced Fruit Delight (page 30) a refreshing light dessert. Instead of sugar, unsweetened apple juice is added to produce a natural sweet taste.

1200 CALORIE WEEKLY MENU PLAN

*Refer to the Index for the page numbers of these recipes.

DAY ONE: TOTAL CALORIES 1199

BREAKFAST: 205 Calories	
½ cup whole bran cereal	65
2 tablespoons raisins	52
1 cup skim milk	88

LUNCH: 380 Calories	
2 ounces roasted turkey breast	100
2 slices whole wheat bread	136
2 teaspoons reduced-calorie mayonnaise	27
2 tomato slices	14
* 1 serving Cucumber-Yogurt Salad	35
2 dried peach halves	68

DINNER: 414 Calories	
* 1 serving Sautéed Liver Supreme	220
1 small baked potato	79
1½ teaspoons reduced-calorie margarine	25
* 1 serving Tropical Carrots	59
* 1 serving Tarragon Asparagus Salad	31

SNACK: 200 Calories	
1 cup vanilla low-fat yogurt	200

DAY TWO: TOTAL CALORIES 1194

BREAKFAST: 230 Calories	
* ½ cup Peach-Yogurt Shake	78
1 poached egg	82
½ whole wheat English muffin	70

LUNCH: 366 Calories	
* 1 cup Ruby Red Borscht	75
* 1 serving Crab and Rice Salad	177
½ cup cooked mixed vegetables	53
1 small apple	61

DINNER: 473 Calories	
* 1 serving Beef Rolls	189
½ cup cooked brown rice	116
1 cup cooked turnip greens	30
½ cup orange sections on lettuce	50
1 cup skim milk	88

SNACK: 125 Calories	
* 1 cup Strawberry-Banana Shake	125

DAY THREE: TOTAL CALORIES 1206

BREAKFAST: 325 Calories	
4 prunes, stewed	104
1¼ cups wheat bran flakes cereal	133
1 cup skim milk	88

LUNCH: 382 Calories	
3 ounces broiled beef patty	186
1 whole wheat hamburger bun	130
2 teaspoons reduced-calorie mayonnaise	27
1 teaspoon mustard	4
1 tomato slice	7
½ cup cooked brussels sprouts	28

DINNER: 308 Calories	
* 1 serving Oven-Fried Fish Fillets	140
* 1 serving Orange Glazed Beets	66
½ cup cooked green beans	16
1 teaspoon reduced-calorie margarine	17
* 1 serving Marinated Tomato Slices	28
½ cup diced fresh pineapple	41

SNACK: 191 Calories	
* 1 Spicy Apple Muffin	103
1 cup skim milk	88

DAY FOUR: TOTAL CALORIES 1206

BREAKFAST: 178 Calories

* 1 cup Fresh Tomato Juice Cocktail	36
* 1 Cottage-Fruit Spread Sandwich	142

LUNCH: 389 Calories

* 1 serving Tuna-Macaroni Salad	181
½ cup steamed broccoli	20
1 medium pear	100
1 cup skim milk	88

DINNER: 464 Calories

* 3 ounces Pineapple-Marinated Pot Roast with ¼ cup sauce	198
½ cup cooked spinach	21
* 1 serving Gazpacho Salad Mold with 2 tablespoons dressing	86
* 1 Shredded Wheat Roll	109
½ banana	50

SNACK: 175 Calories

⅔ cup whole bran cereal	87
1 cup skim milk	88

DAY FIVE: TOTAL CALORIES 1198

BREAKFAST: 260 Calories

½ grapefruit	40
1 cup hot oatmeal	132
1 cup skim milk	88

LUNCH: 382 Calories

* 2 ounces Pineapple-Marinated Pot Roast	127
2 slices whole wheat bread	136
2 teaspoons mustard	8
* 1 serving Zesty Coleslaw	56
1 cup fresh strawberries	55

DINNER: 408 Calories

* 1 serving Spaghetti with Shrimp Sauce	214
½ cup cooked English peas	57
1½ cups leaf lettuce	15
* 1 tablespoon Zesty Italian Dressing	13
* 1 Shredded Wheat Roll	109

SNACK: 148 Calories

1 cup skim milk	88
15 purple grapes	60

DAY SIX: TOTAL CALORIES 1195

BREAKFAST: 258 Calories

* 2 Oatmeal Snack Cakes	170
1 cup skim milk	88

LUNCH: 262 Calories

* 1 serving Minty Cottage Cheese Salad	123
½ cup cooked carrots	24
3 rye wafers	69
½ cup unsweetened fruit cocktail	46

DINNER: 461 Calories

¾ cup tomato juice	35
* 1 serving Vegetable-Meat Loaf	188
* 1 serving Creamed New Potatoes and Peas	117
* 1 serving Citrus Spinach Salad	58
1½ cups cubed watermelon	63

SNACK: 214 Calories

* 1 slice Vanilla Chiffon Cake	126
1 cup skim milk	88

DAY SEVEN: TOTAL CALORIES 1202

BREAKFAST: 201 Calories

5 dried apricot halves, cooked	46
1 scrambled egg (with skim milk)	90
½ cup cooked cream of wheat	65

LUNCH: 415 Calories

* 1 serving Chicken Divan	212
½ cup cooked brown rice	116
½ broiled tomato	14
1½ cups leaf lettuce	15
* 1 tablespoon Zesty Italian Dressing	13
½ cup fresh blueberries	45

DINNER: 465 Calories

* 1½ cups Lentil Stew	174
* 1 serving Marinated Vegetable Salad	39
* 1 slice Oatmeal Bread	108
½ teaspoon reduced-calorie margarine	8
1 cup cubed cantaloupe	48
1 cup skim milk	88

SNACK: 121 Calories

2 squares graham cracker	55
¾ cup skim milk	66

1600 CALORIE WEEKLY MENU PLAN

*Refer to the Index for the page numbers of these recipes.

DAY ONE: TOTAL CALORIES 1595

BREAKFAST: 437 Calories

* 1 cup Fruit Shake	140
1 poached egg	82
1 ounce Canadian bacon, broiled	58
* 1 Whole Wheat English muffin	157

LUNCH: 518 Calories

* 1 cup Potato Soup	116
* 1 serving Easy Sloppy Joes	251
1½ cups diced fresh watermelon	63
1 cup skim milk	88

DINNER: 493 Calories

3 ounces roasted turkey breast	150
* 1 serving Sweet Potatoes in Orange Cups	79
* 1 serving Fancy Green Peas	70
1½ cups leaf lettuce	15
* 1 tablespoon Seasoned Buttermilk Dressing	23
20 seedless green grapes	68
1 cup skim milk	88

SNACK: 147 Calories

* 1 serving Fresh Citrus Dessert	147

DAY TWO: TOTAL CALORIES 1605

BREAKFAST: 268 Calories

¾ cup tomato juice	35
2 slices whole wheat bread	136
1 teaspoon reduced-calorie margarine	17
1 ounce low-fat Cheddar cheese	80

LUNCH: 509 Calories

* 1 serving Tuna Chef Salad	240
3 rye wafers	69
1 cup vanilla low-fat yogurt	200

DINNER: 627 Calories

* 1 cup Peach Soup	104
* 1 serving Veal Marsala	269
½ cup cooked brown rice	116
1 cup steamed broccoli	40
1 cup Romaine lettuce	10
1 cup skim milk	88

SNACK: 201 Calories

½ cup vanilla ice milk	100
1 medium banana	101

DAY THREE: TOTAL CALORIES 1606

BREAKFAST: 389 Calories

5 prunes, stewed	130
* 2 Blueberry Pancakes	82
1 tablespoon reduced-calorie pancake syrup	28
1 ounce lean cooked ham	61
1 cup skim milk	88

LUNCH: 436 Calories

* 1 Open-Face Turkey Sandwich	236
8 asparagus spears, steamed	24
* 1 cup Strawberry Ice Milk	176

DINNER: 575 Calories

* 1 serving Pork Chop and Rice Dinner	290
1 cup cooked turnip greens	30
* 1 serving 3-Bean Salad (refrigerate remainder for Day Four)	71
1 (1-ounce) enriched hard roll	78
* 1 serving Chunky Applesauce	106

SNACK: 206 Calories

* 1 slice Whole Wheat Banana Bread	118
1 cup skim milk	88

DAY FOUR: TOTAL CALORIES 1600

BREAKFAST: 279 Calories
- 1 cup diced cantaloupe 48
- * 1 slice Whole Wheat Banana Bread 118
- 1½ teaspoons reduced-calorie margarine 25
- 1 cup skim milk 88

LUNCH: 508 Calories
- * 1 serving Beef-Stuffed Zucchini 267
- * 1 serving 3-Bean Salad (from Day Three) 71
- 1 cup diced fresh pineapple 82
- 1 cup skim milk 88

DINNER: 648 Calories
- * 1 serving Chicken Cacciatore 249
- 1 cup cooked spinach 42
- 1 cup leaf lettuce 10
- * 2 tablespoons Zesty Italian Dressing 26
- 1 (1-ounce) slice Italian bread 83
- 1 cup vanilla low-fat yogurt 200
- ½ cup unsweetened canned peaches 38

SNACK: 165 Calories
- 2 cups plain unsalted popcorn 46
- * 1 cup Blender Fruit Drink 119

DAY FIVE: TOTAL CALORIES 1595

BREAKFAST: 221 Calories
- 1 cup tomato juice 46
- 1 scrambled egg (with skim milk) 90
- * 1 serving Light Grits Spoonbread 85

LUNCH: 592 Calories
- 2 slices whole wheat bread 136
- 1 tablespoon reduced-calorie margarine 50
- 2 (⅔-ounce) slices low-fat American cheese 100
- * 1 cup Garbanzo Bean Salad 120
- * 2 Lemon Wafers 98
- 1 cup skim milk 88

DINNER: 585 Calories
- * 1 serving Saucy Liver 273
- ½ cup mashed potatoes (with skim milk) 80
- ½ cup cooked brussels sprouts 28
- * 1 serving Cottage Pear Salad 116
- 1 cup skim milk 88

SNACK: 197 Calories
- 6 dried apricot halves 55
- * 1 cup Papaya Cooler 142

DAY SIX: TOTAL CALORIES 1595

BREAKFAST: 326 Calories
- ½ cup grapefruit sections 39
- * 2 Buttermilk Bran Muffins 182
- 1 teaspoon reduced-calorie margarine 17
- 1 cup skim milk 88

LUNCH: 503 Calories
- * 1 serving Tasty Salmon Salad 262
- * 4 Whole Wheat Crackers 84
- ½ cup cooked English peas 57
- 1 medium pear 100

DINNER: 629 Calories
- * 1 serving Stuffed Flounder 193
- 1 medium-size baked potato 103
- * 2 tablespoons Mock Sour Cream 18
- 1½ cups fresh spinach leaves 21
- * 1 tablespoon Seasoned Buttermilk Dressing 23
- * 1 slice Light Beer Bread 88
- * ½ cup Strawberry-Raspberry Ice 95
- 1 cup skim milk 88

SNACK: 137 Calories
- 4 dried peach halves 137

DAY SEVEN: TOTAL CALORIES 1598

BREAKFAST: 293 Calories
- * 1 serving Broiled Grapefruit 76
- * 1 serving Swiss-Zucchini Quiche 197
- 3 tomato slices 20

LUNCH: 626 Calories
- * 3 ounces Savory Roast Beef with 2 tablespoons sauce 195
- 1 cup cooked yellow squash 28
- * 1 serving Tabbouleh 101
- * 1 Whole Wheat Roll 79
- 1 teaspoon reduced-calorie margarine 17
- * 1 cup Chocolate-Marshmallow Freeze 118
- 1 cup skim milk 88

DINNER: 485 Calories
- * 3 ounces Savory Roast Beef 185
- * 2 slices Light Beer Bread 176
- 2 teaspoons reduced-calorie mayonnaise 27
- 1 cup leaf lettuce 10
- * 2 tablespoons Zesty Italian Dressing 26
- 1 small apple 61

SNACK: 194 Calories
- 1 cup wheat bran flakes cereal 106
- 1 cup skim milk 88

MAKE *COOKING LIGHT* WORK FOR YOU!

The goal of *Cooking Light* is to present a nutritious way of eating that can be followed for a lifetime. However, there are a few situations in which dieting should be avoided. During pregnancy a woman should gain 24 to 30 pounds in order to protect herself and her unborn baby's health. Women who are breast-feeding need extra calories to insure nutritious diets for their newborns. Pregnant women and women who are breast-feeding their infants should check with a registered dietitian for instruction on the proper type of meal plan to follow.

Weight-loss diets are usually not advised for children or adolescents because their bodies are growing and developing at a rapid rate. If parents are concerned about a child's weight, they should consult a registered dietitian for assistance in planning a suitable weight control program.

Many of us do need to control our diets in order to reach and maintain an ideal body weight. Whether you are overweight by 5 pounds or 50, you'll probably need to change many of your present eating habits to lose weight and to keep the pounds from returning.

Begin your weight loss program by identifying the eating habits you need to change. Instead of candy bars or other high-calorie snack foods, keep plenty of fresh, low-calorie vegetables on hand for a quick, nutritious snack. Snacks are not bad, but they should be planned as a part of the day's total menu plan.

Many people who enjoy cooking consume extra calories by tasting the food during preparation. Protect yourself against these unwanted calories by chewing sugar-free gum while you're in the kitchen. With gum in your mouth there will be less temptation to taste the food.

A calorie-saving trick for mealtime is to eat from a small luncheon plate instead of a larger dinner plate. A dieter's portion may seem small, but if it's served on a luncheon plate, the portion looks larger.

Make second helpings less tempting by preparing individual plates in the kitchen instead of serving from bowls on the dining table. During the meal, remember to take your time. Studies have shown that rapid eaters tend to eat larger amounts of food than do those who eat more slowly.

Whether eating a meal or a snack, concentrate on eating, not on the television, newspaper, or other diversions. Enjoy chewing each bite of food, and you'll probably feel more satisfied after finishing your meal.

When eating at a restaurant, read the menu carefully and choose the simpler, lower calorie items. Don't hesitate to ask the waiter for a description of how dishes are prepared. By asking that sauces and salad dressings be served on the side, you can better control the amount you eat. Cut out additional calories by asking for the baked potato to be served without butter. Finally, remember that alcohol calories add up quickly. If you do drink, try to limit the amount.

Following the *Cooking Light* approach to menu planning and food preparation encourages you to be creative in your meals while at the same time providing you with the opportunity of serving meals which are nutritious and low in calories. The long range results of *Cooking Light* can be a healthier life-style for you and your family.

Cooking Light
MENUS

BREAKFASTS THROUGH BRUNCHES

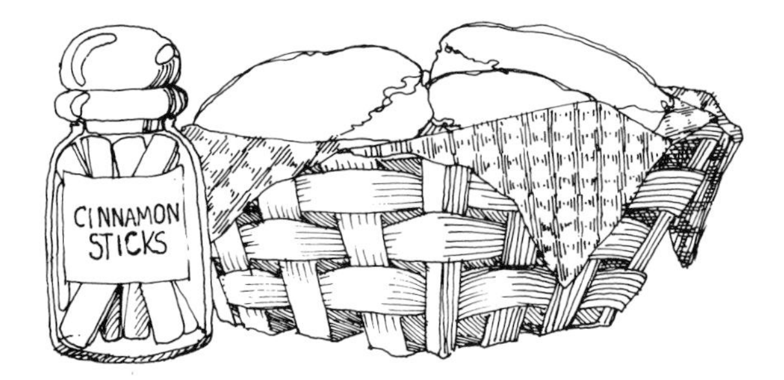

Treat your family to a Weekend Pancake Breakfast: two Feathery Buttermilk Pancakes topped with Fresh Blueberry Sauce. Even with Hot Mocha-Cocoa as the beverage, calories are only 200 per serving. How's that for a delicious, low-calorie breakfast?

Weekend Pancake Breakfast is just one of eight kitchen-tested menus that will help you start every day with a light touch. Follow them to see how a low-calorie breakfast can be more exciting than just poached eggs and dry toast.

Many dieters skip breakfast because they're too busy or because they don't want the calories. But when you skip breakfast, you may be so hungry by lunchtime that you'll forget your good intentions and overeat.

If you're pushed for time in the morning, have a bowl of unsweetened cereal with skim milk and fresh fruit. Or freeze a batch of muffins and heat one to eat with a glass of skim milk for breakfast. Top whole wheat toast with a slice of low-fat cheese and put it under the broiler for a few seconds to melt. Enjoy this easy breakfast with unsweetened fresh fruit or fruit juice.

The asterisks (*) in our menus indicate alternate recipes and the slight change in total calories if the alternate recipe is prepared.

BREAKFAST MINUS THE EGGS

Orange Slush
Mock Sausage Patties
Hash Browns
Hot Tea

Serves 4
Total calories per serving: 323

ORANGE SLUSH

2 cups unsweetened orange juice
½ cup instant nonfat dry milk powder
¼ teaspoon vanilla extract
8 ice cubes

Combine all ingredients in container of electric blender; process until mixture is frothy. Serve immediately. Yield: about 4 cups (about 108 calories per 1-cup serving).

MOCK SAUSAGE PATTIES

½ pound lean ground round
¼ cup beef broth
½ teaspoon grated lemon rind
½ tablespoon lemon juice
2 tablespoons fine, dry breadcrumbs
⅛ teaspoon fennel seeds, crushed
⅛ teaspoon salt
⅛ teaspoon ground ginger
⅛ teaspoon rubbed sage
⅛ teaspoon red pepper
Vegetable cooking spray

Combine all ingredients except cooking spray in a medium bowl; cover and let stand 15 minutes. Shape mixture into 4 patties.

Coat a medium skillet with cooking spray; place over medium-high heat until hot. Place patties in skillet; fry 5 to 6 minutes on each side. Drain patties on paper towels before serving. Yield: 4 servings (about 108 calories per serving).

Note: If a finer texture is desired, grind meat twice.

HASH BROWNS

2 large baking potatoes (about 1½ pounds)
2 tablespoons finely chopped onion
¼ teaspoon garlic salt
¼ teaspoon dried whole thyme
⅛ teaspoon pepper
Vegetable cooking spray

Cook potatoes in boiling water until tender. Cool slightly; peel and shred. Combine potatoes and next 4 ingredients.

Coat a 10-inch nonstick skillet with cooking spray; place over medium heat until hot. Pack potato mixture firmly into skillet; cook 6 to 7 minutes or until bottom is browned.

Invert potato patty onto a plate; return to skillet, cooked side up. Cook over medium heat 6 to 7 minutes or until bottom is browned. Cut into wedges to serve. Yield: 4 servings (about 107 calories per serving).

HIGH-FIBER BREAKFAST

Grapefruit Surprise
Spinach Omelet
or
*Eggs and Wild Rice
Whole Wheat Toast (1 slice)
Apricot Spread (1 tablespoon)
Hot Tea

Serves 6
*Total calories per serving: 340 or *298*

GRAPEFRUIT SURPRISE

3 large grapefruit, halved
2 tablespoons Grand Marnier or other orange-flavored liqueur

Remove seeds, and loosen sections of grapefruit halves; sprinkle 1 teaspoon Grand Marnier over top of each half. Place in a shallow baking pan; bake at 350° for 15 minutes. Serve immediately. Yield: 6 servings (about 61 calories per serving).

SPINACH OMELET

1 (10-ounce) package frozen chopped spinach, thawed and undrained
3 tablespoons chicken broth
1 clove garlic, crushed
⅛ to ¼ teaspoon pepper
¼ cup grated Parmesan cheese
10 eggs
2 tablespoons water
Vegetable cooking spray
2 teaspoons margarine, divided

Combine spinach, broth, garlic, and pepper in a small saucepan; cover and simmer 20 minutes. Stir in Parmesan cheese; cook 1 minute or until cheese is melted, stirring constantly. Set aside.

Combine eggs and water; beat lightly. Coat a 10-inch omelet pan or heavy skillet with cooking spray; add 1 teaspoon margarine. Place pan over medium heat until just hot enough to sizzle a drop of water. Pour half of egg mixture into pan. As mixture starts to cook, gently lift edges of omelet with a spatula and tilt pan so uncooked portion flows underneath.

When mixture is set, spread half of spinach mixture over half of omelet. Loosen omelet with a spatula; fold in half, and slide onto a warm serving platter. Repeat procedure with remaining ingredients. Yield: 6 servings (about 180 calories per serving).

EGGS AND WILD RICE

8 eggs
1 cup cooked wild rice
½ cup skim milk
1½ teaspoons Worcestershire sauce
¼ teaspoon salt
¼ teaspoon hot sauce
Vegetable cooking spray

Combine all ingredients except cooking spray in a large bowl; beat with a fork until ingredients are well blended.

Coat a large nonstick skillet with cooking spray; place over medium-low heat until hot. Pour in egg mixture. As eggs begin to set, stir gently to allow uncooked portions to flow underneath. Cook until eggs are set but still moist. Yield: 6 servings (about 138 calories per serving).

APRICOT SPREAD

1 (11-ounce) package dried apricots
1 cup water

Combine apricots and water in a small saucepan. Bring mixture to a boil; cover, reduce heat, and simmer 15 minutes or until apricots are tender. Cool slightly.

Process apricot mixture in container of an electric blender or food processor until smooth. Spoon into freezer containers; cover and store in refrigerator. Yield: 1¾ cups (about 29 calories per tablespoon).

Note: Spread may be frozen for 6 to 8 months. Thaw to serve.

BREAKFAST FOR A HOLIDAY

Cheese Blintzes
Spiced Oranges and Wine
Almond-Flavored Coffee (1 cup)

Serves 8
Total calories per serving: 283

CHEESE BLINTZES

2 (12-ounce) cartons dry curd cottage cheese
1 egg, beaten
3 tablespoons sugar
1½ teaspoons grated lemon rind
¼ teaspoon vanilla extract
16 Bran Crêpes
Vegetable cooking spray
½ cup reduced-calorie strawberry preserves
Mock Sour Cream (optional)

Combine first 5 ingredients; stir well. Spoon about 3 tablespoons cheese filling in center of each crêpe. Fold right and left sides over filling; then fold bottom and top over filling, forming a square.

Coat a baking sheet with cooking spray. Place blintzes, seam side down, on baking sheet; bake at 350° for 12 minutes or until thoroughly heated. Top each blintz with ½ tablespoon strawberry preserves. Serve with Mock Sour Cream, if desired. Yield: 8 servings (about 208 calories per serving plus 3 calories per teaspoon Mock Sour Cream).

BRAN CRÊPES:

3 eggs
1½ cups skim milk
1 cup all-purpose flour
⅓ cup 100% bran cereal
1 tablespoon sugar
¼ teaspoon salt
2 teaspoons vegetable oil
Vegetable cooking spray

Combine first 7 ingredients in container of an electric blender; process 30 seconds. Scrape down sides of blender container with rubber spatula; process an additional 30 seconds or until smooth. Refrigerate batter 1 hour. (This allows flour particles to swell and soften so that crêpes are light in texture.)

Coat the bottom of a 6-inch crêpe pan or nonstick skillet with cooking spray; place pan over medium heat until just hot, not smoking.

Pour about 2 tablespoons batter into pan. Quickly tilt pan in all directions so that batter covers the pan in a thin film; cook crêpe about 1 minute.

Lift edge of crêpe to test for doneness. Crêpe is ready for flipping when it can be shaken loose from pan. Flip the crêpe, and cook about 30 seconds. (This side is rarely more than spotty brown and is the side on which filling is placed.)

When crêpe is done, place on a towel to cool. Stack between layers of waxed paper to prevent sticking. Repeat procedure until all batter is used, stirring batter occasionally. Yield: 20 crêpes.

MOCK SOUR CREAM:

½ cup low-fat cottage cheese
1 tablespoon skim milk
1½ teaspoons lemon juice

Combine all ingredients in container of an electric blender; process on medium-high speed until smooth and creamy. Cover and chill thoroughly. Yield: ½ cup.

SPICED ORANGES AND WINE

¾ cup light rosé wine
3 (3-inch) sticks cinnamon
8 medium oranges, peeled, sectioned, and seeded

Combine wine and cinnamon sticks in a small saucepan; bring to a boil. Cover, reduce heat, and simmer 5 minutes.

Place orange sections in a serving bowl; pour wine mixture over oranges. Cover and chill thoroughly. Remove cinnamon sticks before serving. Yield: 8 servings (about 54 calories per serving).

ALMOND-FLAVORED COFFEE

1 cup ground coffee (not instant)
½ cup coarsely ground blanched almonds
1 teaspoon ground nutmeg
½ teaspoon vanilla extract
¼ teaspoon almond extract

Combine all ingredients, mixing well. Brew as desired at 1½ times the normal strength. Yield: 14 servings (about 18 calories per serving).

Note: Ground coffee mixture may be stored in an airtight container in the refrigerator for up to 2 weeks.

Choose dairy products made from skim or low-fat milk to keep fat and calories lower. Some examples are skim milk, part-skim mozzarella cheese, Neufchatel cheese, low-fat cottage cheese, and low-fat yogurt.

WEEKEND PANCAKE BREAKFAST

Feathery Buttermilk Pancakes (2 pancakes)
Fresh Blueberry Sauce (⅓ cup)
or
Spicy Apple Dessert Sauce (⅓ cup)
Hot Mocha-Cocoa (1 cup)

Serves 6
Total calories per serving: 200

FEATHERY BUTTERMILK PANCAKES

1 cup all-purpose flour
1 teaspoon sugar
½ teaspoon baking soda
¼ teaspoon salt
2 egg whites
1 cup buttermilk
2 tablespoons reduced-calorie margarine, melted
Vegetable cooking spray

Combine dry ingredients in a medium bowl. Combine egg whites, buttermilk, and margarine; stir into dry ingredients, mixing well.

Coat a skillet or griddle with cooking spray; place over medium heat until hot. For each pancake, pour 2 tablespoons batter onto skillet. Turn pancakes when tops are bubbly and edges are slightly dry. Yield: 12 pancakes (about 53 calories each).

FRESH BLUEBERRY SAUCE

2 tablespoons sugar
1 tablespoon cornstarch
½ cup water
1 tablespoon lemon juice
2 cups fresh blueberries

Combine sugar and cornstarch in a small saucepan; stir in water and lemon juice. Add blueberries; bring to a boil. Reduce heat, and simmer 1 to 2 minutes, stirring constantly, until clear and thickened. Serve sauce warm over pancakes. Yield: 2 cups (about 10 calories per tablespoon).

SPICY APPLE DESSERT SAUCE

2 cups unsweetened apple juice
½ teaspoon ground cinnamon
2 tablespoons cornstarch
¼ cup plus 2 tablespoons water

Combine apple juice and cinnamon in a saucepan. Bring to a boil; reduce heat to low. Combine cornstarch and water; gradually add to apple juice mixture, stirring constantly. Cook until smooth and thickened, stirring constantly.

Serve sauce warm over pancakes or waffles. Yield: 2¼ cups (about 10 calories per tablespoon).

Note: Also good when served chilled over ice milk or plain yogurt.

HOT MOCHA-COCOA MIX

1½ cups instant nonfat dry milk powder
½ cup sugar
½ cup cocoa
¼ cup instant coffee powder
½ teaspoon ground cinnamon
¼ teaspoon ground nutmeg
⅛ teaspoon ground cloves
Boiling water

Combine first 7 ingredients in a large bowl, and mix well. Store mix in an airtight container.

For each serving, place 2 tablespoons mix in a cup. Add 1 cup boiling water, and stir well. Yield: 22 servings (about 41 calories per serving).

SPECIAL FAMILY BREAKFAST

Eggs Florentine
Spiced Fruit Delight
Coffee or Hot Tea

Serves 4
Total calories per serving: 370

EGGS FLORENTINE

2 onion-flavored buns
1 tablespoon plus 1 teaspoon reduced-calorie margarine
1 (10-ounce) package frozen leaf spinach
4 thin slices lean cooked ham
4 slices tomato
4 poached eggs
Tarragon Hollandaise Sauce

Cut onion buns in half; spread each cut side with 1 teaspoon margarine. Place under broiler until lightly browned.

Cook spinach according to package directions, omitting salt; drain well, and keep warm. Place a slice of ham and a slice of tomato on each bun half. Divide spinach evenly on tomatoes; top with a poached egg. Spoon 2 tablespoons Tarragon Hollandaise Sauce over each. Yield: 4 servings (about 267 calories per serving).

TARRAGON HOLLANDAISE SAUCE:

⅓ cup reduced-calorie mayonnaise
2 tablespoons water
2 teaspoons lemon juice
¼ teaspoon dried whole tarragon
Dash of white pepper

Combine all ingredients in a small saucepan; stir with a wire whisk until smooth. Cook mixture over low heat, stirring constantly, 3 to 4 minutes or until thoroughly heated. Serve warm. Yield: ½ cup.

SPICED FRUIT DELIGHT

2 cups unsweetened apple juice
2 (3-inch) sticks cinnamon
1 tablespoon lemon juice
1 apple, cored and cut into thin wedges
1 peach, peeled and cut into thin wedges
1 pear, cored and cut into thin wedges
½ cup pitted fresh sweet cherries
1 cup fresh strawberries, hulled

Combine apple juice and cinnamon in a saucepan; bring to a boil. Boil 10 minutes; cool. Add lemon juice and all fruit except strawberries. Chill. Stir in strawberries just before serving. Yield: 4 servings (about 103 calories per serving).

Note: May be chilled overnight.

Use fresh fruit and fruit juices whenever possible. If not available, look for unsweetened frozen fruit or frozen fruit juice concentrate, fruit canned in water, or unsweetened canned juice.

EASY FAMILY BRUNCH

Cauliflower Quiche
Toasted English Muffin (½ muffin)
Blueberry Fruit Spread (1 tablespoon)
Fruit Shake
or
*Strawberry Cooler

Serves 6
*Total calories per serving: 323 or *319*

CAULIFLOWER QUICHE

1 (8-ounce) package frozen cauliflower
Vegetable cooking spray
½ cup chopped green pepper
⅓ cup finely chopped onion
1 cup (4 ounces) shredded low-fat Cheddar cheese
1 cup skim milk
3 eggs
½ cup biscuit mix
¼ teaspoon paprika
⅛ teaspoon pepper

Cook cauliflower according to package directions, omitting salt; drain well, and coarsely chop. Place cauliflower on paper towels, and squeeze until barely moist.

Coat a 9-inch pieplate with cooking spray. Layer cauliflower, green pepper, onion, and cheese in pieplate.

Combine remaining ingredients in container of electric blender; process 15 seconds or until well blended. Pour into pieplate. Bake at 375° for 30 to 35 minutes or until set. Let stand 5 minutes before serving. Yield: 6 servings (about 167 calories per serving).

BLUEBERRY FRUIT SPREAD

1 teaspoon unflavored gelatin
¼ cup water
2 cups fresh blueberries
½ cup water
2 tablespoons sugar
1 teaspoon lemon juice

Combine gelatin and ¼ cup water, stirring well; set aside.

Combine blueberries, ½ cup water, sugar, and lemon juice in a medium saucepan. Bring to a boil; reduce heat, and simmer uncovered 8 minutes, stirring frequently. Remove saucepan from heat, and add gelatin, stirring until gelatin is dissolved.

Cool to room temperature. Pour into glass jars, and cover tightly. Refrigerate 4 to 6 hours or until mixture is thoroughly chilled. Store in refrigerator up to 1 month. Yield: 2 half pints (about 9 calories per tablespoon).

FRUIT SHAKE

2 cups unsweetened orange juice
½ cup unsweetened crushed pineapple, undrained
1 medium-size ripe banana, sliced
¼ cup instant nonfat dry milk powder
½ teaspoon vanilla extract

Combine all ingredients in container of electric blender; process until smooth. Chill thoroughly before serving. Yield: 3 cups (about 77 calories per ½-cup serving).

STRAWBERRY COOLER

1 cup skim milk
1 cup plain low-fat yogurt
2 tablespoons sugar
2 teaspoons vanilla extract
2 cups frozen whole strawberries

Combine first 4 ingredients in container of an electric blender; process until smooth. Gradually add strawberries; process until smooth and slightly thickened. Yield: 3¾ cups (about 73 calories per ⅝-cup serving).

SUNDAY BRUNCH FOR TWO

Vegetable-Swiss Omelet
Shredded Wheat Biscuits (2 biscuits)
Strawberry Fruit Spread (2 tablespoons)
Coffee

Serves 2
Total calories per serving: 368

VEGETABLE-SWISS OMELET

Vegetable cooking spray
⅓ cup finely chopped zucchini
¼ cup chopped green onions
¼ cup chopped tomato
Dash of pepper
4 eggs, separated
2 tablespoons water
¼ teaspoon dried whole basil
¼ teaspoon celery salt
⅛ teaspoon pepper
¼ cup (1 ounce) shredded Swiss cheese

Coat a 6-inch heavy skillet with cooking spray; place over medium heat until hot. Add zucchini, green onions, and tomato; sauté 2 to 3 minutes or until just tender. Stir in dash of pepper. Remove vegetables from skillet; set aside and keep warm. Wipe skillet dry with a paper towel.

Beat egg whites (at room temperature) until stiff peaks form; set aside. Combine yolks, water, basil, celery salt, and ⅛ teaspoon pepper. Beat until thick and lemon colored. Gently fold egg whites into yolk mixture. Coat skillet with cooking spray; place over medium heat until just hot enough to sizzle a drop of water. Spread half of egg mixture in skillet. Cover, reduce heat to low, and cook 4 to 5 minutes or until omelet is puffed and bottom is golden brown.

Spoon half of zucchini mixture over half of omelet; sprinkle half of cheese over zucchini mixture on omelet. Loosen omelet with a spatula; fold omelet in half. Gently slide omelet onto a warm plate. Repeat procedure with remaining ingredients to make second omelet. Yield: 2 servings (about 224 calories per serving).

SHREDDED WHEAT BISCUITS

1½ cups all-purpose flour
½ cup crushed shredded whole wheat cereal biscuits
2 tablespoons sugar
1 teaspoon baking powder
½ teaspoon baking soda
½ teaspoon salt
3 tablespoons shortening
1 package dry yeast
¼ cup warm water (105° to 115°)
⅔ cup buttermilk
Vegetable cooking spray

Combine flour, cereal, sugar, baking powder, soda, and salt in a medium bowl; cut in shortening using a pastry blender until mixture resembles coarse meal. Dissolve yeast in warm water. Combine yeast mixture and buttermilk; add to flour mixture, blending well. Cover and refrigerate overnight.

Turn dough out on a floured surface, and knead 1 minute. Roll dough to ½-inch thickness; cut with a 2-inch biscuit cutter. Place biscuits on a baking sheet coated with cooking spray. Bake at 425° for about 12 minutes or until golden brown. Yield: 1½ dozen (about 65 calories each).

Note: Biscuit dough may be stored in refrigerator for 3 to 4 days.

Prepare only enough food for one meal, or plan ahead in order to use leftovers. Store leftover food in the refrigerator, freezer, or in opaque containers before you're tempted to eat it.

STRAWBERRY FRUIT SPREAD

1 envelope unflavored gelatin
¼ cup water
3 cups sliced fresh strawberries
3 tablespoons sugar
2 tablespoons water
1½ tablespoons lemon juice

Soften gelatin in ¼ cup water; set aside.

Combine remaining ingredients in a medium saucepan. Bring to a boil; reduce heat, and simmer uncovered 8 minutes, stirring frequently. Remove from heat, and add gelatin mixture, stirring until gelatin is dissolved. Cool to room temperature.

Pour strawberry mixture into sterilized glass jars; cover tightly. Refrigerate at least 4 to 6 hours or until mixture is thoroughly chilled. Store in refrigerator for up to 1 month. Yield: 3 half pints (about 7 calories per tablespoon).

SPECIAL SUMMER BRUNCH

Tomato Juice Appetizer
Eggs Benedict
Sherried Fruit
or
*Brunch Ambrosia
Hot Tea

Serves 6
*Total calories per serving: 398 or *387*

TOMATO JUICE APPETIZER

4 cups tomato juice
1 medium onion, thinly sliced
2 bay leaves
1 teaspoon instant celery flakes
1 teaspoon dried whole basil
¼ teaspoon dried whole rosemary
¼ teaspoon pepper

Combine all ingredients in a pitcher; mix well. Cover and chill overnight. Strain mixture into chilled glasses, discarding herbs. Serve cold. Yield: 4 cups (about 37 calories per ⅔-cup serving).

EGGS BENEDICT

Vegetable cooking spray
6 (1-ounce) slices Canadian bacon
6 poached eggs
3 English muffins, split and toasted
Mock Hollandaise Sauce

Coat a large skillet with cooking spray; place over medium heat until hot. Place Canadian bacon in skillet; cook 3 minutes on each side or until browned. Place on paper towels to drain.

Place 1 slice Canadian bacon and 1 poached egg on each muffin half; top with 2 tablespoons Mock Hollandaise Sauce. Serve immediately. Yield: 6 servings (about 262 calories per serving).

MOCK HOLLANDAISE SAUCE:

½ cup reduced-calorie mayonnaise
3 tablespoons water
1 tablespoon lemon juice
⅛ teaspoon white pepper

Combine all ingredients in a small saucepan; stir with a wire whisk until smooth. Cook mixture over low heat, stirring constantly, 3 to 4 minutes or until thoroughly heated. Serve warm. Yield: ¾ cup.

SHERRIED FRUIT

2 cups halved fresh sweet cherries
2 cups cantaloupe balls
1 cup sliced fresh nectarines
1 cup cubed fresh pineapple
⅓ cup dry sherry
¾ teaspoon chopped fresh mint

Combine fruit in a large bowl. Add sherry and mint, tossing lightly. Cover; chill at least 2 hours or overnight. Yield: 6 servings (about 99 calories per 1-cup serving).

BRUNCH AMBROSIA

2 small apples, sliced
2 medium grapefruit, peeled and sectioned
2 medium oranges, peeled and sectioned
½ cup unsweetened orange juice
2 tablespoons flaked coconut
Mint sprigs (optional)

Combine first 4 ingredients; cover and chill 1 hour. Arrange fruit in individual serving dishes; sprinkle with coconut and garnish with mint, if desired. Yield: 6 servings (about 88 calories per serving).

MIDDAY MEALS

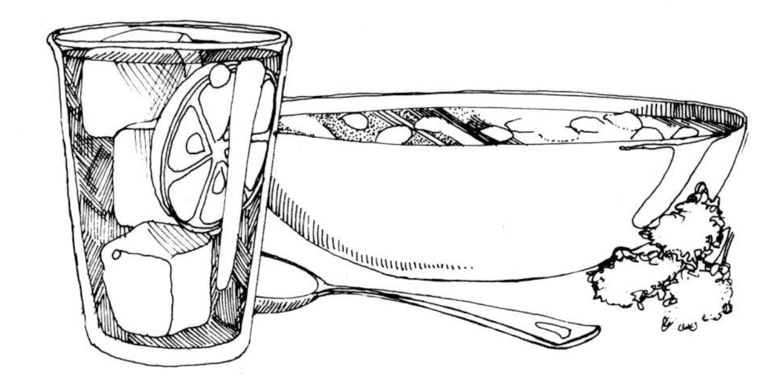

For many people today, lunch means food out of a lunchbox or from a fast-food restaurant. Obviously, you can better control the number of calories you eat by taking your lunch. A sandwich made of whole grain bread and lean meat or poultry is a good lunchbox choice. Be sure to limit the amount of mayonnaise or margarine since each contains about 100 calories per tablespoon. Include fresh, low-calorie vegetables such as raw carrot and celery sticks to eat with your sandwich. Don't tempt yourself with chips!

With our *Cooking Light* Lunchbox Menu, you have a choice of Rye Club Sandwich or Ham Salad Sandwich. Either is hearty and satisfying enough to get you through a busy day. We also suggest a Fresh Vegetable Cocktail for your beverage. Carry it in a thermos so that it will stay cool and refreshing.

In this chapter you'll find a variety of menus to prepare if you're having lunch at home. Our Special Ladies' Luncheon is perfect for a spring or summer day. But if it's cold outside, try our hearty, 400-calorie Lunch for a Chilly Day.

The asterisks (*) in our menus indicate alternate recipes and the slight change in total calories if the alternate recipe is prepared.

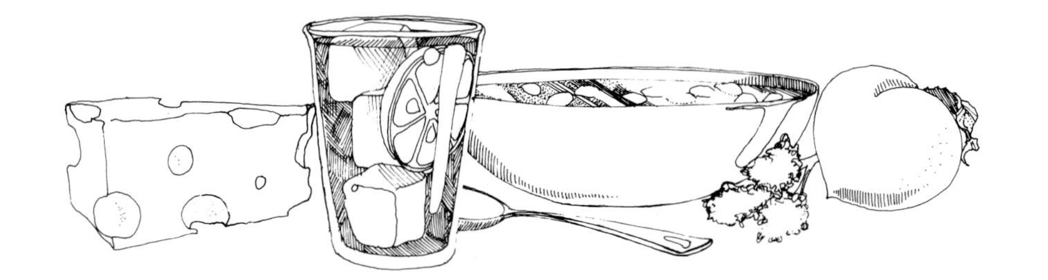

LUNCHBOX MENU

Fresh Vegetable Cocktail
Rye Club Sandwiches
or
*Ham Salad Sandwiches

Serves 4
*Total calories per serving: 464 or *436*

FRESH VEGETABLE COCKTAIL

3 cups unsweetened pineapple juice, chilled
1 medium carrot, sliced
1½ stalks celery, sliced
⅓ cucumber, peeled and sliced
2 slices lemon
Fresh mint (optional)

Combine all ingredients except mint in container of an electric blender. Process until smooth; chill. Serve with fresh mint, if desired. Yield: 4 cups (about 105 calories per 1-cup serving).

Note: Beverage may be made the night before and poured into chilled thermos.

RYE CLUB SANDWICHES

1 cup finely shredded cabbage
¼ cup reduced-calorie mayonnaise
2 tablespoons reduced-calorie chili sauce
1 teaspoon instant minced onion
1 teaspoon lemon juice
4 (1-ounce) slices lean cooked ham
4 (1-ounce) slices cooked turkey
4 (1-ounce) slices Swiss cheese
8 slices rye bread

Combine first 5 ingredients; cover and refrigerate at least 4 hours.

Place 1 slice each of ham, turkey, and cheese on each of 4 slices of bread; top each with equal amounts of coleslaw mixture. Cover with remaining slices of bread. Yield: 4 servings (about 359 calories per serving).

HAM SALAD SANDWICHES

1¼ cups minced lean cooked ham
2 tablespoons dill pickle relish
1 hard-cooked egg, minced
¼ cup minced celery
¼ cup minced apple
2 tablespoons reduced-calorie mayonnaise
1 tablespoon diced pimiento
¼ teaspoon freshly ground pepper
8 slices whole wheat bread
1 tablespoon plus 1 teaspoon reduced-calorie mayonnaise
4 lettuce leaves

Combine first 8 ingredients; chill thoroughly. Spread 4 slices of bread with 1 teaspoon mayonnaise each; top each with a lettuce leaf. Spread about ½ cup ham mixture over each lettuce leaf. Top with remaining bread slices. Yield: 4 servings (about 331 calories per serving).

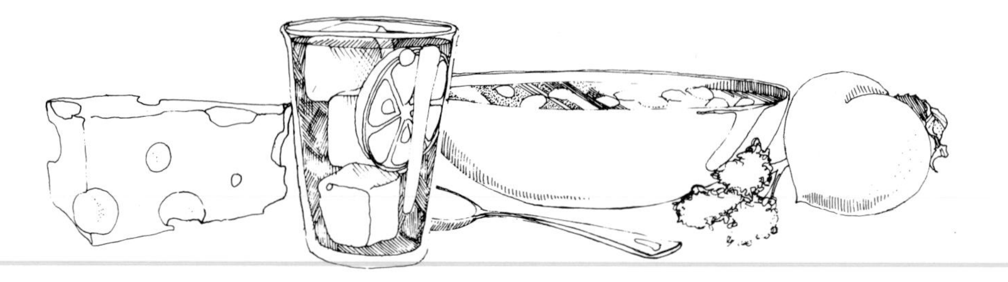

SOUP AND SANDWICH LUNCH

Corn Chowder
Vegetable Salad Rolls
Dutch Peach Crumb Bake
Hot Tea

Serves 4
Total calories per serving: 420

CORN CHOWDER

2 tablespoons reduced-calorie margarine
1 small onion, minced
½ cup minced celery
1 tablespoon all-purpose flour
2¼ cups skim milk
1 (17-ounce) can cream-style corn
¼ teaspoon salt
¼ teaspoon white pepper
⅛ teaspoon ground thyme
Paprika

Melt margarine in a heavy 2-quart saucepan over medium heat; add onion and celery, and sauté 5 minutes or until tender. Stir in flour; cook over low heat 1 minute, stirring constantly. Gradually add milk; cook over medium heat, stirring constantly, until thickened and bubbly. Stir in corn, salt, pepper, and thyme; simmer 20 minutes, stirring occasionally.

To serve, ladle soup into bowls; sprinkle with paprika. Yield: 4½ cups (about 184 calories per 1⅛-cup serving).

VEGETABLE SALAD ROLLS

½ cup chopped green pepper
½ cup chopped cucumber
½ cup chopped tomato
½ cup chopped celery
2 tablespoons chopped onion
2 tablespoons chopped fresh parsley
2 tablespoons chopped dill pickle
⅓ cup low-fat cottage cheese
¼ cup reduced-calorie mayonnaise
⅛ teaspoon garlic powder
8 (1.2-ounce) hard rolls
Leaf lettuce

Combine first 7 ingredients, tossing well; set aside.

Combine cottage cheese, mayonnaise, and garlic powder in container of electric blender; process until smooth. Add to vegetable mixture, tossing gently; chill until ready to serve.

Just before serving, cut a ¾-inch slice from top of each roll; scoop out center, leaving a ½-inch shell (reserve crumbs for other uses). Line inside of rolls with leaf lettuce, and top with vegetable mixture. Yield: 4 servings (about 160 calories per serving).

DUTCH PEACH CRUMB BAKE

2 cups sliced fresh peaches
⅓ cup graham cracker crumbs
½ teaspoon ground cinnamon
Dash of ground nutmeg
2 teaspoons reduced-calorie margarine, melted

Layer peaches in bottom of an 8-inch square baking dish. Combine graham cracker crumbs, cinnamon, and nutmeg, mixing well; blend in margarine. Sprinkle mixture over peaches. Bake, uncovered, at 350° for 30 minutes. Serve warm. Yield: 4 servings (about 76 calories per serving).

Note: Two cups frozen unsweetened peaches, thawed, may be substituted for fresh peaches.

Try to "unlearn" your desire for sweet desserts. Adapt your regular recipes by cutting back on the amount of sugar or by using fresh or unsweetened frozen or canned fruits instead of fruit packed in heavy syrup. You'll gradually learn to appreciate the natural taste of foods more than the sugar-coated taste.

QUICK AND EASY LUNCH FOR TWO

Simple Sloppy Joes
or
*Egg Salad Sandwiches
Carrot Sticks (½ cup)
Spiced Peach Dessert
Skim Milk (1 cup)

Serves 2
*Total calories per serving: 452 or *426*

SIMPLE SLOPPY JOES

½ pound ground chuck
1 cup chopped onion
¼ cup reduced-calorie catsup
1½ tablespoons vinegar
1 tablespoon water
2 teaspoons Worcestershire sauce
1 teaspoon dry mustard
¼ teaspoon salt
¼ teaspoon pepper
1 hamburger bun, split

Cook meat and onion in a large skillet over medium heat until meat is browned and onion is tender; drain in a colander, and pat dry with a paper towel. Wipe pan drippings from skillet with a paper towel.

Return beef mixture to skillet. Stir in remaining ingredients except hamburger bun; cook until thoroughly heated. Spoon mixture evenly over bun halves. Yield: 2 servings (about 290 calories per serving).

EGG SALAD SANDWICHES

2 hard-cooked eggs, chopped
¼ cup finely chopped celery
½ tablespoon chopped fresh parsley
1 teaspoon diced pimiento
⅛ teaspoon salt
Dash of pepper
2 to 3 tablespoons reduced-calorie mayonnaise
6 (¼-inch-thick) slices whole wheat bread
2 slices tomato
2 lettuce leaves

Combine first 6 ingredients; add mayonnaise, and mix well. Spread 2 slices of bread with egg mixture; top each with another slice of bread. Arrange tomato slices and lettuce on top of sandwich. Top with remaining bread.

Cut each sandwich into quarters to serve, using wooden picks to hold layers together. Yield: 2 servings (about 264 calories per serving).

SPICED PEACH DESSERT

1 (16-ounce) can unsweetened peach halves, undrained
½ teaspoon cornstarch
⅛ teaspoon ground cinnamon
Dash of ground nutmeg
Dash of ground cloves
⅛ teaspoon grated orange rind

Drain peaches, reserving juice; set aside. Combine cornstarch, spices, and orange rind in a medium saucepan; stir in reserved peach juice, mixing well. Add peaches; bring to a boil, stirring constantly. Reduce heat, and simmer 2 minutes. Serve warm. Yield: 2 servings (about 52 calories per serving).

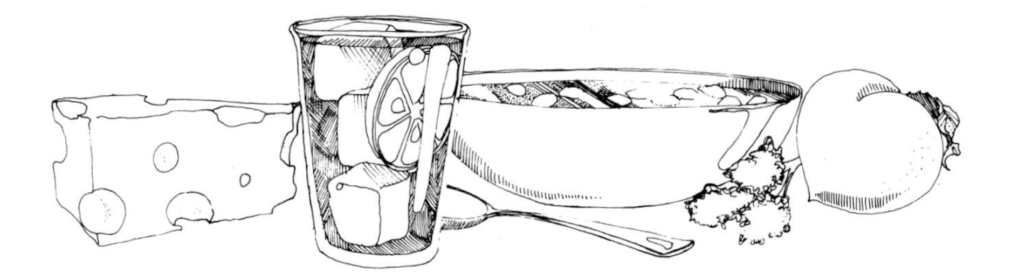

LIGHT SUMMER PICNIC

Pimiento Cheese Sandwiches
Overnight Coleslaw
or
*Zesty Marinated Vegetables
Ginger Cookies (2 cookies)
Iced Tea

Serves 8
*Total calories per serving: 390 or 382**

PIMIENTO CHEESE SANDWICHES

1 (8-ounce) package Neufchatel cheese, softened
2 cups (8 ounces) shredded Colby or Longhorn cheese
1 (4-ounce) jar diced pimiento, drained
3 tablespoons dill pickle juice
Dash of garlic powder
4 (6-inch) whole wheat pocket bread rounds
Leaf lettuce

Combine cheese, mixing well. Add next 3 ingredients, mixing well. Cover and chill at least 1 hour.

Cut pocket bread rounds in half; line each half with lettuce, and fill with ¼ cup cheese mixture. Yield: 8 servings (about 211 calories per serving).

OVERNIGHT COLESLAW

4 cups shredded cabbage
2 cups shredded carrots
¾ cup thinly sliced green onions
¾ cup unsweetened apple juice
⅔ cup cider vinegar
1 tablespoon prepared mustard
1½ teaspoons paprika
1 teaspoon mustard seeds
½ teaspoon garlic salt
½ teaspoon celery seeds
½ teaspoon pepper

Combine cabbage, carrots, and onions in a large bowl. Combine remaining ingredients in a jar; cover tightly, and shake vigorously. Pour over coleslaw mixture; toss lightly to coat. Cover and refrigerate overnight, tossing occasionally. Yield: 8 servings (about 41 calories per serving).

ZESTY MARINATED VEGETABLES

4 medium carrots, scraped and diagonally sliced
1 small head cauliflower, broken into flowerets
2 small zucchini, sliced
¼ pound fresh mushrooms, sliced
1 cup water
⅓ cup vinegar
1 (0.6-ounce) package Italian salad dressing mix

Combine first 4 ingredients in a large shallow dish. Combine water, vinegar, and dressing mix in a jar; cover tightly, and shake vigorously. Pour over vegetables, tossing lightly to coat. Cover and chill overnight. Yield: 8 servings (about 33 calories per serving).

GINGER COOKIES

2 cups all-purpose flour
¼ cup sugar
1 teaspoon baking soda
1 teaspoon ground cinnamon
1 teaspoon ground ginger
½ teaspoon salt
½ teaspoon ground cloves
¾ cup margarine, softened
¼ cup molasses
1 egg, slightly beaten
Sugar

Combine first 7 ingredients, mixing well. Cut in margarine to resemble coarse crumbs. Stir in molasses and egg.

Shape dough into 1-inch balls, and roll lightly in sugar. Place on ungreased baking sheets; bake at 350° for 10 minutes. Remove from baking sheets immediately; cool on wire racks. (Cookies will firm as they cool.) Yield: 3 dozen (about 69 calories each).

Extra calories can add up quickly. Therefore, it's important to divide the total recipe evenly into the number of servings indicated on the recipe. Each serving will be the same size and will contain the number of calories specified.

LUNCH FOR A CHILLY DAY

Hot Ham Sandwiches
or
*Open-Face Sandwiches
Lettuce and Tomato Slices
Curried Fruit
Hot Tea

Serves 6
*Total calories per serving: 408 or *314*

HOT HAM SANDWICHES

¼ cup reduced-calorie margarine, softened
2 tablespoons finely chopped onion
2 tablespoons mustard with horseradish
2 teaspoons poppy seeds or sesame seeds
6 hamburger buns
6 (1-ounce) slices lean cooked ham
6 (1-ounce) slices Swiss cheese

Combine first 4 ingredients; spread on cut sides of hamburger buns. Place 1 slice ham and 1 slice cheese on bottom of each bun; cover with top bun. Wrap each sandwich in foil. Bake at 350° for 25 minutes. Yield: 6 serving (about 328 calories per serving).

OPEN-FACE SANDWICHES

6 (1-ounce) slices cooked turkey breast
6 (1-ounce) slices lean cooked ham
6 slices tomato
6 spears broccoli, cooked
3 English muffins, split
Mock Hollandaise Sauce

Layer 1 slice turkey, 1 slice ham, 1 slice tomato, and 1 spear broccoli on each English muffin half. Spoon 2 tablespoons Mock Hollandaise Sauce over each sandwich. Broil 2 minutes or until sandwiches are heated. Yield: 6 servings (about 234 calories per serving).

MOCK HOLLANDAISE SAUCE:

½ cup reduced-calorie mayonnaise
3 tablespoons water
1 tablespoon lemon juice
⅛ teaspoon white pepper

Combine all ingredients in a small saucepan; stir with a wire whisk until smooth. Cook over low heat, stirring constantly, 3 to 4 minutes or until thoroughly heated. Serve warm. Yield: ¾ cup.

CURRIED FRUIT

1 (8-ounce) can unsweetened sliced pineapple, undrained
1 (16-ounce) can unsweetened peach halves, drained
2 small baking apples, unpeeled, cored, and sliced into rings
1 teaspoon lemon juice
½ to ¾ teaspoon curry powder
⅛ teaspoon ground cinnamon

Drain pineapple slices, reserving juice; set juice aside. Layer fruit in a shallow 2-quart baking dish.

Combine pineapple juice, lemon juice, curry powder, and cinnamon; pour mixture over layered fruit. Bake, uncovered, at 350° for 30 minutes or until apples are tender. Yield: 6 servings (about 60 calories per serving).

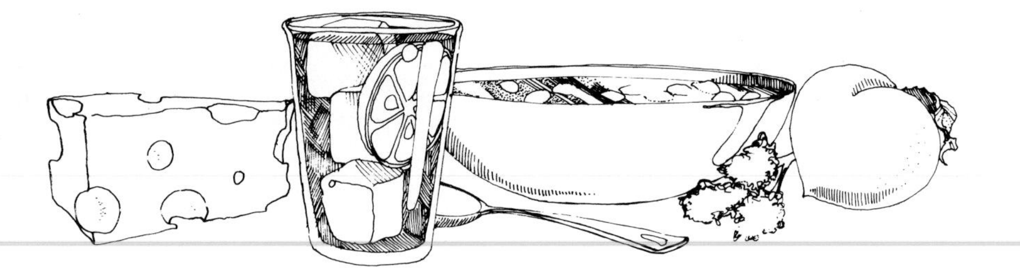

VEGETARIAN LUNCHEON

Light Cream of Celery Soup
Pasta-Stuffed Tomato Salad
Pumpkin Mousse
Iced Tea or Water

Serves 4
Total calories per serving: 494

LIGHT CREAM OF CELERY SOUP

6 stalks celery, coarsely chopped
6 green onions, coarsely chopped
3 medium potatoes, coarsely chopped
1 quart skim milk
½ teaspoon salt
⅛ teaspoon white pepper

Combine all ingredients in a large saucepan. Cook over low heat 30 minutes or until vegetables are tender, stirring occasionally (do not boil).

Pour half of milk mixture into container of electric blender, and process 30 seconds; strain mixture through a sieve into a saucepan. Repeat blending and straining process with remaining mixture. Cook over low heat until thoroughly heated. Serve hot or cold. Yield: 4 cups (about 188 calories per 1-cup serving).

PASTA-STUFFED TOMATO SALAD

¾ cup uncooked corkscrew macaroni
2 small carrots, sliced
2 small green onions, chopped
1 (2-ounce) jar diced pimiento, drained
1 cup drained canned kidney beans
¾ cup sliced celery
¼ cup cooked English peas
2 tablespoons chopped fresh parsley
¼ cup Italian reduced-calorie salad dressing
2 tablespoons reduced-calorie mayonnaise
⅛ teaspoon dried whole marjoram
⅛ teaspoon pepper
4 medium tomatoes

Cook macaroni according to package directions, omitting salt. Drain. Combine with remaining ingredients except tomatoes, tossing well. Chill at least 1 hour.

With stem ends down, cut each tomato into 6 wedges, cutting to, but not through, base of tomato. Spread wedges slightly apart; spoon pasta mixture into tomatoes. Yield: 4 servings (about 222 calories per serving).

PUMPKIN MOUSSE

1 envelope unflavored gelatin
½ cup water
⅔ cup instant nonfat dry milk powder
½ cup mashed canned pumpkin
2 tablespoons sugar
½ teaspoon vanilla extract
¼ teaspoon pumpkin pie spice
6 ice cubes

Combine gelatin and water in a small saucepan; let stand 1 minute. Cook over medium heat 1 minute or until gelatin is dissolved, stirring constantly.

Combine gelatin and remaining ingredients except ice cubes in container of an electric blender; process until smooth. Add ice cubes to container, one at a time, blending well after each addition. Pour into 4 parfait glasses or dessert dishes; cover and refrigerate at least 2 hours. Yield: 4 servings (about 84 calories per serving).

Look for non-traditional ways to include a variety of foods in your diet. If you don't care for milk as a beverage, enjoy a milk-based soup as part of your milk allowance for the day.

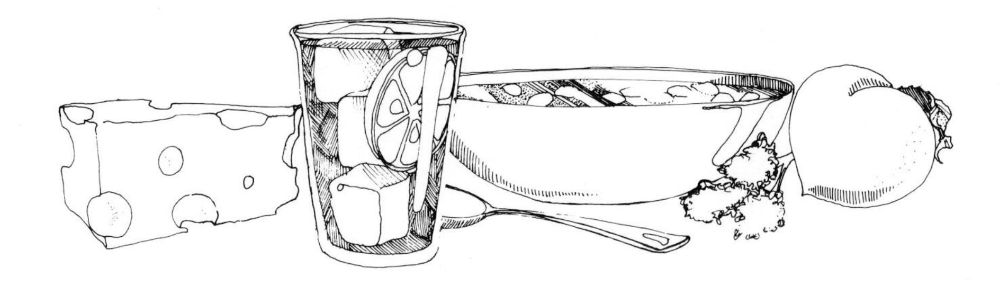

SPECIAL LADIES' LUNCHEON

Shrimp-Crab Salad
Herb-Broiled Tomatoes
Commercial Breadsticks (3 sticks)
Rum Chiffon Delight
Iced Tea or Water

Serves 8
Total calories per serving: 386

SHRIMP-CRAB SALAD

1½ quarts water
2 pounds large unpeeled shrimp
½ pound lump crabmeat
1 (16-ounce) bottle Italian reduced-calorie salad dressing
1 cup chopped celery
1 cup chopped green pepper
¼ cup minced fresh parsley
¼ cup minced shallots
¼ cup finely chopped sweet pickle
1 tablespoon plus 1 teaspoon minced capers
1 tablespoon lemon juice
Lettuce leaves

Bring water to a boil; add shrimp, and return to a boil. Reduce heat, and simmer 3 to 5 minutes. Drain well; rinse with cold water. Peel and devein shrimp.

Combine shrimp and next 9 ingredients in an airtight container; refrigerate overnight.

Spoon crab and shrimp mixture onto lettuce leaves, using a slotted spoon. Yield: 8 servings (about 145 calories per serving).

Fill Vegetable-Swiss Omelet with chopped fresh vegetables and a sprinkling of Swiss cheese. Even with two Shredded Wheat Biscuits and Strawberry Fruit Spread, calories for the entire brunch are under 370 (menu begins on page 32).

HERB-BROILED TOMATOES

4 medium tomatoes
¼ cup grated Parmesan cheese
2 tablespoons fine, dry breadcrumbs
2 tablespoons minced fresh parsley
1 teaspoon dried whole basil
1 teaspoon dried whole oregano
¼ teaspoon salt
¼ teaspoon freshly ground pepper
2 tablespoons reduced-calorie margarine, melted

Remove stems from tomatoes; cut in half crosswise. Combine remaining ingredients; lightly press mixture over cut side of tomato halves. Place tomatoes on baking sheet; broil 6 inches from heat for 3 to 5 minutes or until topping is lightly browned. Yield: 8 servings (about 50 calories per serving).

RUM CHIFFON DELIGHT

1 envelope unflavored gelatin
¼ cup plus 2 tablespoons sugar
2 cups skim milk
4 eggs, separated
2 teaspoons rum flavoring
2 cups sliced fresh strawberries

Combine gelatin and sugar in a medium-size heavy saucepan. Beat together milk and egg yolks; add to gelatin mixture, stirring until smooth. Cook over low heat, stirring constantly, 5 to 7 minutes or until mixture thickens slightly (do not boil). Chill until mixture mounds when dropped from a spoon; stir in rum flavoring.

Beat egg whites (at room temperature) until stiff peaks form; fold gelatin mixture into egg whites. Spoon into 8 parfait or sherbet glasses, alternating with layers of strawberries. Chill at least 1 hour. Yield: 8 servings (about 116 calories per serving).

Treat your dieting friends to a special luncheon of Shrimp-Crab Salad, Herb-Broiled Tomatoes, breadsticks, and Rum Chiffon Delight. When the meal's over, your guests will never believe they've eaten only 386 calories (menu begins on page 46).

FAMILY SUNDAY DINNER

Herbed Pot Roast
Stuffed Potatoes
Congealed Green Salad
Pineapple-Coconut Delight
Skim Milk (1 cup)

Serves 6
Total calories per serving: 500

HERBED POT ROAST

- 1 (3½-pound) boneless bottom-round roast
- Vegetable cooking spray
- ½ teaspoon salt
- ½ teaspoon pepper
- ½ cup water
- ⅓ cup dry sherry
- ¼ cup reduced-calorie catsup
- 1 clove garlic, minced
- ¼ teaspoon dry mustard
- ¼ teaspoon dried whole marjoram
- ¼ teaspoon dried whole rosemary
- ¼ teaspoon dried whole thyme
- 2 medium onions, sliced
- 1 bay leaf
- 2 (8-ounce) cans sliced mushrooms, undrained

Trim all visible fat from meat. Coat a Dutch oven with cooking spray; place over medium heat until hot. Place roast in Dutch oven, and brown on all sides. Sprinkle with salt and pepper.

Combine next 8 ingredients; pour over roast. Add onion and bay leaf. Cover and simmer 2½ to 3 hours or until roast is tender. Add mushrooms; cook until mushrooms are thoroughly heated. Discard bay leaf.

Remove roast from cooking liquid; skim fat from liquid. Serve vegetables and broth with roast. Yield: 12 servings (about 165 calories per 3-ounce serving).

STUFFED POTATOES

- 3 medium baking potatoes (about 1½ pounds)
- ¼ cup plus 2 tablespoons plain low-fat yogurt
- 3 tablespoons minced chives or green onions
- 1½ tablespoons skim milk
- ¼ teaspoon salt
- ⅛ to ¼ teaspoon garlic powder
- ⅛ to ¼ teaspoon white pepper
- 3 tablespoons grated Parmesan cheese
- 1½ teaspoons paprika

Scrub potatoes thoroughly; prick with a fork. Bake at 400° for 1 hour or until tender. Allow potatoes to cool to touch. Cut potatoes in half lengthwise; carefully scoop out pulp, leaving shells intact. Combine potato pulp and next 6 ingredients in a mixing bowl; beat until light and fluffy. Stuff shells with potato mixture.

Combine Parmesan cheese and paprika; sprinkle over potatoes. Bake at 400° for 10 minutes or until thoroughly heated. Yield: 6 servings (about 99 calories per serving).

CONGEALED GREEN SALAD

1 envelope unflavored gelatin
½ cup cold water
2 teaspoons sugar
½ teaspoon salt
⅛ teaspoon pepper
1¼ cups boiling water
¼ cup vinegar
1 tablespoon lemon juice
1 cup finely chopped fresh spinach
1 cup finely chopped celery
¼ cup finely chopped onion
¼ cup shredded carrot
Vegetable cooking spray
Lettuce leaves
Cherry tomatoes

Combine gelatin, cold water, sugar, salt, and pepper in a medium bowl; add boiling water, and stir until gelatin is completely dissolved. Stir in vinegar and lemon juice; chill until the consistency of unbeaten egg white.

Fold next 4 ingredients into gelatin mixture. Spoon into a 4-cup mold coated with cooking spray, and chill until firm. Unmold on lettuce leaves, and garnish with cherry tomatoes. Yield: 6 servings (about 29 calories per serving).

PINEAPPLE-COCONUT DELIGHT

1 (15¼-ounce) can unsweetened crushed pineapple, undrained
1 envelope unflavored gelatin
¼ teaspoon vanilla extract
½ cup instant nonfat dry milk powder
½ cup ice water
2 tablespoons lemon juice
2 tablespoons sugar
½ cup flaked coconut

Drain pineapple well, reserving juice. Add water to pineapple juice to measure 1 cup. Combine juice mixture and gelatin in a small saucepan; let stand 1 minute. Cook over low heat until gelatin is dissolved, stirring constantly. Remove from heat, and stir in pineapple and vanilla. Chill until consistency of unbeaten egg white.

Combine dry milk powder and ice water in a small bowl; beat until foamy. Add lemon juice; continue beating 3 to 4 minutes or until soft peaks form. Gradually add sugar, beating until stiff peaks form. Fold gelatin mixture and coconut into whipped milk. Spoon into 6 (6-ounce) custard cups or dessert dishes. Chill until set. Yield: 6 servings (about 117 calories per serving).

Reduce the number of calories in meat dishes by trimming all visible fat from the meat before cooking.

DINNERS AND SUPPERS

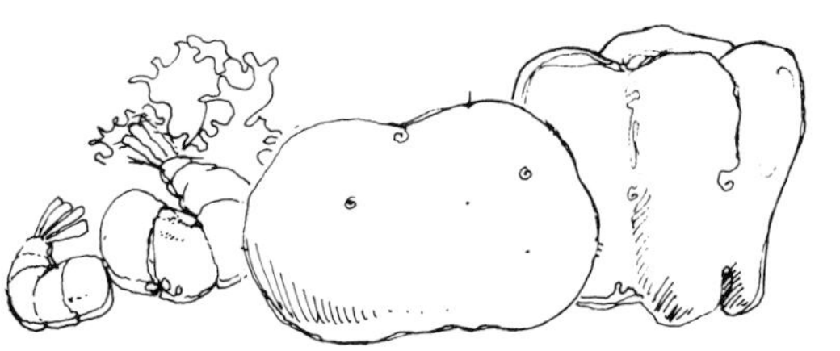

The evening meal is often the main meal of the day. But it shouldn't be a time for indulging in too much food and too many calories. *Cooking Light* shows you how to trim away calories in appetizers, entrées, side dishes, and desserts and still serve delicious dinners or suppers for your family and friends.

In this chapter, you'll find menus with a foreign flavor and dinners to serve two. If you're interested in saving money as well as calories, you should enjoy Supper on a Budget and Gourmet Dining on a Shoestring. Meatless Italian Dinner is hearty, satisfying, and nutritious — even without an ounce of meat.

Use these dinners and suppers as a guide to planning your own menus. Remember to add interest to your meals by including a variety of colors, textures, temperatures, and shapes. Try not to serve the same food more than once in a meal; for instance, do not have a tomato juice appetizer if the entreé contains chopped tomatoes.

Add a simple garnish to your low-calorie plate for extra color and visual appeal. By making your menus varied and attractive, low-calorie dining becomes more enjoyable.

The asterisks (*) in our menus indicate alternate recipes and the slight change in total calories if the alternate recipe is prepared.

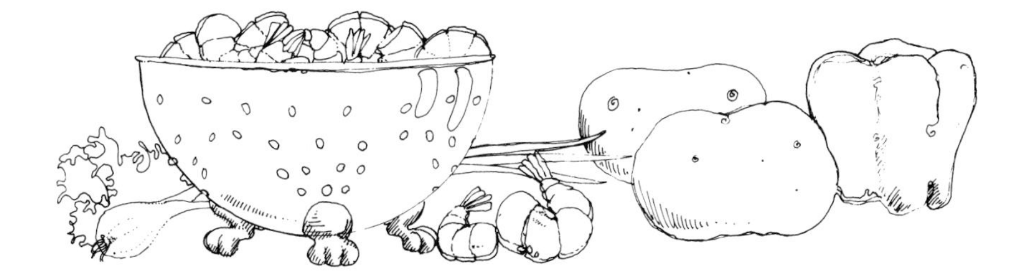

ONE-DISH SUPPER

Vegetable-Pork Chop Dinner
Apple Cider Salad
Vanilla Ice Milk (½ cup)
Chocolate Sauce (2 tablespoons)
Skim Milk (1 cup)

Serves 6
Total calories per serving: 582

VEGETABLE-PORK CHOP DINNER

6 (½-inch-thick) lean pork chops (about 2 pounds)
½ teaspoon salt
¼ teaspoon pepper
Vegetable cooking spray
½ teaspoon dried whole savory, crushed
1 bay leaf
2 cups tomato juice
½ cup water
1 (1¼-pound) cabbage, cut into 6 wedges
6 carrots, scraped and cut into 1-inch slices
1½ cups coarsely chopped onion
6 small new potatoes (about ¾ pound), halved

Trim excess fat from chops; sprinkle with salt and pepper. Coat a Dutch oven with cooking spray; place over medium-high heat until hot. Add pork chops, and cook until browned on both sides. Remove chops, and drain on paper towel; wipe pan drippings from Dutch oven with paper towel.

Return chops to Dutch oven. Add savory, bay leaf, tomato juice, and water; cover and simmer 30 minutes.

Add remaining ingredients; cover and simmer 35 minutes or until vegetables are tender. Remove bay leaf before serving. Yield: 6 servings (about 271 calories per serving).

APPLE CIDER SALAD

- 1 envelope unflavored gelatin
- 2 cups unsweetened apple cider, divided
- 1 tablespoon plus 1 teaspoon lemon juice
- 2 medium apples, unpeeled and finely chopped
- ½ cup finely chopped celery
- Vegetable cooking spray
- Lettuce leaves

Combine gelatin and ½ cup apple cider in a small, heavy saucepan; cook over low heat, stirring constantly until gelatin dissolves. Stir in remaining apple cider and lemon juice; chill until the consistency of unbeaten egg white. Fold in apple and celery.

Spoon apple mixture into a 4-cup mold coated with cooking spray; chill until firm. To serve, unmold on lettuce leaves. Yield: 6 servings (about 69 calories per serving).

CHOCOLATE SAUCE

- ¼ cup plus 2 tablespoons cocoa
- ⅓ cup sugar
- ½ cup skim milk
- ¼ cup water
- ½ to ¾ teaspoon vanilla extract

Combine cocoa and sugar in a small saucepan; stir in milk and water with a wire whisk until smooth. Bring to a boil over medium heat, stirring constantly; cook 1 minute, stirring constantly. Remove from heat; stir in vanilla. Serve warm over ice milk. Yield: about 1 cup (about 26 calories per tablespoon plus 100 calories per ½ cup ice milk).

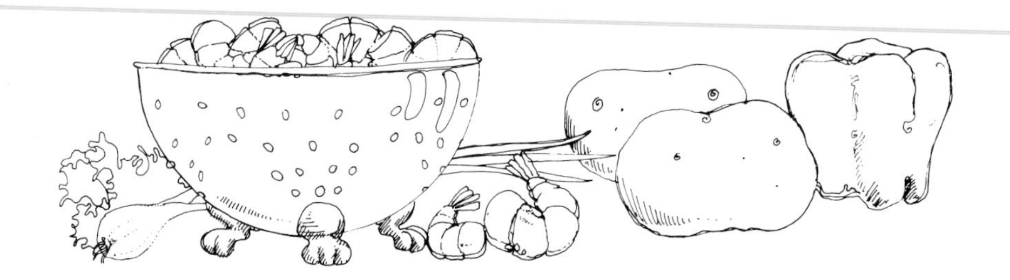

SUPPER ON A BUDGET

Deluxe Pineapple Meat Loaf
Seasoned New Potatoes
Green Salad
Tomato Salad Dressing (2 tablespoons)
Orange-Banana Pops
Skim Milk (1 cup)

Serves 6
Total calories per serving: 521

DELUXE PINEAPPLE MEAT LOAF

1 (8-ounce) can unsweetened crushed pineapple, undrained
3 tablespoons reduced-calorie catsup, divided
1 pound ground chuck
2 slices bread, crumbled
2 eggs, beaten
1 small onion, minced
1 teaspoon prepared horseradish
1 teaspoon soy sauce

Drain pineapple, reserving 2 tablespoons juice. Add 1 tablespoon catsup to reserved juice, mixing well; set aside.

Combine drained pineapple, remaining 2 tablespoons catsup, and next 6 ingredients. Shape into an 8- x 5-inch loaf on rack in broiler pan. Bake at 350° for 45 minutes; remove from oven, and brush with reserved pineapple juice mixture. Bake an additional 15 minutes or until done. Yield: 6 servings (about 207 calories per serving).

SEASONED NEW POTATOES

1½ pounds new potatoes
½ teaspoon dried whole dillweed
3 tablespoons reduced-calorie margarine, melted
3 tablespoons chopped fresh parsley
1 tablespoon minced chives
1 tablespoon lemon juice

Wash potatoes; peel a ½-inch strip around center of each potato. Combine potatoes and dillweed in a medium saucepan. Cover with water, and cook, covered, 20 to 25 minutes or until tender; drain.

Combine remaining ingredients; spoon over hot potatoes, and stir gently until coated. Yield: 6 servings (about 92 calories per serving).

TOMATO SALAD DRESSING

1 (8-ounce) can tomato sauce
½ small onion, diced
¼ cup cider vinegar
1 tablespoon plus 1 teaspoon sugar
2 tablespoons vegetable oil
2 teaspoons Worcestershire sauce
½ teaspoon salt
½ teaspoon dried whole oregano

Combine all ingredients in container of an electric blender; process until smooth. Cover and chill thoroughly. Serve dressing over salad greens. Yield: 1½ cups (about 18 calories per tablespoon).

Including green salads with meals is an effective way of adding fiber and bulk to the diet without adding too many calories. For variety, use different kinds of lettuce. For salad dressing, try a simple sprinkling of vinegar or lemon juice or use a reduced-calorie salad dressing. Regular commercial dressings can turn a simple green salad into a salad high in calories.

ORANGE-BANANA POPS

3 medium bananas, mashed (about 2 cups)
1 cup unsweetened orange juice
¼ cup water
2 tablespoons sugar
1 teaspoon lime or lemon juice

Combine all ingredients, mixing well. Pour mixture into 6 (5-ounce) paper drink cups. Partially freeze; insert a wooden stick or wooden spoon into center of each cup, and freeze until firm.

When ready to serve, let pops stand at room temperature 5 minutes; tear off cups. Yield: 6 servings (about 86 calories per serving).

SPRING SEAFOOD SUPPER

Shrimp Delight
Asparagus Mimosa Salad
Commercial French Bread (1 slice)
Sunshine Fruit Parfaits
Iced Tea or Water

Serves 4
Total calories per serving: 495

SHRIMP DELIGHT

Vegetable cooking spray
1 tablespoon reduced-calorie margarine
½ pound fresh mushrooms, sliced
2 stalks celery, diagonally sliced
2 green onions, sliced
2 cloves garlic, minced
¼ cup finely chopped green pepper
2 tablespoons minced fresh parsley
1½ pounds unpeeled large fresh shrimp
3 tablespoons lemon juice
8 cherry tomatoes, halved
⅛ teaspoon freshly ground pepper
1 teaspoon capers (optional)
2 cups hot cooked vermicelli
Celery leaves (optional)
Lemon rind curl (optional)

Coat a large skillet with cooking spray; add margarine, and place over medium-low heat until margarine is melted. Add next 6 ingredients to skillet; cover and cook 8 to 10 minutes or until vegetables are just tender, stirring occasionally.

Peel and devein shrimp; add shrimp and lemon juice to cooked vegetables. Cook, uncovered, over medium-high heat 4 to 5 minutes or until shrimp are done.

Stir in tomatoes, pepper, and capers, if desired; cook 1 minute or until mixture is thoroughly heated. Serve over vermicelli. Garnish with celery leaves and lemon rind curl, if desired. Yield: 4 servings (about 160 calories per serving plus 90 calories per ½ cup cooked vermicelli).

ASPARAGUS MIMOSA SALAD

1¼ pounds fresh asparagus spears
¼ cup cider vinegar
2 tablespoons water
3 tablespoons minced chives or green onions
1 clove garlic, minced
¼ teaspoon paprika
6 cups shredded lettuce
1 hard-cooked egg yolk
2 tablespoons diced pimiento (optional)

Snap off tough ends of asparagus, and remove scales from stalks with a knife or vegetable peeler. Cook asparagus, covered, in a small amount of boiling water 4 to 6 minutes or until asparagus is crisp-tender; drain.

Arrange asparagus in a shallow baking dish. Combine next 5 ingredients in a glass jar; cover tightly, and shake vigorously. Pour over asparagus; cover and chill 3 to 4 hours.

To serve, arrange asparagus on shredded lettuce; spoon dressing over asparagus and lettuce. Press egg yolk through a sieve; garnish asparagus with sieved egg yolk and chopped pimiento, if desired. Yield: 4 servings (about 42 calories per serving).

SUNSHINE FRUIT PARFAITS

½ cup frozen whipped topping, thawed
¼ cup flaked coconut
2 tablespoons frozen orange juice concentrate, thawed and undiluted
1 large orange, peeled, seeded, and sectioned
1 large banana, sliced
1 cup cubed fresh pineapple
Fresh mint leaves (optional)

Combine whipped topping, coconut, and orange juice concentrate in a small bowl; stir well, and set aside. Combine orange, banana, and pineapple; toss lightly.

Spoon alternate layers of fruit mixture and orange juice mixture into 4 parfait glasses. Garnish with mint, if desired. Yield: 4 servings (about 133 calories per serving).

Always take time to measure and weigh ingredients and individual servings carefully. We recommend a food scale for weighing meat, fish, poultry, and some vegetables, fruit, and breads. Use measuring cups and measuring spoons when appropriate.

SUMMER SUPPER COOKOUT

Deviled Beef Patties
Zucchini and Onion Kabobs
Lettuce Leaves
Dill Pickle (1 medium)
Watermelon Sherbet
Iced Tea or Water

Serves 8
Total calories per serving: 475

DEVILED BEEF PATTIES

2 pounds ground chuck
2 eggs
¼ cup reduced-calorie chili sauce
1 tablespoon instant minced onion
1 tablespoon plus 1 teaspoon Worcestershire sauce
1 tablespoon prepared horseradish
2 teaspoons prepared mustard
¼ teaspoon pepper
8 hamburger buns

Combine all ingredients except hamburger buns; shape into 8 (1-inch-thick) patties. Grill 3 to 5 inches from slow to medium coals 4 to 7 minutes on each side or until desired degree of doneness. Serve on hamburger buns. Yield: 8 servings (about 216 calories per serving plus 120 calories per bun).

ZUCCHINI AND ONION KABOBS

6 medium zucchini, cut into 1½-inch slices
4 medium onions, quartered
¾ cup Italian reduced-calorie salad dressing
3 tablespoons lemon juice

Combine all ingredients in a large baking dish; mix well. Cover and marinate in the refrigerator at least 2 hours.

Remove vegetables from marinade, reserving marinade. Alternate zucchini and onion on skewers. Grill kabobs about 6 inches from medium coals for 20 to 30 minutes or until vegetables are tender, turning and basting frequently with marinade. Yield: 8 servings (about 38 calories per serving).

WATERMELON SHERBET

4 cups diced seeded watermelon
½ cup sugar
3 tablespoons lemon juice
1 envelope unflavored gelatin
¼ cup cold water
1 cup skim milk

Combine watermelon, sugar, and lemon juice; refrigerate 30 minutes. Spoon half of mixture into container of an electric blender; process until smooth. Repeat with remaining watermelon mixture.

Combine gelatin and cold water in a small saucepan; cook over low heat, stirring constantly, until gelatin is dissolved. Gradually add dissolved gelatin to watermelon mixture, stirring well. Add milk, and pour into freezer can of a 1-gallon hand-turned or electric freezer. Freeze according to the manufacturer's instructions. Yield: 1 quart (about 82 calories per ½-cup serving).

SUMMER VEGETABLE SUPPER

Southern-Style Black-Eyed Peas
Oven-Fried Yellow Squash
Tangy Herbed Green Beans
Fresh Tomato (2 slices)
Corn Muffins (2 muffins)
Fresh Peach (1 medium)
Skim Milk (1 cup)

Serves 6
Total calories per serving: 494

SOUTHERN-STYLE BLACK-EYED PEAS

About ¾ pound ham hocks
1 quart water
4 cups shelled fresh black-eyed peas
1 medium onion, minced
½ teaspoon salt
¼ teaspoon pepper

Wash ham hocks, and place in a 3-quart Dutch oven; add water, and bring to a boil. Reduce heat; simmer, uncovered, 30 to 45 minutes or until meat is tender. Remove ham hocks and discard, or reserve any meat for use in other recipes. Strain broth, and chill until fat rises to the surface and hardens. Remove fat and discard.

Place broth, peas, onion, salt, and pepper in a 3-quart Dutch oven; bring to a boil. Reduce heat; cover and simmer 30 minutes or until peas are tender. Add more water if necessary. Yield: 6 servings (about 124 calories per serving).

OVEN-FRIED YELLOW SQUASH

½ cup cornmeal
½ teaspoon salt
¼ teaspoon pepper
1 egg
1 tablespoon water
3 medium-size yellow squash, cut into ¼-inch slices
Vegetable cooking spray

Combine cornmeal, salt, and pepper; set aside. Combine egg and water; beat well. Dip squash in egg mixture; dredge in cornmeal mixture. Lightly coat a 15- x 10- x 1-inch baking pan with cooking spray. Place squash slices in a single layer in pan. Bake at 450° for 30 to 40 minutes or until golden brown, turning once. Yield: 6 servings (about 64 calories per serving).

Note: Green tomatoes may be substituted for squash.

TANGY HERBED GREEN BEANS

1 pound fresh green beans
Vegetable cooking spray
1 large onion, chopped
1 large stalk celery, chopped
½ cup chopped green pepper
¼ cup water
¾ to 1 teaspoon dried whole tarragon
½ teaspoon lemon-pepper seasoning

Remove strings from beans; wash and cut into 2-inch pieces. Set aside.

Coat a large skillet with cooking spray; place over medium heat until hot. Add onion; sauté until tender. Add celery and green pepper; cover and cook over low heat 5 minutes, stirring occasionally. Add green beans and remaining ingredients; cover and cook 20 minutes or until beans are tender. Yield: 6 servings (about 32 calories per serving).

Legumes (dried beans and peas) are valuable sources of fiber, as are leafy vegetables (brussels sprouts, cabbage, lettuce), root vegetables (carrots, turnips, and rutabagas), and vegetables with an edible skin and seeds (potatoes, tomatoes, and cucumbers).

CORN MUFFINS

1 cup cornmeal
½ teaspoon baking soda
½ teaspoon baking powder
¼ teaspoon salt
1 cup buttermilk
1 egg, slightly beaten
1 tablespoon reduced-calorie margarine, melted
Vegetable cooking spray

Combine dry ingredients, mixing well. Stir in buttermilk, egg, and margarine until well blended. Coat muffin pans with cooking spray; spoon batter into muffin pans, filling two-thirds full. Bake at 450° for 10 to 12 minutes. Yield: 1 dozen (about 52 calories each).

ORIENTAL STIR-FRY DINNER

Oriental Spinach Soup
Chinese Beef Stir-Fry
or
*Chicken-Vegetable Stir-Fry
Gingered Fruit
Light Almond Cookies (2 cookies)

Serves 6
*Total calories per serving: 514 or *513*

ORIENTAL SPINACH SOUP

1 (10-ounce) package frozen chopped spinach
1 tablespoon cornstarch
1½ cups water, divided
2 (10½-ounce) cans chicken broth, undiluted
½ cup diagonally sliced celery
2 tablespoons sliced green onions
2 teaspoons soy sauce

Cook spinach according to package directions, omitting salt; drain well. Dissolve cornstarch in ¼ cup water; add to remaining water. Combine cornstarch mixture and broth in a saucepan. Add spinach and remaining ingredients; bring to a boil. Reduce heat, and simmer 5 minutes. Yield: 8 cups (about 55 calories per 1⅓-cup serving).

CHINESE BEEF STIR-FRY

1 pound boneless flank steak
1 tablespoon cornstarch
1½ teaspoons sugar
½ cup water
¼ cup soy sauce
2 tablespoons oyster-flavored sauce
1 medium onion
Vegetable cooking spray
3 stalks celery, diagonally sliced
½ pound fresh mushrooms, sliced
½ cup sliced water chestnuts
½ pound fresh snow peas
3 cups hot cooked rice

Trim excess fat from steak. Partially freeze steak; slice across grain into 2- x ¼-inch strips. Set aside.

Combine cornstarch, sugar, water, soy sauce, and oyster sauce; set aside.

Peel onion, and cut into ¼-inch slices; cut each slice into quarters. Set aside.

Coat wok or skillet well with cooking spray; allow to heat at medium high (325°) for 2 minutes. Add steak, and stir-fry about 3 minutes. Remove meat from wok, reserving pan drippings; set aside.

Place onion, celery, mushrooms, and water chestnuts in wok; stir-fry 2 to 3 minutes. Add meat and snow peas to wok; cover and reduce heat to medium (275°). Simmer 2 to 3 minutes.

Stir in soy sauce mixture. Cook on medium high (325°), stirring constantly, until thickened and bubbly. Serve over rice. Yield: 6 servings (about 176 calories per serving plus 90 calories per ½ cup rice).

CHICKEN-VEGETABLE STIR-FRY

6 chicken breast halves (about 3 pounds), skinned and boned
Vegetable cooking spray
¼ cup plus 1 tablespoon soy sauce
1 (4-ounce) can sliced mushrooms, undrained
1 large onion, coarsely chopped
2 small green peppers, cut into 1-inch strips
1 (8-ounce) can sliced water chestnuts, drained
1 teaspoon cornstarch
½ teaspoon sugar
⅛ teaspoon red pepper
3 cups hot cooked rice

Cut chicken breasts into 1½-inch pieces; set aside.

Coat wok or skillet well with cooking spray; allow to heat at medium high (325°) for 1 to 2 minutes. Add chicken and soy sauce; stir-fry 3 to 4 minutes or until lightly browned. Remove chicken from wok, reserving the pan drippings; set aside.

Drain mushrooms, reserving the liquid; set aside.

Add onion and green pepper to wok; stir-fry 4 minutes or until vegetables are crisp-tender. Return chicken to wok. Stir in water chestnuts and mushrooms.

Combine reserved mushroom liquid, cornstarch, sugar, and red pepper; mix well. Pour over chicken and vegetables, stirring well. Reduce heat to low (225°); simmer 2 to 3 minutes or until slightly thickened. Serve over rice. Yield: 6 servings (about 175 calories per serving plus 90 calories per ½ cup rice).

GINGERED FRUIT

2 medium apples, cored and sliced
2 medium oranges, peeled and sectioned
2 medium bananas, sliced
½ cup unsweetened orange juice
1 tablespoon grated fresh ginger

Combine all ingredients; cover and chill 2 hours. Yield: 6 servings (about 85 calories per serving).

LIGHT ALMOND COOKIES

¼ cup plus 2 tablespoons margarine
¼ cup sugar
1 egg yolk
½ teaspoon almond extract
¼ teaspoon vanilla extract
¼ teaspoon lemon extract
1 cup all-purpose flour
½ teaspoon baking powder
Dash of salt
1 tablespoon almond slices

Cream margarine; gradually add sugar, and beat until light and fluffy. Add egg yolk, and beat well. Stir in flavorings.

Combine dry ingredients; add to creamed mixture, beating well. Shape into 1-inch balls. Place 2 inches apart on ungreased cookie sheets. Press an almond slice in center of each cookie. Bake at 300° for 20 minutes or until edges begin to brown. Remove cookies to wire racks, and cool completely. Yield: 2 dozen (about 54 calories each).

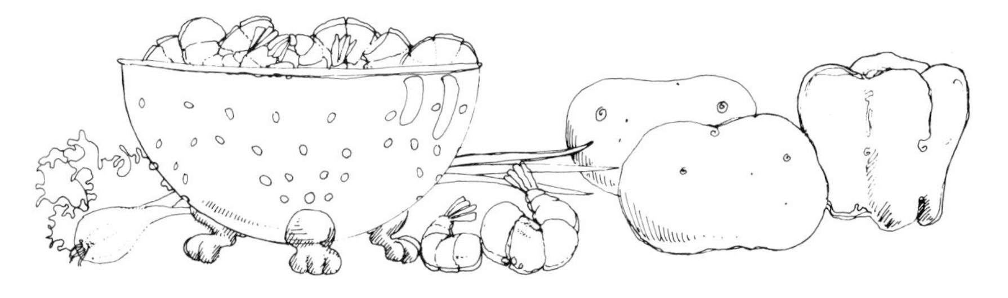

MEATLESS ITALIAN DINNER

Eggplant Lasagna
or
*Italian-Style Spaghetti Squash
Broccoli Salad
Commercial Italian Bread (1 slice)
Fresh Apple (1 medium)
Skim Milk (1 cup)

Serves 6
*Total calories per serving: 473 or *423*

EGGPLANT LASAGNA

Vegetable cooking spray
1¾ cups chopped onion
2 cloves garlic, minced
1 (16-ounce) can whole tomatoes, undrained
¼ cup tomato paste
2 tablespoons chopped fresh parsley
1 teaspoon salt
1 teaspoon dried whole oregano
½ teaspoon dried whole basil
Freshly ground pepper to taste
2 (1½-pound) eggplants, peeled and cut into ¼-inch slices
1 cup (4 ounces) shredded mozzarella cheese
1 (8-ounce) carton low-fat cottage cheese
3 tablespoons grated Parmesan cheese

Coat large skillet with cooking spray. Sauté onion and garlic in skillet over low heat until onion is tender. Stir in next 7 ingredients. Bring to a boil; reduce heat, and simmer uncovered 30 to 40 minutes, stirring occasionally.

Cook eggplant, covered, in a small amount of boiling water 3 to 5 minutes or until just tender (do not overcook); drain well.

Combine mozzarella and cottage cheese, and set aside.

Coat a 13- x 9- x 2-inch baking dish with cooking spray. Place half of eggplant in baking dish. Top with half of sauce mixture and half of cheese mixture; sprinkle with half of Parmesan cheese. Repeat layers. Bake at 350° for 30 minutes. Yield: 6 servings (about 187 calories per serving).

ITALIAN-STYLE SPAGHETTI SQUASH

1 (6-pound) spaghetti squash
Vegetable cooking spray
1 (1-pound) eggplant, peeled and cut into ½-inch cubes
1 small onion, chopped
2 large cloves garlic, minced
1 (28-ounce) can tomatoes, undrained and coarsely chopped
1 (6-ounce) can tomato paste
1 teaspoon dried Italian seasoning
½ teaspoon dried whole basil
½ teaspoon pepper
¼ cup grated Parmesan cheese

Wash squash; pierce several times with a large fork. Place squash in a baking pan. Bake at 350° for 1 hour and 15 minutes or until squash is tender.

Allow squash to cool; cut squash in half, and remove seeds. Using a fork, remove spaghetti-like strands; place strands in a 12- x 8- x 2-inch baking dish, and set aside.

Coat a large skillet with cooking spray; place over medium-low heat until hot. Add eggplant, onion, and garlic to skillet; cover and cook 10 minutes, stirring occasionally. Stir in remaining ingredients except Parmesan cheese. Bring to a boil; reduce heat, and simmer, uncovered, 30 minutes.

Pour sauce over squash strands in baking dish; cover loosely, and bake at 350° for 20 minutes or until thoroughly heated. Sprinkle with Parmesan cheese before serving. Yield: 6 servings (about 137 calories per serving).

BROCCOLI SALAD

1 (10-ounce) package frozen broccoli spears
2 hard-cooked eggs, sliced
2 tablespoons finely chopped onion
½ cup Italian reduced-calorie salad dressing
½ head lettuce, torn into bite-size pieces

Cook broccoli according to package directions just until tender, omitting salt; drain and cool. Cut into 1-inch pieces. Combine broccoli, eggs, onion, and salad dressing; cover and chill. Add lettuce; toss well. Yield: 6 servings (about 56 calories per serving).

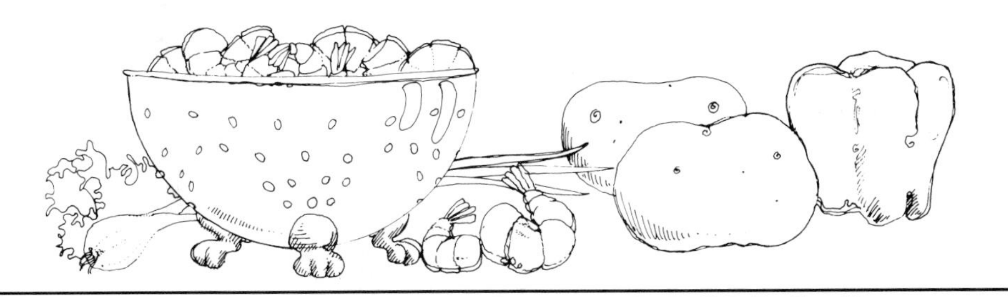

A TASTE OF MEXICO

Chili Con Carne
Mexican Carrot Toss
Mexican Cornsticks
Lemon-Lime Puff
Skim Milk (1 cup)

Serves 6
Total calories per serving: 502

CHILI CON CARNE

Vegetable cooking spray
1 teaspoon vegetable oil
1 medium onion, chopped
1 clove garlic, minced
2 cups thinly sliced celery
½ cup chopped green pepper
1 pound ground round
2 (16-ounce) cans tomatoes, undrained and coarsely chopped
1 (15½-ounce) can kidney beans, drained
2 teaspoons chili powder
1 teaspoon dried whole oregano
½ teaspoon pepper

Coat a Dutch oven with cooking spray; add oil, and place over medium heat until hot. Add next 4 ingredients, and sauté 8 to 10 minutes or until tender. Add ground round, and cook until browned; drain beef mixture in a colander. Wipe pan drippings from pan with a paper towel. Return beef mixture to Dutch oven. Stir in remaining ingredients; cover, reduce heat, and simmer 45 minutes, stirring occasionally. Uncover and simmer 15 minutes to thicken. Yield: 6 cups (about 215 calories per 1-cup serving).

MEXICAN CARROT TOSS

- 2 small zucchini, shredded (about 2½ cups)
- 5 large carrots, scraped and shredded
- 2 tablespoons chopped pimiento-stuffed olives
- 2 tablespoons chopped green onions
- ⅓ cup plain low-fat yogurt
- 1½ tablespoons red wine vinegar
- ½ teaspoon garlic salt
- ½ teaspoon dry mustard
- ⅛ to ¼ teaspoon ground cumin
- Lettuce leaves

Pat zucchini dry on paper towels; place in a medium bowl. Add carrots, olives, and green onions. Combine next 5 ingredients; pour over vegetables, and toss. Serve on lettuce leaves. Yield: 6 servings (about 65 calories per serving).

MEXICAN CORNSTICKS

- ½ cup yellow cornmeal
- 1 tablespoon all-purpose flour
- ½ teaspoon baking soda
- ¼ teaspoon salt
- ⅔ cup buttermilk
- 1 egg white, slightly beaten
- 2 tablespoons finely chopped onion
- 2 tablespoons finely chopped green pepper
- ⅛ teaspoon red pepper
- Vegetable cooking spray

Combine cornmeal, flour, soda, and salt in a small bowl; stir in next 5 ingredients, mixing well.

Coat a cast-iron cornstick pan with cooking spray; place in a 450° oven until hot. Remove pan from oven; spoon cornmeal mixture into pan, filling three-fourths full. Bake at 450° for 15 to 20 minutes or until browned and crisp on the edges. Yield: 6 cornsticks (about 53 calories each).

LEMON-LIME PUFF

- 4 eggs, separated
- 1 tablespoon sugar
- 1 teaspoon grated lemon peel
- ½ teaspoon grated lime peel
- 2 tablespoons lemon juice
- 1 tablespoon lime juice
- 2 tablespoons sugar
- Vegetable cooking spray

Beat egg yolks in a medium bowl. Add next 5 ingredients; continue beating 1 minute. Set aside.

Beat egg whites (at room temperature) until foamy; gradually add 2 tablespoons sugar, beating until stiff peaks form. Fold egg whites into yolk mixture; pour into a 1-quart soufflé dish coated with cooking spray. Bake at 350° for 30 minutes or until lightly browned and firm. Yield: 6 servings (about 79 calories per serving).

> Cut back on the fat and sugar in your favorite bread recipes to keep calories low, or buy the commercial bread brand with the lowest calories per serving.

SPECIAL VEAL DINNER FOR TWO

Tomato Juice (¾ cup)
Veal Scallopini
Herbed New Potatoes
Ginger Carrots
Lettuce Wedge
Tangy Dressing (1 tablespoon)
Fresh Fruit (½ cup)
Light Chablis (6 ounces)

Serves 2
Total calories per serving: 582

VEAL SCALLOPINI

½ pound (¼-inch-thick) veal cutlets
1½ tablespoons all-purpose flour
¼ teaspoon salt
¼ teaspoon freshly ground pepper
Vegetable cooking spray
2 teaspoons vegetable oil
⅓ cup Chablis or other dry white wine
2 tablespoons lemon juice
Lemon twists (optional)

Trim excess fat from veal; place veal on a sheet of waxed paper. Flatten to ⅛-inch thickness, using a meat mallet or rolling pin; cut into 2-inch pieces. Combine flour, salt, and pepper; dredge veal in flour mixture.

Coat a large skillet with cooking spray; add oil to skillet, and place over medium-high heat until hot. Add veal, and cook 1 minute on each side or until lightly browned. Remove veal from skillet, and set aside.

Pour wine and lemon juice into skillet; bring to a boil. Return veal to skillet, turning to coat with sauce; reduce heat, and simmer 1 to 2 minutes or until sauce is slightly thickened and veal is thoroughly heated. Garnish with lemon twists, if desired. Yield: 2 servings (about 225 calories per serving).

HERBED NEW POTATOES

4 small new potatoes
2 teaspoons minced fresh parsley
2 teaspoons minced chives
2 teaspoons reduced-calorie margarine

Peel a ½-inch strip around center of each potato. Cook, covered, in boiling water 20 minutes or until tender. Drain potatoes; add remaining ingredients, tossing to coat. Yield: 2 servings (about 88 calories per serving).

GINGER CARROTS

3 medium carrots, scraped and cut into 3- x ¼-inch strips
1 teaspoon reduced-calorie margarine
1 teaspoon brown sugar
⅛ teaspoon ground ginger

Cook carrots in a small amount of boiling water until crisp-tender; drain and set aside. Melt margarine in saucepan; stir in sugar and ginger. Cook over medium-low heat, stirring constantly, until sugar is dissolved. Add carrots; cook, stirring gently, until carrots are well coated and thoroughly heated. Yield: 2 servings (about 48 calories per serving).

TANGY DRESSING

½ cup reduced-calorie mayonnaise
2 tablespoons lemon juice
2 tablespoons white wine vinegar
1 tablespoon Dijon mustard
2 tablespoons minced fresh parsley
2 tablespoons minced green olives
1 tablespoon minced onion
1 tablespoon minced celery
1 tablespoon minced capers
½ teaspoon freshly ground pepper

Combine mayonnaise, lemon juice, vinegar, and mustard; mix well. Stir in remaining ingredients; cover and chill for 1 hour. Serve dressing over lettuce wedges. Yield: 1 cup (about 26 calories per tablespoon).

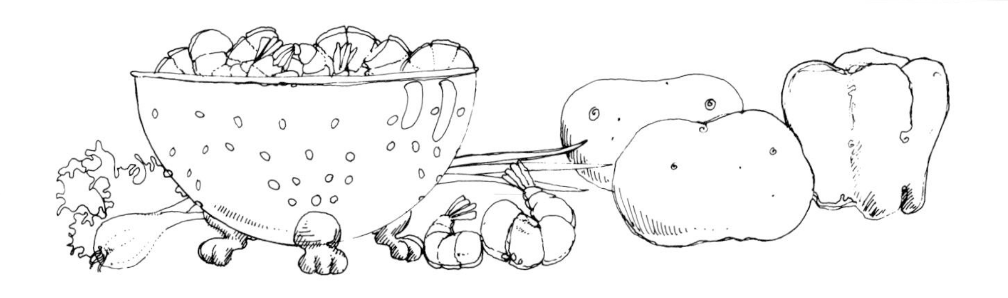

ELEGANT DINNER FOR TWO

Artichokes with Yogurt Dip
Sauterne Scallop Bake
Steamed Broccoli (1 stalk)
Green Salad
Tropical Fruit Meringue Cups

Serves 2
Total calories per serving: 543

ARTICHOKES WITH YOGURT DIP

½ cup plain low-fat yogurt
2 tablespoons reduced-calorie mayonnaise
1 tablespoon reduced-calorie catsup
1½ teaspoons minced onion
1 teaspoon lemon juice
½ teaspoon Worcestershire sauce
4 drops hot sauce
¼ teaspoon garlic powder
¼ teaspoon pepper
2 small artichokes
Lemon wedge

Combine first 9 ingredients, stirring gently; chill.

Wash artichokes by plunging up and down in cold water. Cut off the stem end, and trim about ½ inch from top of each artichoke. Remove any loose bottom leaves. With scissors, trim about ¼ of each outer leaf. Rub top and edges of leaves with a lemon wedge to prevent discoloration.

Place artichokes in a large Dutch oven with about 1 inch of water. Cover tightly, and bring to a boil; reduce heat, and simmer 30 to 40 minutes or until leaves pull out easily. Spread leaves apart; pull out the fuzzy thistle center (choke) with a spoon.

Arrange the artichokes on serving plates, and serve with yogurt dip. Yield: 2 servings (about 42 calories per artichoke plus about 14 calories per tablespoon dip).

SAUTERNE SCALLOP BAKE

¾ cup water
½ cup Sauterne or other dry white wine
¼ teaspoon salt
¼ teaspoon instant minced onion
Dash of pepper
½ pound fresh scallops
½ cup sliced fresh mushrooms
1½ tablespoons reduced-calorie margarine
1½ tablespoons all-purpose flour
½ cup skim milk
⅛ teaspoon pepper
¼ cup (1 ounce) shredded Swiss cheese
Vegetable cooking spray
1 to 2 tablespoons chopped fresh parsley

Combine first 5 ingredients in a medium saucepan; cover and simmer 5 minutes. Stir scallops and mushrooms into liquid mixture; cover and simmer 5 minutes.

Remove scallops and mushrooms from saucepan with a slotted spoon, reserving liquid in pan; set scallops and mushrooms aside. Bring liquid to a boil, and cook, uncovered, 10 minutes or until liquid is reduced to about ½ cup.

Melt margarine in a heavy saucepan over low heat; add flour, and cook 1 minute, stirring constantly (mixture will be dry). Gradually add ½ cup reduced liquid and milk to flour mixture; cook over medium heat, stirring constantly with a wire whisk, until thickened and bubbly. Add ⅛ teaspoon pepper and cheese, stirring until cheese is melted.

Remove sauce from heat; stir scallops and mushrooms into sauce. Coat 2 (10-ounce) custard cups with cooking spray. Spoon scallop mixture into cups; bake at 375° for 15 to 20 minutes. Sprinkle with parsley. Yield: 2 servings (about 198 calories per serving).

TROPICAL FRUIT MERINGUE CUPS

1 egg white
⅛ teaspoon cream of tartar
¼ teaspoon vanilla extract
3½ tablespoons sugar
Vegetable cooking spray
¼ cup unsweetened pineapple juice
1½ teaspoons cornstarch
¼ teaspoon grated lemon rind
1 kiwi, peeled and sliced
1 medium orange, peeled and sectioned

Beat egg white (at room temperature), cream of tartar, and vanilla with an electric mixer until soft peaks form. Gradually add sugar, 1 tablespoon at a time, and beat until stiff peaks form.

Coat a nonstick baking sheet with cooking spray; shape meringue into 2 circles on baking sheet, building up sides to form cups. Bake at 275° for 45 minutes; turn oven off, and let dry in oven 15 minutes. Remove from oven, and let cool to room temperature.

Combine juice, cornstarch, and lemon rind in a saucepan. Cook, stirring constantly, until clear and thickened; chill. Divide glaze in bottoms of meringue shells; arrange kiwi and orange over glaze. Yield: 2 servings (about 175 calories per serving).

COMPANY KABOB DINNER

Marinated Beef Kabobs with Rice
Broccoli with Horseradish Sauce
Cheesy Italian Salad
Glazed Strawberry Dessert

Serves 6
Total calories per serving: 598

MARINATED BEEF KABOBS WITH RICE

1½ pounds lean boneless sirloin steak
1 large purple onion, cut into 1-inch cubes
2 medium-size green peppers, cut into 1-inch squares
1 pound small yellow squash, cut into 1-inch thick slices
1 (8-ounce) bottle Italian reduced-calorie salad dressing
¼ cup Burgundy or other dry red wine
Vegetable cooking spray
3 cups hot cooked rice

Trim all visible fat from meat; cut meat into 1½-inch cubes. Place meat and vegetables in a shallow container; set aside.

Combine salad dressing and wine; pour over meat and vegetables. Cover and marinate in the refrigerator overnight, stirring occasionally. Drain, reserving marinade.

Alternate meat and vegetables on 6 (12-inch) skewers. Coat grill with cooking spray. Grill kabobs over medium-hot coals for 15 minutes or until desired degree of doneness, turning and basting frequently with marinade. Serve over rice. Yield: 6 servings (about 206 calories per serving plus 90 calories per ½ cup cooked rice).

BROCCOLI WITH HORSERADISH SAUCE

1 (1½-pound) bunch fresh broccoli
¼ cup plus 2 tablespoons plain low-fat yogurt
¼ cup plus 2 tablespoons reduced-calorie mayonnaise
1½ teaspoons prepared mustard
½ teaspoon prepared horseradish
Paprika (optional)

Trim off large leaves of broccoli; remove tough ends of lower stalks. Wash broccoli thoroughly, and separate into spears.

Arrange broccoli in steaming rack with stalks to center of rack. Place over boiling water; cover and steam 10 to 15 minutes or to desired degree of doneness. Arrange broccoli spears in serving dish; keep warm.

Combine remaining ingredients except paprika in a small saucepan; cook until thoroughly heated, stirring constantly (do not boil). Spoon sauce over broccoli; sprinkle with paprika, if desired. Yield: 6 servings (about 73 calories per serving).

CHEESY ITALIAN SALAD

3 small zucchini, finely chopped
4 green onions, thinly sliced
6 large fresh mushrooms, finely chopped
1 hard-cooked egg, finely chopped
1 clove garlic, crushed
1 (2-ounce) package blue cheese, crumbled
½ cup Italian reduced-calorie salad dressing
1 small head lettuce

Combine all ingredients except lettuce in a medium bowl. Cover and refrigerate 2 hours, stirring occasionally.

Cut lettuce into 6 wedges; place on serving plates. Divide vegetable mixture on top of lettuce. Yield: 6 servings (about 96 calories per serving).

> Vegetables are rich in the water-soluble vitamins B and C. Steaming vegetables over boiling water preserves more of these vitamins than when vegetables are cooked in boiling water.

GLAZED STRAWBERRY DESSERT

- 7 cups fresh strawberries, divided
- 1 cup water
- ½ cup sugar
- 2 tablespoons cornstarch
- ⅛ teaspoon ground cinnamon
- Fresh mint (optional)

Place 1 cup strawberries and water in container of electric blender; process until pureed. Transfer to a small saucepan, and bring to a boil; cover, reduce heat, and simmer 5 minutes. Strain, reserving liquid; discard pulp. Return liquid to saucepan.

Combine sugar, cornstarch, and cinnamon in a small bowl; add to strawberry liquid, and stir until smooth. Bring to a boil, and cook until mixture thickens, stirring constantly.

Place 1 cup strawberries in each of 6 dessert dishes; spoon sauce over top and chill. Garnish with mint, if desired. Yield: 6 servings (about 133 calories per serving).

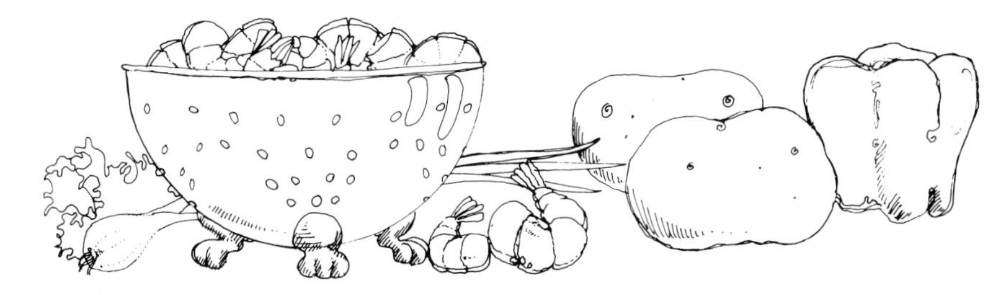

GOURMET DINING ON A SHOESTRING

Fresh Spinach Soup
Baked Chicken Kiev
Cooked Brown Rice (½ cup)
Vegetable Stuffed Squash
Fresh Orange and Grapefruit Sections (½ cup)
Cappuccino Soufflé

Serves 6
Total calories per serving: 571

FRESH SPINACH SOUP

- 1 large onion, chopped
- Vegetable cooking spray
- 1 pound fresh spinach leaves, washed and drained
- 1 medium potato, peeled and quartered
- 2 beef-flavored bouillon cubes
- ¼ teaspoon pepper
- 1 clove garlic, minced
- 3½ cups hot water
- ½ cup skim milk
- 2 tablespoons grated Parmesan cheese

Sauté onion in a large Dutch oven coated with cooking spray. Add next 6 ingredients; bring to a boil. Cover, reduce heat, and simmer 10 to 15 minutes or until potato is tender, stirring occasionally.

Spoon half of spinach mixture into container of an electric blender; process until smooth. Repeat procedure with remaining spinach mixture.

Pour spinach mixture back into Dutch oven; stir in milk. Cook over low heat, stirring constantly, until thoroughly heated. Ladle into bowls; sprinkle each serving with 1 teaspoon Parmesan cheese. Yield: 6 cups (about 56 calories per 1-cup serving).

BAKED CHICKEN KIEV

¼ cup plus 2 tablespoons reduced-calorie margarine, softened
3 tablespoons minced fresh parsley
½ teaspoon dried whole rosemary, crushed
¼ teaspoon garlic salt
Dash of pepper
6 chicken breast halves, skinned and boned
¼ cup skim milk
⅓ cup fine, dry breadcrumbs

Combine first 5 ingredients in a small bowl. Shape margarine mixture into six 2-inch long sticks; freeze until firm.

Place each chicken breast half between 2 sheets of waxed paper; flatten to ¼-inch thickness, using a meat mallet or rolling pin. Place 1 portion margarine mixture in the center of each chicken piece. Fold ends over margarine; roll up, beginning with long side, and secure with wooden picks.

Dip chicken rolls in milk; coat well with breadcrumbs. Place in a baking dish; bake at 400° for 25 to 30 minutes. Pour pan juices over chicken before serving. Yield: 6 servings (about 221 calories per serving).

VEGETABLE STUFFED SQUASH

6 small yellow squash
1 cup finely chopped tomato
½ cup minced onion
½ cup finely chopped green pepper
½ cup (2 ounces) shredded extra-sharp Cheddar cheese
¼ to ½ teaspoon freshly ground pepper
⅛ teaspoon dried whole marjoram

Wash squash thoroughly, and place in a large saucepan. Cover with water, and bring to a boil. Cover, reduce heat, and simmer 5 to 6 minutes or until tender but still firm. Drain and cool slightly. Trim off stems, and cut squash in half lengthwise; gently scoop out pulp, leaving a firm shell.

Drain and chop pulp; combine pulp and remaining ingredients. Place squash shells in a 13- x 9- x 2-inch baking dish; spoon vegetable mixture into shells. Bake at 400° for 20 minutes. Yield: 6 servings (about 68 calories per serving).

CAPPUCCINO SOUFFLÉ

2 (1-ounce) squares semisweet chocolate, coarsely chopped
2 tablespoons sugar
½ teaspoon instant coffee powder
⅛ teaspoon ground cinnamon
⅓ cup boiling water
2 egg yolks
4 egg whites
Vegetable cooking spray

Combine chocolate, sugar, coffee powder, and cinnamon in container of electric blender; process until mixture is a fine powder. Add water, and process 30 seconds. Scrape down sides of container; add egg yolks, and process 15 seconds.

Beat egg whites (at room temperature) in a large bowl until stiff but not dry. Gently fold egg whites into the chocolate mixture. Spoon into a 1-quart soufflé dish coated with cooking spray. Bake at 350° for 30 minutes or until puffed and firm. Yield: 6 servings (about 91 calories per serving).

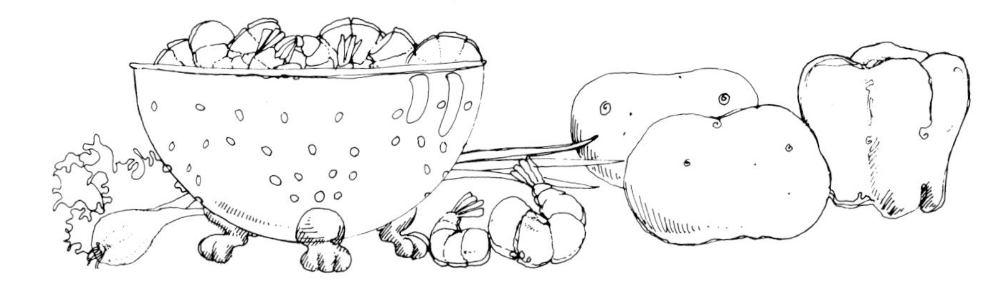

MIDNIGHT BREAKFAST

Potato Omelet
or
*Creamy Scrambled Eggs
Toasted English Muffin (½ muffin)
Fresh Tomato (2 slices)
Gingersnap-Baked Pears
Skim Milk (1 cup)

Serves 4
*Total calories per serving: 523 or *497*

POTATO OMELET

1 medium baking potato, unpeeled
Vegetable cooking spray
1 teaspoon margarine
¼ cup chopped onion
6 eggs
½ cup low-fat cottage cheese
2 tablespoons skim milk
¼ teaspoon salt
⅛ teaspoon pepper
1 cup alfalfa sprouts

Cook potato in boiling water until just tender; let cool to touch. Peel and cut into ½-inch cubes; set aside.

Coat a 10-inch skillet or omelet pan with cooking spray; add margarine to skillet, and place over medium heat until margarine is melted. Add potatoes and onion, and sauté until browned.

Combine next 5 ingredients, mixing until blended; pour over potato mixture in skillet. Reduce heat to low; cover and cook 5 minutes. Uncover and cook until set, gently lifting edges of omelet and tilting pan to allow uncooked portion to flow underneath.

Place alfalfa sprouts on half of omelet; carefully fold omelet in half. Yield: 4 servings (about 187 calories per serving).

CREAMY SCRAMBLED EGGS

2 tablespoons reduced-calorie margarine
1½ tablespoons all-purpose flour
½ cup skim milk
Vegetable cooking spray
5 eggs, beaten
½ cup low-fat cottage cheese
1 tablespoon minced chives
1 teaspoon dried whole chervil
Dash of pepper

Melt margarine in a small heavy saucepan over low heat; add flour, stirring until smooth (mixture will be dry). Cook 1 minute, stirring constantly. Gradually add milk; cook over medium heat, stirring constantly with a wire whisk, until thickened and bubbly. Remove from heat.

Coat a large nonstick skillet with cooking spray; place over medium-low heat until hot. Pour in eggs. As eggs begin to set, stir gently to allow uncooked portions to flow underneath; cook until eggs are softly set. Gently stir in white sauce and remaining ingredients; cook 2 to 3 minutes, stirring often, until eggs are firm but moist. Yield: 4 servings (about 161 calories per serving).

GINGERSNAP-BAKED PEARS

1 (16-ounce) can unsweetened pear halves, drained
12 gingersnaps, finely crushed
2 tablespoons sugar
2 tablespoons reduced-calorie margarine, melted

Arrange pear halves, cut side up, in a 9-inch cakepan. Combine remaining ingredients, mixing well; spread over pears. Bake at 300° for 20 minutes; serve warm. Yield: 4 servings (about 156 calories per serving).

Dieters can enjoy a late night snack or meal provided the calories stay within the total day's plan. The total number of calories eaten per day is important, not when the calories are eaten.

MICROWAVE MENUS

The microwave oven can be a real friend if you're dieting. Since it speeds cooking time, you'll be less tempted to snack before your meal is ready. Also, you can leave off added fat when microwaving foods like chicken and fish and still get a tender, juicy product. Another advantage is that fewer vitamins and minerals are lost from vegetables since less water is needed for cooking.

In the next few pages, you'll find ways to use your microwave at breakfast, lunch, and dinner. The microwave makes egg poaching easy, and the recipe in Breakfast for a Weekday gives exact poaching directions. If an omelet suits your preference, try Sunday Brunch for Two. We've also included a dinner menu calculated for only two servings.

Expecting company for lunch or dinner? Our suggestion is Easy, Elegant Luncheon or Springtime Sunday Dinner. Either menu will help make entertaining less hectic. For the family, try Casual Italian Supper which features Slim Spaghetti Pie as the entrée — perfect for a chilly evening.

We think you'll enjoy these microwave menus; they will help you save calories as well as time.

The asterisks (*) in our menus indicate alternate recipes and the slight change in total calories if the alternate recipe is prepared.

BREAKFAST FOR A WEEKDAY

Egg Scramble
or
*Microwave Poached Eggs
Cheesy Garlic Grits
Fresh Tomato (2 slices)
Toasted English Muffin (½ muffin)
Microwave Peach Jam (1 tablespoon)
Coffee

Serves 4
*Total calories per serving: 335 or *321*

EGG SCRAMBLE

½ cup thinly sliced mushrooms
¼ cup sliced green onions
4 eggs
3 tablespoons skim milk
¼ teaspoon celery salt
⅛ teaspoon pepper

Combine mushrooms and green onions in a 1-quart glass casserole. Cover loosely with heavy-duty plastic wrap, and microwave at HIGH for 3 minutes or until vegetables are tender, stirring once.

Combine remaining ingredients, beating well; add to vegetable mixture in casserole. Cover and microwave at HIGH for 1 minute. Break up set portions of egg with a fork, and push toward center of dish.

Microwave at HIGH for 1 to 2 minutes or until eggs are almost set, stirring once (eggs will be soft and moist).

Cover and let stand 1 to 2 minutes to complete cooking. Yield: 4 servings (about 94 calories per serving).

MICROWAVE POACHED EGGS

½ cup water
1 teaspoon vinegar
4 eggs

Place 2 tablespoons water in each of 4 (6-ounce) custard cups; add ¼ teaspoon vinegar to each. Microwave at HIGH for 2 to 3 minutes or until water is boiling.

Gently break 1 egg into each cup; lightly pierce each yolk with a wooden pick. Cover cups with heavy-duty plastic wrap, and arrange cups in a circle on a microwave-safe platter. Microwave at MEDIUM HIGH (70% power) for 2 to 3 minutes or until almost all of white is opaque (egg will not be completely set). Let eggs stand 2 to 3 minutes to continue cooking. Yield: 4 servings (about 80 calories per serving).

CHEESY GARLIC GRITS

2⅔ cups water
⅔ cup uncooked quick-cooking grits
4 (⅔-ounce) slices low-fat process American cheese, torn into small pieces
1 to 1½ teaspoons Worcestershire sauce
½ teaspoon garlic salt
⅛ to ¼ teaspoon hot sauce
Paprika

Combine water and grits in a 2-quart casserole. Cover with casserole lid or heavy-duty plastic wrap; microwave at HIGH for 8 to 9 minutes, stirring after 4 minutes.

Add next 4 ingredients to grits; mix well. Microwave at HIGH for 30 seconds to 1 minute; stir well. Sprinkle with paprika. Let stand 5 minutes before serving. Yield: 4 servings (about 135 calories per serving).

MICROWAVE PEACH JAM

4 cups frozen unsweetened sliced peaches, thawed
1 (1¾-ounce) package powdered fruit pectin
1 tablespoon sugar
½ teaspoon ascorbic acid
1 tablespoon lemon juice (optional)

Mash peaches with a potato masher. Combine peaches with pectin, sugar, ascorbic acid, and lemon juice, if desired, in a deep 2-quart casserole. Cover with casserole lid, and microwave at HIGH for 2 minutes; stir well. Cover and microwave an additional 3 to 4 minutes or until mixture boils 1 minute. Remove from microwave; continue to stir 2 minutes. Pour into freezer containers; cover and freeze.

To serve, let jam thaw in refrigerator. Store jam in freezer up to 1 year, or in refrigerator up to 1 month. Yield: 2 half pints (about 14 calories per tablespoon).

When preparing poached or hard-cooked eggs in the microwave, be sure to pierce the egg yolk with a wooden pick before microwaving. This releases excess steam which would otherwise burst the yolk.

SUNDAY BRUNCH FOR TWO

Gazpacho
or
*Microwave Tomato Bouillon
Vegetable Omelet
Breakfast Potatoes
Hot Tea

Serves 2
*Total calories per serving: 361 or *335*

GAZPACHO

1 (8-ounce) can whole tomatoes, undrained
1 cup tomato juice
1 small tomato, chopped
¼ cup finely chopped cucumber
¼ cup finely chopped celery
¼ cup finely chopped green pepper
½ tablespoon red wine vinegar
1 clove garlic, crushed
Dash of pepper

Process canned tomatoes in container of an electric blender until smooth. Combine pureed tomatoes and remaining ingredients; cover and refrigerate at least 3 hours. Yield: 3 cups (about 72 calories per 1½-cup serving).

MICROWAVE TOMATO BOUILLON

2 cups tomato juice
1 medium onion, thinly sliced
1 stalk celery, chopped
2 bay leaves, broken
4 peppercorns
2 lemon wedges (optional)

Combine all ingredients except lemon wedges in a 4-cup glass measure. Cover with heavy-duty plastic wrap; let stand at least 1 hour.

Turn back edge of plastic wrap to vent; microwave at HIGH for 2 to 3 minutes or until mixture boils. Strain into mugs, discarding vegetables and herbs; serve hot. Garnish with lemon wedges, if desired. Yield: 2 cups (about 46 calories per 1-cup serving).

VEGETABLE OMELET

½ cup thinly sliced mushrooms
¼ cup chopped green pepper
¼ cup chopped onion
1 tablespoon diced pimiento
3 eggs, separated
2 tablespoons reduced-calorie mayonnaise
¼ teaspoon salt
⅛ teaspoon pepper
Vegetable cooking spray

Combine mushrooms, green pepper, onion, and pimiento in a 1-quart casserole; cover loosely with heavy-duty plastic wrap, and microwave at HIGH for 3 to 3½ minutes or until vegetables are tender. Drain and set aside.

Beat egg whites (at room temperature) until stiff peaks form. Combine egg yolks, mayonnaise, salt, and pepper; beat well. Gently fold egg whites into egg yolk mixture.

Coat a 9-inch pieplate with cooking spray. Pour egg mixture into pieplate, spreading evenly. Microwave at MEDIUM (50% power) for 8 to 10½ minutes or until center is almost set, giving pieplate a half-turn after 5 minutes.

Spread vegetable mixture over half of omelet. Loosen omelet with spatula, and fold in half. Gently slide the omelet onto a warm serving platter. Yield: 2 servings (about 177 calories per serving).

BREAKFAST POTATOES

1 large baking potato
1½ tablespoons reduced-calorie margarine
¼ teaspoon celery salt
¼ teaspoon paprika
⅛ teaspoon pepper
¼ cup finely chopped fresh parsley

Scrub potato, and pat dry; prick several times with a fork. Place potato on paper towel in microwave oven. Microwave at HIGH for 5 to 6 minutes, turning potato after 3 minutes. Let potato stand 5 minutes before checking for doneness. (If potato is not done after standing, microwave briefly, and let stand 2 minutes.) Let cool to touch. Cut potato into ¾-inch cubes; set aside.

Place margarine in a 1½-quart casserole; microwave 30 seconds or until melted. Stir celery salt, paprika, and pepper into margarine; add potatoes and parsley, and toss. Cover with casserole lid, and microwave at HIGH for 2 minutes; stir. Yield: 2 servings (about 112 calories per serving).

Center your elegant, but light, dinner for two around Veal Scallopini, accompanied by Ginger Carrots, Herbed New Potatoes, and Tangy Dressing spooned over wedges of lettuce. Keep calories low with chilled tomato juice for an appetizer and fresh fruit for dessert (menu begins on page 67).

Auto-Cook
TIME
POWER LEVEL
pound
gram

COMPANY LUNCHEON

Microwave Crudité Platter
Fish Teriyaki
Squash Casserole
Spinach-Blue Cheese Salad
Mixed Fresh Fruit (1 cup)
Iced Tea or Water

Serves 6
Total calories per serving: 487

MICROWAVE CRUDITÉ PLATTER

¾ pound fresh brussels sprouts
4 medium carrots, scraped and cut into ½-inch diagonal slices
1 (1-pound) head cauliflower, broken into flowerets
1 small zucchini, cut into ½-inch diagonal slices
2 tablespoons water
3 tablespoons reduced-calorie margarine
2 tablespoons grated Parmesan cheese
½ teaspoon dry mustard
½ teaspoon paprika
¼ teaspoon garlic powder

Wash brussels sprouts; remove loose leaves. Trim stems; cut a cross about ¼-inch deep in the bottom of each sprout. Set aside.

To assemble, arrange carrot slices around the outer edge of a 14-inch round glass platter, reserving 1 slice for center of tray. Arrange brussels sprouts, stem sides down, just inside carrot ring. Place cauliflower inside brussels sprout ring; arrange zucchini slices inside brussels sprouts, placing reserved carrot slice in center of platter.

Sprinkle vegetables with water; cover loosely with heavy-duty plastic wrap. Microwave at HIGH for 10 to 12 minutes or until vegetables are crisp-tender, giving dish a half turn after 5 minutes. Let stand, covered, 5 minutes; carefully pour off water.

Place margarine in a 2-cup glass measure; microwave at HIGH for 30 seconds or until melted. Stir in remaining ingredients; pour over vegetables. Serve with wooden picks as an appetizer. Yield: 6 servings (about 83 calories per serving).

Pour a tasty mixture of herbs, Parmesan cheese, and reduced-calorie margarine over microwaved fresh vegetables for Microwave Crudité Platter. While guests enjoy the attractive appetizer, you can quickly microwave Fish Teriyaki and Squash Casserole (menu above).

FISH TERIYAKI

- 2 pounds flounder fillets
- 3 tablespoons Chablis or other dry white wine
- 2 tablespoons teriyaki sauce
- ½ cup thinly sliced green onions
- 1 teaspoon dried whole basil

Arrange fillets in a shallow 2-quart glass casserole. Combine wine and teriyaki sauce; pour over fillets. Sprinkle with green onions and basil. Cover loosely with heavy-duty plastic wrap; microwave at HIGH for 8 to 9 minutes or until fillets flake with a fork, giving dish a half-turn after 4 minutes. Yield: 6 servings (about 130 calories per serving).

SQUASH CASSEROLE

- 4 medium-size yellow squash (about 1½ pounds), sliced
- ½ cup minced onion
- ¼ cup water
- 1 cup soft whole wheat breadcrumbs (about 3 slices)
- ½ cup (2 ounces) shredded extra-sharp Cheddar cheese
- 1 egg, lightly beaten
- ½ teaspoon garlic salt
- ⅛ teaspoon red pepper
- Paprika

Combine squash, onion, and water in a 2-quart casserole. Cover with casserole lid, and microwave at HIGH for 9 to 10 minutes or until squash is tender, stirring after 4 minutes.

Mash squash mixture with a potato masher. Add next 5 ingredients; stir well.

Cover with casserole lid, and microwave at MEDIUM-HIGH (70% power) for 8 to 10 minutes, stirring after 4 minutes. Let stand 5 minutes before serving. Sprinkle with paprika. Yield: 6 servings (about 113 calories per serving).

SPINACH-BLUE CHEESE SALAD

- 1¼ pounds fresh spinach, torn
- 1 hard-cooked egg, chopped
- 5 water chestnuts, sliced
- ¼ pound fresh mushrooms, sliced
- 1 (2-ounce) jar sliced pimiento, drained
- Blue Cheese Dressing

Combine spinach, egg, water chestnuts, mushrooms, and pimiento in a large bowl; toss. Serve with Blue Cheese Dressing. Yield: 6 servings (about 42 calories per serving plus 19 calories per tablespoon of dressing).

BLUE CHEESE DRESSING:

- ½ cup low-fat cottage cheese
- 2 tablespoons crumbled blue cheese
- ¼ cup plus 2 tablespoons buttermilk
- ¼ teaspoon pepper

Combine all ingredients in container of electric blender; process until smooth. Chill thoroughly. Yield: ⅔ cup.

EASY, ELEGANT LUNCHEON

Company Artichokes
Open-Face Crab Sandwiches
Carrot Sticks (½ cup)
Cinnamon Apple Rings
Iced Tea

Serves 6
Total calories per serving: 363

COMPANY ARTICHOKES

2 (9-ounce) packages frozen artichoke hearts
Yogurt Sauce

Arrange frozen artichokes, icy side up, in a shallow 2-quart glass casserole. Cover with casserole lid or heavy-duty plastic wrap, and microwave at HIGH for 5 minutes; stir, separating artichokes. Cover and microwave at HIGH an additional 4 to 5 minutes or until tender. Let stand 2 minutes.

Serve artichokes hot or chilled with Yogurt Sauce. Yield: 6 servings (about 20 calories per serving plus 16 calories per tablespoon sauce).

YOGURT SAUCE:

1 (8-ounce) carton plain low-fat yogurt
⅓ cup reduced-calorie mayonnaise
2 tablespoons Dijon mustard
1 tablespoon red wine vinegar
1 teaspoon soy sauce
1 clove garlic, crushed
½ teaspoon dried whole marjoram

Combine all ingredients in a small bowl; mix well. Cover and chill at least 1 hour. Yield: about 1½ cups.

OPEN-FACE CRAB SANDWICHES

⅔ cup finely chopped celery
¼ cup reduced-calorie mayonnaise
2 teaspoons lemon juice
2 (6-ounce) packages frozen crabmeat, thawed and drained
¼ cup finely chopped onion
3 English muffins, split and toasted
1 large tomato, cut into 6 slices
Freshly ground pepper
¼ cup plus 2 tablespoons shredded Cheddar cheese

Combine celery, mayonnaise, and lemon juice; set aside.

Combine crabmeat and onion in a small glass bowl. Cover loosely with heavy-duty plastic wrap; microwave at HIGH for 1½ to 2 minutes or until mixture is thoroughly heated, stirring once.

Place English muffin halves, cut side up, in a 12- x 8- x 2-inch glass baking dish. Spoon hot crabmeat mixture onto each muffin half.

Place tomato slices over crabmeat mixture; spoon celery mixture evenly over tomato slices. Sprinkle each sandwich with pepper, and top with 1 tablespoon cheese.

Microwave at HIGH for 2 to 3 minutes or until cheese begins to melt, giving dish a half-turn after 1½ minutes. Yield: 6 servings (about 182 calories per serving).

CINNAMON APPLE RINGS

6 medium cooking apples, unpeeled, cored, and cut into ½-inch rings
½ cup unsweetened apple juice
1 tablespoon lemon juice
¼ teaspoon ground cinnamon
⅛ teaspoon ground nutmeg

Place apple slices in a 12- x 8- x 2-inch baking dish. Combine remaining ingredients; pour over apples. Cover loosely with heavy-duty plastic wrap. Microwave at HIGH 2 minutes; rearrange apples, and give dish a half-turn. Microwave at HIGH 4 to 5 minutes or until apples are tender. Let stand 2 minutes before serving. Yield: 6 servings (about 76 calories per serving).

Heavy-duty plastic wrap holds in steam and heat and is recommended for microwaving vegetables and fish. It is also useful for bowls that have no covers. Place the wrap loosely over the dish, and fold back one corner to prevent excessive steam buildup.

SPRINGTIME SUNDAY DINNER

Ham with Pineapple Sauce
Creamy Green Beans (½ cup)
Potato Salad
Spicy Choco-Crunch Parfaits
Skim Milk (1 cup)

Serves 8
Total calories per serving: 594

HAM WITH PINEAPPLE SAUCE

1 (3-pound) boneless, fully cooked ham
1 (15¼-ounce) can unsweetened pineapple tidbits, undrained
1 tablespoon cornstarch
2 tablespoons dry sherry
1 tablespoon red wine vinegar
2 to 3 teaspoons Dijon mustard
2 to 3 teaspoons prepared horseradish
2 teaspoons Worcestershire sauce

Place ham in a deep 2½-quart glass casserole; cover loosely with heavy-duty plastic wrap. Microwave at MEDIUM (50% power) for 8 to 10 minutes per pound or until thoroughly heated, turning ham over and giving dish a half-turn after 12 minutes. Let stand 10 minutes before slicing.

Combine pineapple and cornstarch in a 4-cup glass measure; stir in remaining ingredients. Cover loosely with heavy-duty plastic wrap; microwave at HIGH for 4 to 5 minutes or until clear and thickened, stirring after 2 minutes and then at 1-minute intervals. Serve ham with pineapple sauce. Yield: 12 servings (about 165 calories per 3 ounces cooked ham plus 10 calories per tablespoon sauce).

CREAMY GREEN BEANS

2 (10-ounce) packages frozen cut green beans
2 tablespoons reduced-calorie mayonnaise
1 (4-ounce) can sliced mushrooms, drained
1 (4-ounce) jar diced pimiento, drained
2 teaspoons lemon juice
½ teaspoon dried whole basil
½ teaspoon dried whole marjoram
⅛ to ¼ teaspoon pepper

Remove wrappers from green bean boxes; place boxes in a flat baking dish, and pierce with a fork. Microwave at HIGH for 12 to 15 minutes, rearranging boxes once. Drain beans, and place in a 1½-quart casserole. Add remaining ingredients; mix well. Cover and microwave at HIGH for 2 minutes or until thoroughly heated. Yield: 8 servings (about 35 calories per serving).

POTATO SALAD

- 3 medium potatoes (about 1¼ pounds), peeled and cut into ¾-inch cubes
- 1 cup water
- 2 eggs
- ½ cup sliced celery
- ⅓ cup sliced green onions
- ½ cup reduced-calorie mayonnaise
- 1 tablespoon vinegar
- ½ teaspoon salt
- ½ teaspoon dried Italian seasoning
- ½ teaspoon dry mustard
- ¼ teaspoon pepper
- Leafy lettuce (optional)

Combine potatoes and water in a 2-quart casserole. Cover loosely with heavy-duty plastic wrap or casserole lid; microwave at HIGH for 10 to 13 minutes or until tender, stirring after 5 minutes. Drain well, and set aside.

Gently break each egg into a 6-ounce custard cup; pierce yolks with a wooden pick. Cover each cup with heavy-duty plastic wrap. Arrange cups about 2 inches apart in center of microwave oven. Microwave at MEDIUM (50% power) for 1 to 2 minutes or until eggs are almost set, giving cups a half-turn after 1 minute.

Test eggs with a wooden pick (yolks should be just firm and whites almost set). Let eggs stand, covered, for 1 to 2 minutes to complete cooking. If eggs are not desired degree of doneness after standing, cover and continue microwaving briefly. Let eggs cool. Remove yolks, and mash; chop whites.

Combine potatoes, egg whites, celery, and green onions in a large bowl. Combine egg yolks and remaining ingredients except lettuce; stir into potato mixture. Cover and chill at least 3 hours. Serve in a lettuce-lined bowl, if desired. Yield: 8 servings (about 107 calories per ½-cup serving).

SPICY CHOCO-CRUNCH PARFAITS

- 2 tablespoons reduced-calorie margarine
- 1¼ cups quick-cooking oats, uncooked
- 2 tablespoons light brown sugar
- 2 pints chocolate ice milk
- 1½ teaspoons pumpkin pie spice
- 1¼ teaspoons brandy flavoring

Place margarine in a 9-inch glass pieplate; microwave at HIGH for 45 seconds or until melted. Stir in oats and sugar, mixing well; spread in bottom of pieplate. Microwave at HIGH for 4 minutes or until toasted, stirring at 1-minute intervals. Let mixture cool to room temperature.

Spoon ice milk into a large glass bowl; cover loosely with heavy-duty plastic wrap. Microwave at MEDIUM (50% power) for 40 to 50 seconds or just until softened. Add pumpkin pie spice and brandy flavoring, stirring until smooth.

Spoon half of ice milk mixture in bottom of 8 chilled parfait glasses; sprinkle with half of oat mixture. Repeat layers. Cover and freeze until firm. Yield: 8 servings (about 177 calories per serving).

> Many frozen vegetables can be microwaved in the box. Before microwaving remove the wrapper and pierce or slit the box several times to prevent steam build-up.

SPECIAL CHICKEN DINNER

Spinach-Stuffed Chicken Rolls
Hot Cooked Vermicelli (½ cup)
Marinated Squash
Pineapple-Orange Chiffon
Skim Milk (1 cup)

Serves 8
Total calories per serving: 590

SPINACH-STUFFED CHICKEN ROLLS

1 small onion, chopped
¼ pound fresh mushrooms, sliced
1 (10-ounce) package frozen chopped spinach, thawed
¼ cup grated Parmesan cheese
½ teaspoon dried whole basil
½ teaspoon grated lemon rind
¼ teaspoon salt
¼ teaspoon hot sauce
8 chicken breast halves (about 4 pounds), skinned and boned
1 (16-ounce) can whole tomatoes, drained and chopped
⅓ cup finely chopped onion
1 clove garlic, crushed
½ teaspoon dried whole basil
¼ teaspoon freshly ground pepper
2 to 3 tablespoons tomato paste

Combine small onion and mushrooms in a 1½-quart casserole. Cover and microwave at HIGH for 4 to 4½ minutes or until onion is tender; drain.

Place spinach on paper towels, and squeeze until barely moist. Add spinach, Parmesan cheese, ½ teaspoon basil, lemon rind, salt, and hot sauce to onion mixture; mix well.

Place chicken breasts between 2 sheets of waxed paper; flatten to ¼-inch thickness using a meat mallet. Place ¼ cup spinach mixture in center of each chicken piece; roll up, and secure with a wooden pick. Place rolls, seam side down, in a shallow 2-quart casserole.

Combine next 5 ingredients; pour evenly over chicken rolls. Cover with waxed paper, and microwave at HIGH for 12 to 14 minutes or until done; rotate dish after 5 minutes, and rearrange rolls so uncooked portions are to outside of dish.

Transfer chicken rolls to a warm serving platter. Stir tomato paste into liquid in casserole; cover and microwave at HIGH for 1½ to 2 minutes or until thoroughly heated. Pour sauce over chicken rolls. Yield: 8 servings (about 228 calories per serving).

MARINATED SQUASH

4 medium-size yellow squash
1 medium-size green pepper, cut into thin strips
2 green onions, sliced
⅔ cup unsweetened apple juice
⅓ cup cider vinegar
¼ teaspoon pepper
¼ teaspoon dry mustard
⅛ teaspoon dried whole basil
Lettuce leaves

Slice squash into ⅛-inch slices; place in a 12- x 8- x 2-inch baking dish with green pepper and onions.

Combine apple juice, vinegar, and herbs in a 4-cup glass measure. Cover with heavy-duty plastic wrap, and microwave at HIGH for 2½ to 3 minutes or until mixture boils. Pour over squash; let cool. Cover and refrigerate overnight. Serve on lettuce leaves. Yield: 8 servings (about 31 calories per serving).

PINEAPPLE-ORANGE CHIFFON

1 (15¼-ounce) can unsweetened sliced pineapple, undrained
4 eggs, separated
1 envelope unflavored gelatin
1 tablespoon cornstarch
3 tablespoons Cointreau or other orange-flavored liqueur
2 teaspoons lime juice
2 tablespoons sugar
1½ cups frozen whipped topping, thawed
Vegetable cooking spray
1 (11-ounce) can mandarin oranges, drained
Fresh mint sprigs (optional)

Drain pineapple, reserving juice; add water to juice to measure 1¼ cups. Combine juice mixture, egg yolks, gelatin, and cornstarch in a 4-cup glass measure; beat well. Cover loosely with heavy-duty plastic wrap; microwave at HIGH for 3 to 4 minutes or until thickened, stirring with a whisk after 2 minutes and then at 1-minute intervals. Stir in liqueur and lime juice; let cool to room temperature.

Beat egg whites (at room temperature) in a large bowl until soft peaks form; add sugar, 1 tablespoon at a time, beating until stiff peaks form. Fold beaten egg whites and whipped topping into custard.

Coat a 2-quart bowl or mold with cooking spray; arrange pineapple slices and orange sections in bottom of bowl. Pour chiffon mixture over fruit in bowl. Cover and refrigerate 3 hours or until set. To serve, unmold onto a serving platter. Garnish with fresh mint, if desired. Yield: 8 servings (about 151 calories per serving).

A time range for microwaving is given in each recipe to allow for the difference in wattage of microwave ovens. To prevent overcooking, always check for doneness at the lower end of the ranges since food continues to cook after removal from the microwave.

CASUAL ITALIAN SUPPER

Slim Spaghetti Pie
Spinach Salad
Orange-Poached Pears
Skim Milk (1 cup)

Serves 6
Total calories per serving: 547

SLIM SPAGHETTI PIE

4 ounces vermicelli
¼ cup grated Parmesan cheese
1 egg, well beaten
Vegetable cooking spray
¾ pound ground chuck
½ cup chopped onion
¼ cup chopped green pepper
1 (8-ounce) can stewed tomatoes, undrained
1 (6-ounce) can tomato paste
¾ teaspoon dried whole oregano
½ teaspoon garlic salt
¼ teaspoon salt
½ cup low-fat cottage cheese
¼ cup (1 ounce) shredded mozzarella cheese
2 teaspoons chopped fresh parsley

Cook vermicelli according to package directions, omitting salt; drain. Stir Parmesan cheese into hot vermicelli. Add egg, stirring well. Spoon mixture into a 9-inch pieplate coated lightly with cooking spray. Use a spoon to shape the vermicelli into a pie shell. Microwave at HIGH, uncovered, 2 minutes or until set. Set aside.

Crumble beef in a shallow 2-quart casserole; stir in onion and green pepper. Cover with heavy-duty plastic wrap, and microwave at HIGH about 5 minutes, stirring at 2-minute intervals; drain well in a colander, and pat dry with paper towels. Wipe pan drippings from casserole with a paper towel.

Return meat to casserole. Stir in tomatoes, tomato paste, and seasonings. Cover and microwave at HIGH about 3½ minutes, stirring once; set aside.

Spread cottage cheese evenly over pie shell. Top with meat sauce. Cover with heavy-duty plastic wrap, and microwave at HIGH about 6 minutes; sprinkle with mozzarella cheese. Microwave, uncovered, at HIGH about 30 seconds or until cheese begins to melt.

Sprinkle parsley on top. Let stand 10 minutes before serving. Yield: 6 servings (about 267 calories per serving).

SPINACH SALAD

2 eggs
¼ cup red wine vinegar
1 tablespoon olive oil
1 tablespoon Dijon mustard
½ teaspoon fines herbs
1 pound fresh spinach, trimmed and torn
⅔ cup sliced green onions

Gently break each egg into a separate 6-ounce custard cup; pierce yolks with a wooden pick. Cover each cup with heavy-duty plastic wrap. Arrange cups about 2 inches apart in center of microwave oven. Microwave at MEDIUM (50% power) for 1 to 2 minutes or until eggs are almost set, giving cups a half-turn after 1 minute.

Test eggs with a wooden pick (yolks should be just firm and whites should be almost set). Let eggs stand, covered, for 1 to 2 minutes to complete cooking. If eggs are not desired degree of doneness after standing, cover and continue microwaving briefly. Let eggs cool; chop finely, and set aside.

Combine next 4 ingredients in a 1-cup glass measure; cover and microwave at HIGH for 1 minute or until boiling.

Combine spinach, eggs, and green onions in a large bowl. Pour hot dressing over spinach; toss and serve immediately. Yield: 6 servings (about 72 calories per serving).

ORANGE-POACHED PEARS

6 medium-size ripe pears
¾ cup unsweetened orange juice
¼ to ½ teaspoon grated lemon rind
1½ tablespoons lemon juice
1 (3-inch) stick cinnamon
6 whole cloves
1¼ teaspoons cornstarch
1½ tablespoons cold water
Orange rind strips (optional)

Peel pears; remove core, leaving stem end intact. Cut a small slice from bottom of each pear, and arrange upright in a deep 2½-quart casserole.

Combine next 5 ingredients; pour over pears. Cover with casserole lid or heavy-duty plastic wrap, and microwave at HIGH for 7 to 10 minutes or until pears are fork-tender, rearranging pears at 3-minute intervals. Discard cinnamon and cloves.

Transfer pears to a shallow serving dish. Combine cornstarch and water, stirring until blended; stir into juice mixture in casserole. Cover and microwave at HIGH for 1½ to 3 minutes or until mixture is clear and slightly thickened, stirring after 45 seconds.

Pour orange sauce over pears; garnish each serving with a strip of orange rind, if desired. Yield: 6 servings (about 118 calories per serving).

Pierce vegetables (potatoes and acorn squash) that are microwaved whole in their skins. This allows excess steam to escape which would otherwise cause the vegetable to burst.

SATURDAY NIGHT SUPPER FOR TWO

Cheesy Meat Patties
Glazed Acorn Rings
or
*Orange-Glazed Carrots
Lettuce Wedge
Special Thousand Island Dressing (2 tablespoons)
Banana (1 small)
Iced Tea or Water

Serves 2
*Total calories per serving: 551 or *505*

CHEESY MEAT PATTIES

- ½ pound lean ground beef
- ¼ cup soft whole wheat breadcrumbs
- 2 tablespoons reduced-calorie catsup
- 1 egg, slightly beaten
- 1 tablespoon chopped fresh parsley
- ⅛ teaspoon garlic salt
- ⅛ teaspoon dried whole oregano
- ⅛ teaspoon pepper
- ¼ cup (1 ounce) shredded mozzarella cheese
- 2 teaspoons Parmesan cheese

Combine first 8 ingredients. Divide mixture into 4 portions; shape into 4-inch patties. Top 2 meat patties with mozzarella cheese, and place remaining meat patties over cheese. Press edges to seal.

Place meat patties on a microwave bacon rack; cover with waxed paper. Microwave at HIGH for 2 to 3 minutes; turn patties over, and sprinkle each with 1 teaspoon Parmesan cheese. Cover and microwave at HIGH 2 to 3 minutes or until desired degree of doneness. Yield: 2 servings (about 310 calories per serving).

GLAZED ACORN RINGS

1 (1-pound) acorn squash
⅓ cup unsweetened apple juice
½ teaspoon cornstarch
¼ teaspoon ground cinnamon

Pierce squash 4 to 5 times with a fork, and place on paper towel in microwave oven. Microwave at HIGH for 6 to 7 minutes or until soft to the touch, turning squash over after 3 minutes. Let stand 5 minutes.

Cut squash crosswise into 1-inch-thick rings; discard ends and seeds. Arrange rings in an 8-inch square baking dish. Combine apple juice, cornstarch, and cinnamon, stirring until blended; pour around squash.

Cover dish with waxed paper. Microwave at HIGH for 3 minutes or until squash is tender and sauce is thickened; rearrange squash and stir sauce after 2 minutes. Spoon sauce over squash to serve. Yield: 2 servings (about 105 calories per serving).

ORANGE-GLAZED CARROTS

3 medium carrots, scraped and cut into ¼-inch-thick slices
3 tablespoons unsweetened orange juice
1 teaspoon cornstarch
3 tablespoons unsweetened orange juice
¼ teaspoon grated orange rind
⅛ teaspoon ground mace

Combine carrots and 3 tablespoons orange juice in a 1-quart casserole; cover with casserole lid, and microwave at HIGH for 5 to 6 minutes or until carrots are crisp-tender, stirring at 2-minute intervals.

Combine cornstarch, 3 tablespoons orange juice, orange rind, and mace, stirring until blended; stir into carrot mixture, mixing well. Cover and microwave at HIGH for 1 minute or until thickened, stirring after 30 seconds. Yield: 2 servings (about 59 calories per serving).

SPECIAL THOUSAND ISLAND DRESSING

1 cup low-fat cottage cheese
¼ cup chili sauce
¼ cup plus 2 tablespoons skim milk
1 teaspoon paprika
½ teaspoon salt
2 hard-cooked eggs, finely chopped
2 tablespoons finely chopped celery
2 tablespoons finely chopped green pepper
1 tablespoon sweet pickle relish
1 tablespoon finely chopped onion

Combine first 5 ingredients in container of electric blender; process until smooth. Stir in remaining ingredients. Chill. Yield: 2 cups (about 13 calories per tablespoon).

Cooking Light
RECIPES

APPETIZERS AND BEVERAGES

Many hostesses put out a lavish array of rich foods for a special party. That's unfortunate for their dieting guests who may abandon good intentions and indulge in sweet punch, canapés, and calorie-laden chips and dips. You may want to try a different approach. Instead of weighing your party down with the usual high-calorie fare, treat your guests to such specialties as Lemon-Marinated Mushrooms, Creamy Egg Dip, and Holiday Cranberry Punch.

We have kept the calories low in our recipes by starting with low-fat cottage cheese, yogurt, or reduced-calorie mayonnaise instead of the usual higher-calorie ingredients. If a dip recipe calls for cream cheese, we suggest using Neufchatel cheese; it has about one-third fewer calories than cream cheese. Regular snack crackers and chips are generally high in calories and salt. So be sure to offer your guests fresh vegetables or melba toast as dippers.

Before opening the wine bottle for the special occasion, remember that alcohol calories add up quickly. A 6-ounce glass of Chablis contains about 130 calories, compared to 90 for a 6-ounce glass of apple cider. Try a little calorie-free club soda in grape or apple juice to add a bubbly sparkle and make the fruit juice calories go further.

Most commercial snack foods such as chips, candy, and cookies add almost nothing to the diet but calories and salt. However, you don't have to avoid snacks altogether. Nutritious, low-calorie snacks are helpful in preventing excessive hunger between meals. Unsweetened fruit, raw vegetables, and unsalted popcorn are good low-calorie, high-fiber snacks to have on hand.

MONTEREY JACK QUICHE SQUARES

3 eggs
¼ cup plus 2 tablespoons all-purpose flour
¾ teaspoon baking powder
¼ teaspoon salt
1½ cups (6 ounces) shredded Monterey Jack cheese
1 cup plus 2 tablespoons low-fat cottage cheese
1 (4-ounce) can diced green chiles, drained
Vegetable cooking spray

Beat eggs (at room temperature) with electric mixer 3 minutes or until thick. Combine flour, baking powder, and salt; add to eggs, and beat until smooth. Stir in cheese and green chiles.

Pour mixture into a 9-inch square baking pan coated with cooking spray. Bake at 350° for 30 to 35 minutes. Cool in pan 10 minutes before serving; cut into 2¼-inch squares. Yield: 16 appetizers (about 76 calories each).

CRAB-STUFFED CHERRY TOMATOES

36 cherry tomatoes
Salt
¼ cup low-fat cottage cheese
1½ teaspoons minced onion
1½ teaspoons lemon juice
½ teaspoon prepared horseradish
Dash of garlic salt
½ pound fresh crabmeat, drained and flaked
¼ cup minced celery
1 tablespoon finely chopped green pepper

Cut top off each tomato; scoop out pulp, reserving pulp for other uses. Sprinkle inside of tomatoes lightly with salt, and invert on paper towels to drain.

Place cottage cheese in container of electric blender; process until smooth. Add onion, lemon juice, horseradish, and garlic salt, blending well. Stir in remaining ingredients. Spoon crabmeat mixture into tomatoes. Chill before serving. Yield: 36 appetizers (about 12 calories each).

CELERY STUFFED WITH SHRIMP

1 (4¼-ounce) can shrimp, drained and chopped
⅓ cup reduced-calorie mayonnaise
¼ cup unsweetened crushed pineapple, drained
2 teaspoons minced fresh parsley
1½ teaspoons lemon juice
1½ teaspoons finely chopped onion
Dash of hot sauce
8 (8-inch) stalks celery

Combine all ingredients except celery; chill. Cut celery crosswise into 2-inch pieces. Stuff mixture into celery sticks. Yield: 32 appetizers (about 13 calories each).

LEMON-MARINATED MUSHROOMS

1 pound small fresh mushrooms
½ cup lemon juice
¼ cup water
2 tablespoons minced fresh parsley
2 tablespoons Dijon mustard
1 tablespoon olive oil
1 teaspoon dried whole oregano
2 teaspoons Worcestershire sauce
¼ teaspoon garlic salt
⅛ teaspoon red pepper

Wipe mushrooms clean with damp paper towels; place in a shallow bowl.

Combine remaining ingredients in a jar; cover tightly, and shake vigorously. Pour marinade over mushrooms, tossing to coat. Cover mushrooms and refrigerate overnight, stirring occasionally. Yield: 8 appetizer servings (about 41 calories per serving).

VEGETABLES VINAIGRETTE

1 (1¼-pound) bunch broccoli
1 (1½-pound) head cauliflower, broken into flowerets
1 pound fresh brussels sprouts
¾ pound baby carrots, scraped
½ pound fresh mushrooms
1 pint cherry tomatoes
1 large cucumber, sliced
2 cups water
1 cup white wine vinegar
2 teaspoons sugar
1 teaspoon dry mustard
1 teaspoon paprika
1 teaspoon dried whole oregano
¼ teaspoon dried whole thyme
4 whole cloves garlic, crushed

Trim off leaves of broccoli; discard tough ends of lower stalks. Cut broccoli into bite-size pieces.

Steam broccoli, cauliflower, brussels sprouts, and carrots separately until crisp-tender; drain well, and chill. Place mushrooms, tomatoes, cucumber, and steamed vegetables in a large, shallow glass or plastic container.

Combine remaining ingredients in a jar. Cover and shake vigorously. Pour over vegetables; cover and refrigerate overnight. Drain vegetables, and arrange on a serving platter. Yield: 20 appetizer servings (about 45 calories per serving).

FRESH FRUIT WITH LEMON SAUCE

2 unpeeled Delicious apples, cut into wedges
2 tablespoons lemon juice
3 kiwi, peeled and sliced crosswise
3 medium oranges, peeled and sliced crosswise
1 medium pineapple, peeled and cubed
1 pound seedless green grapes
1 head romaine lettuce, shredded
¼ cup flaked coconut
Lemon Sauce

Toss apple wedges in lemon juice. Arrange apple wedges and other fruit on a bed of lettuce. Sprinkle with coconut, and serve with Lemon Sauce. Yield: 20 appetizer servings (about 61 calories per serving plus 20 calories per tablespoon sauce).

LEMON SAUCE:

1 (1¾-ounce) package powdered fruit pectin
1 cup unsweetened pineapple juice
2 tablespoons honey
½ teaspoon grated lemon rind
1 tablespoon lemon juice

Combine all ingredients, mixing well. Cover and refrigerate 2 hours or until thoroughly chilled. Yield: 1¼ cups.

PEARS STUFFED WITH CHEESE

6 large ripe pears
1 (8-ounce) package Neufchatel cheese, softened
½ cup low-fat cottage cheese
¼ cup crumbled blue cheese

Wash pears, and pat dry; cut out center of each pear with an apple corer. Combine remaining ingredients, mixing well. Fill pears with cheese mixture; cover and chill thoroughly.

Just before serving, cut each stuffed pear into 8 wedges. Yield: 48 appetizers (about 30 calories each).

CREAMY EGG DIP

1 (8-ounce) package Neufchatel cheese, softened
3 tablespoons skim milk
3 hard-cooked eggs, finely chopped
2 tablespoons reduced-calorie mayonnaise
2 teaspoons chopped chives
1 teaspoon prepared mustard
⅛ teaspoon pepper

Combine cheese and milk in a small mixing bowl; beat until creamy. Add remaining ingredients, mixing well. Serve with fresh vegetables. Yield: 2 cups (about 28 calories per tablespoon).

CREAMY CUCUMBER DIP

2 medium cucumbers, unpeeled and grated
1 small onion, grated
1 (8-ounce) package Neufchatel cheese, softened
2 tablespoons reduced-calorie mayonnaise
½ teaspoon seasoned salt
¼ teaspoon garlic powder
¼ teaspoon garlic salt
¼ teaspoon lemon juice

Place cucumber and onion on paper towels, and squeeze until barely moist.

Beat Neufchatel cheese until smooth; stir in grated vegetables and remaining ingredients. Chill. Serve with fresh vegetables. Yield: about 2 cups (about 23 calories per tablespoon).

SPINACH-VEGETABLE DIP

1 cup low-fat cottage cheese
½ cup reduced-calorie mayonnaise
½ cup chopped green onions
½ cup chopped fresh parsley
1 tablespoon dried whole dillweed
1 (10-ounce) package frozen spinach, thawed
¼ teaspoon hot sauce

Combine all ingredients in container of electric blender; process on high speed 1 to 2 minutes or until smooth. Chill mixture overnight. Serve with fresh vegetables. Yield: 2½ cups (about 14 calories per tablespoon).

LOW-FAT CHICKEN SPREAD

1½ pounds chicken breasts, skinned
¼ (8-ounce) package Neufchatel cheese, softened
1 tablespoon reduced-calorie mayonnaise
1 tablespoon grated onion
1 tablespoon sweet pickle juice
½ cup finely chopped celery
Dash of curry powder
¼ teaspoon salt
¼ teaspoon pepper
½ tablespoon chopped pimiento
Dash of hot sauce
Dash of garlic powder
Vegetable cooking spray
Leaf lettuce
Radishes (optional)

Cook chicken in unsalted water to cover until tender. Remove from broth, reserving 2 tablespoons broth; cool. Bone chicken, and chop fine. Set aside.

Combine Neufchatel cheese and mayonnaise, beating until smooth. Add onion, pickle juice, celery, curry powder, salt, pepper, pimiento, hot sauce and garlic powder; mix well. Stir in chicken and reserved chicken broth. Lightly coat four ½-cup molds or one 2-cup mold with cooking spray; press in chicken mixture, and chill.

Unmold on lettuce-lined serving plate; garnish with radishes, if desired. Serve with melba toast or celery sticks. Yield: 2 cups (about 22 calories per tablespoon).

Note: The chicken will remain moist if cooked and boned the day before using and placed in the broth to chill.

COTTAGE-FRUIT SPREAD SANDWICH

1 cup low-fat cottage cheese
¼ cup chopped dates
¼ cup chopped pecans
Dash of ground cinnamon
8 (1-ounce) slices raisin bread
8 fresh strawberries, sliced
1 small banana, sliced

Combine first 4 ingredients; spread about 3 tablespoons mixture on each slice of bread. Top each sandwich with strawberry and banana slices. Serve immediately. Yield: 8 servings (about 142 calories per serving).

TASTY LOW-FAT SANDWICH SPREAD

1 cup low-fat cottage cheese
2 teaspoons lemon juice
1 tablespoon skim milk
½ teaspoon salt
½ teaspoon ground celery seeds
½ teaspoon dry mustard
1 hard-cooked egg, quartered

Combine all ingredients in container of electric blender; process until smooth, scraping sides of container often. Chill. Serve as a sandwich or hors d'oeuvre spread. Yield: 1⅛ cups (about 14 calories per tablespoon).

SMOKY SALMON BALL

1 (15½-ounce) can red salmon, drained and flaked
1 (8-ounce) package Neufchatel cheese, softened
1 tablespoon instant minced onion
1 tablespoon lemon juice
1 teaspoon prepared horseradish
½ teaspoon Worcestershire sauce
¼ to ½ teaspoon liquid smoke
⅓ cup finely chopped celery

Combine all ingredients except celery. Shape mixture into a ball; chill about 2 hours or until firm. Roll ball in chopped celery. Serve with crackers or fresh vegetables. Yield: 1 salmon ball (about 36 calories per tablespoon).

SHERRIED LIVER PÂTÉ

3 tablespoons reduced-calorie margarine
1 pound chicken livers
½ pound mushrooms, finely chopped
2 cloves garlic, crushed
¼ cup dry sherry
1 teaspoon dry mustard
½ teaspoon dried whole thyme
¼ teaspoon salt
¼ teaspoon ground nutmeg
⅓ cup minced green onions
½ teaspoon freshly ground pepper
Vegetable cooking spray

Melt margarine in a large skillet over medium-high heat. Add chicken livers, mushrooms, and garlic; sauté 10 minutes or until livers are browned. Stir in sherry, mustard, thyme, salt, and nutmeg; bring to a boil. Reduce heat, and simmer 2 minutes. Let cool.

Process chicken liver mixture in container of an electric blender until smooth. Combine liver mixture with green onions and pepper, mixing until well blended; spoon liver mixture into a crock or bowl coated with cooking spray. Cover and refrigerate at least 4 hours. Unmold to serve. Serve with melba toast or celery sticks. Yield: about 2 cups (about 26 calories per tablespoon).

GRAPE SPRITZER

8 lime slices
5⅓ cups club soda, chilled
2⅔ cups unsweetened grape juice, chilled

Place 1 lime slice in each of 8 glasses. Combine club soda and grape juice; mix well. Pour 1 cup mixture over lime slice in each glass. Yield: 8 cups (about 55 calories per 1-cup serving).

BLENDER FRUIT DRINK

1 medium-size ripe banana
1 (16-ounce) can unsweetened apricot halves, undrained
1 cup unsweetened orange juice
½ cup skim milk

Peel banana, and cut into 2-inch slices. Combine banana and remaining ingredients in container of an electric blender; process until smooth. Chill thoroughly. Yield: 4 cups (about 119 calories per 1-cup serving).

FRESH TOMATO JUICE COCKTAIL

2 quarts ripe tomatoes (about 5 pounds)
2 medium onions, quartered
1 cup water
2 large bay leaves
7 whole cloves
¼ to ½ teaspoon red pepper
2 tablespoons vinegar
2 tablespoons lemon juice

Wash tomatoes thoroughly. Remove blemishes and stem ends; cut into quarters. Combine tomatoes, onion, water, bay leaves, cloves, and red pepper in large saucepan or Dutch oven. Cook, uncovered, over low heat 45 minutes.

Remove from heat, and press tomato mixture through a fine sieve; discard pulp. Add vinegar and lemon juice. Chill before serving. Yield: 2 quarts (about 36 calories per 1-cup serving).

PAPAYA COOLER

1 papaya, peeled, seeded, and cubed (about 2 cups)
1 cup fresh strawberries
1½ cups skim milk
¼ cup honey
1 tablespoon lemon juice
4 ice cubes

Combine all ingredients in container of electric blender; process until smooth. Serve immediately. Yield: 4 cups (about 142 calories per 1-cup serving).

STRAWBERRY-BANANA SHAKE

1 medium-size ripe banana
1 cup frozen unsweetened strawberries
1 cup skim milk
1 teaspoon vanilla extract

Peel banana; place in a freezer bag. Freeze until firm.

Slice banana; place banana and remaining ingredients in container of electric blender, and process until smooth. Serve immediately. Yield: 2 servings (about 125 calories per serving).

FRUIT SHAKE

1 (8-ounce) can unsweetened crushed pineapple, undrained
2 medium-size ripe bananas, sliced
1 medium carrot, scraped and sliced
½ cup sliced fresh peaches
½ cup sliced fresh strawberries

Combine all ingredients in container of an electric blender; process until smooth. Chill thoroughly. Yield: 3 cups (about 140 calories per 1-cup serving).

PEACH-YOGURT SHAKE

2½ cups peeled, diced peaches
1 cup skim milk
1 (8-ounce) carton vanilla low-fat yogurt
Fresh mint leaves (optional)

Combine all ingredients except mint in container of an electric blender; process until smooth. Garnish with mint, if desired. Yield: 3½ cups (about 156 calories per 1-cup serving).

BANANA NOG

6 medium-size ripe bananas
1 quart skim milk
1 teaspoon rum extract
Ground nutmeg

Peel bananas; place in a freezer bag, and freeze until firm.

Combine 3 bananas, 2 cups milk, and ½ teaspoon rum extract in container of electric blender; process until smooth and thick. Repeat with remaining bananas, milk, and rum extract.

Sprinkle individual servings with nutmeg; serve immediately. Yield: 7½ cups (about 63 calories per ½-cup serving).

SPICY APPLE CIDER

2 cups water
2 (3-inch) sticks cinnamon
1 tablespoon whole cloves
½ teaspoon whole allspice
2 quarts unsweetened apple cider
1 lemon, thinly sliced
1 orange, thinly sliced

Combine water and spices in a large Dutch oven; bring to a boil. Reduce heat, and simmer 10 minutes. Strain mixture, discarding spices; return water to Dutch oven. Add apple cider, lemon, and orange to Dutch oven; cook over low heat until thoroughly heated. Serve warm. Yield: 10 cups (about 47 calories per ½-cup serving).

HOT APRICOT PUNCH

1 (12-ounce) can apricot nectar
2 cups water
1½ cups unsweetened apple cider
1½ tablespoons lemon juice
6 whole cloves
Cinnamon sticks (optional)

Combine first 5 ingredients in a 3-quart saucepan; cover and bring to a boil. Remove from heat; let stand about 2 hours (flavor is improved if mixture stands). Reheat before serving. Serve with cinnamon sticks, if desired. Yield: 5 cups (about 35 calories per ½-cup serving).

HOLIDAY CRANBERRY PUNCH

4 cups fresh cranberries
1 quart unsweetened apple juice
1 quart water
2 tablespoons grated orange rind
6 (3-inch) sticks cinnamon
12 whole cloves
1 quart unsweetened orange juice

Wash and sort cranberries; drain well. Combine cranberries, apple juice, water, orange rind, cinnamon, and cloves in a Dutch oven; bring to a boil. Reduce heat, and simmer 5 minutes or until cranberries pop.

Strain punch mixture, discarding pulp and spices; return to Dutch oven, and add orange juice. Cook over medium heat until thoroughly heated. Serve hot. Yield: 11 cups (about 51 calories per ½-cup serving).

SPECIAL HOT CHOCOLATE

½ cup plus 1 tablespoon cocoa
¼ cup sugar
1 teaspoon ground cinnamon
6 cups skim milk, divided
2 eggs, beaten
2 teaspoons vanilla extract

Combine cocoa, sugar, and cinnamon in a saucepan; gradually add ½ cup milk, stirring until mixture is smooth. Stir in remaining milk. Cook over medium heat, stirring constantly, until mixture is thoroughly heated.

Gradually stir a small amount of hot mixture into eggs. Add eggs to saucepan; cook over low heat 2 to 3 minutes, stirring constantly. Remove from heat; add vanilla, and beat on medium speed of an electric mixer until frothy. Yield: 7 cups (about 145 calories per 1-cup serving).

BREADS, GRAINS, AND PASTA

There's no reason to give up bread, rice, spaghetti, or macaroni just because you're dieting. Although some diet books tell you these carbohydrate foods should be avoided, it's actually the rich sauces, butter, and mayonnaise that increase the number of calories.

Whether you use commercially baked bread or make your own, you'll get more fiber if the bread contains whole grain ingredients such as whole wheat flour, buckwheat flour, bran, and oats. The fibrous outer coating of the wheat kernel is stripped away when whole grain flour is refined to make white flour; valuable nutrients are lost in the process. Although some nutrients are added back when refined flour is enriched, whole grain flour is still in the lead nutritionally because of the fiber and the certain trace vitamins and minerals that it contains.

Dieters should feel free to experiment with different sizes, shapes, and flavors of pasta. Pasta has about 100 calories per half-cup portion if cooked just to the *al dente* stage (barely tender). When cooked a few more minutes (until tender), the pasta absorbs more water and swells, decreasing the calorie count to 80 per half-cup serving.

Brown rice, with its chewy texture and nutty flavor, contains more fiber and nutrients than white rice. When you do use white rice, the best choice is parboiled (or converted) rice. Parboiled white rice is hulled under special conditions, keeping the nutrient composition close to that of brown rice.

Add some variety to your menu with wild rice. While wild rice is not a true rice (it comes from a wild water grass), the texture and flavor are similar to that of brown rice. Wild rice is lower in calories than white or brown rice and contains about 70 calories per half-cup serving.

WHOLE WHEAT BUTTERMILK BISCUITS

½ cup whole wheat flour
½ cup all-purpose flour
1 teaspoon sugar
1½ teaspoons baking powder
¼ teaspoon baking soda
¼ teaspoon salt
2½ tablespoons margarine, softened
¼ cup plus 3 tablespoons buttermilk
Vegetable cooking spray

Combine flour, sugar, baking powder, soda, and salt; cut in margarine using a pastry blender until mixture resembles coarse meal. Add buttermilk, stirring until dry ingredients are moistened. Turn dough out on a lightly floured surface; knead lightly 4 or 5 times.

Roll dough to ½-inch thickness, and cut into 2-inch circles using a floured biscuit cutter. Place biscuits on a baking sheet coated with cooking spray. Bake at 400° for 10 minutes or until biscuits are lightly browned. Yield: 10 biscuits (about 71 calories each).

BUTTERMILK BRAN MUFFINS

1½ cups whole bran cereal
1½ cups buttermilk
1 egg, beaten
2 tablespoons reduced-calorie margarine, melted
1¼ cups all-purpose flour
2 tablespoons sugar
2 teaspoons baking powder
½ teaspoon baking soda
¼ teaspoon salt
Vegetable cooking spray

Combine cereal and buttermilk; let stand 5 minutes. Stir in egg and margarine, mixing well.

Combine flour, sugar, baking powder, soda, and salt in a large bowl; make a well in center of mixture. Add bran mixture to dry ingredients, stirring just until moistened.

Coat muffin pans with cooking spray. Spoon batter into pans, filling two-thirds full. Bake at 400° for 20 to 25 minutes. Yield: 1 dozen (about 91 calories each).

REFRIGERATOR BRAN MUFFINS

8 cups wheat bran flakes cereal
5 cups all-purpose flour
1 cup sugar
1 tablespoon baking soda
2 teaspoons salt
4 eggs, beaten
1 quart buttermilk
½ cup vegetable oil
Vegetable cooking spray

Combine cereal, flour, sugar, soda, and salt in a very large bowl; make a well in center of mixture. Add eggs, buttermilk, and oil; stir just until moistened. Cover tightly, and store in refrigerator until ready to bake. (Batter can be kept in refrigerator up to 3 weeks.)

When ready to bake, coat muffin pans with cooking spray. Spoon 3 tablespoons batter into each muffin cup. Bake at 400° for 12 to 15 minutes or until lightly browned. Yield: 45 muffins (about 116 calories each).

LIGHT WHEAT MUFFINS

1 cup all-purpose flour
1 cup whole wheat flour
2 tablespoons sugar
2½ teaspoons baking powder
¼ teaspoon salt
1 egg, beaten
1 cup skim milk
¼ cup vegetable oil
Vegetable cooking spray

Combine first 5 ingredients in a large bowl; make a well in center of mixture. Combine egg, milk, and oil, stirring well; add to dry ingredients, stirring just until moistened.

Coat muffin pans with cooking spray; spoon batter into pans, filling one-half full. Bake at 425° for 20 to 25 minutes. Yield: 10 muffins (about 157 calories each).

WHOLE WHEAT MUFFINS

2 cups whole wheat flour
2 tablespoons brown sugar
2 teaspoons baking powder
½ teaspoon ground cinnamon
¼ teaspoon salt
1 egg, beaten
1 cup plus 2 tablespoons skim milk
3 tablespoons reduced-calorie margarine, melted
Vegetable cooking spray

Combine first 5 ingredients in a large bowl; make a well in center of mixture. Combine egg, milk, and margarine; add to dry ingredients, stirring just until moistened.

Coat muffin pans with cooking spray. Spoon mixture into muffin pans, filling two-thirds full. Bake at 400° for 20 to 25 minutes. Yield: 1 dozen (about 102 calories each).

SPICY APPLE MUFFINS

1⅔ cups all-purpose flour
3 tablespoons sugar
2½ teaspoons baking powder
1 teaspoon ground cinnamon
½ teaspoon ground nutmeg
¼ teaspoon salt
1 egg, beaten
1 cup skim milk
2 tablespoons vegetable oil
1 cup finely chopped apple
Vegetable cooking spray

Combine flour, sugar, baking powder, cinnamon, nutmeg, and salt in a large bowl; make a well in center of mixture. Combine egg, milk, and oil; pour into center of dry ingredients, stirring just until moistened. Fold in apple.

Coat muffin pans with cooking spray. Spoon batter into pans, filling one-half full. Bake at 400° for 25 minutes. Yield: 1 dozen (about 103 calories each).

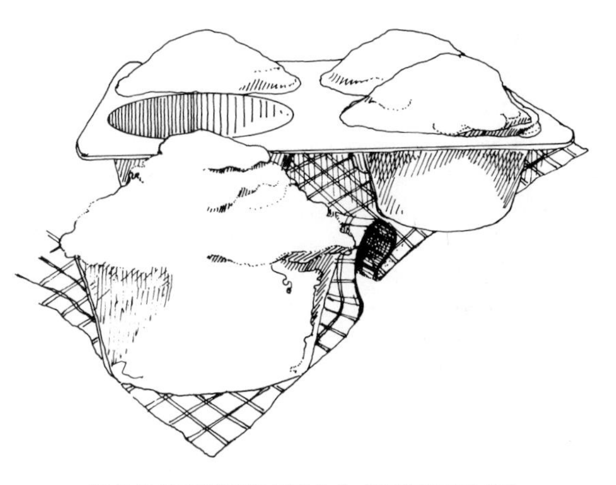

BLUEBERRY MUFFINS

2⅓ cups all-purpose flour
2 tablespoons sugar
1 tablespoon baking powder
½ teaspoon ground cinnamon
¼ teaspoon salt
1 cup skim milk
¼ cup reduced-calorie margarine, melted
1 egg, beaten
1 teaspoon vanilla extract
1½ cups fresh or frozen blueberries, thawed and drained
Vegetable cooking spray

Combine first 5 ingredients in a large bowl; make a well in center of mixture. Combine milk, margarine, egg, and vanilla; add to dry ingredients, stirring just until moistened. Fold in blueberries.

Spoon batter into muffin pans coated with cooking spray, filling two-thirds full. Bake at 400° for 20 to 25 minutes or until golden brown. Yield: 16 muffins (about 95 calories each).

WHOLE WHEAT BANANA BREAD

2 cups whole wheat flour
¼ cup wheat germ
1 teaspoon baking soda
½ teaspoon salt
1½ cups mashed ripe banana
¼ cup vegetable oil
¼ cup honey
2 eggs
1 teaspoon vanilla extract
Vegetable cooking spray

Combine flour, wheat germ, baking soda, and salt in a large bowl; make a well in center of mixture. Combine banana, oil, honey, eggs, and vanilla; add to dry ingredients, stirring just until moistened.

Coat a 9- x 5- x 3-inch loafpan with cooking spray. Spoon batter into pan, and bake at 350° for 1 hour or until a wooden pick inserted in center comes out clean. Yield: 1 loaf (about 118 calories per ½-inch slice).

OATMEAL SNACK CAKES

1¼ cups quick-cooking oats, uncooked
½ cup raisins
½ cup chopped dates
¼ cup whole bran cereal
½ cup unsweetened crushed pineapple, undrained
1 medium apple, peeled, cored, and chopped
1 egg
2 tablespoons reduced-calorie margarine, melted
1½ teaspoons baking powder
1 teaspoon vanilla extract
¼ teaspoon salt
Vegetable cooking spray

Combine oats, raisins, dates, and cereal in a large bowl; set aside.

Combine remaining ingredients except cooking spray in container of electric blender; process until smooth. Add pineapple mixture to dry ingredients, stirring until well blended.

Spoon batter evenly into muffin pans coated with cooking spray. Bake at 350° for 35 minutes. (Snack cakes do not rise during baking.) Yield: 1 dozen (about 85 calories each).

WHOLE WHEAT CRACKERS

¾ cup whole wheat flour
½ cup all-purpose flour
2 tablespoons sugar
1 teaspoon baking powder
½ teaspoon baking soda
¼ teaspoon cream of tartar
¼ teaspoon salt
¼ cup margarine, softened
⅓ cup buttermilk

Combine dry ingredients in a medium bowl. Cut in margarine with pastry blender until mixture resembles coarse meal. Sprinkle buttermilk evenly over surface, stirring with a fork until all dry ingredients are moistened. Shape mixture into a ball.

Roll dough to 1/8-inch thickness on a floured surface. Cut with a 2-inch biscuit cutter, and prick tops with a fork; place on ungreased baking sheets. Bake at 350° for 12 to 15 minutes or until crisp and lightly browned. Cool in pan 10 minutes. Remove to wire racks; cool completely. Yield: 4 dozen (about 21 calories each).

BLUEBERRY PANCAKES

1 cup all-purpose flour
1½ teaspoons baking powder
½ teaspoon baking soda
¼ teaspoon salt
1 egg, beaten
1 cup buttermilk
1 tablespoon reduced-calorie margarine, melted
½ cup fresh blueberries, rinsed and drained
Vegetable cooking spray

Combine dry ingredients in a medium bowl; set aside. Combine egg, buttermilk, and margarine; add to dry ingredients, stirring just until moistened. Fold in blueberries.

For each pancake, pour 2 tablespoons batter onto hot griddle or skillet coated with cooking spray. Turn pancakes when tops are covered with bubbles and edges are brown. Yield: 16 pancakes (about 41 calories each).

WHOLE WHEAT WAFFLES

1 cup all-purpose flour
1 cup whole wheat flour
2 teaspoons sugar
¼ teaspoon salt
2 eggs
1¾ cups skim milk
¼ cup vegetable oil
Vegetable cooking spray

Combine dry ingredients; set aside. Beat eggs at medium speed of an electric mixer until light and fluffy. Add flour mixture, skim milk, and oil to beaten eggs; beat until smooth.

Coat a waffle iron with cooking spray. Allow waffle iron to pre-heat.

Pour about 1 cup plus 2 tablespoons batter into hot waffle iron. Bake until steaming stops (about 6 minutes). Repeat procedure until all batter is used. Yield: 12 (4-inch) waffles (about 140 calories each).

MEXICAN CORNBREAD

1 cup self-rising cornmeal
¼ teaspoon red pepper
½ cup chopped onion
½ cup chopped green pepper
½ cup (2 ounces) shredded low-fat Cheddar cheese
1 cup skim milk
2 eggs, beaten
1 (8½-ounce) can cream-style corn
Vegetable cooking spray

Combine cornmeal and red pepper; add remaining ingredients except cooking spray, mixing well.

Spoon batter into an 8-inch square baking pan coated with cooking spray. Bake at 450° for 25 minutes or until golden. Cut into 2-inch squares. Yield: 16 servings (about 62 calories per serving).

LIGHT GRITS SPOONBREAD

2 cups skim milk
⅓ cup uncooked regular grits
½ teaspoon salt
3 eggs, separated
Vegetable cooking spray

Combine milk, grits, and salt in a heavy 3-quart saucepan. Bring to a boil; reduce heat, and cook, stirring constantly, 10 to 12 minutes or until very thick. Beat egg yolks until thick and lemon colored. Gradually stir about one-fourth of hot mixture into yolks; add to remaining hot mixture, stirring constantly. Beat egg whites (at room temperature) until stiff peaks form; fold into grits mixture.

Coat a 1½-quart casserole with cooking spray; spoon grits mixture into casserole. Bake at 375° for 35 to 40 minutes or until lightly browned. Yield: 6 servings (about 85 calories per serving).

> Let leftovers be leftovers. Don't eat them while clearing the table.

LIGHT BEER BREAD

1 (12-ounce) can light beer
½ cup water
3 tablespoons vegetable oil
4½ to 5 cups all-purpose flour, divided
1½ cups whole wheat flour
2 packages dry yeast
3 tablespoons sugar
1½ teaspoons salt
Vegetable cooking spray

Combine beer, water, and oil in a saucepan; heat to 120° to 130°. Set aside.

Combine 1½ cups all-purpose flour, whole wheat flour, yeast, sugar, and salt in a large mixing bowl; add beer mixture, and beat 5 minutes at medium speed of an electric mixer. Stir in enough remaining flour to make a soft dough.

Turn dough out onto a lightly floured surface; knead until smooth and elastic (about 8 to 10 minutes). Place dough in a bowl coated with cooking spray, turning to grease top. Cover and let rise in a warm place (85°), free from drafts, 1 hour or until doubled in bulk.

Punch dough down, and divide in half. Shape each half into a loaf; place in two 9- x 5- x 3-inch loafpans coated with cooking spray. Cover and let rise in a warm place, free from drafts, 45 minutes or until doubled in bulk. Bake at 375° for 30 to 35 minutes or until loaves sound hollow when tapped. Yield: 2 loaves (about 88 calories per ½-inch slice).

Note: Wrap any leftovers in foil, and freeze. To reheat, thaw in unopened foil package. Bake in foil at 350° for 30 minutes or until hot.

CARAWAY BREAD

2 packages dry yeast
3 cups warm water (105° to 115°)
About 4 cups unbleached all-purpose flour
About 4 cups whole wheat flour
About 1 cup rye flour
2 teaspoons salt
¼ cup caraway seeds
Vegetable cooking spray

Dissolve yeast in warm water in a large mixing bowl; set mixture aside.

Combine flour. Gradually add about 1 cup flour mixture, salt, and caraway seeds to yeast mixture; mix well. Stir in enough remaining flour to make a soft dough.

Turn dough out onto a floured surface, and knead until smooth and elastic (about 5 minutes). Place in a bowl coated with cooking spray, turning to grease top. Cover and let rise in a warm place (85°), free from drafts, 1 to 1½ hours or until doubled in bulk.

Punch dough down; turn out onto a floured surface, and knead 1 minute. Return to bowl coated with cooking spray, turning to grease top. Cover and let rise in a warm place (85°), free from drafts, 1 hour or until doubled in bulk.

Punch dough down; divide in half. Shape each half into a loaf; place in two 9- x 5- x 3-inch loafpans coated with cooking spray. Cover and let rise 20 minutes.

Cut ¼-inch-deep crisscross slashes in top of each loaf with a sharp knife. Place a pan of water on lower oven rack. Bake at 400° for 5 minutes. Reduce temperature to 375°; bake 1 hour or until loaves sound hollow when tapped. Yield: 2 loaves (about 104 calories per ½-inch slice).

FRENCH BREAD

5¼ cups all-purpose flour, divided
1 cup plus 2 tablespoons water
2 packages dry yeast
½ teaspoon sugar
¾ teaspoon shortening
Vegetable cooking spray
¾ cup water
1¼ teaspoons salt
1 tablespoon plus ¾ teaspoon sugar
1 tablespoon shortening
1 egg white
1 tablespoon water

Combine 3¼ cups flour and next 4 ingredients in a large mixing bowl; mix with a heavy-duty electric mixer at high speed for 5 minutes. Place dough in a large bowl coated with cooking spray, turning to grease top. Cover dough, and let rise in a warm place (85°), free from drafts, 1½ hours or until doubled in bulk.

Return dough to mixing bowl. Add remaining 2 cups flour, ¾ cup water, salt, 1 tablespoon plus ¾ teaspoon sugar, and 1 tablespoon shortening; beat at high speed 10 to 12 minutes.

Coat 2 baking sheets with cooking spray; set aside. Turn dough out onto a floured surface, and divide into 2 equal portions; shape each portion into a 14-inch loaf. Place loaves on prepared baking sheets.

Combine egg white and 1 tablespoon water, and beat until frothy; gently brush over loaf (do not allow egg white mixture to drip onto baking sheet). Place a pan of boiling water on the lower rack of oven to obtain steam. Bake at 425° for 30 minutes or until golden brown. Yield: 2 loaves or 56 slices (about 48 calories per 1-ounce slice).

OATMEAL BREAD

1 cup plus 2 tablespoons skim milk
2 tablespoons margarine
2½ tablespoons honey
1¼ teaspoons salt
1 package dry yeast
¼ cup warm water (105° to 115°)
1 cup regular oats, uncooked
3 to 3¼ cups all-purpose flour
Vegetable cooking spray

Scald milk; add margarine, honey, and salt, stirring until margarine melts. Let mixture cool to 105° to 115°.

Combine yeast and warm water in a large bowl; let stand 5 minutes. Add milk mixture, oats, and 2 cups flour; mix well. Stir in enough remaining flour to make a soft dough.

Turn dough out onto a lightly floured surface; knead until smooth and elastic (about 8 to 10 minutes). Place dough in a large bowl coated with cooking spray, turning to grease top. Cover and let rise in a warm place (85°), free from drafts, 1 hour or until doubled in bulk.

Punch dough down; cover and let dough stand 10 minutes.

Turn dough out onto a lightly floured surface. Roll into a 15- x 9-inch rectangle. Roll up, jellyroll fashion, beginning at narrow edge. Pinch seam and ends together to seal; place roll, seam side down, in a 9- x 5- x 3-inch loafpan coated with cooking spray.

Cover and let rise 50 minutes or until doubled in bulk. Bake at 375° for 40 to 45 minutes or until loaf sounds hollow when tapped. Remove from pan; cool on wire rack. Yield: 1 loaf (about 108 calories per ½-inch slice).

WHOLE WHEAT ROLLS

¼ cup vegetable oil
2 tablespoons sugar
¾ teaspoon salt
1 package dry yeast
1 teaspoon sugar
¾ cup warm water (105° to 115°)
1 egg, slightly beaten
1½ cups all-purpose flour
1 cup whole wheat flour
½ cup graham cracker crumbs
Vegetable cooking spray

Combine oil, 2 tablespoons sugar, and salt in a large mixing bowl; set aside. Dissolve yeast and 1 teaspoon sugar in warm water. Add yeast mixture and egg to oil mixture. Stir in flour and cracker crumbs, blending well.

Place dough in a bowl coated with cooking spray, turning to grease top. Cover and let rise in a warm place (85°), free from drafts, 1 hour or until doubled in bulk.

Roll dough to ¼-inch thickness on a floured surface; cut into 2½-inch circles using a floured biscuit cutter. Place on baking sheets coated with cooking spray. Let rise in a warm place (85°), free from drafts, 45 minutes or until doubled in bulk. Bake at 350° for 15 to 20 minutes. Yield: about 2 dozen (about 79 calories each).

Leftover rolls can be sliced in half and toasted for breakfast.

SHREDDED WHEAT ROLLS

1 package dry yeast
1 cup warm water (105° to 115°)
3 tablespoons sugar
2 tablespoons vegetable oil
1 egg
¾ teaspoon salt
3 to 3½ cups all-purpose flour, divided
¾ cup shredded whole wheat cereal biscuits (about 2), crumbled
Vegetable cooking spray

Dissolve yeast in warm water in a large bowl. Add sugar, oil, egg, salt, and 1½ cups flour; beat at low speed of electric mixer until smooth. Add cereal; mix well. Stir in enough of remaining flour to make a very soft dough.

Place dough in a large bowl coated with cooking spray, turning to grease top. Cover and let rise in a warm place (85°), free from drafts, 1 hour or until doubled in bulk.

Coat muffin pans with cooking spray; set aside. Punch dough down; turn out onto a floured surface, and knead 4 or 5 times. Shape into 1-inch balls; place 3 balls in each muffin cup. Cover and let rise in a warm place, free from drafts, 40 minutes or until doubled in bulk. Bake at 400° for 12 to 15 minutes or until browned. Yield: 1½ dozen (about 109 calories each).

WHOLE WHEAT ENGLISH MUFFINS

1⅔ cups skim milk
3 tablespoons margarine
1 tablespoon sugar
1 teaspoon salt
1 package dry yeast
¼ cup warm water (105° to 115°)
2⅔ to 2¾ cups all-purpose flour, divided
2⅓ cups whole wheat flour
Vegetable cooking spray
Cornmeal

Combine skim milk, margarine, sugar, and salt in a small saucepan; cook over low heat until margarine is melted. Let cool to lukewarm.

Dissolve yeast in warm water in a large bowl; let stand 5 minutes. Stir milk mixture into dissolved yeast. Gradually beat in 2⅓ cups all-purpose flour and whole wheat flour at low speed of electric mixer. Knead in enough of remaining all-purpose flour to make a soft dough (do not overwork dough).

Place dough in a large bowl coated with cooking spray, turning to grease top. Cover and let rise in a warm place (85°), free from drafts, 1 hour or until doubled in bulk. Turn dough out onto a heavily floured surface; roll to ½-inch thickness. Cut into 3-inch circles using a floured biscuit cutter. Cover and let rest on floured surface 30 minutes.

Coat an electric griddle or skillet with cooking spray. Allow to heat at medium (350°) until hot; sprinkle lightly with cornmeal. Transfer muffins to griddle; bake 12 minutes. Turn and bake an additional 15 to 18 minutes. Cool muffins completely on wire racks. Store in an airtight container. To serve, split muffins, and toast until lightly browned. Yield: 16 muffins (about 157 calories each).

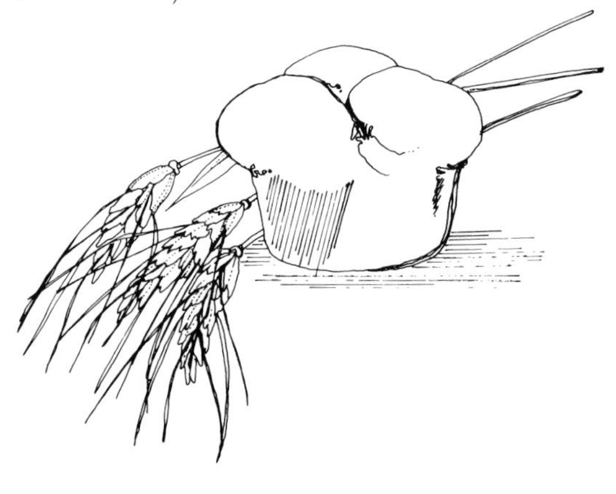

FRIED RICE

Vegetable cooking spray
1 teaspoon vegetable oil
3 cups cooked rice
½ cup diagonally sliced celery
½ cup sliced water chestnuts
⅓ cup sliced green onions
2 teaspoons soy sauce

Coat a large nonstick skillet with cooking spray; add oil, and place over medium-high heat until hot. Add rice to skillet; stir-fry 3 to 4 minutes. Stir in celery and water chestnuts; stir-fry 3 minutes or just until celery is tender. Add green onions and soy sauce, and toss. Yield: 8 servings (about 90 calories per serving).

HERBED RICE SAUTÉ

Vegetable cooking spray
1 tablespoon reduced-calorie margarine
1 cup uncooked regular rice
1 cup chopped onion
2¼ cups water
1 teaspoon dried whole rosemary
½ teaspoon dried whole marjoram
½ teaspoon dried whole savory
2 chicken-flavored bouillon cubes

Coat a large heavy skillet with cooking spray; add margarine, and place over medium-high heat until margarine is melted. Add rice and onion; sauté until rice is lightly browned. Stir in remaining ingredients. Bring to a boil, stirring to dissolve bouillon; cover, reduce heat, and simmer 20 to 25 minutes or until rice is tender and water is absorbed. Yield: 7 servings (about 113 calories per serving).

PEPPERED RICE

2½ cups water
1 beef-flavored bouillon cube
1¼ cups uncooked regular rice
¼ teaspoon garlic powder
¼ teaspoon pepper
1½ tablespoons chopped fresh parsley

Combine water and bouillon cube in a medium saucepan; bring water to a boil, stirring to dissolve cube. Stir in rice, garlic powder, and pepper. Reduce heat; cover and simmer 20 to 25 minutes or until rice is tender. Remove from heat. Add parsley and toss. Yield: 8 servings (about 105 calories per serving).

CONFETTI RICE

1 (4-ounce) can sliced mushrooms, undrained
1 (10¾-ounce) can chicken broth, undiluted
⅛ teaspoon garlic powder
⅛ teaspoon pepper
1 cup uncooked regular rice
1 (2-ounce) jar diced pimiento, drained
½ cup sliced water chestnuts

Drain mushrooms, reserving liquid; set mushrooms aside. Add water to mushroom liquid to equal ¾ cup. Combine mushroom liquid mixture, broth, garlic powder, and pepper in a medium saucepan; bring to a boil. Stir in mushrooms and remaining ingredients; cover, reduce heat, and simmer 20 to 25 minutes or until rice is tender and liquid is absorbed. Yield: 7 servings (about 119 calories per serving).

SEASONED ONION RICE

Vegetable cooking spray
1 medium onion, finely chopped
1 cup uncooked regular rice
1 (10¾-ounce) can chicken broth, undiluted
¾ cup water
1 tablespoon Worcestershire sauce
1 beef-flavored bouillon cube
¼ teaspoon pepper

Coat a medium saucepan with cooking spray; add onion, and sauté 5 minutes. Add chicken broth, water, Worcestershire sauce, bouillon cube and pepper; bring to a boil.

Coat a 1½-quart casserole with vegetable cooking spray; add rice mixture. Cover and bake at 350° for 1 hour. Yield: 6 servings (about 136 calories per serving).

When grains, such as rice, are served together with dried beans or peas, they complement each other, providing a source of high quality protein.

VEGETABLE RICE

Vegetable cooking spray
¼ cup chopped onion
1 cup water
½ cup uncooked regular rice
¼ cup Chablis or other dry white wine
½ teaspoon chicken-flavored bouillon granules
⅛ teaspoon pepper
2 small carrots, scraped and diagonally sliced
2 tablespoons chopped green pepper

Coat a medium saucepan with cooking spray; place over medium heat until hot.

Add onion, and sauté 5 minutes. Add next 5 ingredients, and bring to a boil. Cover, reduce heat, and simmer 10 minutes. Stir in remaining ingredients, and simmer an additional 10 to 15 minutes or until rice is tender and liquid is absorbed. Yield: 4 servings (about 101 calories per serving).

COLORFUL RICE CASSEROLE

Vegetable cooking spray
1½ pounds zucchini, thinly sliced
¾ cup chopped green onions
1 (17-ounce) can corn, drained
1 (16-ounce) can tomatoes, undrained and chopped
3 cups cooked regular rice
¼ cup chopped fresh parsley
½ teasoon salt
¼ teaspoon pepper
¼ teaspoon dried whole oregano

Coat an electric skillet with cooking spray; heat at 350° until hot. Add zucchini and onions; sauté about 5 minutes or until crisp-tender. Stir in remaining ingredients; cover, reduce heat, and simmer 15 minutes. Yield: 12 servings (about 84 calories per ½-cup serving).

BROWN RICE PILAF

1¼ cups chicken broth
½ cup uncooked brown rice
½ cup chopped onion
1 (2½-ounce) jar sliced mushrooms, drained
¼ teaspoon pepper
⅛ teaspoon dried whole thyme
½ cup thinly sliced celery

Combine all ingredients except celery in a 1-quart casserole. Cover and bake rice mixture at 350° for 1 hour.

Add celery to rice mixture; cover and bake 10 to 15 minutes or until celery is just tender and liquid is absorbed. Yield: 4 servings (about 119 calories per serving)

SEASONED BROWN RICE

Vegetable cooking spray
2 tablespoons chopped onion
¼ teaspoon minced garlic
1 cup uncooked brown rice
1⅓ cups water
1 (10¾-ounce) can chicken broth, undiluted
Dash of pepper
1 bay leaf
1 tablespoon chopped fresh parsley
¼ teaspoon ground thyme

Coat a medium saucepan with cooking spray. Place over medium heat until hot; add onion and garlic, and sauté until onion is tender.

Add remaining ingredients, and bring to a boil. Cover, reduce heat, and simmer 45 to 50 minutes or until rice is tender and liquid is absorbed. Remove mixture from heat, and discard bay leaf. Yield: 6 servings (about 145 calories per serving).

ORANGE RICE

Vegetable cooking spray
1 cup uncooked regular rice
¾ cup chopped celery
1 tablespoon chopped onion
2 cups unsweetened orange juice
2 teaspoons grated orange rind
½ teaspoon salt

Coat a large skillet with cooking spray, and place over medium heat until hot. Add rice, celery, and onion; cook, stirring occasionally, until rice is lightly browned. Add remaining ingredients, and bring to a boil. Pour mixture into a 1½-quart casserole.

Cover and bake at 350° for 25 to 30 minutes. Yield: 7 servings (about 130 calories per serving).

CURRIED PINEAPPLE RICE

1 small onion, chopped
1½ cups water
1 (10½-ounce) can beef broth, undiluted
1 cup uncooked regular rice
¾ teaspoon curry powder
⅛ teaspoon garlic powder
1 (8-ounce) can unsweetened pineapple chunks, drained

Combine first 3 ingredients in a medium saucepan; bring to a boil. Stir in rice, curry powder, and garlic powder. Cover, reduce heat, and simmer 20 to 25 minutes. Add pineapple to rice; cook an additional 5 minutes or until rice is tender and water is absorbed. Yield: 8 servings (about 103 calories per serving).

WILD RICE CASSEROLE

Vegetable cooking spray
1 (6-ounce) package long-grain and wild rice mix
6 green onions, chopped
8 medium mushrooms, sliced
2 cups chicken broth
1 (8-ounce) can sliced water chestnuts, drained

Coat a medium skillet with cooking spray; place over medium heat until hot. Add rice; cook until lightly browned, stirring occasionally. Stir in remaining ingredients, and spoon mixture into a 1¾-quart casserole.

Cover casserole and bake at 350° for 1 hour or until rice is done. Yield: 6 servings (about 134 calories per serving).

SEASONED BULGUR

1 cup uncooked bulgur wheat
1 (10¾-ounce) can chicken broth, undiluted
¾ cup water
¼ teaspoon dried whole marjoram
2 tablespoons thinly sliced green onions
1 tablespoon minced fresh parsley

Combine wheat, chicken broth, water, and marjoram in a medium saucepan. Bring to a boil; cover, reduce heat, and simmer 20 to 25 minutes or until liquid is absorbed and bulgur is tender. Stir in green onions and parsley. Yield: 6 servings (about 117 calories per serving).

BAKED MACARONI AND CHEESE

1 cup uncooked elbow macaroni
2 eggs, beaten
1 cup skim milk
1 cup low-fat cottage cheese
¼ cup (1 ounce) shredded extra-sharp Cheddar cheese
½ teaspoon salt
¼ teaspoon freshly ground pepper
Vegetable cooking spray
1 tablespoon fine, dry breadcrumbs

Cook macaroni according to package directions, omitting salt; drain. Combine macaroni and next 6 ingredients.

Spoon mixture into a 1-quart baking dish coated with cooking spray; sprinkle with breadcrumbs. Bake at 350° for 1 hour. Yield: 6 servings (about 158 calories per serving).

SPINACH MANICOTTI

10 manicotti shells
2 (6-ounce) cans tomato paste
3 cups water
½ cup finely chopped onion
2 cloves garlic, crushed
½ teaspoon dried whole basil
½ teaspoon dried whole oregano
¼ teaspoon salt
¼ teaspoon pepper
2 (10-ounce) packages frozen chopped spinach
1 (16-ounce) carton low-fat cottage cheese
⅓ cup grated Parmesan cheese
¼ teaspoon ground nutmeg
Pepper to taste
Vegetable cooking spray
Chopped fresh parsley

Cook manicotti shells according to package directions, omitting salt; drain and set aside.

Combine next 8 ingredients; cover and cook over low heat 1 hour.

Cook spinach according to package directions, omitting salt. Drain; place on paper towels, and squeeze until barely moist. Combine spinach, cottage cheese, Parmesan cheese, nutmeg, and pepper. Stuff manicotti shells with spinach mixture, and arrange in a 13- x 9- x 2-inch baking dish coated with cooking spray.

Pour tomato sauce over manicotti. Bake at 350° for 45 minutes. Garnish with parsley. Yield: 5 servings (about 300 calories per serving).

GARDEN PASTA

Vegetable cooking spray
1 cup chopped green onions
½ cup chopped fresh parsley
2 cloves garlic, crushed
2 cups finely shredded cabbage
2 cups peeled, chopped tomato
½ cup sliced radishes
½ cup chopped carrot
½ cup chicken broth
¼ cup tomato paste
1 teaspoon dried whole basil
Freshly ground pepper to taste
1 large tomato, cut into wedges
4 ounces uncooked vermicelli
1 cup (4-ounce) shredded Cheddar cheese

Coat a 10-inch skillet with cooking spray; place over medium heat until hot. Add onions, parsley, and garlic; sauté until tender. Add cabbage, chopped tomato, radishes, carrot, chicken broth, tomato paste, basil, and pepper. Cover and simmer 10 minutes. Stir in tomato wedges; cook just until thoroughly heated.

Cook vermicelli according to package directions, omitting salt; drain.

Serve vegetable sauce over hot vermicelli. Top each serving with ¼ cup shredded cheese. Yield: 4 servings (about 292 calories per serving).

Even if you're dieting, there's no reason to avoid bread—provided you choose breads low in fat and sugar. For starters, try one of these selections. From top: Whole Wheat Muffins (page 105), French Bread (page 108), Whole Wheat Crackers (page 106), and Whole Wheat Banana Bread (page 106).

DESSERTS

The look and taste of our desserts in *Cooking Light* may say "fattening," but they're not. In the following pages, you'll find delicious desserts such as Glazed Peach Pie and Chocolate-Marshmallow Freeze. Each recipe has been stripped of extra calories by cutting back on the amounts of sugar, honey, butter, cream, and other high-calorie ingredients.

Skim milk is used in recipes which traditionally call for whole milk or heavy cream. One cup of skim milk contains only 90 calories. An equal amount of whole milk provides 170 calories, while 1 cup of whipping cream totals a whopping 830 calories! (That's not counting calories from sugar when the cream is whipped and sweetened.)

Dieters often get tired of living by a list of desserts which should be avoided. However, fruit is a natural dessert that everyone should eat more often. Fresh fruit and unsweetened fruit juice are used in many of our recipes to replace some, if not all, of the sugar. When using recipes that call for fresh fruit, remember that the riper fruit usually has a sweeter flavor.

Fresh fruit is loaded with vitamins, minerals, and fiber. If fresh fruit is not available, unsweetened frozen or canned is a good choice. Avoid fruit packed in heavy syrup since the fruit absorbs the sugar making it almost impossible to drain or even rinse the extra calories away.

Some of our light dessert recipes call for low-fat yogurt. Contrary to popular belief, yogurt is not always low in calories. Dieters should be wary of whole milk yogurt and yogurt filled with sweetened fruit. Yogurt with sweetened fruit can contain up to 270 calories per cup. This compares to only 140 calories per cup of plain low-fat yogurt.

If none of the fruit recipes satisfy your sweet tooth, look through the last few pages in this section. You'll find some taste-tempting desserts that are surprisingly low in calories.

Cranberry-Apple Ice (page 130) contains only 91 calories per half-cup serving. Make it during the winter, when fresh cranberries are in season, to serve your diet-conscious holiday guests.

STUFFED BAKED APPLES

4 medium cooking apples
¼ cup raisins
¾ cup water
1 teaspoon lemon juice
Ground cinnamon

Core apples to within ½-inch of bottom, leaving a 1-inch wide cavity. Peel around top third of each apple.

Arrange apples in an 8-inch square or 9-inch round baking pan. Fill cavity of each apple with 1 tablespoon raisins. Combine water and lemon juice; pour over apples. Sprinkle lightly with cinnamon. Cover and bake at 375° for 50 to 60 minutes or until apples are tender. Yield: 4 servings (about 109 calories per serving).

CHUNKY APPLESAUCE

4 medium cooking apples (about 1½ pounds)
½ cup unsweetened apple juice
¼ teaspoon ground cinnamon
⅛ teaspoon ground nutmeg

Peel, core, and quarter apples; combine apples and apple juice in a saucepan. Cook, uncovered, over medium-low heat 10 to 15 minutes or until apples are tender, stirring occasionally to break up apples.

Stir in spices. Serve warm or chilled. Yield: 4 servings (about 106 calories per serving).

Note: Add more water, if needed, to achieve desired consistency.

BANANAS FOSTER

½ cup unsweetened pineapple juice
¼ teaspoon ground cinnamon
3 large firm bananas
1 (8-ounce) can unsweetened sliced pineapple, drained
¼ cup rum
1 quart vanilla ice milk

Combine pineapple juice and cinnamon in a medium skillet. Peel bananas, and slice in half crosswise; then quarter each piece lengthwise. Quarter each pineapple slice. Add bananas and pineapple to juice mixture; cook over medium heat until bananas are slightly soft, basting constantly with juice.

Place rum in a small, long-handled pan; heat just until warm. Ignite rum with a long match, and pour over fruit. Serve immediately over ice milk. Yield: 8 servings (about 64 calories per serving plus 100 calories per ½-cup ice milk).

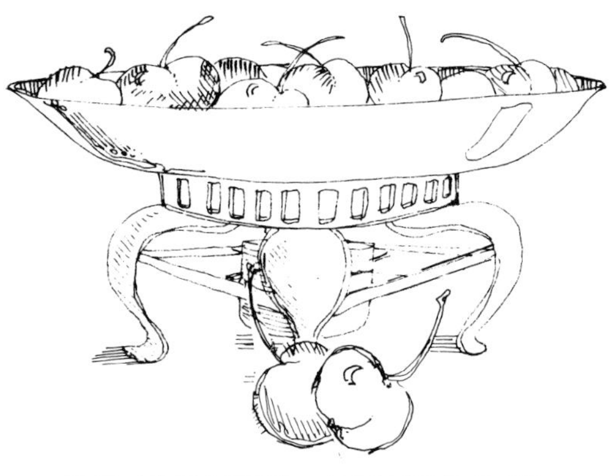

BRANDIED CHERRIES JUBILEE

1 tablespoon cornstarch
1 tablespoon sugar
½ teaspoon grated orange rind
½ cup unsweetened orange juice
½ cup water
1 pound fresh sweet cherries, pitted
¼ cup brandy
1½ quarts vanilla ice milk

Combine cornstarch, sugar, and orange rind in a large skillet; stir in orange juice and water. Bring to a boil; add cherries, and simmer 10 minutes. Transfer mixture to a chafing dish to keep warm.

Heat brandy in a small, long-handled pan to produce fumes (do not boil). Ignite brandy with a long match, and pour over cherries. Spoon cherries over ice milk. Yield: 12 servings (about 36 calories per ⅓ cup sauce plus 100 calories per ½ cup ice milk).

FRESH CITRUS DESSERT

4 medium oranges, peeled, seeded, and sectioned
2 medium grapefruit, peeled, seeded, and sectioned
1 (15¼-ounce) can unsweetened pineapple chunks, drained
1 pint lemon or pineapple sherbet

Combine first 3 ingredients; cover and chill. Divide fruit evenly into 8 sherbet glasses; top each serving with ¼ cup sherbet. Yield: 8 servings (about 147 calories per serving).

FRESH FRUIT COMPOTE

1 (15¼-ounce) can unsweetened pineapple tidbits, undrained
3 tablespoons cornstarch
2 teaspoons sugar
½ teaspoon ground nutmeg
1 cup water
3 tablespoons lemon juice
2 medium oranges, peeled, seeded, and sectioned
2 medium apples, unpeeled and chopped
2 medium bananas, sliced
1 medium-size yellow apple, unpeeled and chopped
1 medium pear, unpeeled and chopped
1 cup seedless green grapes, halved
1 cup red grapes, halved and seeded

Drain pineapple, reserving juice; set aside. Combine cornstarch, sugar, and nutmeg in a medium saucepan; gradually add water, stirring until smooth. Cook over medium heat, stirring constantly, until mixture comes to a boil; boil 1 minute. Remove from heat, and stir in reserved pineapple juice and lemon juice; cool.

Combine reserved pineapple and remaining ingredients in a large bowl; pour dressing over top, tossing gently to coat. Cover and chill thoroughly. Yield: 12 servings (about 105 calories per 1-cup serving).

FRUIT-FILLED CANTALOUPE

2 medium cantaloupes (about 2¼ pounds each)
2 cups fresh strawberries, halved
1 cup fresh blueberries
¼ cup gin
1½ tablespoons lemon juice
2 teaspoons sugar
Fresh mint leaves (optional)

Cut each cantaloupe in half, and remove seeds; prick cavities with a fork (do not puncture rind). Combine strawberries, blueberries, gin, lemon juice, and sugar; toss lightly. Spoon fruit mixture into cantaloupe halves; chill at least 2 hours. Garnish with mint leaves, if desired. Yield: 4 servings (about 172 calories per serving).

WINE-FRUIT COMPOTE

Ascorbic-citric powder
2 medium pears, unpeeled and sliced
2 medium apples, unpeeled and sliced
2 medium bananas, peeled and sliced
1 (16-ounce) package frozen unsweetened peaches, thawed and drained
1 tablespoon plus 1 teaspoon sugar
½ cup Sauterne or other dry white wine
2 tablespoons flaked coconut

Prepare an ascorbic-citric solution according to manufacturer's directions. Toss pears, apples, and bananas separately in prepared solution; drain fruit.

Layer fruit (in order listed) in a 3-quart serving bowl, sprinkling each layer with 1 teaspoon sugar. Pour wine over fruit, and sprinkle with coconut. Refrigerate fruit mixture at least 2 hours before serving. Yield: 10 servings (about 90 calories per 1-cup serving).

TROPICAL FRUIT DELIGHT

1 medium-size ripe banana
½ cup fresh cranberries
3 tablespoons skim milk
½ cup plain low-fat yogurt
2 tablespoons sugar
¼ teaspoon ground ginger
2 medium pears, unpeeled and chopped
2 medium apples, unpeeled and chopped
1 medium pineapple, peeled and cubed

Combine first 3 ingredients in container of an electric blender; process until finely chopped. Add yogurt, sugar, and ginger; process until well blended. Chill thoroughly.

Divide fruit evenly into 8 dessert bowls; spoon 3 tablespoons sauce over each serving. Yield: 8 servings (about 117 calories per serving).

FRESH FRUIT WITH HONEY CREAM

1 large orange
1 cup unpeeled, chopped apple
1 cup unpeeled, chopped pear
1 tablespoon lemon juice
½ cup low-fat cottage cheese
2 tablespoons skim milk
1 tablespoon honey
Lime slices (optional)

Peel and section orange; remove membranes and seeds. Cut each section in half crosswise. Combine fruit and lemon juice; toss.

Combine cottage cheese, milk, and honey in container of an electric blender; process at medium speed until smooth. To serve, spoon fruit into individual serving dishes; divide cottage cheese mixture evenly over fruit. Garnish with lime slices, if desired. Yield: 6 servings (about 79 calories per serving).

FRUIT-YOGURT DESSERT

2 medium bananas, sliced
2 medium apples, cored and cut into ½-inch cubes
½ cup unsweetened orange juice
1 (15¼-ounce) can unsweetened pineapple chunks, drained
1 (8-ounce) carton peach low-fat yogurt
¼ teaspoon ground ginger

Combine bananas, apples, and orange juice in a large bowl; toss to coat. Add pineapple; cover and chill 1 to 2 hours. Drain well.

Combine yogurt and ginger, blending well; pour over fruit, and toss gently. Serve immediately in dessert dishes. Yield: 6 servings (about 123 calories per serving).

SPICED FRUIT DESSERT

1 orange
1 (15¼-ounce) can unsweetened pineapple chunks, undrained
2 (16-ounce) cans unsweetened pear halves, drained
1 (16-ounce) can unsweetened apricot halves, drained
2 (2-inch) sticks cinnamon
6 whole cloves

Peel orange, reserving rind; divide orange into sections, removing membrane. Drain pineapple, reserving juice. Combine orange sections, pineapple, pears, and apricots in a bowl; set aside.

Combine rind, pineapple juice, cinnamon, and cloves in a small saucepan; simmer 5 minutes. Strain juice, and pour over fruit; cover and chill dessert several hours. Yield: 6 servings (about 116 calories per serving).

BROILED GRAPEFRUIT

3 medium grapefruit, halved
2 tablespoons reduced-calorie margarine
2 tablespoons brown sugar

Remove seeds, and loosen sections of grapefruit halves. Spread each half with 1 teaspoon margarine, and sprinkle with 1 teaspoon sugar.

Place grapefruit halves in a baking pan; broil 6 inches from heat for 3 minutes or until sugar is melted and grapefruit is thoroughly heated. Serve immediately. Yield: 6 servings (about 76 calories per serving).

HONEYDEW-BERRY DESSERT

½ cup reduced-calorie strawberry jam
¼ teaspoon grated orange rind
½ cup unsweetened orange juice
Dash of ground cinnamon
1 tablespoon cornstarch
2 tablespoons water
1 cup sliced fresh strawberries
¼ teaspoon almond extract
4 cups honeydew balls
Grated orange rind

Combine first 4 ingredients in a small saucepan. Combine cornstarch and water, stirring until blended; add to strawberry jam mixture. Bring to a boil over medium heat, stirring frequently; reduce heat, and simmer until the strawberry jam melts and mixture is thickened. Remove sauce from heat; stir in the sliced strawberries and almond extract. Cool sauce to room temperature.

Spoon 1 cup honeydew balls into each of 4 individual serving dishes; divide sauce evenly over fruit, and sprinkle with grated orange rind. Yield: 4 servings (about 140 calories per serving).

KIWI JUBILEE

½ cup unsweetened apple juice
½ teaspoon grated orange rind
4 kiwis, peeled and sliced
¼ cup rum
3 cups vanilla ice milk

Combine apple juice and orange rind in a small skillet; bring to a boil. Add kiwi; reduce heat, and simmer just until thoroughly heated.

Place rum in a small, long-handled pan; heat just until warm. Ignite with a long match, and pour over kiwi mixture. Serve sauce over ½-cup servings of ice milk. Yield: 6 servings (about 157 calories per serving).

ORANGE DATE-NUT DESSERT

4 medium bananas, sliced
4 medium oranges, peeled and sectioned
1 (8-ounce) can unsweetened pineapple chunks, drained
1 cup chopped dates
¼ cup chopped walnuts or pecans
¼ cup unsweetened orange juice
1 tablespoon lemon juice
1 tablespoon honey
½ teaspoon ground ginger

Combine fruit and walnuts in a medium bowl. Combine remaining ingredients, stirring until blended. Pour dressing over fruit mixture, and toss gently; spoon into individual dessert dishes to serve. Yield: 10 servings (about 150 calories per serving).

BAKED PEARS WITH LEMON SAUCE

4 medium pears, peeled
3 tablespoons water
1 tablespoon honey
2 whole cloves
Lemon Sauce

Cut pears in half lengthwise; remove cores. Arrange pears, cut side up, in a glass baking dish.

Combine water, honey, and cloves; pour over pears. Cover and bake at 350° for 25 to 30 minutes. Serve warm pears with chilled Lemon Sauce. Yield: 4 servings (about 115 calories per serving plus 10 calories per tablespoon sauce).

LEMON SAUCE:

2 teaspoons cornstarch
¾ cup skim milk, divided
1 (3-inch) stick cinnamon
½ teaspoon grated lemon rind
3 tablespoons lemon juice
1 tablespoon honey

Combine cornstarch and ¼ cup milk in a small saucepan, stirring until blended. Add remaining ½ cup milk and cinnamon; cook over medium heat 6 to 8 minutes, stirring constantly, until mixture is thickened.

Reduce heat, and stir in remaining ingredients until well blended. Remove from heat; cool to room temperature. Cover and refrigerate 3 hours or until thoroughly chilled. Remove cinnamon stick before serving. Yield: 1 cup.

POACHED PEARS WITH PINEAPPLE SAUCE

4 medium pears
2 cups unsweetened pineapple juice
¼ teaspoon ground nutmeg
1 tablespoon cornstarch
2 tablespoons water
1 teaspoon grated unsweetened chocolate

Peel pears, removing core from bottom end but leaving stems intact.

Combine pineapple juice and nutmeg in a 2-quart saucepan; place pears in juice mixture. Bring to a boil; cover, reduce heat, and simmer 10 to 15 minutes or until tender. Transfer pears to serving dish with a slotted spoon.

Combine cornstarch and water, stirring until blended; stir into juice mixture. Cook over medium heat, stirring constantly, until mixture is clear and thickened.

Place pears in individual dessert dishes. Pour pineapple sauce over pears; chill thoroughly. Just before serving, garnish each pear with ¼ teaspoon grated chocolate. Yield: 4 servings (about 178 calories per serving).

STRAWBERRIES À LA ORANGE

2 cups fresh strawberries
1 tablespoon sugar
½ teaspoon grated orange rind
½ cup unsweetened orange juice, chilled
2 tablespoons Cointreau or other orange-flavored liqueur

Combine strawberries and sugar in a medium bowl; toss. Cover and refrigerate at least 1 hour.

To serve, add remaining ingredients to strawberries; mix well, and spoon into individual serving dishes. Yield: 2 servings (about 148 calories per serving).

STRAWBERRY-ORANGE CUPS

2 large oranges
2 cups fresh strawberries, sliced
2 tablespoons Triple Sec or other orange-flavored liqueur
2 egg whites
2 tablespoons sugar
Fresh mint leaves (optional)

Cut oranges in half crosswise. Gently remove pulp, leaving shells intact. Remove membrane from pulp and shells (do not puncture shells); set shells aside.

Combine orange pulp, strawberries, and Triple Sec; cover and chill at least 1 hour.

Fill orange shells with strawberry mixture. Beat egg whites (at room temperature) until foamy; gradually add sugar, beating until stiff peaks form. Spread meringue over opening of each orange shell, sealing to edge of shells; place on a baking sheet. Broil shells 8 inches from heat for 1 minute or until meringue is lightly browned. Garnish with mint, if desired. Yield: 4 servings (about 124 calories per serving).

RHUBARB AND STRAWBERRY GLAZE

3 cups sliced fresh rhubarb (about ¾ pound)
3 tablespoons sugar
1 cup water
1 tablespoon cornstarch
¼ cup water
1 teaspoon lemon juice
2 cups sliced fresh strawberries

Place rhubarb in a saucepan with sugar and 1 cup water. Bring to a boil; reduce heat, and simmer 2 minutes. Remove from heat; drain, reserving liquid. Add enough water to reserved liquid to make 1¼ cups.

Combine cornstarch and ¼ cup water in a small saucepan, stirring until blended; add 1¼ cups reserved liquid mixture. Bring to a boil; reduce heat, and cook 2 minutes, stirring constantly. Remove from heat; allow to cool. Stir in lemon juice, strawberries, and rhubarb; chill thoroughly. Yield: 4 servings (about 87 calories per serving).

Note: 3 cups frozen sliced rhubarb may be substituted for fresh rhubarb.

HEAVENLY FRUIT HALO

1 envelope unflavored gelatin
2 tablespoons sugar
¼ cup cold water
1¼ cups skim milk
1 cup Mock Cream Cheese
½ teaspoon almond extract
1 cup frozen whipped topping, thawed
Vegetable cooking spray
2 cups fresh strawberries, sliced

Combine gelatin, sugar, and water in a small saucepan; let stand 1 minute. Cook over low heat, stirring constantly, until gelatin and sugar are dissolved. Remove from heat, and let cool slightly. Stir in next 3 ingredients; fold in whipped topping. Pour mixture into a 4-cup ring mold coated with cooking spray; refrigerate 3 to 4 hours or until firm.

Unmold onto a serving plate; spoon strawberries into center of mold. Yield: 6 servings (about 138 calories per serving).

MOCK CREAM CHEESE:

1½ cups ricotta cheese
1 cup low-fat cottage cheese
⅔ cup plain low-fat yogurt

Combine all ingredients in container of electric blender or food processor; process until smooth. Store in a covered container in refrigerator up to 1 week. Yield: 3⅓ cups.

Note: Mock Cream Cheese may be used instead of sour cream on baked potatoes. Each tablespoon provides 16 calories.

CHILLED ORANGE SQUARES

2 envelopes unflavored gelatin
¼ cup sugar
1½ cups unsweetened orange juice, divided
2 eggs, separated
3 cups low-fat cottage cheese
1 teaspoon grated orange rind
1 teaspoon vanilla extract
¼ cup sugar
¼ cup graham cracker crumbs
2 cups sliced fresh strawberries

Combine gelatin, ¼ cup sugar, and ¾ cup orange juice in a small saucepan; let stand 1 minute. Cook over low heat, stirring constantly, until gelatin is dissolved.

Combine ¾ cup orange juice, egg yolks, cottage cheese, orange rind, and vanilla in container of electric blender; process until smooth.

Combine cottage cheese mixture and gelatin mixture in a large bowl; let cool. Beat egg whites (at room temperature) until foamy. Add ¼ cup sugar, 1 tablespoon at a time, beating until stiff peaks form. Fold into cottage cheese mixture, blending with a wire whisk until smooth.

Sprinkle graham cracker crumbs evenly over bottom of a 13- x 9- x 2-inch baking dish; pour filling over crumbs. Chill until firm. Cut into squares; serve with fresh strawberries. Yield: 12 servings (about 120 calories per serving).

PETITS POTS DE CHOCOLAT

1 envelope unflavored gelatin
1½ cups skim milk, divided
3 eggs, separated
¼ cup sugar
⅓ cup sifted cocoa
⅛ teaspoon salt
1 teaspoon vanilla extract
¼ cup sugar
½ cup frozen whipped topping, thawed
1 teaspoon chocolate shavings

Combine gelatin and ½ cup milk in a medium saucepan, stirring well; let stand 1 minute. Cook over medium heat, stirring constantly, until gelatin is completely dissolved (about 1 minute).

Combine remaining 1 cup milk and egg yolks, beating well. Add yolk mixture, ¼ cup sugar, cocoa, and salt to saucepan; stir well. Cook over medium heat, stirring constantly, until smooth and thickened (about 5 minutes). Remove from heat; stir in vanilla, and chill 20 minutes.

Beat egg whites (at room temperature) in a mixing bowl until foamy; gradually add ¼ cup sugar, 1 tablespoon at a time, beating until stiff peaks form. Gradually add chilled chocolate mixture to beaten egg whites, folding gently.

Divide evenly into 8 (4-ounce) serving dishes. Chill at least 2 hours. Garnish each serving with 1 tablespoon whipped topping and ⅛ teaspoon chocolate shavings. Yield: 8 servings (about 117 calories per serving).

CHILLED CHOCOLATE DESSERT

1 envelope unflavored gelatin
⅔ cup skim milk
¼ cup sugar
3 tablespoons cocoa
¼ cup skim milk
1 (12-ounce) carton low-fat cottage cheese
2 eggs, separated
1½ teaspoons vanilla extract
2 tablespoons sugar
⅓ cup graham cracker crumbs
¼ teaspoon ground cinnamon
1 tablespoon reduced-calorie margarine
1 cup frozen whipped topping, thawed
1 cup fresh strawberries

Combine gelatin and ⅔ cup milk in a small saucepan; let stand 1 minute. Cook over medium heat, stirring constantly, about 1 minute or until gelatin is dissolved; set aside to cool

Combine ¼ cup sugar and cocoa in a small bowl; gradually add ¼ cup milk, stirring until smooth. Combine cocoa mixture, cottage cheese, egg yolks, and vanilla in container of an electric blender; process until smooth. Add gelatin mixture, blending well. Set aside.

Beat egg whites (at room temperature) until foamy. Gradually add 2 tablespoon sugar, 1 tablespoon at a time, beating until stiff peaks form. Fold one-fourth of the chocolate mixture into egg whites; fold in the remaining mixture.

Combine graham cracker crumbs and cinnamon; cut into margarine with a pastry blender or fork. Firmly press mixture evenly into bottom of an 8 or 9-inch springform pan. Pour chocolate mixture over crust; cover and chill 4 hours or until firm. Spread whipped topping over top of dessert and garnish with strawberries. Yield: 8 servings (about 157 calories per serving).

LAYERED LEMON PUDDING

2 eggs, beaten
¼ cup sugar
1 tablespoon grated lemon rind
¼ cup lemon juice
1 tablespoon margarine
1 (1.25-ounce) envelope whipped topping mix
½ cup skim milk
½ teaspoon vanilla extract
Lemon twists

Combine first 5 ingredients in a small saucepan; cook over low heat until thickened. Cool slightly. Spoon 1 tablespoon into each of 5 dessert cups; set aside remaining lemon mixture.

Combine whipped topping mix, milk, and vanilla; beat 2 minutes at low speed of electric mixer. Beat at high speed until stiff peaks form. Spoon 3 tablespoons whipped topping over lemon layer in each dessert cup.

Gently fold remaining whipped topping into remaining lemon mixture; spoon evenly into dessert cups. Cover and chill. Garnish each serving with a lemon twist. Yield: 5 servings (about 142 calories per serving).

BAKED VANILLA CUSTARD

3 eggs, slightly beaten
¼ cup sugar
¼ teaspoon salt
½ to 1 teaspoon vanilla extract
2 cups skim milk, scalded
Ground nutmeg (optional)

Combine first 4 ingredients, beating well; gradually add milk, stirring constantly. Pour into 6 (6-ounce) custard cups. Sprinkle with nutmeg, if desired.

Place custard cups in a 13- x 9- x 2-inch baking pan; pour hot water into pan to a depth of 1 inch. Bake at 325° for 40 to 45 minutes or until knife inserted halfway between center and edges of custard comes out clean. Remove cups from water; cool. Chill thoroughly. Yield: 6 servings (about 101 calories per serving).

STRAWBERRY-LEMON MOUSSE

¾ cup sugar
½ cup cornstarch
3 cups skim milk
1½ teaspoons grated lemon rind
½ cup lemon juice
4 egg whites
¼ cup sugar
2½ cups sliced fresh strawberries, chilled

Combine ¾ cup sugar and cornstarch in a medium saucepan; gradually stir in milk. Cook over medium heat, stirring constantly, until smooth and thickened. Remove milk mixture from heat, and stir in lemon rind and juice; cool, stirring occasionally.

Beat egg whites (at room temperature) until foamy. Gradually add ¼ cup sugar, 1 tablespoon at a time, beating until soft peaks form. Fold into lemon mixture. Spoon ½-cup portions into individual serving dishes; chill until firm. Top each serving with ¼ cup sliced strawberries. Yield: 10 servings (about 153 calories per serving).

LIGHT RASPBERRY MOUSSE

2½ cups fresh raspberries
1 envelope unflavored gelatin
1⅓ cups unsweetened orange juice, divided
2 tablespoons sugar
2 tablespoons Triple Sec or other orange-flavored liqueur
¾ cup evaporated skim milk, chilled
1 teaspoon vanilla extract
2 egg whites, stiffly beaten
Orange twists (optional)

Process raspberries in food mill or container of an electric blender. Strain raspberries, reserving 1 cup juice; discard seeds.

Soften gelatin in ⅓ cup orange juice. Combine raspberry juice, gelatin mixture, remaining 1 cup orange juice, and sugar in a saucepan; bring to a boil, stirring constantly until sugar dissolves. Remove from heat, and cool.

Stir Triple Sec into raspberry mixture; chill until consistency of unbeaten egg white.

Combine evaporated skim milk and vanilla in a large cold bowl; beat until stiff peaks form. Beat egg whites (at room temperature) until stiff peaks form. Fold whipped milk mixture and egg whites into raspberry mixture. Spoon into a 1½-quart soufflé dish or 6 individual serving dishes; chill until firm. Garnish with orange twists, if desired. Yield: 6 servings (about 123 calories per serving).

LIGHT COCONUT SOUFFLÉ

3 tablespoons reduced-calorie margarine
3 tablespoons all-purpose flour
¾ cup skim milk
3 egg yolks
3 tablespoons sugar
1 teaspoon vanilla extract
¾ cup flaked coconut
4 egg whites
Vegetable cooking spray
2 tablespoons flaked coconut

Melt margarine in a small heavy saucepan over low heat; add flour, stirring until smooth. Cook 1 minute, stirring constantly (mixture will be dry). Gradually add milk; cook over medium heat, stirring constantly with a wire whisk, until smooth and thickened.

Beat egg yolks and sugar until thick and lemon colored. Gradually stir about one-fourth of hot mixture into yolks; add to remaining hot mixture, stirring constantly. Stir in vanilla and ¾ cup coconut. Set aside.

Beat egg whites (at room temperature) in a large bowl until stiff but not dry; gently fold into coconut mixture. Pour mixture into a 1-quart soufflé dish coated with cooking spray; sprinkle with 2 tablespoons coconut. Place in a shallow pan containing about 1 inch warm water. Bake at 375° for 40 to 45 minutes or until puffy and golden brown. Serve immediately. Yield: 6 servings (about 172 calories per serving).

ORANGE SOUFFLÉ

1 envelope unflavored gelatin
½ cup unsweetened orange juice
⅓ cup sugar
1 tablespoon all-purpose flour
3 eggs, separated
1 cup skim milk
1 tablespoon reduced-calorie margarine
2 teaspoons grated orange rind
6 ladyfingers, split

Soften gelatin in orange juice; set aside. Combine sugar and flour in a medium saucepan, mixing well. Combine egg yolks and milk; stir into sugar mixture. Add margarine; cook over low heat, stirring constantly, 8 to 10 minutes. Remove from heat; add gelatin mixture and orange rind, stirring until well blended.

Beat egg whites (at room temperature) until soft peaks form. Fold egg whites into orange mixture.

Line the sides of a 1-quart soufflé dish with ladyfingers; spoon soufflé mixture into prepared dish. Chill several hours or until set. Yield: 8 servings (about 121 calories per serving).

BLUEBERRY PARFAIT

3 eggs, separated
½ cup skim milk
1 tablespoon lemon juice
1 cup fresh blueberries
3 tablespoons sugar
1 envelope unflavored gelatin
½ teaspoon grated lemon rind
Lemon twists (optional)

Combine egg yolks, and next 4 ingredients in electric blender; process until smooth. Transfer to a small saucepan; sprinkle gelatin over blueberry mixture to soften. Cook over medium heat, stirring constantly, about 5 minutes or until gelatin is dissolved and mixture coats a spoon.

Remove blueberry mixture from heat, and stir in lemon rind; let cool to room temperature. Cover and refrigerate 30 to 45 minutes or until mixture is the consistency of unbeaten egg white.

Beat egg whites (at room temperature) until stiff peaks form; fold into blueberry mixture. Spoon evenly into 6 parfait glasses. Chill 2 hours. Garnish with lemon twists, if desired. Yield: 6 servings (about 90 calories per serving).

PEACH PARFAIT

1 envelope plus 1 teaspoon unflavored gelatin
½ cup cold water
¼ cup sugar
1 (12-ounce) can peach nectar
2 tablespoons water
1 tablespoon lemon juice
4 medium peaches, peeled and cut into ¾-inch cubes
¼ cup plus 2 tablespoons frozen whipped topping, thawed (optional)
Additional peach slices (optional)

Dissolve gelatin in ½ cup cold water; bring to a boil, stirring constantly. Remove from heat; stir in sugar and peach nectar. Chill until consistency of unbeaten egg white.

Combine 2 tablespoons water and lemon juice in a medium bowl; add cubed peaches, tossing gently to coat. Drain peaches, and combine with thickened nectar mixture; spoon evenly into 6 parfait glasses. Chill until firm.

Just before serving, top each parfait with 1 tablespoon whipped topping and an additional peach slice, if desired. Yield: 6 parfaits (about 98 calories per serving plus 14 calories per tablespoon whipped topping).

STRAWBERRY PUFF

1 (16-ounce) package frozen whole strawberries
2 egg whites
¼ cup sugar
1 tablespoon lemon juice
1 cup frozen whipped topping, thawed
½ (16-ounce) package frozen whole strawberries, partially thawed

Combine first 4 ingredients in a large mixing bowl. Beat at high speed of electric mixer 10 to 12 minutes or until stiff peaks form. Add whipped topping; beat until smooth. Spoon into individual serving dishes, and freeze until firm.

Crush remaining strawberries with a fork. Spoon over dessert. Yield: 8 servings (about 110 calories per serving).

FROZEN FRUIT DESSERT

2 cups mashed ripe bananas
1 (8-ounce) can unsweetened crushed pineapple, undrained
2 cups unsweetened orange juice
2 tablespoons lemon juice

Combine all ingredients, and pour into an 8- or 9-inch square baking pan; freeze mixture until almost firm.

Spoon mixture into a large mixing bowl, and beat with an electric mixer until smooth and creamy. Spoon mixture back into pan, and freeze until firm. Yield: 5 cups (about 75 calories per ½-cup serving).

FROZEN FRUIT CREAM

1 (8-ounce) can unsweetened pineapple chunks, undrained
2⅓ cups Mock Cream Cheese (recipe on page 123)
1 (12-ounce) carton frozen whipped topping, thawed
1 teaspoon lemon juice
1 (11-ounce) can mandarin oranges, drained
1 cup frozen unsweetened cherries, thawed and drained
1 cup seedless green grapes, halved
¼ cup chopped pecans

Drain pineapple, reserving juice. Combine reserved juice, Mock Cream Cheese, whipped topping, and lemon juice in a large bowl; stir until well blended.

Fold pineapple chunks and remaining ingredients into cream cheese mixture; pour into a 13- x 9- x 2-inch baking pan, and freeze until firm.

Let stand at room temperature 10 to 15 minutes before slicing. Yield: 15 servings (about 148 calories per serving).

CHOCOLATE-MARSHMALLOW FREEZE

1 (13-ounce) can evaporated skim milk
⅓ cup cocoa
¼ cup sugar
16 marshmallows

Reserve ½ cup milk; pour remaining milk into a large bowl, and chill thoroughly.

Combine cocoa and sugar in a medium-size heavy saucepan; gradually stir in ½ cup reserved evaporated milk until blended. Add marshmallows to cocoa mixture; cook over low heat, stirring constantly, until marshmallows are melted. Cool to room temperature.

Beat chilled milk with electric mixer until stiff peaks form; fold in cocoa mixture. Pour into a 9-inch square baking pan; cover and freeze 4 hours or until firm. Yield: 8 servings (about 118 calories per 1-cup serving).

LEMON FREEZE

1 cup evaporated skim milk
2 eggs, separated
¼ cup lemon juice
¼ cup sugar
1 teaspoon grated lemon rind
¼ cup lemon juice
¼ cup graham cracker crumbs

Place evaporated milk in a 9-inch square baking pan; freeze 1½ hours or until slushy.

Combine egg yolks, ¼ cup lemon juice, sugar, and lemon rind; beat until smooth, and set aside.

Combine frozen milk and egg whites in a large cold bowl; beat with electric mixer until foamy. Add ¼ cup lemon juice, and beat until stiff peaks form. Gently fold reserved yolk mixture into beaten milk mixture. Pour into baking pan; sprinkle with graham cracker crumbs. Freeze 4 hours or until firm. Yield: 9 servings (about 73 calories per serving).

PINEAPPLE-ORANGE BARS

⅔ cup plus 2 tablespoons graham cracker crumbs, divided
2 tablespoons margarine, softened
½ cup instant nonfat dry milk powder
½ cup unsweetened orange juice, chilled
1 egg white
1 tablespoon lemon juice
¼ cup sugar
1 (8-ounce) can unsweetened crushed pineapple, drained

Combine ⅔ cup graham cracker crumbs and margarine. Press mixture into an 8-inch square pan; set aside.

Combine next 4 ingredients; beat at high speed of electric mixer for 3 minutes. Add sugar, and beat an additional 3 minutes; fold in pineapple, and spoon into prepared pan. Sprinkle remaining graham cracker crumbs on top.

Freeze 8 hours or overnight. Let stand at room temperature 15 minutes before serving. Yield: 9 servings (about 92 calories per serving).

ORANGE ALASKA

8 large oranges
1 pint orange sherbet, softened
2 (8-ounce) cartons peach low-fat yogurt
⅓ cup Cointreau or other orange-flavored liqueur
2 teaspoons grated orange rind
3 egg whites
½ teaspoon vanilla extract
¼ teaspoon cream of tartar
¼ cup sugar

Cut a small slice from the top of each orange. Clip membranes, and carefully remove pulp (do not puncture bottom). Strain pulp, reserving ½ cup juice.

Combine ½ cup orange juice, sherbet, yogurt, Cointreau, and orange rind in a large bowl; pour into orange shells. Place shells on a baking sheet; freeze about 4 hours.

Beat the egg whites (at room temperature), vanilla, and cream of tartar until foamy. Gradually add sugar, 1 tablespoon at a time, beating until stiff peaks form.

Spread meringue over top opening of each orange shell making sure edges are sealed. Freeze until ready to serve.

When ready to serve, broil orange shells 6 inches from heat for 1 or 2 minutes or until tops are golden brown. Yield: 8 servings (about 188 calories per serving).

STRAWBERRY ICE MILK

1 envelope unflavored gelatin
½ cup skim milk, divided
3 eggs
¾ cup sugar
3½ cups skim milk
2 teaspoons vanilla extract
4 cups fresh strawberries

Combine gelatin and ½ cup milk in a small saucepan; let stand 1 minute. Cook over medium heat, stirring constantly, about 1 minute or until gelatin is dissolved. Set aside.

Combine eggs and sugar in a large bowl; beat with electric mixer at high speed 4 to 5 minutes or until thick and doubled in volume. Stir in gelatin mixture, 3½ cups milk, and vanilla. Pour into a 13- x 9- x 2-inch baking pan; cover and freeze 2 to 3 hours or until mixture is slushy.

Place strawberries in container of an electric blender; process until pureed. Remove all but one-third of strawberries from blender container, and set aside.

Add one-third of the frozen mixture to strawberries in container of blender; process until smooth and well blended. Pour mixture into a large bowl. Repeat blending procedure with remaining strawberries and frozen mixture. Return blended strawberry mixture to baking dish; cover and freeze 3 hours or until firm. Yield: 8 cups (about 88 calories per ½-cup serving).

CAPPUCCINO ICE

3 cups strong, brewed coffee
2 cups frozen whipped topping, thawed
2 tablespoons sugar
2 tablespoons cocoa

Combine all ingredients in a container of an electric blender; process at low speed until smooth. Pour into an 8-inch square baking pan; cover and freeze until firm.

Let frozen mixture stand at room temperature 30 minutes. Spoon into blender container; process until smooth. Return mixture to baking pan; cover and freeze until firm.

To serve, let stand 5 minutes at room temperature; spoon into serving dishes. Yield: 6 servings (about 98 calories per serving).

CRANBERRY-APPLE ICE

2 pounds fresh cranberries
4 cups unsweetened apple juice, divided
¾ cup sugar
1 teaspoon grated orange rind

Wash cranberries; combine with 2 cups apple juice and sugar in a large saucepan. Cook 7 to 10 minutes or until cranberries pop; put through a food mill. Add remaining apple juice and orange rind to cranberry mixture. Chill.

Pour mixture into freezer can of a 1-gallon hand-turned or electric freezer. Freeze according to manufacturer's instructions. Yield: 2 quarts (about 91 calories per ½-cup serving).

Note: Ice may be stored in freezer compartment of refrigerator until serving time. Let stand at room temperature 10 to 15 minutes before serving.

STRAWBERRY-RASPBERRY ICE

4 cups fresh strawberries
4 cups fresh raspberries
2 cups unsweetened white grape juice
1 envelope unflavored gelatin
½ cup sugar
1 tablespoon lemon juice (optional)

Rinse strawberries and raspberries. Press fruit through a sieve; reserve juice, and discard seeds. Set juice aside.

Combine grape juice and gelatin in a small saucepan; let stand 1 minute. Add sugar; cook over low heat, stirring constantly, until gelatin and sugar are dissolved.

Combine berry juice, grape juice mixture, and lemon juice, if desired. Pour into freezer can of a 1-gallon hand-turned or electric freezer; freeze according to manufacturer's instructions. Yield: 7 cups (about 95 calories per ½-cup serving).

Note: Leftover ice may be stored in freezer compartment of refrigerator; let stand at room temperature 10 minutes before serving.

MIXED FRUIT SHERBET

2 (16-ounce) cans unsweetened apricot halves, undrained
5 large very ripe bananas, mashed
3 cups water
1 (15-ounce) can unsweetened crushed pineapple, undrained
1 (12-ounce) can frozen unsweetened orange juice concentrate, thawed and undiluted

Drain apricots, reserving ¼ cup apricot juice; chop apricots.

Combine apricots, ¼ cup reserved juice, and remaining ingredients in the freezer can of a 1-gallon hand-turned or electric freezer. Freeze according to manufacturer's instructions. Let ripen at least 1 hour before serving. Yield: 1 gallon (about 59 calories per ½-cup serving).

BLUEBERRY-KIRSCH SORBET

2 cups unsweetened apple juice
2 tablespoons sugar
4 cups fresh blueberries
½ cup kirsch
½ tablespoon lemon juice
Lemon rind strips (optional)

Combine apple juice and sugar in a small saucepan; bring to a boil, and boil 1 minute.

Process blueberries in container of an electric blender until smooth. Combine blueberries, apple juice mixture, kirsch, and lemon juice; pour into freezer can of a 1-gallon hand-turned or electric freezer, and freeze according to manufacturer's directions. Garnish each serving with lemon rind strips, if desired. Yield: 7½ cups (about 68 calories per ½-cup serving).

VANILLA CHIFFON CAKE

1 cup sifted all-purpose flour
½ cup sugar
1½ teaspoons baking powder
¼ teaspoon salt
4 eggs, separated
¼ cup vegetable oil
¼ cup water
1 teaspoon vanilla extract
½ teaspoon cream of tartar
½ cup sugar

Combine flour, ½ cup sugar, baking powder, and salt in a small mixing bowl. Make a well in center; add egg yolks, oil, water, and vanilla. Beat at high speed of electric mixer 5 minutes or until satin smooth.

Combine egg whites (at room temperature) and cream of tartar in a large mixing bowl; beat until soft peaks form. Add ½ cup sugar, 2 tablespoons at a time, and beat about 4 minutes at medium speed or until stiff peaks form (peaks should stand up straight when beaters are lifted from bowl).

Pour egg yolk mixture in a thin, steady stream over entire surface of egg whites; gently fold yolk mixture into whites.

Pour batter into an ungreased 10-inch tube pan, spreading batter evenly with a spatula. Bake at 325° for 1 hour or until cake springs back when touched lightly. Remove from oven; invert pan, and cool cake completely before removing from pan. Yield: 16 servings (about 126 calories per serving).

LEMON PUDDING CAKE

3 eggs, separated
¼ cup lemon juice
2 tablespoons margarine, melted
¼ cup all-purpose flour
2 tablespoons sugar
1 teaspoon grated lemon rind
¼ cup sugar
Citrus-Cheese Sauce

Beat egg yolks, lemon juice, and margarine in a large bowl. Add flour, 2 tablespoons sugar, and lemon rind to egg yolk mixture, beating until mixture is smooth.

Beat egg whites (at room temperature) until foamy. Gradually add ¼ cup sugar, 1 tablespoon at a time, beating until stiff peaks form. Fold egg whites into egg yolk mixture. Pour batter into an ungreased 8-inch square baking pan; place in a larger pan, and add about 1 inch warm water to larger pan. Bake at 350° for 35 to 40 minutes. Serve warm or chilled with Citrus-Cheese Sauce. Yield: 9 servings (about 93 calories per serving plus about 60 calories per ¼ cup sauce).

CITRUS-CHEESE SAUCE:

½ (8-ounce) package Neufchatel cheese, softened
3 tablespoons sugar
1 teaspoon grated orange rind
1 tablespoon orange juice
½ teaspoon grated lemon rind
1 tablespoon lemon juice
⅓ cup instant nonfat dry milk powder
⅓ cup ice water

Beat cheese in a medium bowl until fluffy; add next 5 ingredients, beating until mixture is smooth. Combine milk powder and water in a small cold bowl; beat until stiff peaks form. Fold whipped milk mixture into cheese mixture. Serve immediately. Yield: 2¼ cups.

Make it your rule not to taste test cake batter or other mixtures while preparing desserts. Calories can add up quickly.

STRAWBERRY-YOGURT CRÊPES

2 (8-ounce) cartons vanilla low-fat yogurt
16 (6-inch) crêpes (recipe follows)
Strawberry Sauce

Spoon 2 tablespoons yogurt in center of each crêpe; roll up, and place on individual serving plates. Top each crêpe with about 2 tablespoons Strawberry Sauce. Yield: 8 servings (about 190 calories per serving).

CRÊPES:

3 eggs
1½ cups skim milk
1⅓ cups all-purpose flour
½ teaspoon salt
2 teaspoons vegetable oil
Vegetable cooking spray

Combine eggs, milk, flour, salt, and oil in container of an electric blender; process 30 seconds. Scrape down sides of blender container with rubber spatula; process an additional 30 seconds or until mixture is smooth. Refrigerate batter 1 hour. (This allows flour particles to swell and soften so crêpes are light in texture.)

Coat the bottom of a 6-inch crêpe pan or nonstick skillet with cooking spray; place over medium heat until just hot, not smoking.

Pour about 2 tablespoons batter into pan; quickly tilt pan in all directions so batter covers pan in a thin film. Cook about 1 minute.

Lift edge of crêpe to test for doneness. Crêpe is ready for flipping when it can be shaken loose from pan. Flip the crêpe, and cook about 30 seconds on the other side. (This side is rarely more than spotty brown and is the side on which filling is placed.)

When crêpe is done, place on a towel to cool. Stack crêpes between layers of waxed paper to prevent sticking. Repeat procedure until all batter is used, stirring batter occasionally. Yield: 20 (6-inch) crêpes.

Note: To freeze crêpes, stack between layers of wax paper; place in freezer container and freeze.

STRAWBERRY SAUCE:

3 cups fresh strawberries, sliced
2½ tablespoons sugar
2½ teaspoons cornstarch
¼ teaspoon almond extract

Combine strawberries and sugar; cover and refrigerate several hours or overnight. Drain the strawberries, reserving juice; set aside.

Add enough water to strawberry juice to make ¾ cup. Combine juice and cornstarch in a saucepan, stirring until cornstarch is dissolved. Cook over medium heat, stirring constantly, until smooth and thickened. Stir in strawberries and almond extract. Chill. Yield: 2 cups.

LIGHT CRÊPES SUZETTES

2 cups unsweetened orange juice
2 tablespoons cornstarch
1 tablespoon grated orange rind
2 medium oranges, peeled and sectioned
16 (6-inch) crêpes (recipe follows)
¼ cup Grand Marnier or other orange-flavored liqueur

Combine first 3 ingredients in a large skillet; cook over medium heat until mixture comes to a boil, stirring constantly. Boil 1 minute. Stir in orange sections, and cool slightly.

Dip both sides of crêpe in orange sauce; fold in half, then in quarters. Repeat procedure.

Arrange crêpes in remaining sauce; place over low heat until thoroughly heated. Heat Grand Marnier in a saucepan over medium heat. (Do not boil.) Ignite and pour over crêpes. After flames die down, serve immediately. Yield: 8 servings (about 146 calories per serving).

CRÊPES:

3 eggs
1½ cups skim milk
1⅓ cups all-purpose flour
½ teaspoon salt
2 teaspoons vegetable oil
Vegetable cooking spray

Combine first 5 ingredients in container of an electric blender; process 30 seconds. Scrape down sides of blender container with rubber spatula; process an additional 30 seconds or until smooth. Refrigerate batter 1 hour. (This allows flour particles to swell and soften so crêpes are light in texture).

Coat the bottom of a 6-inch crêpe pan or nonstick skillet with cooking spray; place pan over medium heat until just hot, not smoking.

Pour about 2 tablespoons batter into pan. Quickly tilt pan in all directions so batter covers pan in a thin film; cook about 1 minute.

Lift edge of crêpe to test for doneness. Crêpe is ready for flipping when it can be shaken loose from pan. Flip the crêpe, and cook about 30 seconds on the other side. (This side is rarely more than spotty brown and is the side on which the filling is placed.)

When crêpe is done, place on a towel to cool. Stack between layers of waxed paper to prevent sticking. Repeat until all batter is used, stirring batter occasionally. Yield: 20 crêpes.

LEMON WAFERS

½ cup margarine
¾ cup firmly packed light brown sugar
1 egg
2 teaspoons grated lemon rind
1½ tablespoons lemon juice
1½ cups all-purpose flour
½ teaspoon baking soda
¼ teaspoon salt
Vegetable cooking spray

Cream margarine; gradually add sugar, beating until light and fluffy. Add egg, lemon rind, and lemon juice, beating well.

Combine flour, soda, and salt; add to creamed mixture, mixing just until blended.

Drop dough by rounded teaspoonfuls about 2 inches apart on cookie sheets coated with cooking spray. Bake at 400° for 8 to 10 minutes. Remove from cookie sheet immediately, and cool on wire rack. Yield: 3½ dozen (about 49 calories each).

LAYERED STRAWBERRY CHEESECAKE PIE

1 cup graham cracker crumbs
2 tablespoons sugar
3 tablespoons reduced-calorie margarine, melted
½ cup water
4 eggs
1 (16-ounce) carton low-fat cottage cheese
½ cup sugar
½ cup instant nonfat dry milk powder
¼ cup all-purpose flour
1 tablespoon lemon juice
2 teaspoons vanilla extract
⅛ teaspoon salt
4 cups fresh strawberries, washed and hulled
1 tablespoon cornstarch
1 cup unsweetened orange juice

Combine first 3 ingredients; press evenly into bottom of a 9-inch springform pan.

Combine next 9 ingredients in container of electric blender; process 1 minute or until smooth. Pour into crust. Bake at 300° for 1 hour. Turn off heat, and leave in oven 1 hour. Set aside to cool.

Arrange strawberries on top of pie. Combine cornstarch and orange juice in a saucepan, stirring well. Cook over low heat 1 minute or until thickened and clear, stirring constantly. Cool.

Pour glaze over strawberries; chill. Yield: 12 servings (about 180 calories per serving) or 10 servings (about 216 calories per serving).

DEEP-DISH APPLE PIES

2½ cups peeled, diced apple
2 tablespoons brown sugar
1 teaspoon quick-cooking tapioca
⅛ teaspoon ground nutmeg
⅛ teaspoon ground cinnamon
⅓ cup all-purpose flour
⅛ teaspoon salt
1 tablespoon plus 2 teaspoons shortening
1 tablespoon cold water

Combine apple, sugar, tapioca, nutmeg, and cinnamon; divide evenly among 4 (8-ounce) custard cups. Set aside.

Combine flour and salt in a small bowl; cut in shortening with fork or pastry blender until mixture resembles coarse meal. Sprinkle cold water evenly over surface; stir with a fork until dry ingredients are moistened.

Divide dough into 4 equal portions. Roll out each portion on a lightly floured surface to fit custard cups; place pastry over apples.

Cut slits in pastry to allow steam to escape. Bake at 400° for 30 minutes. Serve immediately. Yield: 4 servings (about 139 calories per serving).

FRESH PEACH PIE

¼ cup sugar
3 tablespoons cornstarch
½ cup unsweetened white grape juice
1½ cups mashed fresh peaches
3 cups sliced fresh peaches
Crunchy Whole Wheat Pastry Shell

Combine sugar and cornstarch in a medium saucepan; stir in grape juice and mashed peaches. Bring to a boil; reduce heat, and simmer about 5 minutes or until mixture is thickened, stirring constantly. Set aside to cool.

Place sliced peaches in Crunchy Whole Wheat Pastry Shell. Spoon cooled peach mixture over sliced peaches; chill thoroughly. Yield: 8 servings (about 195 calories per serving).

CRUNCHY WHOLE WHEAT PASTRY SHELL:

¾ cup whole wheat flour
½ cup regular oats, uncooked
1 tablespoon sugar
1 teaspoon ground cinnamon
½ cup reduced-calorie margarine, melted
2 tablespoons water
Vegetable cooking spray

Combine flour, oats, sugar, and cinnamon in a small bowl. Combine margarine and water; sprinkle over dry ingredients. Mix with a fork until mixture forms a ball.

Coat a 9-inch pieplate with cooking spray; press whole wheat pastry mixture evenly and firmly into pieplate with lightly floured hands. Bake at 450° for 12 to 15 minutes; cool. Yield: one 9-inch pastry shell.

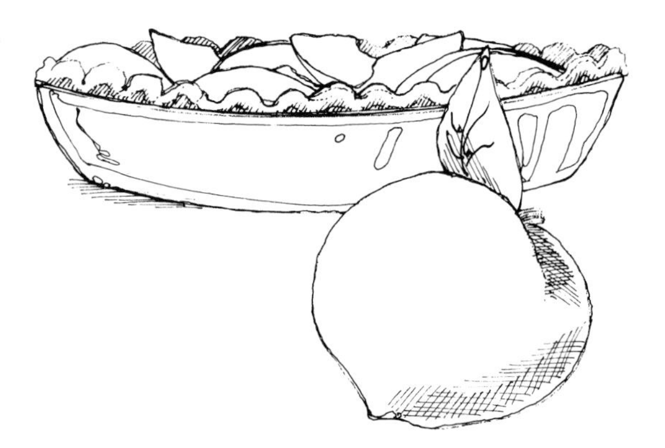

LIGHT BLUEBERRY COBBLER

1 (8-ounce) carton lemon low-fat yogurt
1 teaspoon grated lemon rind
4 cups fresh blueberries
½ cup all-purpose flour
¼ cup sugar
¼ teaspoon ground cinnamon
3 tablespoons reduced-calorie margarine

Combine yogurt and lemon rind; cover and refrigerate until serving time.

Place blueberries in an 8-inch square or 9-inch round cake pan. Combine flour, sugar, and cinnamon in a small bowl. Cut margarine into flour mixture with fork or pastry blender until mixture resembles coarse meal; sprinkle over berries.

Bake at 350° for 40 minutes or until topping is golden brown. Let cool 5 minutes before serving; top each serving with about 2½ tablespoons yogurt mixture. Yield: 6 servings (about 182 calories per serving).

Note: 4 cups frozen unsweetened blueberries, thawed and drained, may be substituted for fresh blueberries.

PINEAPPLE-APRICOT KUCHEN

1 (16-ounce) can unsweetened apricot halves, drained
1 (8-ounce) can unsweetened pineapple tidbits, drained
2 tablespoons sugar
1 teaspoon grated lemon rind
¼ teaspoon ground cinnamon
1 egg, beaten
¾ cup vanilla low-fat yogurt
1 (10-ounce) can refrigerated flaky biscuits

Cut each apricot half into thirds. Combine apricots, pineapple, sugar, lemon rind, and cinnamon; set aside.

Combine egg and yogurt in a small bowl; blend well, and set aside.

Separate each biscuit into 2 layers; place biscuit halves, sides touching, in bottom of a 13- x 9- x 2-inch baking pan. Pat biscuits evenly onto bottom and ¾-inch up sides of pan, sealing biscuit edges together. Bake biscuit crust at 375° for 10 minutes.

Spoon fruit mixture onto biscuit crust; top with yogurt mixture, spreading evenly over fruit. Bake an additional 20 minutes. Cool in pan 10 minutes; cut into squares to serve. Yield: 12 servings (about 132 calories per serving).

FANCY FRUIT TART

1 cup all-purpose flour
¼ cup cornstarch
¼ cup sugar
⅓ cup margarine
1 egg, beaten
Vegetable cooking spray
1 cup sliced fresh strawberries
1 cup sliced fresh peaches
½ cup seedless green grapes, halved
¼ cup fresh blueberries
Citrus Glaze

Combine flour, cornstarch, and sugar; cut in margarine with fork or pastry blender until mixture resembles coarse meal. Add beaten egg, and stir with a fork until all ingredients are thoroughly moistened.

Coat a 14½- x 12-inch baking sheet with cooking spray. Shape dough into a ball, and place directly on baking sheet. Roll pastry into a 10½-inch circle; trim edges. Bake at 400° for 8 to 10 minutes or until lightly browned. Cool on baking sheet 10 minutes; then carefully remove to wire rack to complete cooling.

Place pastry on a serving platter, and arrange fruit attractively over top; spoon Citrus Glaze evenly over fruit. Refrigerate tart at least 1 hour before serving. Yield: 10 servings (about 170 calories per serving).

CITRUS GLAZE:

1 tablespoon cornstarch
¼ cup water
¾ cup unsweetened orange juice
1 tablespoon lemon juice
¼ teaspoon grated lemon rind

Combine cornstarch, water, and orange juice in a small saucepan, stirring until blended. Bring mixture to a boil; cook over medium heat 1 minute, stirring constantly.

Remove from heat; stir in lemon juice and rind. Cover surface with waxed paper or plastic wrap; let cool. Yield: about 1 cup glaze.

FISH AND SHELLFISH

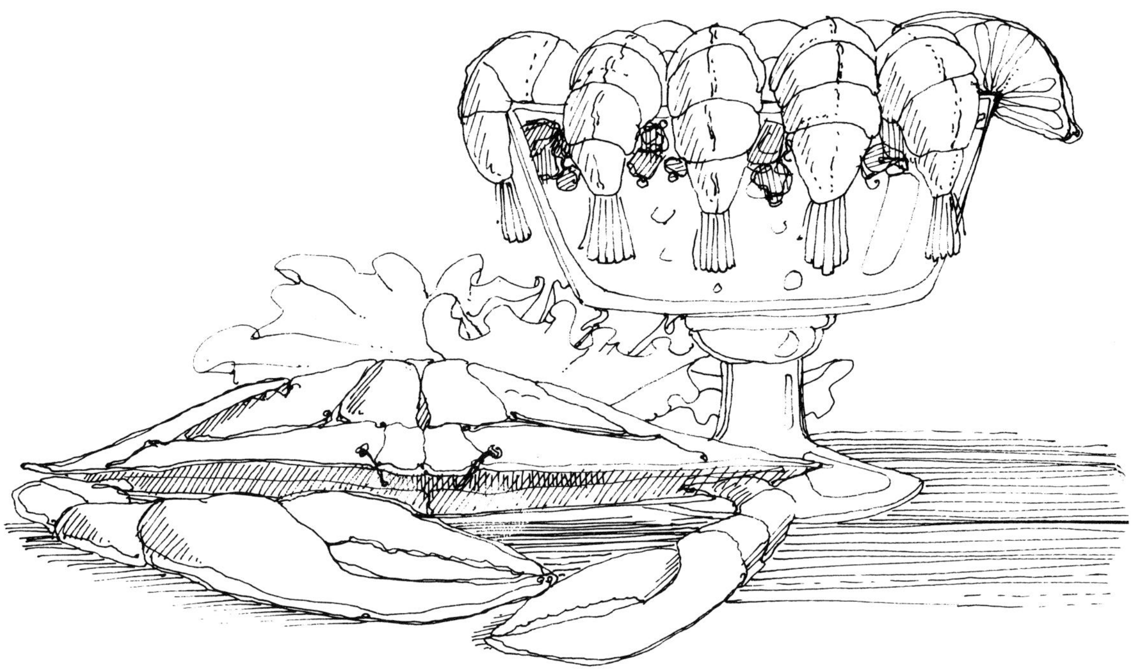

When it comes to protein foods, fish should be at the top of a dieter's list. Fish is a real bargain, calorically-speaking. It is an important source of protein and several vitamins and minerals, and raw boneless fish can contain as few as 360 calories per pound. (For comparison, boneless beef sirloin can contain as many as 1500 calories per pound.)

However, there's a wide range in fat content among the different varieties of fish. It is best to choose one of the leaner types such as flounder, sole, cod, snapper, haddock, halibut, shrimp, or scallops. Mackerel, mullet, salmon, and pompano are higher in fat. Fish canned in oil, such as tuna and sardines, are also high in fat. By choosing water-packed tuna you'll save about 300 calories per 6½-ounce can.

Fresh fish is very perishable and must be handled carefully before it is cooked. Wrap fish in moisture-proof paper or place it in a tightly covered container. Store the fish in the coldest part of the refrigerator, but for no longer than one or two days before cooking.

Frozen, unbreaded fish is a good choice for dieters and should be handled with care before cooking. Be sure to keep frozen fish solidly frozen. Once thawed, the fish should be cooked immediately. It is best to thaw frozen fish in the refrigerator instead of at room temperature.

Our *Cooking Light* recipes suggest baking, broiling, or poaching fish rather than dredging the fish in breadcrumbs and frying. During frying, fish acts as a sponge, soaking up the high-calorie oil. In preparing fish recipes, we use a variety of herbs and spices to season the fish instead of the usual high-calorie and salty seasonings. Avoid overcooking, since it tends to make the texture of the fish tough and dry.

VEGETABLE-FISH ROLLS

2 large carrots, scraped
2 large stalks celery
Vegetable cooking spray
1 large onion, finely chopped
1 clove garlic, minced
1 tablespoon reduced-calorie margarine
4 flounder or sole fillets (about 1 pound)
¾ teaspoon dried whole dillweed
¼ teaspoon pepper
1 lemon, sliced
½ cup Chablis or other dry white wine
2 tablespoons lemon juice

Cut carrots and celery into 2- x ⅛-inch strips; set aside.

Coat a large skillet with cooking spray; place over medium-high heat until hot. Add onion and garlic; sauté 3 minutes or until just tender. Remove from skillet, and set aside. Melt margarine in skillet; add carrots and celery, and sauté 3 minutes or until crisp-tender.

Place one-fourth of carrot and celery strips on short end of each fillet; roll up fillets, and place, seam side down, in an 8-inch square baking dish. Combine onion mixture, dillweed, and pepper. Spoon mixture over and around rolls; top with lemon slices.

Combine wine and lemon juice; pour around fillets. Cover and bake at 375° for 15 to 20 minutes or until fillets flake easily with a fork. Yield: 4 servings (about 143 calories per serving).

CELERY-FISH ROLL-UPS

Vegetable cooking spray
½ cup finely chopped onion
1 clove garlic, minced
1 (16-ounce) can stewed tomatoes, undrained
5 cups sliced celery (sliced ¼-inch thick)
¼ cup chopped fresh parsley
1 teaspoon dried whole oregano
1 teaspoon dried whole rosemary, crushed
¼ teaspoon salt
¼ teaspoon pepper
6 flounder fillets (about 2 pounds)

Coat a large skillet with cooking spray; place over medium heat until hot. Add onion and garlic; sauté 3 to 4 minutes or until onion is just tender. Stir in remaining ingredients except fillets; bring to a boil. Reduce heat, and simmer, uncovered, 3 minutes.

Spoon about ¼ cup celery mixture in center of each fillet; roll up, and place, seam side down, in a shallow 2-quart casserole. Spoon remaining celery mixture around fish rolls. Cover and bake at 350° for 25 minutes or until fillets flake easily with a fork. Yield: 6 servings (about 164 calories per serving).

POACHED FISH CREOLE

Vegetable cooking spray
¼ cup minced onion
¼ cup minced green pepper
1 clove garlic, minced
1 (16-ounce) can tomatoes, undrained and coarsely chopped
2 teaspoons Worcestershire sauce
2 teaspoons red wine vinegar
½ teaspoon dried whole basil
¼ teaspoon pepper
⅛ teaspoon hot sauce
1 pound flounder or sole fillets

Coat a large skillet with cooking spray; place over medium heat until hot. Add onion and green pepper to skillet; sauté 3 to 4 minutes or until tender.

Add remaining ingredients to skillet except fillets, and bring to a boil. Add fillets, spooning sauce over fillets. Cover, reduce heat, and simmer 2 minutes; uncover and simmer an additional 8 to 10 minutes or until fillets flake easily with a fork. Yield: 4 servings (about 124 calories per serving).

> Since fish is naturally tender, it can be prepared using either dry- or moist-heat methods of cooking.

OVEN-FRIED FISH FILLETS

1 pound flounder or sole fillets
1 tablespoon reduced-calorie mayonnaise
6 tablespoons fine, dry breadcrumbs
2 tablespoons minced fresh parsley
½ teaspoon paprika
Vegetable cooking spray
Lemon wedges

Coat fillets with mayonnaise. Combine breadcrumbs, parsley, and paprika. Dredge coated fillets in breadcrumb mixture.

Arrange fillets on a baking sheet coated with cooking spray; bake at 450° for 12 minutes or until fillets flake easily with a fork. Serve with lemon wedges. Yield: 4 servings (about 140 calories per serving).

BAKED FLOUNDER VINAIGRETTE

1 pound flounder fillets
3 tablespoons Italian reduced-calorie salad dressing
Paprika
1 large tomato, thinly sliced
1 tablespoon minced chives
¼ cup (1 ounce) shredded Cheddar cheese

Arrange fillets in a shallow baking dish; brush salad dressing over fillets. Sprinkle with paprika. Arrange tomato slices over fillets; sprinkle with chives. Bake, uncovered, at 450° for 10 minutes. Sprinkle with cheese, and bake an additional 2 to 3 minutes or until fillets flake with a fork. Yield: 4 servings (about 132 calories per serving).

> Even if the recipe seems to require a little extra work, it is important to follow the directions completely in order to decrease calories in the finished product.

PARMESAN FLOUNDER FILLETS

1 pound flounder fillets
Vegetable cooking spray
1 (8-ounce) carton plain low-fat yogurt
¼ cup grated Parmesan cheese
2 tablespoons chopped fresh parsley
1 tablespoon instant minced onion
1 tablespoon lemon juice
½ teaspoon garlic salt

Arrange fillets in a 13- x 9- x 2-inch baking pan coated with cooking spray. Combine remaining ingredients; spread mixture evenly over fillets. Bake at 375° for 12 to 15 minutes. Yield: 4 servings (about 161 calories per serving).

FOIL-BAKED FLOUNDER FILLETS

Vegetable cooking spray
1 tablespoon reduced-calorie margarine
½ pound fresh mushrooms, chopped
2 tablespoons minced onion
3 tablespoons Chablis or other dry white wine
1 tablespoon lemon juice
2 tablespoons minced fresh parsley
4 flounder or sole fillets (about 1¼ pounds)
Freshly ground black pepper

Coat a skillet with cooking spray; add margarine. Melt margarine over medium heat. Add mushrooms and onion; sauté 5 minutes or until tender. Stir in next 3 ingredients; cook 5 minutes or until most of the liquid has evaporated.

Cut four 12-inch square pieces of heavy-duty aluminum foil; place a fillet, skin side down, in center of each piece of foil. Pepper each fillet; top with one-fourth of mushroom mixture.

Fold aluminum foil over fillets, and seal edges securely. Place foil packages on a baking sheet; bake at 400° for 20 to 25 minutes or until fillets flake easily with a fork. Yield: 4 servings (about 147 calories per serving).

BROILED FLOUNDER FILLETS WITH MUSTARD

1½ pounds flounder or sole fillets
Vegetable cooking spray
2 tablespoons reduced-calorie mayonnaise
1 tablespoon Dijon mustard
1 tablespoon chopped fresh parsley
⅛ teaspoon freshly ground pepper
Lemon wedges (optional)

Arrange fillets on a baking sheet coated with cooking spray. Combine remaining ingredients except lemon wedges; spread evenly over fillets. Broil 3 to 4 inches from heat for 4 minutes or until fillets flake easily with a fork. Garnish with lemon wedges, if desired. Yield: 6 servings (about 107 calories per serving).

STUFFED FLOUNDER

Vegetable cooking spray
1 teaspoon reduced-calorie margarine
½ pound fresh mushrooms, thinly sliced
1 cup finely chopped celery
4 slices whole wheat bread, toasted
⅔ cup chicken broth
2 tablespoons minced fresh parsley
2 tablespoons instant minced onion
1 teaspoon poultry seasoning
¼ teaspoon pepper
4 flounder or sole fillets (about 2 pounds)
2 teaspoons lemon juice

Coat a medium skillet with cooking spray; add margarine. Place skillet over medium heat until margarine is melted. Add mushrooms and celery; sauté 5 to 6 minutes or until vegetables are tender and liquid is evaporated.

Crumble bread in a medium bowl; add sautéed vegetables and next 5 ingredients, mixing well. Arrange 2 fillets in a 13- x 9- x 2-inch baking dish coated with cooking spray. Top with stuffing mixture; cover with remaining 2 fillets.

Sprinkle lemon juice evenly over fillets; bake, uncovered, at 350° for 25 to 30 minutes or until fillets flake easily with a fork. Yield: 6 servings (about 193 calories per serving).

CUCUMBER-STUFFED RED SNAPPER ROLLS

¼ cup sliced green onions
2 tablespoons reduced-calorie margarine, melted
1½ cups French bread cubes (½-inch cubes), toasted
2 cups peeled, seeded, and chopped cucumber
2 tablespoons plain low-fat yogurt
1 tablespoon minced fresh parsley
2 teaspoons lemon juice
½ teaspoon dried whole dillweed
¼ teaspoon salt
8 (⅓-pound) red snapper fillets with skin

Sauté onions in margarine until tender. Combine onions and next 7 ingredients; set aside.

Cut each fillet in half lengthwise. Spread ¼ cup stuffing over each fillet, leaving a ½-inch margin. Starting at narrow end, roll up fillets, jellyroll fashion; secure with wooden picks.

Stand rolls vertically in large glass baking dish; cover and bake at 350° for 30 to 35 minutes or until fillets flake easily with a fork. Yield: 8 servings (about 183 calories per serving).

POACHED SNAPPER

1 cup Chablis or other dry white wine
½ to 1 cup water
1 lemon, sliced
5 green onions, sliced
5 sprigs fresh parsley
4 peppercorns
2 bay leaves
½ teaspoon salt
1½ pound dressed red snapper, head intact
Additional lemon slices

Combine first 8 ingredients in a fish poacher or large skillet; bring to a boil, and add snapper. Cover, reduce heat, and simmer 20 minutes or until the snapper flakes easily.

Remove the snapper from skillet carefully, and garnish with additional lemon slices. Yield: 3 servings (about 109 calories per serving).

SALMON CAKES WITH MUSTARD SAUCE

1 (7¾-ounce) can salmon, drained and flaked
¼ cup fine, dry breadcrumbs
2 eggs, slightly beaten
2 tablespoons lemon juice
¼ teaspoon pepper
Vegetable cooking spray
½ cup finely chopped celery
⅓ cup finely chopped green onions
Mustard Sauce

Combine first 6 ingredients; set aside.

Coat a large nonstick skillet with cooking spray; place over medium heat until hot. Add celery and green onions; sauté until tender. Add to salmon mixture; mix well.

Coat skillet again with cooking spray; place over medium-high heat until hot. For each salmon cake, spoon about ¼ cup mixture onto skillet; shape into patty with a spatula. Cook about 2 minutes or until browned on each side. Serve immediately with Mustard Sauce. Yield: 4 servings (about 147 calories per serving plus 15 calories per tablespoon sauce).

MUSTARD SAUCE:

2 tablespoons reduced-calorie margarine
1½ tablespoons all-purpose flour
1 cup skim milk
1 teaspoon dry mustard
1 teaspoon lemon juice
¼ teaspoon salt

Melt margarine over low heat; add flour, stirring until smooth. Cook 1 minute, stirring constantly. Gradually add milk; cook over medium heat, stirring constantly, until thickened and bubbly. Remove from heat; stir in mustard, lemon juice, and salt. Yield: 1 cup.

POACHED SALMON

1½ cups Chablis or other dry white wine
½ cup water
1 onion, sliced
1 lemon, sliced
4 sprigs fresh parsley
1 teaspoon dried whole dillweed
¼ teaspoon pepper
4 (1-inch-thick) salmon steaks (about 1½ pounds)

Combine first 7 ingredients in a large skillet. Bring to a boil; cover, reduce heat, and simmer 10 minutes. Add salmon steaks; cover and simmer 8 minutes or until salmon flakes easily. Yield: 4 servings (about 266 calories per serving).

CUCUMBER-TUNA SALAD

3 tablespoons reduced-calorie mayonnaise
2 tablespoons plain low-fat yogurt
1 to 1½ tablespoons capers
½ teaspoon dried whole dillweed
½ teaspoon prepared horseradish
1 small cucumber, peeled, seeded, and diced
1 (6½-ounce) can water-packed tuna, drained and flaked
Lettuce leaves
1 medium tomato, cut into wedges

Combine first 5 ingredients in a medium bowl; stir in cucumber and tuna. Chill. Serve on lettuce leaves, and garnish with tomato wedges. Yield: 2 servings (about 204 calories per serving).

BROCCOLI-TUNA CRÊPES

1 (10-ounce) package frozen chopped broccoli
2 tablespoons reduced-calorie margarine
1 medium onion, chopped
1 cup sliced fresh mushrooms
2 tablespoons all-purpose flour
1 cup skim milk
2 teaspoons Dijon mustard
½ teaspoon dried whole marjoram
¼ teaspoon pepper
1 (6½-ounce) can water-packed tuna, drained and flaked
12 (6-inch) crêpes (recipe follows)
Cheese Sauce

Cook broccoli according to package directions, omitting salt; drain and set aside.

Melt margarine in a 2-quart saucepan; add onion and mushrooms, and sauté until tender. Add flour, stirring until vegetables are coated; cook over low heat 1 minute, stirring constantly. Gradually add milk, mustard, marjoram, and pepper, stirring until smooth; cook over medium heat, stirring constantly, until thickened and bubbly. Add broccoli and tuna, and cook until thoroughly heated.

To serve, spoon about ¼ cup tuna mixture into center of each crêpe; roll up. Serve Cheese Sauce over crêpes. Yield: 6 servings (about 194 calories per serving plus 22 calories per tablespoon sauce).

CRÊPES:

3 eggs
1½ cups skim milk
1⅓ cups all-purpose flour
¼ teaspoon salt
Vegetable cooking spray

Combine first 4 ingredients in container of an electric blender; process 30 seconds. Scrape down sides of blender container with rubber spatula; process an additional 30 seconds or until smooth. Refrigerate batter 1 hour. (This allows flour particles to swell and soften so crêpes are light in texture.)

Coat the bottom of a 6-inch crêpe pan or nonstick skillet with cooking spray; place pan over medium heat until just hot, not smoking.

For each crêpe, pour 2 tablespoons batter into pan; quickly tilt pan in all directions so batter covers pan in a thin film. Cook about 1 minute.

Lift edge of crêpe to test for doneness. Crêpe is ready for flipping when it can be shaken loose from pan. Flip the crêpe, and cook about 30 seconds on the other side. (This side is rarely more than spotty brown and is the side on which the filling is placed.)

When crêpe is done, place on a towel to cool. Repeat cooking procedure with remaining batter, stirring batter occasionally. Stack crêpes between layers of paper towels or waxed paper to prevent sticking. Freeze any unused crêpes for other uses. Yield: 22 (6-inch) crêpes.

CHEESE SAUCE:

1½ tablespoons reduced-calorie margarine
1 tablespoon all-purpose flour
½ cup skim milk
¼ cup (1 ounce) shredded extra sharp Cheddar cheese
½ teaspoon Dijon mustard
1 (2-ounce) jar diced pimiento, drained

Melt margarine in a small heavy saucepan over low heat; add flour, stirring until smooth. (Mixture will be dry.) Cook 1 minute, stirring constantly. Gradually add milk, stirring with a wire whisk; cook over medium heat, stirring constantly, until thickened and bubbly. Add cheese and mustard, stirring until cheese melts. Stir in pimiento. Yield: about ¾ cup.

By using water-packed tuna instead of tuna packed in oil, you'll save about 300 calories per 6½-ounce can.

TUNA-BROCCOLI LOAF

1 (10-ounce) package frozen chopped broccoli
4 eggs
½ cup skim milk
1 cup soft whole wheat breadcrumbs
2 (6½-ounce) cans water-packed tuna, drained and flaked
1 small onion, finely chopped
½ cup (2 ounces) shredded Swiss cheese
2 teaspoons lemon juice
Vegetable cooking spray
Swiss Cheese Sauce

Cook broccoli according to package directions, omitting salt. Drain well, and set aside.

Combine eggs and milk in a large bowl; beat well. Stir in breadcrumbs; let stand 5 minutes. Stir in broccoli, tuna, onion, cheese, and lemon juice, mixing well; pack into an 8½- x 4½- x 3-inch loafpan coated with cooking spray.

Bake loaf at 350° for 1 hour; let stand 5 minutes. Unmold onto serving platter, and cut into 1-inch slices; serve with Swiss Cheese Sauce. Yield: 8 servings (about 159 calories per serving plus 23 calories per tablespoon sauce).

SWISS CHEESE SAUCE:

1 tablespoon reduced-calorie margarine
1 tablespoon all-purpose flour
¾ cup skim milk
¼ teaspoon dry mustard
⅛ teaspoon salt
⅛ teaspoon white pepper
½ cup (2 ounces) shredded Swiss cheese

Melt margarine in a small saucepan over low heat; add flour, stirring until smooth. Cook 1 minute, stirring constantly. (Mixture will be dry.) Gradually add milk, stirring with a wire whisk until smooth. Cook over medium heat, stirring constantly, until thickened and bubbly. Add mustard, salt, pepper, and cheese, stirring until cheese is melted. Yield: 1 cup.

CHEESY TUNA POTATO

1 medium baking potato
1 (3¼-ounce) can water-packed tuna, drained and flaked
1 tablespoon minced onion
1 tablespoon finely chopped celery
1 tablespoon finely chopped green pepper
3 tablespoons reduced-calorie mayonnaise
¼ teaspoon seasoned pepper
Paprika
2 tablespoons shredded low-fat Cheddar cheese

Wash potato; bake at 375° for 45 to 60 minutes or until done. Let stand until cool enough to handle. Cut potato in half lengthwise; scoop out pulp, leaving a ¼-inch-thick shell.

Mash potato pulp in a medium bowl with a potato masher or fork; stir in next 6 ingredients, mixing well. Divide mixture evenly into potato shells, mounding top; sprinkle each with paprika. Place on a baking sheet; bake at 350° for 10 minutes. Remove from oven, and sprinkle with cheese. Bake an additional 5 minutes or until thoroughly heated. Yield: 2 servings (about 206 calories per serving).

LINGUINI WITH CLAM SAUCE

Vegetable cooking spray
½ cup finely chopped onion
½ cup finely chopped celery
2 cloves garlic, minced
3 (6½-ounce) cans minced clams, undrained
1 (14½-ounce) can whole tomatoes, undrained and chopped
½ teaspoon dried whole basil
¼ teaspoon dried whole oregano
¼ teaspoon hot sauce
⅓ cup minced fresh parsley
2 cups hot cooked linguini

Coat a large saucepan with cooking spray; place over medium heat until hot. Add onion, celery, and garlic; sauté until tender.

Drain clams, reserving liquid; add clam liquid, tomatoes, basil, oregano, and hot sauce to saucepan. Bring to a boil; reduce heat, and simmer, uncovered, 45 minutes.

Stir in clams and parsley; cook until thoroughly heated. Serve over linguini. Yield: 4 servings (about 128 calories per serving plus 90 calories per ½ cup cooked linguini).

DELUXE CRAB IMPERIAL

1 pound fresh crabmeat, drained and flaked
1 egg, beaten
½ cup reduced-calorie mayonnaise
2 tablespoons skim milk
2 tablespoons capers
¼ teaspoon pepper
Vegetable cooking spray
3 tablespoons grated Parmesan cheese

Combine all ingredients except cooking spray and cheese; stir gently until well mixed.

Coat 6 crab shells or custard cups with cooking spray; spoon mixture evenly into shells, and sprinkle with cheese. Place crab shells on baking sheet; bake at 350° for 25 to 30 minutes. Yield: 6 servings (about 160 calories per serving).

DEVILED CRAB

Vegetable cooking spray
1 teaspoon reduced-calorie margarine
1 cup chopped celery
½ cup finely chopped onion
1 pound fresh crabmeat, drained and flaked
1 cup diced whole wheat bread
1 egg, beaten
3 tablespoons chopped fresh parsley
2 tablespoons dry sherry
1 teaspoon dried whole thyme
½ teaspoon pepper

Coat a large skillet with cooking spray; add margarine, and place skillet over medium heat until margarine is melted. Add celery and onion; sauté 5 minutes or until tender. Remove from heat; stir in remaining ingredients, mixing well.

Divide mixture evenly into 6 crab shells or ramekins coated with cooking spray; place on baking sheet. Bake at 350° for 20 to 25 minutes. Yield: 6 servings (about 123 calories per serving).

SAUCY BARBECUED OYSTERS

2 (12-ounce) containers fresh Select oysters, undrained
¼ cup tomato paste
2 tablespoons reduced-calorie chili sauce
2 tablespoons lemon juice
1 tablespoon Worcestershire sauce
1 teaspoon prepared horseradish
¼ teaspoon onion powder
⅓ cup crushed whole wheat crackers

Drain oysters, reserving 2 tablespoons liquid. Pat oysters dry with paper towels, and place in an 8-inch square baking dish.

Combine 2 tablespoons oyster liquid and remaining ingredients except crackers; spoon over oysters. Sprinkle cracker crumbs over top of sauce; bake at 350° for 25 minutes. Yield: 6 servings (about 103 calories per serving).

SCALLOPS AU VIN

1½ pounds fresh scallops
¼ teaspoon salt
½ teaspoon freshly ground pepper
½ pound fresh mushrooms, chopped
¼ cup plus 2 tablespoons minced fresh parsley
¼ cup plus 2 tablespoons dry white wine
2 tablespoons reduced-calorie margarine

If scallops are large, cut in half; divide evenly into 6 (10-ounce) custard cups or ramekins. Sprinkle scallops with salt and pepper.

Divide mushrooms over scallops; sprinkle 1 tablespoon parsley and 1 tablespoon wine over mushrooms in each cup. Dot each with 1 teaspoon margarine. Bake, uncovered, at 450° for 15 minutes or until scallops are done. Yield: 6 servings (about 124 calories per serving).

VEGETABLE-SCALLOP KABOBS

1 pound fresh scallops
2 large green peppers, cut into 1-inch squares
1 pint cherry tomatoes
16 medium-size fresh mushroom caps
1 (8-ounce) bottle Italian reduced-calorie salad dressing

Combine all ingredients in a large shallow dish. Cover and marinate at least 3 hours in the refrigerator, stirring occasionally.

Alternate scallops and green peppers on skewers; place on a broiler rack. Alternate tomatoes and mushrooms on skewers; place on broiler rack. Brush with remaining dressing.

Broil 4 inches from heat 5 to 7 minutes for scallop skewers and 2 to 4 minutes for tomato skewers. Turn skewers; baste with dressing often. Yield: 4 servings (about 159 calories per serving).

GRILLED SCALLOP KABOBS

1 (15¼-ounce) can unsweetened pineapple chunks, undrained
¼ cup Chablis or other dry white wine
¼ cup soy sauce
2 tablespoons lemon juice
2 tablespoons chopped fresh parsley
½ teaspoon pepper
¼ teaspoon garlic powder
1 pound fresh scallops
18 medium-size fresh mushrooms
2 large green peppers, cut into 1-inch squares
18 cherry tomatoes

Drain pineapple, reserving ¼ cup plus 2 tablespoons juice. Combine pineapple juice and next 6 ingredients in a large shallow dish. Add pineapple, scallops, and vegetables; toss well to coat, and marinate in the refrigerator 1 to 1½ hours.

Alternate pineapple, scallops, and vegetables on skewers. Place kabobs 4 to 5 inches from hot coals; grill 10 to 12 minutes, turning the kabobs and basting them frequently with the marinade. Yield: 6 servings (about 149 calories per serving).

SPECIAL BOILED SHRIMP

4 large bay leaves
20 peppercorns
12 whole cloves
1 teaspoon mustard seeds
1 teaspoon crushed red pepper
1 teaspoon dried whole marjoram
½ teaspoon dried whole basil
¼ teaspoon dried whole thyme
⅛ teaspoon caraway seeds
⅛ teaspoon cumin seeds
⅛ teaspoon fennel seeds
⅛ teaspoon celery seeds
2 quarts water
1 lemon, quartered
4 cloves garlic
2½ pound unpeeled medium or large fresh shrimp
Seafood Sauce

Combine first 12 ingredients in a doubled cheesecloth bag, and tie securely with string.

Combine water, lemon, garlic, and herb bag in a Dutch oven. Bring to a boil; reduce heat, and simmer 2 minutes. Stir in shrimp; return to a boil, and cook 3 to 5 minutes. Drain well; chill. Serve with Seafood Sauce. Yield: 6 servings (about 119 calories per serving plus 7 calories per tablespoon sauce).

SEAFOOD SAUCE:

1½ cups reduced-calorie catsup
2 tablespoons lemon juice
1 to 2 teaspoons prepared horseradish
½ teaspoon garlic powder
½ teaspoon ground celery seeds
¼ teaspoon hot sauce

Combine all ingredients; mix well, and chill. Serve with boiled shrimp. Yield: 1⅔ cups sauce.

Don't think you always have to clean your plate. Enjoy what you eat, but stop when you feel satisfied.

LEMON BARBECUED SHRIMP

2½ pounds unpeeled large fresh shrimp
½ cup lemon juice
¼ cup Italian reduced-calorie salad dressing
¼ cup water
¼ cup soy sauce
3 tablespoons minced fresh parsley
3 tablespoons minced onion
1 clove garlic, crushed
½ teaspoon freshly ground pepper

Peel and devein shrimp; place in a large shallow baking dish.

Combine remaining ingredients in a jar; cover tightly, and shake vigorously. Pour marinade over shrimp. Cover and refrigerate 4 hours.

Thread shrimp onto skewers. Broil or grill 5 to 6 inches from medium heat 3 to 4 minutes on each side, basting frequently with marinade. Yield: 6 servings (about 139 calories per serving).

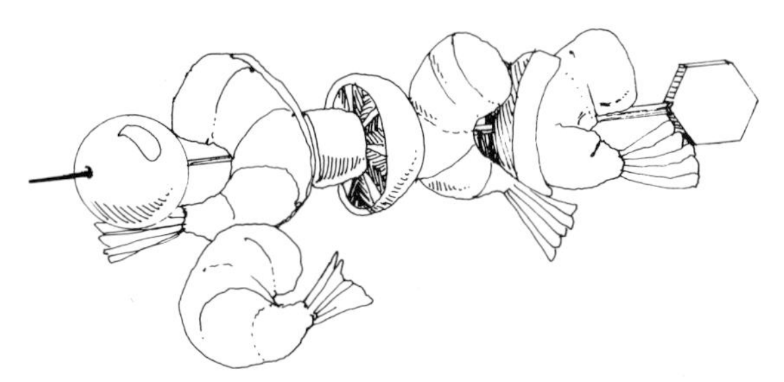

MARINATED SHRIMP KABOBS

1 large green pepper, cut into 1-inch pieces
1 pound unpeeled medium-size fresh shrimp
1 (8-ounce) can unsweetened pineapple chunks, undrained
¼ cup prepared mustard
12 to 16 cherry tomatoes
½ pound fresh mushroom caps

Pour boiling water over green pepper; let stand 5 minutes. Drain.

Peel and devein shrimp; set aside.

Drain pineapple, reserving juice. Combine pineapple juice and mustard in a large shallow dish; add shrimp. Cover and marinate 3 to 4 hours in refrigerator, stirring occasionally.

Remove shrimp from marinade, reserving marinade. Alternate shrimp, pineapple chunks, and vegetables on skewers. Brush with sauce. Broil or grill 4 inches from heat 3 to 4 minutes on each side or until shrimp are done, brushing often with sauce. Yield: 4 servings (about 155 calories per serving).

SHRIMP EGG FOO YUNG

4 eggs, beaten
1 cup fresh bean sprouts
½ cup thinly sliced celery
½ cup chopped green onions
1 (10-ounce) package frozen cooked shrimp, thawed and drained
1 teaspoon chicken-flavored bouillon granules
Vegetable cooking spray
Sauce (recipe follows)

Combine first 6 ingredients. Let mixture stand 10 minutes.

Coat a large nonstick skillet with cooking spray; place over medium heat until hot. For each patty, spoon ¼ cup egg mixture into skillet; shape into patty with a spatula as it cooks. Cook until patty is lightly browned on one side; turn and cook until patty is set and lightly browned on other side. Repeat until all egg mixture is used. Serve with sauce. Yield: 6 servings (about 109 calories per serving plus 3 calories per tablespoon sauce).

SAUCE:

2 tablespoons cornstarch
¼ cup water
1¾ cups water
1 tablespoon soy sauce
1 teaspoon chicken-flavored bouillon granules

Combine cornstarch and ¼ cup water in a small saucepan, stirring until blended; add remaining ingredients. Cook over medium heat, stirring constantly, until bouillon dissolves and sauce is thickened. Yield: 2 cups.

SHRIMP CHOW MEIN

1½ tablespoons cornstarch
2 tablespoons water
1 large onion, sliced
1 (2-ounce) can mushroom stems and pieces, undrained
½ cup chicken broth
3 tablespoons soy sauce
1½ pounds unpeeled small fresh shrimp
1 (8-ounce) can sliced water chestnuts, drained
2 cups fresh bean sprouts
1 red or green pepper, cut into 1-inch squares
2 stalks celery, diagonally sliced

Combine cornstarch and water, stirring until blended. Set aside.

Combine onion, mushrooms, broth, and soy sauce in a large skillet; cover and cook over medium-low heat 4 minutes or until onion is tender. Peel and devein shrimp; add shrimp and next 4 ingredients to skillet. Cook, stirring frequently, 4 to 5 minutes or until shrimp are done.

Stir in reserved cornstarch mixture; cook, stirring constantly, 1 to 2 minutes or until mixture thickens. Yield: 4 servings (about 191 calories per serving).

SHRIMP CREOLE

1 (8-ounce) can tomato sauce
1 (4½-ounce) jar sliced mushrooms, drained
½ cup Sauterne or other dry white wine
½ cup chopped onion
1 clove garlic, minced
½ cup chopped green pepper
½ cup chopped celery
2 bay leaves
⅛ to ¼ teaspoon red pepper
1 pound unpeeled medium-size fresh shrimp
2 cups hot cooked rice

Combine tomato sauce, mushrooms, wine, onion, garlic, green pepper, celery, bay leaves, and red pepper in a large skillet. Bring to a boil; cover, reduce heat, and simmer 10 minutes.

Peel and devein shrimp; add to tomato sauce mixture. Cook, uncovered, 3 to 4 minutes or until shrimp are done. Serve warm over rice. Yield: 4 servings (about 118 calories per serving plus 90 calories per ½ cup cooked rice).

CURRIED SHRIMP

6 cups water
2 pounds unpeeled fresh shrimp
⅓ cup chopped onion
1 clove garlic, minced
¼ cup chopped green pepper
3 tablespoons reduced-calorie margarine, melted
3 tablespoons all-purpose flour
2 teaspoons curry powder
¼ to ½ teaspoon salt
⅛ teaspoon white pepper
⅛ teaspoon ground ginger
⅛ teaspoon chili powder
1½ cups skim milk
1 tablespoon lemon juice
3 cups hot cooked rice

Bring water to a boil; add shrimp, and return to a boil. Reduce heat, and simmer 3 to 5 minutes.

Drain well; rinse with cold water. Peel and devein shrimp; set aside.

Sauté onion, garlic, and green pepper in margarine until vegetables are tender. Combine flour and seasonings; add to vegetable mixture, stirring until smooth. Cook over low heat 1 minute, stirring constantly. Gradually stir in milk; cook over medium heat, stirring constantly with a wire whisk, until thickened and bubbly.

Add shrimp and lemon juice to sauce; cook until thoroughly heated. Serve over rice. Yield: 6 servings (about 161 calories per serving plus 90 calories per ½ cup cooked rice).

POLYNESIAN SHRIMP AND PINEAPPLE

6 cups water
2 pounds unpeeled large fresh shrimp
Vegetable cooking spray
1 teaspoon reduced-calorie margarine
1 medium-size green pepper, cut into 1-inch cubes
1 (15¼-ounce) can unsweetened pineapple chunks, undrained
2 tablespoons cornstarch
1 (10½-ounce) can beef broth, undiluted
1 tablespoon soy sauce
1 teaspoon lemon juice
1 (6-ounce) package frozen Chinese pea pods, thawed and drained
3 cups hot cooked rice

Bring water to a boil; add shrimp, and return to a boil. Reduce heat, and simmer, uncovered, 3 to 5 minutes. Drain well, and rinse shrimp with cold water; peel and devein.

Coat a large skillet with cooking spray. Add margarine, and place over medium heat until margarine is melted. Add green pepper to skillet; sauté until tender. Remove pepper, and set aside.

Drain pineapple, reserving ½ cup juice. Combine ½ cup pineapple juice, cornstarch, beef broth, soy sauce, and lemon juice in skillet. Bring to a boil, and cook until smooth and slightly thickened, stirring constantly.

Add shrimp, green pepper, pineapple chunks, and pea pods to sauce; cook until thoroughly heated. Serve over rice. Yield: 6 servings (about 178 calories per serving plus 90 calories per ½ cup cooked rice).

GARLIC SHRIMP

6 cups water
2 pounds unpeeled large fresh shrimp
Vegetable cooking spray
¼ cup chopped scallions or green onions
2 teaspoons minced garlic
¼ cup dry white wine
¼ cup water
1 teaspoon lemon juice
½ teaspoon salt
⅛ to ¼ teaspoon coarsley ground black pepper
1 teaspoon dried whole dillweed
1 teaspoon chopped fresh parsley
3 cups hot cooked rice

Bring 6 cups water to a boil; add shrimp, and return to a boil. Reduce heat, and simmer 3 to 5 minutes. Drain well; rinse with cold water. Peel and devein shrimp.

Coat a large skillet with cooking spray; place over medium heat until hot. Add scallions and garlic, and sauté until scallions are tender.

Add shrimp, white wine, water, lemon juice, salt, and pepper; cook over medium heat about 5 minutes, stirring occasionally. Stir in dillweed and parsley; serve over rice. Yield: 6 servings (about 100 calories per serving plus 90 calories per ½ cup cooked rice).

Season fish and shellfish with herbs, spices, onion, garlic, vinegar, lemon, or lime juice instead of the usual fattening and salty seasonings.

SHRIMP THERMIDOR

4 cups water
1 pound unpeeled fresh shrimp
Vegetable cooking spray
1 cup sliced fresh mushrooms
2 tablespoons reduced-calorie margarine
2 tablespoons all-purpose flour
½ teaspoon dry mustard
¼ teaspoon salt
¼ teaspoon white pepper
1½ cups skim milk
2 tablespoons grated Parmesan cheese
Paprika

Bring water to a boil; add shrimp, and return to a boil. Reduce heat, and simmer 3 to 5 minutes. Drain well; rinse with cold water. Peel and devein shrimp; set aside.

Coat a medium-size heavy saucepan with cooking spray; place over medium heat until hot. Add mushrooms; sauté 3 to 4 minutes. Remove from saucepan, and set aside.

Melt margarine in saucepan over low heat. Combine flour, dry mustard, salt, and pepper; add to margarine, and cook 1 minute, stirring constantly. (Mixture will be dry.) Gradually add milk, stirring with a wire whisk until smooth. Cook over medium heat, stirring constantly, until thickened and bubbly. Stir in shrimp and mushrooms; cook until thoroughly heated.

Coat 4 ramekins or 10-ounce custard cups with cooking spray; divide mixture evenly among ramekins. Sprinkle with Parmesan cheese and paprika. Bake at 400° for 10 to 12 minutes. Yield: 4 servings (about 165 calories per serving).

SPAGHETTI WITH SHRIMP SAUCE

Vegetable cooking spray
1 medium onion, chopped
1 medium-size green pepper, chopped
½ cup chopped green onions
¼ cup chopped celery
4 cloves garlic, minced
1 (8-ounce) can tomato sauce
½ (10-ounce) can tomatoes with green chiles, undrained and chopped
¼ teaspoon salt
¼ teaspoon pepper
¼ teaspoon dried whole oregano
Pinch of dried whole rosemary
Pinch of dried whole thyme
¼ cup water
1 pound unpeeled fresh shrimp
4 ounces uncooked spaghetti

Coat a large skillet with cooking spray; place over medium-high heat until hot. Add onion, green pepper, green onions, celery, and garlic; sauté until vegetables are tender. Add tomato sauce, tomatoes, seasonings, and water; cover and simmer 30 minutes, stirring occasionally.

Peel and devein shrimp; add shrimp to skillet, and simmer, covered, an additional 10 minutes.

Cook spaghetti according to package directions, omitting salt; drain. Serve shrimp sauce over spaghetti. Yield: 4 servings (about 124 calories per serving plus 90 calories per ½ cup cooked spaghetti).

Keep calories low in Poached Snapper by poaching red snapper in a mixture of Chablis, lemon, green onions, parsley, peppercorns, and bay leaves (page 140).

CHEES
10 oz

MEATS

Sirloin or round? Ground beef or ground chuck? Spareribs or pork chops? These are important decisions a dieter must face at the meat counter. The cut of meat which you select will make a big difference in how successful you are at cooking and eating light. The more tender cuts of meat from the loin, sirloin, and rib areas usually contain more fat and are higher in calories. Cuts of meat from the round, chuck, and flank areas are usually less tender, contain less fat, and are lower in calories.

The cooking method you choose for meat is an important factor in cutting back on calories. Meat contains visible and invisible particles of fat. It's best to bake, broil, or roast meat on a rack so that excess fat drips away. Remove extra fat in ground beef or chuck by draining the meat in a colander after browning.

Less tender cuts of meat becomes more tender and flavorful if marinated for several hours in an acidic liquid such as wine, lemon juice, orange juice, tomato juice, or vinegar. The meat will become even more tender when cooked slowly in liquid rather than quickly broiled or pan-fried.

The reputation of pork has changed over the past few years. Today's pork is much leaner and can be included on a low-calorie diet. Be sure to purchase the leanest cuts of pork such as pork chops instead of spareribs, and use a low-fat method of cooking.

Add lamb or veal to your menu for an occasional change of pace. When trimmed of excess fat, a 3-ounce portion of roasted leg of lamb provides only 163 calories. A 3-ounce portion of broiled veal round provides 184 calories.

Pizza on a diet? Each slice of Whole Wheat Pizza (page 164) has only 171 calories. And since the crust is made with whole wheat flour, this pizza also provides fiber.

SAVORY ROAST BEEF

1 (5-pound) beef eye-of-round roast
2 large cloves garlic, cut into 6 slivers each
1 teaspoon dried whole thyme
1 teaspoon freshly ground pepper
1 (8-ounce) bottle Italian reduced-calorie salad dressing
1 cup dry red wine
2 bay leaves
Sauce (recipe follows)

Trim excess fat from roast. Cut 12 slits, 1 inch deep, across top of roast; place 1 sliver of garlic in each slit. Combine thyme and pepper; rub over entire surface of meat. Place meat in a large shallow baking dish. Combine salad dressing, wine, and bay leaves; pour over roast. Cover and refrigerate 12 hours or overnight, turning occasionally.

Remove roast, reserving ½ cup marinade for sauce; place roast on rack in a broiler pan. Insert meat thermometer into thickest part of roast; cover roast with aluminum foil, and bake at 450° for 20 minutes. Uncover and bake an additional 30 to 35 minutes or until thermometer registers 140° for rare or 160° for medium doneness.

Let roast stand at room temperature about 15 minutes before carving. Slice thinly to serve. Serve with sauce. Yield: 14 servings (about 185 calories per 3-ounce serving plus 5 calories per tablespoon sauce).

SAUCE:

½ cup reserved marinade
2 tablespoons all-purpose flour
1 teaspoon beef-flavored bouillon granules
½ cup water
½ cup dry red wine
¼ teaspoon dried whole thyme
Dash of pepper

Combine marinade, flour, and bouillon granules in a jar; cover tightly, and shake vigorously, blending until smooth. Pour into a small saucepan; stir in remaining ingredients. Cook over medium heat, stirring constantly, until thickened and bubbly. Yield: 1½ cups.

PINEAPPLE-MARINATED POT ROAST

1 (4½-pound) lean round roast
1 cup sliced fresh mushrooms
1 cup unsweetened pineapple juice
¼ cup soy sauce
1½ teaspoons ground ginger
1 large onion, sliced
1 tablespoon cornstarch
2 tablespoons water

Trim excess fat from roast. Place roast and mushrooms in a Dutch oven. Combine pineapple juice, soy sauce, and ginger; pour over roast. Cover and refrigerate 1 hour, turning once.

Add onion to Dutch oven; place over high heat, and bring to a boil. Cover, reduce heat, and simmer 2½ hours or until roast is tender.

Remove roast and vegetables to a warm serving dish. Skim off fat from liquid in Dutch oven. Combine cornstarch and water, stirring until blended; stir into liquid in Dutch oven. Cook over medium-high heat, stirring constantly, until thickened and bubbly.

Slice roast, and serve with sauce. Yield: 12 servings (about 190 calories per 3-ounce serving plus 2 calories per tablespoon sauce).

BEEF ROLLS

4 beef cube steaks (about 1 pound)
¼ teaspoon pepper
½ teaspoon dried Italian seasoning
1 small carrot, scraped
1 medium-size green pepper
Vegetable cooking spray
½ cup beef broth
½ cup dry red wine
1 teaspoon paprika
¼ teaspoon hot sauce
1 small onion, chopped

Sprinkle steaks with pepper and Italian seasoning. Cut carrot and green pepper into 3- x ¼-inch strips. Arrange an even number of vegetable strips in center of each steak. Roll up steaks; tie with string or fasten with wooden picks.

Coat a large nonstick skillet with cooking spray; place over medium-high heat until hot. Add steak rolls, and brown on all sides.

Combine broth, wine, paprika, and hot sauce; pour over steak rolls. Add onion to skillet. Bring to a boil; cover, reduce heat, and simmer 1 hour or until steak is tender. Yield: 4 servings (about 189 calories per serving).

BROILED FLANK STEAK

2 pounds lean beef flank steak
¾ cup dry red wine
1½ teaspoons lemon pepper seasoning
Vegetable cooking spray

Place steak in a large shallow baking dish. Combine wine and lemon pepper seasoning; pour over steaks. Cover and refrigerate 24 hours, turning occasionally.

Coat a broiler rack with cooking spray.

Remove steak from marinade, and place on rack. Broil 3 to 4 inches from heat for 5 to 7 minutes on each side or to desired doneness. To serve, slice steak across grain into thin slices. Yield: 8 servings (about 153 calories per serving).

STEAK KABOBS

2 pounds lean boneless sirloin steak, cut into 1½-inch cubes
¾ cup Italian reduced-calorie salad dressing
3 tablespoons soy sauce
¼ teaspoon garlic powder
16 large mushrooms
16 cherry tomatoes
1 large green pepper, cut into 1-inch squares

Trim excess fat from steak; place in a shallow baking dish. Combine dressing, soy sauce, and garlic powder; pour over meat. Cover and marinate steak overnight in the refrigerator.

Remove meat from marinade, reserving marinade. Alternate meat and vegetables on skewers. Brush with marinade. Broil 4 inches from heat 5 minutes on each side, brushing frequently with marinade. Yield: 8 servings (about 215 calories per serving).

BEEF IN GREEN PEPPERCORN SAUCE

1 pound lean top round steak (½-inch-thick)
Vegetable cooking spray
1½ cups beef broth
½ cup dry red wine
2 large cloves garlic, crushed
2 bay leaves
1 tablespoon green peppercorns, drained
1 tablespoon cornstarch
2 tablespoons water

Trim excess fat from steak; cut into serving-size pieces. Place each piece of meat between 2 sheets of waxed paper, and flatten to ⅛-inch thickness using a meat mallet or rolling pin.

Coat a large skillet with cooking spray; place over medium-high heat until hot. Add meat to skillet; cook 2 to 3 minutes on each side or until browned. Add next 5 ingredients; bring to a boil. Cover mixture, reduce heat, and simmer 20 minutes. Remove meat from skillet; set aside. Discard bay leaves.

Combine cornstarch and water, stirring until blended; stir into broth mixture. Cook over medium heat, stirring constantly, until thickened. Return meat to skillet; cook until thoroughly heated. Yield: 4 servings (about 192 calories per serving).

BEEF WITH TOMATOES

2 pounds lean round steak
1 tablespoon vegetable oil
2 cups water
1 medium onion, chopped
1 medium-size green pepper, chopped
1 teaspoon sugar
1 teaspoon ground allspice
½ teaspoon dried whole basil
1 slice lemon
1 cup chopped fresh tomato

Trim excess fat from meat; cut into serving-size pieces.

Brown meat on both sides in hot oil in a large Dutch oven. Drain on paper towels, and wipe pan dry with paper towels.

Return meat to Dutch oven, and add remaining ingredients except tomato; cover and simmer 2 to 2½ hours or until meat is tender.

Remove steak and vegetables to platter; top with tomatoes. Yield: 8 servings (about 195 calories per serving).

SWISS STEAK

1½ pounds lean round steak
2 tablespoons all-purpose flour
½ teaspoon seasoned salt
Vegetable cooking spray
½ cup beef broth
½ cup vegetable juice
¼ teaspoon dried whole thyme
1 medium onion, sliced
2 carrots, cut into thin strips
2 stalks celery, cut into thin strips
1 large leek, cut into thin strips
1 tablespoon minced fresh parsley

Trim excess fat from steak; cut into serving-size pieces. Combine flour and seasoned salt; dredge steak in flour mixture, and pound into steak with a meat mallet or rolling pin.

Coat a large skillet with cooking spray; place over medium-high heat until hot. Brown steak on both sides in skillet; remove from skillet, and drain on paper towels. Wipe pan drippings from skillet with a paper towel.

Combine broth, vegetable juice, and thyme in skillet; bring to a boil. Return meat to skillet, and add onion. Cover, reduce heat, and simmer 1 hour, basting frequently.

Add carrot, celery, and leek to skillet; simmer, uncovered, an additional 15 minutes or until vegetables are just tender. Sprinkle with parsley just before serving. Yield: 6 servings (about 206 calories per serving).

BEEF STROGANOFF

1 pound lean round steak
3 tablespoons all-purpose flour
¼ teaspoon pepper
Vegetable cooking spray
1 teaspoon vegetable oil
½ pound fresh mushrooms, halved
1 large onion, sliced
2 cups beef broth
2 tablespoons dry sherry
2 tablespoons tomato paste
1 teaspoon dry mustard
¼ teaspoon dried whole oregano
⅛ teaspoon dried whole dillweed
⅓ cup plain low-fat yogurt
3 cups hot cooked noodles

Trim excess fat from steak. Partially freeze steak; slice across grain into thin strips. Combine flour and pepper, mixing well. Dredge meat in flour mixture; set aside.

Coat a small Dutch oven with cooking spray; add oil, and place over medium heat until hot. Add mushrooms and onion to Dutch oven; cover and cook 5 minutes or until onion is tender, stirring frequently. Remove vegetables from Dutch oven, and set aside.

Add meat to Dutch oven; increase heat to medium-high, and cook until browned. Stir in mushrooms, onion, and remaining ingredients except yogurt and noodles. Bring to a boil; cover, reduce heat, and simmer 15 minutes.

Uncover and simmer an additional 15 minutes. Remove from heat, and stir in yogurt. Cook meat and sauce until thoroughly heated (do not boil). Serve over noodles. Yield: 6 servings (about 162 calories per serving plus 100 calories per ½ cup cooked noodles).

BEEF BOURGUIGNON CRÊPES

1½ pounds lean round steak
1 pound pearl onions
Vegetable cooking spray
2 tablespoons all-purpose flour
¼ cup dry sherry
1 (10¾-ounce) can beef broth, undiluted
1 cup Burgundy or other dry red wine
1 bay leaf
Pinch of frozen chopped chives
Pinch of dried whole thyme
Pinch of whole dried tarragon
Pinch of chopped fresh parsley
1 pound small fresh mushrooms
12 Whole Wheat Crêpes

Trim excess fat from steak. Partially freeze steak; slice into 2- x ½-inch strips.

Brown meat and onions in a heavy Dutch oven coated with cooking spray. Combine flour and sherry, stirring until well blended; stir mixture into Dutch oven.

Add next 7 ingredients to Dutch oven; cover and simmer over low heat 45 minutes. Add mushrooms; cover and simmer an additional 15 minutes. Discard bay leaf.

Spoon ⅓ cup meat filling in center of each crêpe, using a slotted spoon; roll up. Spoon remaining sauce over crêpes. Yield: 6 servings (about 351 calories per serving).

Note: Filled crêpes may be heated, if necessary. Place in a shallow baking dish. Cover with foil, and bake at 375° for 10 to 12 minutes or until thoroughly heated.

WHOLE WHEAT CRÊPES

1½ cups whole wheat flour
3 eggs
¾ cup skim milk
¾ cup water
¼ teaspoon salt
1 tablespoon vegetable oil
Vegetable cooking spray

Combine first 6 ingredients in an electric blender; process 30 seconds. Scrape down sides of blender container with rubber spatula; process an additional 30 seconds or until smooth. Refrigerate batter 1 hour. (This allows flour particles to swell and soften so crêpes are light in texture.)

Coat the bottom of a 10-inch crêpe pan or nonstick skillet with cooking spray; place pan over medium heat until just hot, not smoking.

Pour about 3 tablespoons batter into pan. Quickly tilt pan in all directions so batter covers pan in a thin film; cook about 1 minute.

Lift edge of crêpe to test for doneness. Crêpe is ready for flipping when it can be shaken loose from pan. Flip the crêpe, and cook about 30 seconds. (This side is rarely more than spotty brown and is the side on which filling is placed.)

When crêpe is done, place on a towel to cool. Stack between layers of waxed paper to prevent sticking. Repeat until all batter is used, stirring batter occasionally. Yield: 15 (10-inch) crêpes.

Try using a variety of herbs and spices as a substitute for salt in meat and vegetable dishes.

CHINESE BEEF AND GREEN BEANS

¾ pound boneless lean sirloin steak
1½ pounds fresh green beans
Vegetable cooking spray
1 large onion, coarsely chopped
2 cloves garlic, minced
1½ cups beef broth
1½ tablespoons cornstarch
3 tablespoons water
1 tablespoon soy sauce
2 cups hot cooked rice

Trim excess fat from steak. Partially freeze steak; slice across grain into 3- x ¼-inch strips. Set aside.

Remove strings from beans; wash and cut into 1-inch pieces. Set aside.

Coat a skillet with cooking spray; place over medium-high heat until hot. Add meat, onion, and garlic; stir-fry until meat is browned. Add beans and broth; cover. Reduce heat, and simmer 8 minutes or until beans are crisp-tender.

Combine cornstarch, water, and soy sauce, stirring until blended; stir into meat mixture. Cook, stirring constantly, until thickened. Serve over rice. Yield: 4 servings (about 212 calories per serving plus 90 calories per ½ cup cooked rice).

ORIENTAL BEEF AND BROCCOLI

2 pounds lean round steak
¼ cup soy sauce
2 cloves garlic, minced
1 (1½ pound) bunch fresh broccoli
Vegetable cooking spray
1 teaspoon vegetable oil
2 low-sodium beef-flavored bouillon cubes
1¼ cups boiling water
1 (4-ounce) can mushroom stems and pieces, drained
1 tablespoon cornstarch
2 tablespoons water
4 cups hot cooked rice

Trim excess fat from steak. Partially freeze steak; slice across the grain into 3- x ¼-inch strips. Combine meat, soy sauce, and garlic in a medium bowl; stir well, and set aside.

Trim off large leaves of broccoli; remove tough ends of lower stalks, and wash thoroughly. Cut broccoli stems from buds, separate buds into small sections, and slice stems diagonally into ¼-inch pieces. Set broccoli aside.

Coat a wok with cooking spray; allow to heat at medium high (325°) for 2 minutes. Pour oil around top of wok. Add meat mixture to wok, and stir-fry to desired doneness. Remove from wok and set aside.

Dissolve bouillon cubes in boiling water. Add broccoli, bouillon mixture, and mushrooms to wok; bring to a boil. Cover, reduce heat to low (225°), and simmer 4 minutes or until broccoli is crisp-tender.

Dissolve cornstarch in 2 tablespoons water; stir into broccoli mixture. Return meat mixture to wok; stir-fry until thoroughly heated and slightly thickened. Serve with rice. Yield: 8 servings (about 197 calories per serving plus 90 calories per ½ cup cooked rice).

ORIENTAL BEEF AND VEGETABLES

1½ pounds (1-inch-thick) lean round steak
¼ cup soy sauce
2 tablespoons dry sherry
¼ teaspoons ground ginger
Vegetable cooking spray
1 small head Chinese or green cabbage (1 to 1½ pounds), cut into ½-inch slices
1 pound fresh mushrooms, sliced
1 (8-ounce) can sliced bamboo shoots, drained
8 green onions, cut into 2-inch slices
2 tablespoons cornstarch
3 tablespoons water
1 pint cherry tomatoes
4 cups hot cooked rice

Trim excess fat from steak. Partially freeze steak; slice across grain into 3- x ¼-inch strips.

Combine meat, soy sauce, sherry, and ginger; mix well, and let stand 20 minutes.

Coat a large Dutch oven with cooking spray; place over medium-high heat until hot. Add meat mixture to Dutch oven; cook, stirring frequently, until meat is browned. Add cabbage, mushrooms, bamboo shoots, and onions. Cover, reduce heat, and simmer 4 to 5 minutes or until vegetables are crisp-tender.

Dissolve cornstarch in water; add to meat mixture. Add tomatoes, and cook, stirring constantly, until thickened. Serve over rice. Yield: 8 servings (about 184 per serving plus 90 calories per ½ cup cooked rice).

SUKIYAKI

1 pound lean beef flank steak
1 beef-flavored bouillon cube
½ cup boiling water
3 tablespoons soy sauce
2 teaspoons sugar
Vegetable cooking spray
3 cups thinly sliced Chinese cabbage
5 large green onions, diagonally sliced into 1-inch pieces
1 cup diagonally sliced celery
1 medium-size green pepper, thinly sliced
2 cups fresh bean sprouts
1 (8-ounce) can sliced bamboo shoots, drained
1 (8-ounce) can sliced water chestnuts, drained
4 ounces fresh tofu, cubed (about ¾ cup)
½ pound fresh mushrooms, sliced
3 cups hot cooked rice

Trim excess fat from steak. Partially freeze steak; slice across the grain into thin strips, and set aside.

Dissolve bouillon cube in water; stir in soy sauce and sugar, and set aside.

Coat a wok with cooking spray; allow to heat at medium high (325°) for 2 minutes. Add Chinese cabbage, green onions, celery, and green pepper; stir-fry 2 minutes. Add next 4 ingredients; stir-fry 1 minute. Remove vegetables, and set aside.

Add meat and mushrooms to wok; stir-fry 2 minutes or to desired doneness. Stir in bouillon mixture and vegetables; cook until thoroughly heated. Serve over rice. Yield: 6 servings (about 189 calories per serving plus 90 calories per ½ cup cooked rice).

PEPPERS AND STEAK

2 pounds lean round steak, cut ½-inch thick
1 cup beef broth
¼ cup soy sauce
½ teaspoon garlic powder
½ teaspoon ground ginger
Vegetable cooking spray
1 cup water
3 large green peppers, cut into thin strips
1 (2-ounce) jar diced pimiento, drained
3 tablespoons cornstarch
¼ cup water
4 cups hot cooked rice

Trim excess fat from steak. Partially freeze steak; slice across grain into 2- x ¼-inch strips.

Combine next 4 ingredients in a shallow container; add meat, tossing to coat. Cover and refrigerate overnight.

Drain meat well, reserving ½ cup marinade; set aside.

Coat a large skillet with cooking spray; place over medium-high heat until hot. Add meat, and cook until lightly browned. Add reserved ½ cup marinade and 1 cup water. Reduce heat to low; cover and simmer 45 minutes. Add green pepper and pimiento, stirring well; cook 15 minutes or until meat is tender.

Combine cornstarch and ¼ cup water, stirring until blended; add to meat mixture. Cook, stirring constantly, until thickened. Serve over rice. Yield: 8 servings (about 195 calories per serving plus 90 calories per ½ cup cooked rice).

Partially freezing meat makes it easier to cut the meat into thin strips or cubes.

MUSHROOM BURGERS

1½ pounds ground chuck
1 (2-ounce) can mushroom stems and pieces, drained and finely chopped
1 tablespoon minced onion
1 tablespoon soy sauce
¼ teaspoon pepper
Vegetable cooking spray

Combine all ingredients except cooking spray, mixing lightly. Shape mixture into 6 patties about 1½-inches thick.

Coat a broiler pan and rack with cooking spray. Place patties on rack; broil 3 to 5 inches from heat 5 to 7 minutes on each side. Yield: 6 servings (about 192 calories per serving).

HAMBURGERS FLORENTINE

1 (10-ounce) package frozen chopped spinach
2 pounds ground round
1 medium onion, finely chopped
1 egg
¼ cup seasoned, dry breadcrumbs
2 tablespoons grated Parmesan cheese
½ teaspoon dried whole oregano
½ teaspoon pepper
Vegetable cooking spray
1 (8-ounce) can tomato sauce
½ cup beef broth

Cook spinach according to package directions, omitting salt; drain well. Finely chop spinach. Combine spinach and next 7 ingredients in a large bowl; shape into 8 patties.

Coat a large skillet with cooking spray; place over medium heat until hot. Cook patties, 4 at a time, 3 to 4 minutes on each side or until browned. Remove from skillet, and place on paper towels to drain. Wipe pan drippings from skillet with paper towels.

Combine tomato sauce and broth in skillet; heat to boiling. Arrange patties in skillet, turning to coat with sauce. Reduce heat; simmer, uncovered, 20 minutes, basting frequently. Yield: 8 servings (about 241 calories per serving).

EASY SLOPPY JOES

2½ pounds ground chuck
2 cups chopped onion
1 (6-ounce) can tomato paste
½ cup catsup
¼ cup tomato juice
2 tablespoons Worcestershire sauce
2 tablespoons prepared mustard
2 tablespoons lemon juice
1 teaspoon salt
¼ teaspoon pepper
6 hamburger buns, split and toasted

Combine ground chuck and onion in a large skillet; cook until meat is browned and onion is tender. Pour mixture into a colander, and pat dry with a paper towel; wipe pan drippings from skillet with a paper towel.

Return meat mixture to skillet, and add remaining ingredients except buns; simmer 15 to 20 minutes, stirring frequently.

To serve, spoon ½ cup meat mixture over each bun half. Yield: 12 servings (about 251 calories per serving).

Note: Sloppy Joe mixture freezes well. When ready to serve, just thaw in refrigerator and heat.

SWEET-AND-SOUR MEATBALLS

1½ cups tomato juice
2 teaspoons instant minced onion
2 teaspoons green pepper flakes
2 teaspoons Worcestershire sauce
1 teaspoon vinegar
½ teaspoon dried Italian seasoning
⅛ teaspoon garlic powder
⅛ teaspoon ground cinnamon
⅛ teaspoon pepper
1 (4-ounce) can sliced mushrooms, undrained
1 cup sliced carrots
Meatballs (recipe follows)
1½ cups hot cooked rice

Combine all ingredients except meatballs and rice in a large skillet. Bring to a boil; cover, reduce heat, and simmer 15 to 20 minutes or until carrots are tender. Add meatballs; simmer, uncovered, until thoroughly heated. Serve over rice. Yield: 3 servings (about 231 calories per serving plus 90 calories per ½ cup cooked rice).

MEATBALLS:

½ pound ground chuck
½ cup drained unsweetened crushed pineapple
1 slice whole wheat bread, crumbled
1 teaspoon instant minced onion
1 teaspoon Worcestershire sauce
⅛ teaspoon garlic powder
⅛ teaspoon dry mustard
Dash of pepper

Combine all ingredients; shape mixture into meatballs, using 1 heaping tablespoon mixture for each. Place meatballs on rack in a baking pan. Bake at 350° for 30 minutes or until done. Yield: 12 meatballs.

SAUCY MEATBALLS

1 pound ground chuck
1 tablespoon cornstarch
2 tablespoons beef broth
2 tablespoons Worcestershire sauce
¼ teaspoon dried whole thyme
Vegetable cooking spray
½ pound pearl onions, peeled
1½ cups beef broth
¼ teaspoon dried whole thyme
⅛ teaspoon pepper
¼ cup water
2 tablespoons cornstarch
2 tablespoons chopped fresh parsley
3 cups hot cooked noodles

Combine first 5 ingredients, mixing lightly; shape into 1¼-inch meatballs. Broil 6 inches from heat 5 minutes; turn meatballs, and broil an additional 5 minutes or until browned. Drain well on paper towels.

Coat a large skillet with cooking spray; place over medium heat until hot. Add onions; cook 2 minutes, stirring constantly. Add meatballs, 1½ cups beef broth, ¼ teaspoon thyme, and pepper. Bring to a boil; cover, reduce heat, and simmer 20 minutes.

Combine water and 2 tablespoons cornstarch, stirring until blended. Stir cornstarch mixture into broth mixture; cook until thickened and bubbly. Stir in parsley. Serve over noodles. Yield: 6 servings (about 174 calories per serving plus 100 calories per ½ cup cooked noodles).

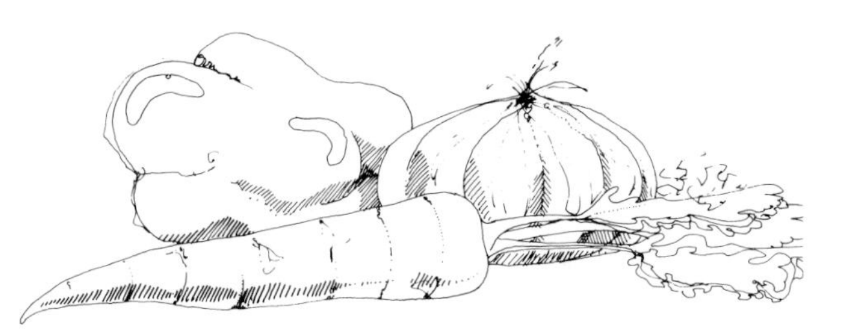

VEGETABLE-MEAT LOAF

1 pound ground chuck
1 cup soft whole wheat breadcrumbs
¼ cup shredded carrot
¼ cup thinly sliced celery
2 tablespoons finely chopped onion
2 tablespoons finely chopped green pepper
1 egg, slightly beaten
1 teaspoon parsley flakes
½ teaspoon dry mustard
¼ teaspoon salt
¼ teaspoon pepper
1 (16-ounce) can whole tomatoes, drained and chopped
Vegetable cooking spray
2 tablespoons reduced-calorie catsup

Combine all ingredients except cooking spray and catsup.

Coat a broiler pan and rack with cooking spray. Place meat mixture on broiler rack, and shape into a 10- x 6-inch loaf. Spread catsup over meat loaf. Bake at 350° for 1 hour and 10 minutes or until done. Yield: 6 servings (about 188 calories per serving).

BEEFY-VEGETABLE SUPPER

Vegetable cooking spray
½ pound lean ground beef
½ cup chopped onion
1 clove garlic, minced
1 medium zucchini, cut into thin strips
6 medium-size fresh mushrooms, quartered
1 cup fresh bean sprouts
1 cup thinly sliced Chinese cabbage
⅓ cup diagonally sliced celery
1 teaspoon dried whole basil
¼ teaspoon dried whole oregano
¼ teaspoon salt
⅛ teaspoon freshly ground pepper
1 large tomato, coarsely chopped

Coat a small Dutch oven with cooking spray; place over medium-high heat until hot. Combine meat, onion, and garlic in Dutch oven; sauté 6 to 7 minutes or until meat is browned and onion is tender. Drain meat mixture in a colander, and pat dry with a paper towel. Wipe pan drippings from pan with a paper towel.

Return meat mixture to Dutch oven; add remaining ingredients except tomato. Sauté over medium heat 4 to 5 minutes or until vegetables are crisp-tender. Stir in tomato, and cook an additional 2 minutes. Yield: 4 servings (about 150 calories per serving)

CABBAGE-BEEF ROLLS

1 pound ground chuck
1 egg
¾ cup soft whole wheat breadcrumbs
⅓ cup chopped onion
2 teaspoons Worcestershire sauce
1½ teaspoons paprika
¼ teaspoon pepper
1 (8-ounce) can tomato sauce, divided
8 large cabbage leaves
¼ cup water

Combine first 7 ingredients; add ½ cup tomato sauce. Mix well, and set aside.

Blanch cabbage leaves in boiling water for 3 to 4 minutes; drain. Place about ⅓ cup meat mixture in center of each cabbage leaf. Fold ends of each cabbage leaf over; roll up, and secure with wooden picks.

Place cabbage rolls in a large skillet. Combine remaining tomato sauce and water; pour over cabbage rolls. Bring to a boil; cover, reduce heat, and simmer 30 minutes. To serve, remove cabbage rolls to a serving platter; discard liquid. Yield: 4 servings (about 270 calories per serving).

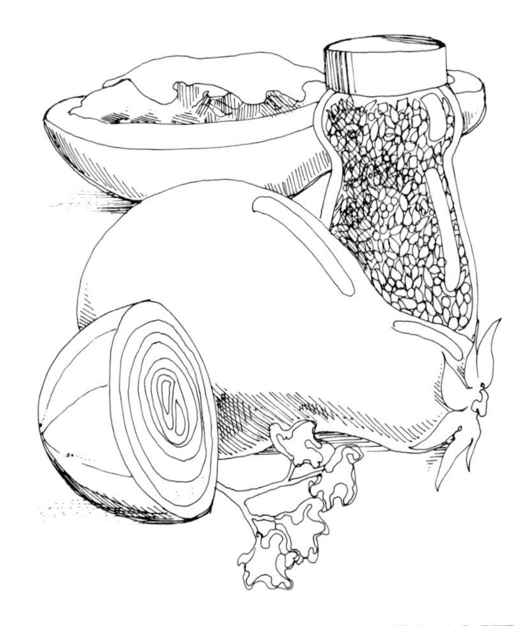

BEEF-STUFFED EGGPLANT

2 (¾-pound) eggplants
1 pound ground chuck
1 cup finely chopped onion
1 cup finely chopped fresh mushrooms
1 (8-ounce) can tomato sauce
¼ cup wheat germ
1 teaspoon garlic salt
½ teaspoon dried whole chervil
½ teaspoon dried whole basil
½ teaspoon dried whole oregano
½ teaspoon freshly ground pepper
2 tablespoons grated Parmesan cheese
2 tablespoons chopped fresh parsley

Wash eggplant, and wrap in aluminum foil. Bake at 350° for 1 hour; unwrap and let cool to touch. Cut each eggplant in half lengthwise. Remove pulp, leaving a ¼-inch shell; mash pulp, and set aside. Arrange shells in a large baking dish.

Cook ground chuck, onion, and mushrooms in a large skillet until meat is browned. Drain well in a colander, and pat dry with paper towels; wipe pan drippings from skillet with paper towels.

Return meat mixture to skillet. Stir in eggplant pulp and remaining ingredients except cheese and parsley.

Spoon mixture evenly into eggplant shells; sprinkle with cheese. Bake at 350° for 20 to 25 minutes or until thoroughly heated. Sprinkle with parsley before serving. Yield: 4 servings (about 311 calories per serving).

BEEF-STUFFED ZUCCHINI

4 medium zucchini (about 1½ pounds)
¾ pound ground chuck
¼ cup fine, dry breadcrumbs
¼ cup grated Parmesan cheese
¼ cup tomato juice
2 eggs, beaten
2 tablespoons minced fresh parsley
½ teaspoon dried whole rosemary, crushed
¼ teaspoon garlic salt
⅛ teaspoon pepper
Vegetable cooking spray

Cook whole zucchini in boiling water in a large skillet 7 minutes or until tender but still firm. Drain and let cool to touch. Cut each zucchini in half lengthwise; remove pulp, and chop, leaving a ¼-inch shell. Set aside.

In same skillet, brown meat, stirring to crumble. Drain meat in a colander, and pat dry with a paper towel. Wipe pan drippings from skillet with a paper towel. Combine zucchini pulp, meat, and remaining ingredients except cooking spray; fill zucchini shells with mixture.

Place stuffed zucchini in a large baking pan coated with cooking spray. Bake at 350° for 25 to 30 minutes. Yield: 4 servings (about 267 calories per serving).

ZUCCHINI-BEEF LASAGNA

Vegetable cooking spray
½ pound lean ground beef
⅓ cup chopped onion
1 (15-ounce) can tomato sauce
½ teaspoon dried whole oregano
¼ teaspoon dried whole basil
¼ teaspoon pepper
1 cup low-fat cottage cheese
1 egg
4 medium zucchini
2 tablespoons all-purpose flour
1 cup (4 ounces) shredded mozzarella cheese

Coat a large skillet with cooking spray; place over medium-high heat until hot. Cook ground beef and onion in skillet 8 minutes or until meat is browned and onion is tender.

Drain meat mixture in a colander, and pat dry with a paper towel. Wipe pan drippings from skillet with a paper towel.

Return meat mixture to skillet; add tomato sauce, oregano, basil, and pepper, and bring to a boil. Reduce heat, and simmer, uncovered, 5 minutes, stirring occasionally.

Combine cottage cheese and egg; set aside.

Cut zucchini lengthwise into ¼-inch thick slices. Arrange half of zucchini in a 12- x 8- x 2-inch glass baking dish; sprinkle with 1 tablespoon flour. Spread cottage cheese mixture evenly over zucchini; top with half of meat mixture. Layer remaining zucchini and 1 tablespoon flour over meat mixture. Sprinkle evenly with mozzarella cheese, and cover with remaining meat mixture.

Bake lasagna at 350° for 40 to 45 minutes or until zucchini is tender. Let stand 10 minutes before serving. Yield: 6 servings (about 223 calories per serving).

SPANISH RICE WITH BEEF

1 pound lean ground beef
1 medium onion, chopped
1 medium-size green pepper, chopped
2 (16-ounce) cans stewed tomatoes, undrained
1 cup water
1 cup uncooked regular rice
1½ teaspoons chili powder
¾ teaspoon dried whole oregano
½ teaspoon salt
¼ teaspoon red pepper
⅛ teaspoon garlic powder

Cook ground beef, onion, and green pepper in a small Dutch oven until meat is browned. Drain in a colander; pat dry with a paper towel. Wipe pan drippings from pan with a paper towel.

Return meat mixture to Dutch oven, and stir in remaining ingredients. Bring to a boil; cover, reduce heat, and simmer 30 minutes or until rice is tender, stirring occasionally. Yield: 6 servings (about 283 calories per serving).

SPINACH-BEEF LASAGNA

6 lasagna noodles
Vegetable cooking spray
1 pound ground chuck
1 medium onion, chopped
2 cloves garlic, minced
1½ cups tomato puree
1 teaspoon dried whole basil
1 teaspoon dried whole oregano
¼ teaspoon salt
¼ teaspoon pepper
2 (10-ounce) packages frozen chopped spinach, thawed
1 (12-ounce) carton low-fat cottage cheese
3 tablespoons grated Parmesan cheese
1 egg, beaten
¼ teaspoon salt
¼ teaspoon pepper
⅛ teaspoon ground nutmeg

Cook noodles according to package directions, omitting salt; drain and set aside.

Coat a large skillet with cooking spray; place over medium heat until hot. Add meat, onion, and garlic; sauté until meat is browned and onion is tender.

Drain meat mixture well in a colander; wipe pan drippings from skillet with paper towels.

Return meat mixture to skillet. Add tomato puree, basil, oregano, ¼ teaspoon salt, and pepper; bring to a boil. Reduce heat, and simmer mixture 5 minutes.

Place spinach on paper towels, and squeeze until barely moist. Combine spinach and next 6 ingredients in a medium bowl, stirring until blended. Spread half of spinach mixture evenly in a 12- x 8- x 2-inch baking dish; layer 3 noodles over spinach. Spread half of meat mixture over noodles; repeat layers, ending with meat mixture. Cover and bake at 350° for 45 minutes. Let stand 5 to 10 minutes before serving. Yield: 8 servings (about 251 calories per serving).

SPAGHETTI WITH VEGETABLE-MEAT SAUCE

½ pound lean ground beef
Vegetable cooking spray
1 medium onion, chopped
2 medium zucchini, cut into ¼-inch-thick slices
½ cup shredded carrot
2 (16-ounce) cans tomatoes, undrained and chopped
1 (8-ounce) can tomato sauce
1 (6-ounce) can tomato paste
1 (4-ounce) can mushroom stems and pieces, undrained
1 teaspoon salt
2 teaspoons dried whole oregano
1 teaspoon dried whole basil
1 teaspoon dried Italian seasoning
½ teaspoon garlic powder
¼ teaspoon pepper
2 tablespoons grated Romano cheese
3 cups hot cooked spaghetti

Cook ground beef in a Dutch oven over medium heat until meat is browned, stirring to crumble. Drain meat in a colander, and pat dry with a paper towel. Wipe pan drippings from Dutch oven with a paper towel.

Coat Dutch oven with cooking spray; place over medium heat until hot. Add onion; sauté until almost tender. Add zucchini and carrot, and sauté 5 minutes. Remove vegetables from Dutch oven, and set aside.

Combine meat and remaining ingredients except sautéed vegetables, cheese, and spaghetti in Dutch oven; simmer, uncovered, for 30 minutes. Stir in vegetables and cheese, and cook just until heated. Serve sauce over spaghetti. Yield: 6 servings (about 174 calories per serving plus 90 calories per ½ cup cooked spaghetti).

MEATY SPAGHETTI

1½ pounds ground chuck
1 medium onion, chopped
1 cup chopped celery
½ cup chopped green pepper
2 cloves garlic, minced
1 (15-ounce) can tomato sauce
1 (6-ounce) can tomato paste
¾ cup water
1 (4-ounce) can mushroom stems and pieces, undrained
1½ teaspoons dried whole oregano
½ teaspoon salt
½ teaspoon pepper
1 (12-ounce) package thin spaghetti

Cook ground chuck in a Dutch oven over medium heat, stirring to crumble, until meat is browned. Drain meat in a colander, and pat dry with a paper towel. Wipe pan drippings from pan with a paper towel.

Return meat to Dutch oven; add onion, celery, green pepper, and garlic. Cook over low heat, stirring frequently, 5 minutes. Add remaining ingredients except spaghetti, and stir well; bring to a boil. Cover, reduce heat, and simmer 1½ hours, stirring occasionally.

Cook spaghetti according to package directions; drain. Spoon meat sauce over spaghetti. Yield: 8 servings (about 330 calories per serving).

STUFFED SHELLS WITH BEEF-TOMATO SAUCE

18 jumbo pasta shells (about 5¼ ounces)
Vegetable cooking spray
½ pound ground chuck
1 small onion, chopped
1 clove garlic, minced
1 (15-ounce) can tomato sauce
1 (6-ounce) can tomato paste
¾ teaspoon dried whole oregano
½ teaspoon pepper
1½ cups low-fat cottage cheese
¼ cup grated Parmesan cheese
1 egg, beaten
2 tablespoons minced fresh parsley
Dash of ground nutmeg

Cook pasta shells according to package directions, omitting salt; drain and set aside.

Coat a large skillet with cooking spray; place over medium heat until hot. Add meat, onion, and garlic. Cook until meat is lightly browned. Drain meat mixture in a colander, and pat dry with paper towels; wipe pan drippings from skillet with paper towels.

Return meat mixture to skillet. Stir in tomato sauce, tomato paste, oregano, and pepper; bring to a boil. Reduce heat, and simmer, uncovered, 15 minutes.

Combine cheese, egg, parsley, and nutmeg in a medium bowl; fill each shell with 1 slightly heaping tablespoon of cheese mixture.

Spread tomato sauce mixture in a 12- x 8- x 2-inch baking dish; arrange shells over sauce. Cover and bake at 350° for 40 minutes. Yield: 6 servings (about 294 calories per serving).

LEAN PASTICHIO

¾ pound ground chuck
½ cup chopped onion
1 cup uncooked elbow macaroni
1 (8-ounce) can tomato sauce
2 tablespoons grated Parmesan cheese
½ teaspoon dried whole thyme
¼ teaspoon ground cinnamon
½ cup skim milk
3 tablespoons all-purpose flour
¼ teaspoon salt
¼ teaspoon white pepper
1 cup skim milk
¼ cup plus 2 tablespoons Parmesan cheese
2 eggs, beaten
Ground cinnamon

Cook meat and onion in a large skillet over medium-high heat until meat is browned; drain meat in a colander, and pat dry with paper towels.

Cook macaroni according to package directions, omitting salt. Combine meat mixture, macaroni, and next 4 ingredients; spread in bottom of a 10- x 6- x 2-inch baking dish.

Combine ½ cup milk, flour, salt, and pepper in a jar; cover tightly, and shake vigorously to blend. Pour into a small saucepan; stir in 1 cup milk. Cook over medium heat, stirring constantly, until mixture is thickened and bubbly. Remove from heat, and stir in ¼ cup plus 2 tablespoons Parmesan cheese. Let cool to room temperature.

Stir eggs into thickened milk mixture; pour evenly over meat mixture. Sprinkle lightly with cinnamon. Bake at 375° for 30 to 35 minutes or until knife inserted near center comes out clean. Let stand 10 minutes before serving. Yield: 6 servings (about 305 calories per serving).

When purchasing meat, select the leanest cut of meat. The label on ground beef will indicate if the meat is lean.

WHOLE WHEAT PIZZA

½ cup warm water (105° to 115°)
1 tablespoon vegetable oil
1 teaspoon sugar
½ teaspoon salt
½ package (about 1 teaspoon) dry yeast
¾ cup all-purpose flour
¾ cup whole wheat flour
Vegetable cooking spray
½ pound ground chuck
½ teaspoon salt
1 cup Pizza Sauce
1 cup (4 ounces) shredded mozzarella cheese, divided
¾ cup sliced fresh mushrooms
¼ cup sliced green onions
1 green pepper, sliced into thin rings (optional)
2 tablespoons grated Parmesan cheese
Crushed red pepper (optional)

Combine water, oil, sugar, and ½ teaspoon salt in a medium mixing bowl. Sprinkle yeast over mixture, stirring until dissolved. Gradually add flour, mixing well after each addition.

Turn dough out onto a lightly floured surface, and knead about 4 minutes or until smooth and elastic. Shape into a ball, and place in a bowl coated with cooking spray, turning to grease top. Cover and let rise in a warm place (85°), free from drafts, 1 hour or until doubled in bulk.

Coat a 12-inch pizza pan with cooking spray; set aside. Punch dough down. Lightly coat hands with cooking spray, and pat dough evenly into pizza pan. Bake at 425° for 5 minutes.

Combine ground chuck and ½ teaspoon salt in a skillet; cook over medium heat until meat is browned, stirring to crumble. Drain well on paper towels.

Spread 1 cup Pizza Sauce evenly over pizza crust, leaving a ½-inch border around edges. Sprinkle ¾ cup mozzarella cheese over top.

Sprinkle meat over cheese on pizza crust; top with mushrooms, green onions, and green pepper, if desired. Bake at 425° for 15 minutes.

Sprinkle with remaining ¼ cup mozzarella cheese and Parmesan cheese; bake 5 minutes. Sprinkle with crushed red pepper, if desired. Yield: 10 slices (about 171 calories per slice).

PIZZA SAUCE:

1 (28-ounce) can whole tomatoes, undrained
1 (6-ounce) can tomato paste
1 large onion, chopped
3 tablespoons chopped fresh parsley
2 cloves garlic, minced
1 small green pepper, chopped
1½ teaspoons dried whole oregano
¼ teaspoon pepper

Place tomatoes in container of an electric blender; process until smooth. Pour into a small Dutch oven. Stir in remaining ingredients; bring to a boil. Reduce heat, and simmer, uncovered, 1 hour or until sauce is reduced to about 3 cups. Divide into 1-cup portions; freeze 2 portions for later use. Yield: 3 cups or enough sauce for 3 (12-inch) pizzas.

SAUTÉED LIVER SUPREME

½ pound thinly sliced beef liver
1 tablespoon all-purpose flour
Vegetable cooking spray
1 large onion, chopped
1 large green pepper, chopped
1 (4½-ounce) jar sliced mushrooms, undrained
2 cups water
⅔ cup uncooked regular rice
1 beef-flavored bouillon cube
1 tablespoon Worcestershire sauce
¼ teaspoon garlic powder
¼ teaspoon pepper

Cut liver into 3- x ½-inch strips; dredge liver in flour. Coat a small Dutch oven with cooking spray; place over medium heat until hot. Add liver, onion, and green pepper to skillet; sauté until liver is brown and vegetables are tender.

Stir in remaining ingredients. Bring to a boil; cover, reduce heat, and simmer 20 to 25 minutes or until rice is tender, stirring occasionally. Yield: 4 servings (about 220 calories per serving).

SAUCY LIVER

1 (28-ounce) can whole tomatoes, undrained and chopped
1 small onion, thinly sliced and separated into rings
1 cup chopped fresh mushrooms
⅓ cup chopped green pepper
2 tablespoons diced pimiento
2 cloves garlic, crushed
1 teaspoon paprika
½ teaspoon chili powder
¼ teaspoon salt
¼ teaspoon pepper
6 slices beef liver (about 1¾ pounds)
3 tablespoons all-purpose flour
Vegetable cooking spray
1 tablespoon plus 1 teaspoon olive or vegetable oil, divided

Combine first 10 ingredients in a medium saucepan. Bring to a boil; reduce heat, and simmer, uncovered, 20 minutes.

Dredge liver in flour, and set aside. Coat a large skillet with cooking spray; add 2 teaspoons oil, and place skillet over medium-high heat until hot.

Add half of liver to skillet; cook 4 minutes on each side or until browned. Remove from skillet, and set aside. Repeat procedure with remaining oil and liver.

Add sauce to skillet; bring to a boil, scraping to loosen clinging particles. Return liver to skillet; reduce heat, and simmer 5 minutes or until sauce is thickened. Yield: 6 servings (about 273 calories per serving).

PORK CHOP AND RICE DINNER

4 (½-inch-thick) lean pork chops
¼ teaspoon pepper
Vegetable cooking spray
¼ cup diced onion
¼ cup diced green pepper
½ cup uncooked regular rice
1 (28-ounce) can whole tomatoes, undrained and chopped
¼ cup water
½ teaspoon salt
½ teaspoon prepared mustard

Trim excess fat from chops; sprinkle with pepper. Coat a large skillet with cooking spray; place over medium heat until hot. Add chops, and cook until browned on both sides. Remove chops, and drain on paper towels; wipe pan drippings from skillet with a paper towel.

Coat skillet with additional cooking spray; add onion and green pepper to skillet, and sauté until tender. Stir in rice, tomatoes, water, salt, and mustard; add pork chops. Bring to a boil; cover, reduce heat, and simmer 25 to 30 minutes or until rice is tender and pork chops are done. Yield: 4 servings (about 290 calories per serving).

FRUITED PORK CHOP AND RICE SKILLET

6 (½-inch-thick) lean pork chops
Vegetable cooking spray
1 cup unsweetened apple juice
¾ cup chicken broth
2 tablespoons soy sauce
1 teaspoon ground ginger
1 teaspoon prepared mustard
¼ teaspoon salt
¼ teaspoon pepper
⅔ cup uncooked regular rice
¼ cup raisins
2 small cooking apples, unpeeled

Trim excess fat from pork chops. Coat a large skillet with cooking spray. Place over medium heat until hot; add chops, and cook until browned on both sides. Remove chops, and pat dry with paper towels. Wipe pan drippings from skillet with paper towels.

Return chops to skillet. Add next 7 ingredients; cover and simmer 20 minutes.

Add rice and raisins to skillet, arranging chops on top of rice. Cover and cook over low heat an additional 20 minutes.

Core apples; cut crosswise into ¼- to ½-inch slices. Place apple rings on top of chops; cover and cook until apples are crisp-tender and liquid is absorbed. Yield: 6 servings (about 302 calories per serving).

ORIENTAL PORK CHOP BAKE

6 (½-inch-thick) lean pork chops
Vegetable cooking spray
¾ cup unsweetened orange juice
¼ cup soy sauce
2 tablespoons lemon juice
1 (4-ounce) can whole mushrooms, drained
½ teaspoon ground ginger
¼ teaspoon garlic powder
¼ teaspoon pepper
1 green pepper, chopped
1 medium onion, chopped
½ cup sliced water chestnuts
1 lemon, thinly sliced
3 cups hot cooked rice

Trim excess fat from chops; brown chops on both sides in a large skillet coated with cooking spray. Remove chops from skillet, and pat dry with paper towels. Place in a 13- x 9- x 2-inch baking dish.

Combine next 7 ingredients, and pour over chops. Cover and bake at 350° for 30 to 35 minutes. Arrange green pepper, onion, water chestnuts, and lemon slices over chops; cover and bake an additional 15 minutes. Serve with rice. Yield: 6 servings (about 210 calories per serving plus 90 calories per ½ cup cooked rice).

ORIENTAL OVEN-FRIED PORK CHOPS

1 egg, beaten
3 tablespoons soy sauce
1 tablespoon dry sherry
4 (1-inch-thick) lean pork chops
¼ cup fine, dry breadcrumbs
½ teaspoon garlic powder
⅛ teaspoon ground ginger
Vegetable cooking spray

Combine egg, soy sauce, and sherry in a shallow baking dish. Trim excess fat from pork chops; add chops to egg mixture, turning to coat. Cover and let stand 1 hour.

Combine breadcrumbs, garlic powder, and ginger. Dredge pork chops in breadcrumb mixture; arrange in a shallow baking dish coated with cooking spray. Bake at 350° for 30 minutes; turn pork chops, and bake an additional 25 to 30 minutes or until done. Yield: 4 servings (about 239 calories per serving).

ITALIAN-STYLE PORK CHOPS

4 (1-inch-thick) lean pork chops
Salt (optional)
Pepper
Vegetable cooking spray
½ pound fresh mushrooms, sliced
1 medium onion, chopped
1 clove garlic, crushed
2 medium-size green peppers, cut into thin strips
2 (8-ounce) cans tomato sauce
¼ cup dry sherry
1 tablespoon lemon juice
¼ teaspoon dried whole oregano
¼ teaspoon dried whole basil

Trim excess fat from pork chops; sprinkle lightly with salt, if desired, and pepper. Brown chops on both sides in a large skillet coated with cooking spray. Drain pork chops on paper towels; transfer to a shallow 2-quart baking dish. Cover pork chops with mushrooms, and set aside.

Add onion, garlic, and green pepper to skillet; sauté over medium-high heat until onion is just tender. Stir in remaining ingredients, and simmer, uncovered, 5 minutes; pour over chops. Cover and bake at 350° for 1 hour or until done. Yield: 4 servings (about 262 calories per serving).

SWEET-AND-SOUR PORK

1 (20-ounce) can unsweetened pineapple chunks, undrained
Vegetable cooking spray
1½ pounds lean boneless pork, cut into 1-inch cubes
½ cup chicken broth
¼ cup vinegar
1 tablespoon brown sugar
1 tablespoon plus 1 teaspoon soy sauce
½ teaspoon ground ginger
1 medium-size green pepper, cut into thin strips
1 small onion, cut into thin wedges
2 tablespoons cornstarch
2 tablespoons dry sherry
4 cups hot cooked rice

Drain pineapple, reserving juice; set aside.

Coat a large nonstick skillet with cooking spray; place over medium-high heat until hot. Add pork, and cook until browned on all sides. Remove pork, and drain on paper towels; wipe skillet dry with paper towels.

Return pork to skillet; stir in reserved pineapple juice, broth, vinegar, sugar, soy sauce, and ginger. Bring to a boil; cover, reduce heat, and simmer 20 to 25 minutes or until pork is tender.

Add reserved pineapple, green pepper, and onion; cover and simmer 4 to 5 minutes or until vegetables are crisp-tender.

Combine cornstarch and sherry, stirring until blended; pour over pork mixture. Cook, stirring constantly, until thickened and bubbly. Serve over rice. Yield: 8 servings (about 277 calories per serving plus 90 calories per ½ cup cooked rice).

ORIENTAL PORK AND MUSHROOMS

2 pounds lean boneless pork, cut into ¼-inch strips
2½ tablespoons sherry
2½ tablespoons soy sauce
¼ teaspoon pepper
Vegetable cooking spray
½ pound fresh mushrooms, sliced
2 teaspoons cornstarch
½ cup chicken broth
4 cups hot cooked rice

Combine pork, sherry, soy sauce, and pepper, tossing lightly; let stand 15 to 20 minutes. Drain pork mixture.

Coat a large skillet with cooking spray; place over medium-high heat until hot. Add pork, and cook 4 to 6 minutes or until meat is browned, stirring constantly. Remove pork, and pat dry with paper towels; set aside.

Cook mushrooms in skillet over medium heat 2 to 3 minutes or until tender, stirring constantly. Add meat to mushrooms, mixing well. Combine cornstarch and broth, stirring until blended; add to meat mixture. Cook over medium heat, stirring constantly, until thickened. Serve over rice. Yield: 8 servings (about 173 calories plus 90 calories per ½ cup rice).

CURRIED HAM LOAF

1 (8-ounce) can unsweetened sliced pineapple, undrained
1 pound ground lean ham
½ pound ground lean pork
1 egg, slightly beaten
1 medium-size green pepper, finely chopped
1 cup soft whole wheat breadcrumbs
¼ cup skim milk
1 tablespoon prepared mustard
½ teaspoon curry powder
¼ teaspoon pepper
Vegetable cooking spray

Drain pineapple, reserving juice; set pineapple aside. Combine juice and next 9 ingredients in a large bowl; mix well.

Coat a 9- x 5- x 3-inch loafpan with cooking spray. Cut pineapple slices in half; arrange in bottom of loafpan. Spoon ham mixture into loafpan, packing lightly; bake at 350° for 1 hour or until done. Pour off pan drippings; let stand 10 minutes before unmolding and slicing. Yield: 8 servings (about 268 calories per serving).

ORANGE LAMB CHOPS

½ cup unsweetened orange juice
1 tablespoon grated orange rind
½ teaspon dried whole thyme
⅛ teaspoon freshly ground pepper
4 (½-inch-thick) lamb chops (about 1¼ pounds)
Vegetable cooking spray
1 tablespoon margarine
1 cup sliced fresh mushrooms
½ cup Chablis or other dry white wine

Combine first 4 ingredients in a shallow baking dish. Trim excess fat from lamb chops. Place chops in dish; spoon orange juice mixture over chops. Cover and refrigerate 3 hours.

Coat a large skillet with cooking spray; place over medium-high heat until hot.

Remove chops from marinade, reserving liquid; arrange in skillet. Brown lamb chops on both sides. Remove chops from skillet, and drain on paper towels.

Melt margarine in skillet over medium heat; add mushrooms, and sauté just until tender. Stir in reserved marinade and wine; bring to a boil. Return lamb chops to skillet; cover, reduce heat, and simmer 10 minutes. Uncover and simmer an additional 10 minutes or until sauce is reduced to about ½ cup. Yield: 4 servings (about 170 calories per serving).

MARINATED LAMB KABOBS

1½ pounds lean boneless lamb, cut into 1½-inch cubes
½ cup Italian reduced-calorie salad dressing
¼ cup lemon juice
1 teaspoon dried whole oregano, crushed
¼ teaspoon pepper

Place lamb in a shallow dish; combine remaining ingredients, and pour over lamb. Cover and refrigerate overnight.

Remove meat from marinade; thread onto skewers. Broil 7 to 8 inches from heat for 18 to 20 minutes, turning occasionally and basting with marinade. Yield: 6 servings (about 133 calories per serving).

VEAL MARSALA

1½ pounds (¼-inch-thick) veal cutlets
Pepper
Vegetable cooking spray
1 (28-ounce) can whole tomatoes, undrained
½ cup Marsala wine
¼ cup minced fresh parsley
1 clove garlic, minced
1 teaspoon dried whole basil
½ pound fresh mushrooms, sliced
1 large green pepper, cut into thin strips
1 large onion, sliced and separated into rings
¼ cup grated Parmesan cheese

Trim excess fat from veal. Place veal between waxed paper; flatten to ⅛-inch thickness using a meat mallet. Cut veal into 2-inch squares.

Sprinkle veal with pepper. Coat a large nonstick skillet with cooking spray; place over medium-high heat until hot. Sauté veal, a few pieces at a time, 2 to 3 minutes on each side or until browned. Remove from skillet; set aside.

Drain and chop tomatoes, reserving ½ cup juice. Add tomatoes, reserved ½ cup juice, wine, parsley, garlic, and basil to skillet; bring to a boil. Stir in mushrooms, green pepper, and onion; cover, reduce heat, and simmer 5 minutes. Uncover and simmer 5 to 7 minutes.

Return veal to skillet, stirring well. Simmer, uncovered, 3 to 4 minutes. Transfer veal and vegetables to a serving dish; pour liquid over all. Sprinkle with cheese. Yield: 6 servings (about 269 calories per serving).

VEAL SCALLOPINI WITH MUSHROOMS

1 pound (¼-inch-thick) veal cutlets
Freshly ground pepper
Vegetable cooking spray
1 tablespoon reduced-calorie margarine
½ pound fresh mushrooms, sliced
1 large green pepper, cut into ½-inch strips
½ cup Chablis or other dry white wine
¼ cup water
1 tablespoon lemon juice
1 chicken-flavored bouillon cube
1 tablespoon cornstarch
2 tablespoons water
2 tablespoons chopped fresh parsley
2 cups hot cooked vermicelli

Trim excess fat from veal; cut into serving-size pieces. Place veal between two sheets of waxed paper; flatten veal to ⅛-inch thickness, using a meat mallet. Sprinkle veal lightly with pepper.

Coat a large nonstick skillet with cooking spray; add margarine, and place over medium heat until margarine is melted. Add veal, a few pieces at a time; cook 2 to 3 minutes on each side or until veal is lightly browned. Remove from skillet, and keep warm.

Add mushrooms and green pepper to skillet; sauté 2 to 3 minutes or until pepper is crisp-tender. Stir in next 4 ingredients. Bring to a boil, stirring to dissolve bouillon; boil 1 minute.

Combine cornstarch and water, stirring until blended; add to mushroom mixture in skillet. Cook, stirring constantly, until thickened. Remove from heat, and stir in parsley. Spoon sauce over veal. Serve with vermicelli. Yield: 4 servings (about 263 calories per serving plus 90 calories per ½ cup cooked vermicelli).

POULTRY

Southerners love to eat chicken — "Southern-Fried Chicken," that is. Chicken is naturally low in calories compared to some protein foods. However, when chicken is dipped in batter and fried golden brown, the calories add up quickly.

Most of the fat in chicken is found in the skin, so you should always remove the skin before cooking. Grill, broil, or bake chicken on a rack to allow extra fat to drip away. Whatever cooking method you choose, be sure to keep calories low by using low-calorie seasonings, sauces, and marinades. Experiment with various wines and herbs to add delicious flavor without adding salt.

Although chicken is low in cholesterol, chicken livers are high in cholesterol. Unless you're on a cholesterol-restricted diet, you should be able to include chicken livers in your meal plan occasionally. They are a valuable source of vitamin A and iron and contain only 141 calories per 3-ounce serving.

Try Cornish hens if you're in need of a special entrée for company. Season the hens with wine, orange juice, or herbs before roasting. You can count on two servings for each 1½-pound hen. Just slice the hen with a sharp carving knife or electric knife after cooking.

Another type of poultry that's ideal for light cooking is turkey, especially turkey breast. The white meat of a turkey contains only 50 calories per ounce of cooked meat and is good by itself, in casseroles and salads, or on sandwiches. Make good use of turkey bones and the bony pieces of chicken by boiling them in water to make broth for soups, stews, and other recipes calling for broth. If you chill the broth, you can easily remove the high-calorie fat that rises to the top.

PARMESAN CHICKEN

4 chicken breast halves (about 2 pounds), skinned and boned
⅓ cup fine, dry breadcrumbs
¼ teaspoon dried whole basil
⅛ teaspoon pepper
1 egg, slightly beaten
Vegetable cooking spray
1 (8-ounce) can tomato sauce
¼ teaspoon garlic powder
¼ teaspoon dried whole basil
¼ cup grated Parmesan cheese
¼ cup (1 ounce) shredded mozzarella cheese

Place each chicken breast between 2 sheets of waxed paper; flatten to ¼-inch thickness using a meat mallet or rolling pin.

Combine breadcrumbs, ¼ teaspoon basil, and pepper. Dip chicken pieces in egg; dredge in breadcrumb mixture.

Coat a large nonstick skillet with cooking spray; place over medium-high heat until hot. Place chicken breasts in skillet, and cook until lightly browned on both sides. Remove from skillet, and arrange chicken breasts in a 12- x 8- x 2- inch baking dish.

Combine tomato sauce, garlic powder, and ¼ teaspoon basil; pour over chicken. Sprinkle with Parmesan cheese. Cover and bake at 350° for 30 minutes. Uncover and sprinkle with mozzarella cheese; bake an additional 5 minutes. Yield: 4 servings (about 298 calories per serving).

HERB-BAKED CHICKEN

1 teaspoon dried whole rosemary, crushed
¼ teaspoon pepper
1 (3-pound) broiler-fryer, cut up and skinned
½ cup unsweetened pineapple juice
¼ teaspoon ground ginger
5 shallots, minced
Paprika

Rub rosemary and pepper into the chicken; arrange, meaty side up, in a 9-inch baking dish. Combine pineapple juice and ginger; pour over chicken. Sprinkle with shallots and paprika.

Cover and bake at 350° for 30 minutes; remove cover, and bake 25 to 30 minutes or until done. Yield: 6 servings (about 145 calories per serving).

MARSALA-BAKED CHICKEN

¼ cup fine, dry breadcrumbs
¼ cup grated Parmesan cheese
2 tablespoons minced fresh parsley
¼ teaspoon paprika
8 chicken thighs (about 2½ pounds), skinned
Vegetable cooking spray
2 tablespoons reduced-calorie margarine
⅓ cup Marsala wine

Combine first 4 ingredients, stirring well; dredge chicken in breadcrumb mixture.

Arrange chicken in a shallow baking pan coated with cooking spray. Dot with margarine; cover and bake at 350° for 30 minutes. Pour wine over chicken. Cover and bake 15 minutes; uncover and bake 15 minutes. Yield: 8 servings (about 151 calories per serving).

WINE-BAKED CHICKEN BREASTS

8 chicken breast halves (about 4 pounds), skinned
1 pound fresh mushrooms, halved
1 cup Chablis or other dry white wine
⅓ cup chopped fresh parsley
1 teaspoon dried whole tarragon
½ teaspoon salt
½ teaspoon freshly ground pepper

Arrange chicken breasts, bone side down, in a 13- x 9- x 2-inch baking dish. Arrange mushrooms around chicken. Pour wine over chicken; sprinkle with parsley, tarragon, salt, and pepper. Cover and bake at 350° for 50 to 60 minutes or until done. Yield: 8 servings (about 154 calories per serving).

CHICKEN IN ORANGE SAUCE

2 chicken breast halves (about 1 pound), skinned
1 small onion, sliced and separated into rings
⅔ cup unsweetened orange juice
2 tablespoons dry sherry
1 tablespoon minced fresh parsley
½ tablespoon all-purpose flour
¾ teaspoon grated orange rind
Paprika
Orange slices

Place chicken in a shallow 1-quart casserole; arrange onion slices over each piece. Combine next 5 ingredients in a small saucepan; bring to a boil, stirring constantly.

Pour sauce over chicken; cover and bake at 350° for 30 minutes. Uncover and bake an additional 25 to 30 minutes or until chicken is tender, basting occasionally with sauce. Sprinkle with paprika, and garnish with orange slices. Yield: 2 servings (about 207 calories per serving).

CHICKEN TERIYAKI

6 chicken breast halves (about 3 pounds), skinned
1 cup dry white wine
½ cup water
⅓ cup soy sauce
½ teaspoon garlic powder
½ teaspoon ground ginger
Vegetable cooking spray

Place chicken in a large, shallow dish. Combine next 5 ingredients; pour over chicken. Cover and marinate in refrigerator overnight.

Coat a broiler rack with cooking spray. Remove chicken from marinade; place on rack. Broil 8 to 10 inches from heat for 10 to 15 minutes on each side, basting occasionally with marinade. Yield: 6 servings (about 183 calories per serving).

OVEN-BARBECUED CHICKEN

1 (3-pound) broiler-fryer, cut into serving-size pieces and skinned
½ cup water
½ cup reduced-calorie chili sauce
⅓ cup vinegar
1 tablespoon Worcestershire sauce
2 teaspoons onion powder
½ teaspoon salt
½ teaspoon pepper
¼ teaspoon garlic powder
¼ teaspoon dry mustard
Vegetable cooking spray

Place chicken in a shallow 2-quart baking dish; set aside.

Combine next 9 ingredients in a small saucepan; bring to a boil. Pour chili sauce mixture over chicken; cover and refrigerate at least 4 hours, turning chicken occasionally.

Coat a broiler pan and rack with cooking spray; place chicken on rack. Broil 7 inches from heat for 20 to 30 minutes or until done, turning once and basting often with marinade. Yield: 6 servings (about 151 calories per serving).

MARINATED BARBECUED CHICKEN

1 (3-pound) broiler-fryer, quartered and skinned
1 (8-ounce) can tomato sauce
½ cup Italian reduced-calorie salad dressing
½ cup unsweetened orange juice
1 teaspoon dried whole oregano
¼ teaspoon salt
¼ teaspoon pepper
1 clove garlic, crushed

Place chicken in a shallow pan. Combine remaining ingredients; pour over chicken. Cover; marinate 8 hours or overnight in the refrigerator, turning occasionally.

Remove chicken from marinade, reserving marinade. Place chicken, bone side down, on grill over medium-hot coals. Grill 1 hour to 1 hour and 15 minutes or until desired degree of doneness, turning chicken and basting with marinade about every 15 minutes. Yield: 4 servings (about 255 calories per serving).

MARINATED SESAME CHICKEN

8 chicken thighs (about 2½ pounds), skinned
½ cup Russian reduced-calorie salad dressing
¼ cup soy sauce
2 tablespoons instant minced onion
1 tablespoon sesame seeds
2 tablespoons water
½ teaspoon ground ginger
¼ teaspoon instant minced garlic
⅛ teaspoon red pepper
Vegetable cooking spray

Place chicken in a large, shallow baking dish. Combine next 8 ingredients; pour over chicken, turning chicken to coat well. Cover and refrigerate at least 12 hours, turning occasionally.

Remove chicken from marinade, and arrange on grill coated with cooking spray. Grill over slow coals 45 to 50 minutes or until chicken is tender, turning and basting with marinade every 15 minutes. Yield: 8 servings (about 149 calories per serving).

Note: Chicken thighs may be cooked on a broiler rack coated with cooking spray. Broil 8 inches from heat for 10 minutes on each side or until tender, turning and basting with marinade occasionally.

SESAME CHICKEN KABOBS

4 chicken breast halves (about 2 pounds), skinned
¼ cup soy sauce
¼ cup Russian reduced-calorie salad dressing
1 tablespoon sesame seeds
2 tablespoons lemon juice
¼ teaspoon garlic powder
¼ teaspoon ground ginger
1 large green pepper, cut into 1-inch pieces
2 medium onions, cut into eighths
3 small zucchini, cut into ¾-inch pieces
1 pint cherry tomatoes
Vegetable cooking spray

Cut chicken breasts into 1-inch pieces; place chicken in a shallow container, and set aside.

Combine next 6 ingredients in a jar; cover tightly, and shake vigorously. Pour over chicken; cover and marinate in the refrigerator 2 hours.

Remove chicken from marinade, reserving marinade. Alternate chicken and vegetables on skewers. Coat grill with cooking spray. Grill kabobs about 6 inches from medium-hot coals for 15 to 20 minutes or until done, turning and basting often with marinade. Yield: 6 servings (about 190 calories per serving).

When eating a meal or snack, concentrate on eating. Make it a rule to eat only at the kitchen or dining room table instead of while doing other things around the house.

OVEN-FRIED SESAME CHICKEN

3 tablespoons sesame seeds
2 tablespoons all-purpose flour
¼ teaspoon pepper
4 chicken breast halves (about 2 pounds), skinned
2 tablespoons soy sauce
2 tablespoons reduced-calorie margarine, melted

Combine sesame seeds, flour, and pepper. Dip chicken pieces into soy sauce; dredge in sesame seed mixture.

Arrange chicken, bone side down, in a large, shallow baking dish; drizzle margarine over chicken. Bake at 400° for 40 to 45 minutes or until chicken is tender. Yield: 4 servings (about 221 calories per serving).

PARMESAN OVEN-FRIED CHICKEN

½ cup fine, dry breadcrumbs
⅓ cup grated Parmesan cheese
2 tablespoons chopped fresh parsley
¼ teaspoon garlic salt
¼ teaspoon pepper
6 chicken breast halves (about 3 pounds), skinned
¼ cup Italian reduced-calorie salad dressing
Vegetable cooking spray

Combine first 5 ingredients; set aside.

Dip chicken in salad dressing; dredge in breadcrumb mixture. Place chicken, bone side down, in a 13- x 9- x 2-inch baking pan coated with cooking spray. Bake, uncovered, at 350° for 45 minutes or until tender. Yield: 6 servings (about 232 calories per serving).

MEXICAN OVEN-FRIED CHICKEN

1 (3-pound) broiler-fryer, cut into serving-size pieces, and skinned
1½ cups Bloody Mary mix
½ cup crushed corn flakes cereal
½ teaspoon dried whole oregano
½ teaspoon ground cumin
½ teaspoon chili powder
½ teaspoon paprika
¼ teaspoon onion salt
⅛ teaspoon garlic powder
Vegetable cooking spray

Combine chicken and Bloody Mary mix in a large bowl; cover chicken and refrigerate 6 hours or overnight.

Combine next 7 ingredients. Drain chicken, and dredge in cereal mixture. Arrange chicken pieces in a jellyroll pan coated with cooking spray. Bake at 350° for 50 to 60 minutes or until done. Yield: 6 servings (about 178 calories per serving).

CHICKEN DIJON

4 chicken breast halves (about 2 pounds), skinned and boned
Vegetable cooking spray
½ cup chicken broth
¼ cup Chablis or other dry white wine
2 cups sliced fresh mushrooms
2 tablespoons chopped fresh parsley
2 tablespoons minced onion
⅛ teaspoon pepper
2 tablespoons chopped fresh parsley
1 tablespoon Dijon mustard

Place each piece of chicken between 2 sheets of waxed paper, and flatten to ¼-inch thickness using a meat mallet or rolling pin.

Coat a large nonstick skillet with cooking spray; place over medium-high heat until hot. Add chicken to skillet; cook 2 to 3 minutes on each side or until lightly browned. Remove from skillet, and set aside.

Combine chicken broth, wine, mushrooms, 2 tablespoons parsley, onion, and pepper in a skillet; cook over medium heat 1 minute. Return chicken to skillet; cover and cook 10 minutes.

Remove chicken and vegetables to a serving platter using a slotted spoon; keep warm. Cook broth mixture over medium-high heat until sauce is reduced to about ⅓ cup. Remove from heat; stir in parsley and mustard with a wire whisk. Spoon sauce over chicken. Serve warm. Yield: 4 servings (about 192 calories per serving).

CHICKEN PAPRIKA

Vegetable cooking spray
1 large onion, minced
1 medium-size green pepper, cut into thin strips
1 cup sliced fresh mushrooms
1 cup water
2 tablespoons paprika
2 tablespoons lemon juice
½ teaspoon salt (optional)
¼ teaspoon freshly ground pepper
4 chicken breast halves (about 2 pounds), skinned
1 tablespoon reduced-calorie margarine
1 tablespoon all-purpose flour
1 (8-ounce) carton plain low-fat yogurt

Coat a large skillet with cooking spray; place over medium heat until hot. Add onion, green pepper, and mushrooms to skillet; sauté until tender. Stir in water, paprika, lemon juice, salt, if desired, and pepper. Add chicken; cover and simmer 30 minutes or until chicken is tender. Remove chicken and vegetables to a serving platter using a slotted spoon; keep warm.

Combine margarine and flour; blend well, making a paste. Add to sauce mixture in skillet, stirring with a wire whisk until smooth. Cook over medium heat, stirring constantly, until thickened and bubbly.

Stir in yogurt; cook 1 minute or until thoroughly heated (do not boil). Pour over chicken and vegetables. Yield: 4 servings (about 242 calories per serving).

FRUITED BARBECUED CHICKEN

1 (8-ounce) can tomato sauce
1 (8-ounce) can unsweetened crushed pineapple, drained
1 tablespoon brown sugar
2 tablespoons vinegar
1 teaspoon instant minced onion
1 teaspoon paprika
1 teaspoon Worcestershire sauce
⅛ teaspoon garlic powder
Dash of pepper
1 (3-pound) chicken, cut into serving-size pieces, and skinned
1 tablespoon water
2 teaspoons cornstarch
1 (11-ounce) can mandarin oranges, drained

Combine first 9 ingredients in a large skillet; add chicken pieces. Bring to a boil; cover, reduce heat, and simmer 40 minutes or until chicken is tender, basting chicken occasionally.

Remove chicken to serving platter. Combine water and cornstarch, stirring until blended; stir into sauce in skillet. Add mandarin oranges; cook, stirring constantly, until mixture thickens. Pour sauce over chicken. Yield: 6 servings (about 182 calories per serving).

Remove the skin from chicken before, not after, cooking. Otherwise, fat from the skin is absorbed by the meat.

CHICKEN IN WHITE WINE

2 chicken breast halves (about 1 pound) skinned and boned
¼ teaspoon ground nutmeg
⅛ teaspoon salt
Vegetable cooking spray
⅔ cup Chablis or other dry white wine
¼ pound fresh mushrooms, quartered
2 tablespoons minced onion
1 teaspoon cornstarch
2 teaspoons Chablis or other dry white wine
1 cup hot cooked rice

Sprinkle chicken with nutmeg and salt.

Coat a heavy skillet with cooking spray; place over medium heat until hot. Place chicken in skillet, and cook until browned on both sides. Add ⅔ cup wine, mushrooms, and onion. Bring to a boil; cover, reduce heat, and simmer 15 minutes. Remove chicken, and keep warm.

Combine cornstarch and 2 teaspoons wine; stir into mushroom mixture in skillet. Cook, stirring constantly, until thickened and bubbly.

Serve chicken and wine sauce over hot cooked rice. Yield: 2 servings (about 209 calories per serving plus 90 calories per ½ cup cooked rice).

SPICED CHICKEN IN WINE

4 chicken breast halves (about 2 pounds), skinned
½ lemon
½ teaspoon ground ginger
¼ teaspoon ground allspice
¼ teaspoon ground cinnamon
¼ teaspoon salt
⅛ teaspoon pepper
Vegetable cooking spray
2 small onions, sliced
2 cloves garlic, minced
½ cup Chablis or other dry white wine
½ cup water

Rub chicken pieces with cut side of lemon half; reserve lemon. Combine next 5 ingredients; sprinkle over chicken, and rub in gently.

Coat a large heavy skillet with cooking spray; place over medium heat until hot. Place chicken, bone side down, in skillet; squeeze reserved lemon half over chicken. Cook over medium heat 15 minutes, turning once. Remove chicken from skillet, and set aside.

Add onion and garlic to skillet; sauté 5 minutes or until onion is tender. Return chicken to skillet; stir in wine and water. Cover and cook over low heat 30 minutes or until chicken is tender, basting with wine mixture. Spoon onion slices and wine sauce over chicken before serving. Yield: 4 servings (about 189 calories per serving).

CHICKEN-VEGETABLE CRÊPES

6 chicken breast halves (about 3 pounds), skinned and boned
½ teaspoon garlic powder
1 tablespoon soy sauce
1 teaspoon cornstarch
½ teaspoon salt
¼ teaspoon pepper
Vegetable cooking spray
1 tablespoon vegetable oil
1 large green pepper, coarsely chopped
1 cup diagonally sliced celery
4 scallions, sliced
1 (6-ounce) package frozen Chinese pea pods, thawed and drained
1 tablespoon soy sauce
2 tablespoons plus 2 teaspoons cornstarch
¾ cup water
⅛ teaspoon ground ginger
¾ teaspoon chicken-flavored bouillon granules
2 medium tomatoes, peeled and coarsely chopped
12 crêpes (recipe follows)
Mushroom Sauce

Cut chicken breasts into ¾-inch pieces.

Combine garlic powder, soy sauce, cornstarch, salt, pepper, and chicken; mix well, and let stand 20 minutes at room temperature.

Coat wok with cooking spray; add oil. Allow to heat at medium-high (325°) for 2 minutes. Add green pepper, and stir-fry 2 minutes. Add celery, scallions, and pea pods; stir-fry 2 minutes. Remove vegetables from wok, and set aside.

Combine 1 tablespoon soy sauce and 2 tablespoons plus 2 teaspoons cornstarch; stir in water, ginger, and bouillon granules. Set mixture aside.

Add chicken to wok, and stir-fry 3 minutes; add stir-fried vegetables, tomatoes, and bouillon mixture. Stir-fry over low heat (225°) 3 minutes or until thickened and bubbly.

Spoon ½ cup chicken mixture in center of each crêpe; roll up. Spoon Mushroom Sauce evenly over crêpes, and serve immediately. Yield: 6 servings (about 309 calories per serving).

CRÊPES:

3 eggs
1½ cups skim milk
1⅓ cups all-purpose flour
½ teaspoon salt
2 teaspoons vegetable oil
Vegetable cooking spray

Combine first 5 ingredients in container of an electric blender; process 30 seconds. Scrape down sides of blender container with rubber spatula; process an additional 30 seconds or until smooth. Refrigerate batter 1 hour. (This allows flour particles to swell and soften so crêpes are light in texture.)

Coat the bottom of a 10-inch crêpe pan or nonstick skillet with cooking spray; place pan over medium heat until just hot, not smoking.

Pour about 3 tablespoons batter into pan. Quickly tilt pan in all directions so batter covers pan in a thin film; cook about 1 minute.

Lift edge of crêpe to test for doneness. Crêpe is ready for flipping when it can be shaken loose from pan. Flip the crêpe, and cook about 30 seconds on the other side. (This side is rarely more than spotty brown and is the side on which the filling is placed.)

When crêpe is done, place on a towel to cool. Stack between layers of waxed paper to prevent sticking. Repeat until all batter is used, stirring batter occasionally. Yield: 14 (10-inch) crêpes.

MUSHROOM SAUCE:

1 cup sliced fresh mushrooms
Vegetable cooking spray
1 tablespoon cornstarch
1 teaspoon chicken-flavored bouillon granules
1 cup water

Sauté mushrooms until tender in a small skillet coated with cooking spray; remove mushrooms from skillet, and set aside. Combine cornstarch, bouillon granules, and water in a small saucepan. Bring to a boil, and cook 1 minute, stirring constantly. Stir in sautéed mushrooms. Yield: 1⅓ cups.

Note: Filled crêpes may be heated if necessary. Place in a shallow baking dish; cover with foil, and bake at 375° for 10 to 12 minutes or until thoroughly heated.

CHICKEN AND ENGLISH PEA BAKE

1 tablespoon reduced-calorie margarine, melted
2 teaspoons soy sauce
1½ teaspoons paprika
½ teaspoon dried whole rosemary, crushed
4 chicken thighs (about 1¼ pounds), skinned
¼ pound fresh mushrooms, sliced
½ cup chicken broth
1 (10-ounce) package frozen English peas, thawed and drained

Combine first 4 ingredients in a shallow 2-quart casserole. Place chicken thighs in casserole, turning to coat.

Add mushrooms; pour broth around chicken. Cover and bake at 350° for 50 minutes. Add peas; cover and bake an additional 10 minutes or until peas are tender. Yield: 4 servings (about 179 calories per serving).

CHICKEN DIVAN

2 (10-ounce) packages frozen broccoli spears
4 chicken breast halves (about 2 pounds), skinned
¼ teaspoon dried whole rosemary, crushed
¼ teaspoon salt
¼ teaspoon pepper
1 cup water
2 tablespoons reduced-calorie margarine
2 tablespoons all-purpose flour
1 cup skim milk
1 egg yolk, beaten
½ teaspoon grated lemon rind
1 tablespoon lemon juice
⅛ teaspoon white pepper
2 tablespoons reduced-calorie mayonnaise
Vegetable cooking spray
2 tablespoons grated Parmesan cheese

Cook broccoli according to package directions, omitting salt. Drain and set aside.

Place chicken, rosemary, salt, pepper, and water in a saucepan; bring to a boil. Cover, reduce heat, and simmer 15 to 20 minutes or until chicken is tender. Drain, reserving ½ cup broth. Bone and chop chicken; set aside.

Melt margarine in a small saucepan over low heat; add flour, stirring until smooth (mixture will be dry). Cook 1 minute, stirring constantly. Gradually stir in milk and reserved chicken broth; cook over medium heat, stirring constantly with a wire whisk, until thickened and bubbly.

Combine egg yolk, lemon rind, lemon juice, and pepper in a small bowl. Gradually stir mixture into egg yolk mixture; stir egg yolk mixture into saucepan. Cook 1 minute, stirring constantly. Add mayonnaise, mixing well.

Coat a shallow 2-quart casserole with cooking spray; layer half of the broccoli, chicken, and sauce in casserole. Repeat layers; sprinkle with cheese. Bake at 350° for 30 minutes. Yield: 6 servings (about 212 calories per serving).

CHICKEN-SHRIMP JAMBALAYA

Vegetable cooking spray
2 medium onions, chopped
2 cloves garlic, minced
2 stalks celery, chopped
1 large green pepper, chopped
⅔ cup uncooked regular rice
2 cups chicken broth
1 cup chopped cooked chicken
1 (16-ounce) can stewed tomatoes
1 (4¼-ounce) can shrimp, rinsed and drained
½ teaspoon hot sauce
¼ teaspoon pepper

Coat a large skillet with cooking spray; place over medium heat until hot. Add onion, garlic, celery, and green pepper; sauté until tender.

Stir in remaining ingredients. Bring to a boil; cover, reduce heat, and simmer 25 minutes or until rice is done, stirring occasionally. Yield: 4 servings (about 266 calories per serving).

CREAMED CHICKEN

3 small chicken breast halves (about 1¼ pounds), skinned
Vegetable cooking spray
1 teaspoon margarine
½ cup sliced fresh mushrooms
¼ cup chopped green pepper
1 tablespoon chopped celery
1 tablespoon minced onion
1 tablespoon margarine
2 tablespoons all-purpose flour
1 cup skim milk
1 hard-cooked egg, thinly sliced
2 tablespoons diced pimiento
½ teaspoon salt
⅛ teaspoon pepper
3 English muffins, split and toasted
Paprika

Cook chicken in unsalted boiling water 30 minutes; drain. Remove chicken from bone; coarsely chop, and set aside.

Coat a medium skillet with cooking spray; add 1 teaspoon margarine. Sauté mushrooms, green pepper, celery, and onion over low heat until vegetables are tender but not brown. Remove vegetables from skillet; drain and set aside.

Melt 1 tablespoon margarine in skillet over low heat; add flour, stirring until smooth (mixture will be dry). Cook 1 minute, stirring constantly. Gradually add milk; cook over medium heat, stirring constantly with a wire whisk, until thickened and bubbly. Add chicken, sautéed vegetables, egg, pimiento, salt, and pepper; stir gently.

Spoon chicken mixture over English muffins; sprinkle with paprika. Yield: 6 servings (about 197 calories per serving).

CHICKEN AND SPINACH NOODLES

4 chicken breast halves (about 2 pounds), skinned
Water
2 teaspoons salt
8 ounces spinach noodles
¾ cup cooked English peas
1 (2½-ounce) jar sliced mushrooms, drained
1 (4-ounce) jar sliced pimiento, drained
2 egg yolks
1 cup skim milk
½ cup freshly grated Parmesan cheese
Freshly ground pepper

Place chicken and 1 cup water in saucepan; cover and cook until tender. Drain and remove chicken from bone; cut chicken into strips, and set aside.

Bring 3 quarts water and salt to a boil in a large Dutch oven. Gradually stir in noodles; return water to a boil. Boil 14 to 15 minutes; drain and return to Dutch oven. Add chicken, peas, mushrooms, and pimiento.

Beat egg yolks and milk with a fork until foamy; gradually add to noodles in Dutch oven, stirring well. Add Parmesan cheese and pepper; cook over medium-high heat, stirring gently, until mixture thickens. Yield: 8 servings (about 267 calories per serving).

CHICKEN CACCIATORE

2 (16-ounce) cans whole tomatoes, undrained and chopped
1 (8-ounce) can tomato sauce
1 (4-ounce) can mushroom stems and pieces, drained
½ cup chopped onion
3 cloves garlic, minced
¼ cup chopped green pepper
¼ cup chopped celery
2 bay leaves
1 tablespoon Worcestershire sauce
2 teaspoons dried whole oregano
½ teaspoon pepper
2 pounds boneless chicken breast halves, skinned
4 cups hot cooked vermicelli

Combine all ingredients except chicken and vermicelli in a small Dutch oven; bring to a boil. Add chicken; cover, reduce heat, and simmer 30 minutes. Uncover and simmer an additional 30 minutes. Discard bay leaves; serve chicken and sauce over vermicelli. Yield: 8 servings (about 159 calories per serving plus 90 calories per ½ cup cooked vermicelli).

HOT CHICKEN SALAD

2 cups cubed cooked chicken or turkey breast
1 cup chopped celery
1 cup chopped green pepper
⅔ cup sliced green onions
⅓ cup shredded sharp Cheddar cheese
1 (4-ounce) jar diced pimiento, drained
⅓ cup reduced-calorie mayonnaise
1 tablespoon lemon juice
1 teaspoon Worcestershire sauce
¼ teaspoon hot sauce
Vegetable cooking spray
3 tablespoons fine, dry breadcrumbs
1 tablespoon reduced-calorie margarine, melted

Combine first 6 ingredients in a large bowl; toss. Combine mayonnaise, lemon juice, Worcestershire sauce, and hot sauce; add to chicken mixture, mixing well. Spoon mixture into a 1½-quart casserole coated with cooking spray.

Combine breadcrumbs and margarine; sprinkle evenly over chicken mixture. Bake at 350° for 20 to 25 minutes or until thoroughly heated. Yield: 4 servings (about 261 calories per serving).

CHICKEN-GARDEN SKILLET

6 chicken breast halves (about 3 pounds), skinned and boned
Vegetable cooking spray
¼ cup chicken broth
¼ cup Chablis or other dry white wine
1 (9-ounce) package frozen artichoke hearts, thawed
1 medium onion, sliced
1 medium-size green pepper, sliced
½ teaspoon dried whole tarragon
¼ teaspoon white pepper
2 teaspoons cornstarch
1 tablespoon cold water
2 medium tomatoes, cut into wedges

Cut chicken into 1-inch pieces. Coat a nonstick skillet with cooking spray; place over medium-high heat until hot. Add chicken to skillet; sauté until lightly browned.

Add next 7 ingredients, stirring well; bring to a boil. Cover, reduce heat, and simmer 5 to 7 minutes or until chicken is done and vegetables are just tender.

Combine cornstarch and water. Stir cornstarch mixture and tomatoes into chicken mixture. Cook, stirring constantly, until mixture is thickened. Yield: 6 servings (about 203 calories per serving).

CHICKEN AND VEGETABLE STIR-FRY

2 pounds boneless chicken breasts, skinned
1 teaspoon paprika
¼ teaspoon salt
¼ teaspoon pepper
⅛ teaspoon garlic powder
Vegetable cooking spray
1 large onion, thinly sliced
1½ large green peppers, cut into thin strips
½ cup diagonally sliced carrots
½ cup diagonally sliced celery
1¼ cups chicken broth, divided
2 tablespoons cornstarch
3 tablespoons soy sauce
2 large tomatoes, cut into wedges
4 cups hot cooked rice

Cut chicken into thin strips; sprinkle with paprika, salt, pepper, and garlic powder.

Coat a wok or large skillet with cooking spray; allow to heat at medium-high (325°) for 2 minutes. Add chicken, and stir-fry 3 to 4 minutes or until lightly browned. Add onion, green pepper, carrots, celery, and ½ cup chicken broth; cover and cook 1½ minutes.

Combine remaining ¾ cup chicken broth, cornstarch, and soy sauce, stirring until blended; mix well. Add broth mixture to wok or skillet, stirring well. Add tomatoes; cook 2 to 3 minutes or until sauce thickens. Serve over rice. Yield: 8 servings (about 159 calories per serving plus 90 calories per ½ cup cooked rice).

CHICKEN LIVER SAUTÉ

3 tablespoons reduced-calorie margarine
1 pound chicken livers
½ pound fresh mushrooms, sliced
1 medium onion, chopped
2 cloves garlic, crushed
1 tablespoon all-purpose flour
1 (14½-ounce) can whole tomatoes, drained and coarsely chopped
½ cup dry vermouth
¼ cup minced fresh parsley
½ teaspoon dried whole rosemary, crushed
½ teaspoon dried whole thyme
¼ teaspoon salt
2 cups hot cooked rice or vermicelli

Melt margarine in a large skillet over medium-high heat; add chicken livers, and sauté 5 minutes or until browned. Remove chicken livers, and set aside.

Add mushrooms, onion, and garlic to skillet; sauté 4 to 5 minutes or until onion is tender. Stir in flour; cook 1 minute over low heat, stirring constantly. Stir in next 6 ingredients. Bring to a boil; reduce heat, and simmer 5 minutes.

Stir in livers; simmer an additional 5 minutes, stirring occasionally. Serve over rice. Yield: 4 servings (about 235 calories per serving plus about 90 calories per ½ cup cooked rice).

TURKEY À LA KING

3 tablespoons reduced-calorie margarine
½ cup chopped onion
½ cup chopped green pepper
2 tablespoons all-purpose flour
1½ cups skim milk
1 teaspoon chicken-flavored bouillon granules
¼ teaspoon white pepper
2 cups chopped cooked turkey breast
1 (4-ounce) can sliced mushrooms, drained
1 (2-ounce) jar diced pimiento, drained
2 cups hot cooked rice

Melt margarine in a medium-size heavy saucepan over medium heat; add onion and green pepper, and sauté 5 to 6 minutes or until green pepper is tender. Add flour, stirring until vegetables are coated; cook 1 minute over low heat, stirring constantly.

Gradually add milk, bouillon granules, and pepper; cook over medium heat, stirring constantly, until thickened and bubbly. Stir in turkey, mushrooms, and pimiento; cook until thoroughly heated. Serve over rice. Yield: 4 servings (about 226 calories per serving plus 90 calories per ½ cup cooked rice).

OPEN-FACE TURKEY SANDWICHES

2 cups diced cooked turkey breast
1 (8-ounce) can unsweetened pineapple tidbits, drained
¾ cup diced celery
¾ cup chopped apple
⅓ cup reduced-calorie mayonnaise
¼ teaspoon white pepper
¼ teaspoon curry powder
6 slices whole wheat bread
2 tablespoons reduced-calorie mayonnaise
Lettuce leaves

Combine first 7 ingredients, stirring until well mixed. Cover and refrigerate 2 hours.

Spread each bread slice with 1 teaspoon mayonnaise; top with lettuce. Spoon turkey mixture evenly on each sandwich. Yield: 6 servings (about 236 calories per serving).

HERBED CORNISH HENS

4 (1-pound 6-ounce) Cornish hens
1½ cups light rosé wine
½ teaspoon garlic powder
½ teaspoon onion powder
½ teaspoon celery seeds
½ teaspoon poultry seasoning
½ teaspoon paprika
½ teaspoon dried whole basil
½ teaspoon pepper
½ cup light rosé wine

Remove giblets from hens; reserve for other uses. Rinse hens with cold water, and pat dry. Split each hen lengthwise using an electric knife. Place the hens, cavity side up, on a rack in a shallow roasting pan.

Pour 1½ cups wine over hens in pan. Combine seasonings; sprinkle half of seasoning mixture over cavity of hens. Cover and marinate in refrigerator 2 hours. Bake, uncovered, at 350° for 1 hour. Remove from oven, and turn hens breast side up. Pour ½ cup wine over hens; sprinkle with remaining seasoning mixture. Bake an additional 30 minutes, basting every 10 minutes with wine mixture in pan. Yield: 8 servings (about 157 calories per serving).

CORNISH HENS WITH APPLE GLAZE

4 (1-pound 6-ounce) Cornish hens
1 (12-ounce) can unsweetened apple juice concentrate, thawed and undiluted
3 tablespoons water
1 tablespoon cornstarch
½ teaspoon ground cinnamon
3 lemon slices

Remove giblets from hens; discard or reserve for other uses. Rinse hens with cold water, and pat dry. Split each hen lengthwise using an electric knife. Place hens, cavity side up, on a rack in a shallow roasting pan.

Dilute ½ cup apple juice concentrate with 3 tablespoons water. Set aside remaining juice.

Pour diluted juice over hens in pan. Bake, uncovered, at 350° for 45 minutes. Remove from oven, and turn hens breast side up.

Combine remaining apple juice concentrate, cornstarch, and cinnamon in a small saucepan, mixing well; add lemon slices. Cook over medium heat, stirring constantly, until thickened. Brush hens with sauce. Return to oven, and bake an additional 15 minutes or until done. Yield: 8 servings (about 244 calories per serving).

Serve Cornish Hens with Apple Glaze atop Vegetable Rice (page 112). Add Marinated Vegetable Salad (page 194) and steamed broccoli for a total calorie count around 400 for the meal.

SALADS AND SALAD DRESSINGS

Salads, especially green salads which are high in fiber and bulk, are excellent food choices for dieters. Salads can help to fill you up without adding too many calories. In this chapter you will find a variety of salads which can be served as appetizers or to complement the main course. A hearty salad, such as Chicken-Fruit Salad or Garbanzo Bean Salad, is filling and can be served as the main dish in a meal. Some of our fruit salads are so refreshing and naturally sweet that they can be served as a dessert.

You can create your own salads by using the recipes on the following pages as guides. Try combining two or more low-calorie vegetables such as celery, cucumbers, summer squash, green pepper, mushrooms, broccoli, cauliflower, and bean sprouts. For variety, use different kinds of lettuce, remembering that the darker greens contain more nutrients. For a change, use fresh spinach in your salad instead of lettuce.

While fresh salads are great for dieters, regular salad dressings should be avoided. One tablespoon of most commercial dressings contains about 60 calories—that's approximately the same number of calories as in a whole pound of lettuce. Mayonnaise is even higher, containing about 100 calories per tablespoon.

Instead of adding unwanted calories to your salads with regular salad dressings, try our light versions of Miracle French Dressing, Celery Seed Dressing, and Seasoned Buttermilk Dressing. These are made with tomato juice, unsweetened fruit juice, and reduced-calorie mayonnaise instead of oil. At only 5 to 23 calories per tablespoon, they're delightful alternatives to the higher-calorie regular commercial salad dressings.

Keep calories low in fresh vegetable and fruit salads without giving up flavor. Toss the salad with one of these light salad dressings. Clockwise from back: Miracle French Dressing (page 197), Zesty Italian Dressing (page 198), Seasoned Buttermilk Dressing (page 196), Tangy Fruit Dressing (page 197), and Celery Seed Dressing (page 197).

FRESH CHERRY SALAD

2 cups fresh cherries, pitted
2 cups cantaloupe balls
2 nectarines, cut into wedges
Lettuce leaves
Lime Dressing

Combine cherries, cantaloupe balls, and nectarines; place in a lettuce-lined bowl. Serve with Lime Dressing. Yield: 8 servings (about 63 calories per serving plus 35 calories per tablespoon dressing).

LIME DRESSING:

½ cup reduced-calorie mayonnaise
½ teaspoon grated lime rind
2 tablespoons lime juice
1 tablespoon honey

Combine all ingredients, mixing well. Cover and chill. Yield: ⅔ cup.

GRAPE SALAD MOLD

1 envelope unflavored gelatin
2 cups unsweetened white grape juice, divided
1½ cups green grapes, halved
Vegetable cooking spray
Lettuce leaves

Soften gelatin in 1 cup grape juice; let stand 10 minutes. Bring remaining grape juice to a boil; add gelatin, stirring until dissolved. Chill until consistency of unbeaten egg white. Stir in grapes.

Coat five ½-cup molds with cooking spray; pour gelatin mixture into molds. Chill until firm. Unmold on lettuce leaves. Yield: 5 servings (about 105 calories per serving).

MAIN DISH FRUIT SALAD

½ cup reduced-calorie mayonnaise
1 tablespoon lemon juice
2 teaspoons sugar
2 medium bananas, sliced
1½ cups cantaloupe balls
1 medium peach, peeled and cubed
1 cup cubed fresh pineapple
1 cup seedless green grapes
1 cup fresh strawberries, halved
1½ cups watermelon balls
Lettuce leaves
3 cups low-fat cottage cheese
6 fresh strawberries

Combine mayonnaise, lemon juice, and sugar; stir well, and set aside.

Combine next 7 ingredients; toss gently. Spoon fruit into 6 individual lettuce-lined serving dishes, and top each with ½ cup cottage cheese. Slice 6 strawberries lengthwise, keeping stem end intact; place atop each salad. Serve with mayonnaise dressing. Yield: 6 servings (about 178 calories per serving plus 40 calories per tablespoon dressing).

SPECIAL WALDORF SALAD

1 cup unpeeled, chopped yellow Delicious apple
1 cup unpeeled, chopped red Delicious apple
1 to 2 tablespoons lemon juice
1 cup chopped celery
1 (8-ounce) can unsweetened pineapple tidbits, drained
¼ cup reduced-calorie mayonnaise
3 tablespoons raisins
Lettuce leaves

Toss apple in lemon juice; add remaining ingredients except lettuce, and mix well. Cover and chill at least 1 hour. Serve on lettuce leaves. Yield: 6 servings (about 80 calories per serving).

MINTY COTTAGE CHEESE SALAD

1 (12-ounce) carton low-fat cottage cheese
1 teaspoon sugar
1 teaspoon finely chopped fresh mint
2 cups diced fresh pineapple
Lettuce leaves
1 medium orange, peeled and sectioned
Fresh mint sprigs

Combine cottage cheese, sugar, and chopped mint; cover and chill at least 2 hours.

Just before serving, add pineapple to cottage cheese mixture; spoon into a lettuce-lined bowl. Top with orange sections, and garnish with fresh mint sprigs. Yield: 4 servings (about 123 calories per serving).

COTTAGE PEAR SALAD

½ cup low-fat cottage cheese
¼ cup reduced-calorie mayonnaise
2 teaspoons honey
1½ teaspoons lemon juice
2 (16-ounce) cans unsweetened pear halves, drained and chilled
Lettuce leaves
Grated lemon rind

Combine cottage cheese, mayonnaise, honey, and lemon juice; chill. Arrange pear halves on lettuce leaves. Fill each pear half with 1 tablespoon dressing. Sprinkle with grated lemon rind before serving. Yield: 5 servings (about 116 calories per serving).

TANGY WILTED LETTUCE SALAD

1 small bunch leaf lettuce, finely shredded (about 4 cups)
½ cup sliced green onions
¼ cup unsweetened pineapple juice
2 tablespoons vinegar
2 teaspoons olive oil
½ teaspoon soy sauce
¼ teaspoon dry mustard
⅛ teaspoon curry powder
⅛ teaspoon pepper

Combine lettuce and green onions in a large bowl. Combine remaining ingredients in a small saucepan; bring to a boil. Pour over lettuce, and toss well. Serve immediately. Yield: 4 servings (about 43 calories per serving).

GREEN GARDEN SALAD

1 (¾-pound) head romaine lettuce
1 (½-pound) head red leaf lettuce
⅓ pound fresh spinach, trimmed
1 (10-ounce) package frozen English peas, thawed
2 large green onions, sliced
1 medium cucumber, sliced
2 stalks celery, thinly sliced
⅓ cup white vinegar
2 tablespoons chopped fresh parsley
2 tablespoons vegetable oil
1 teaspoon sugar
½ teaspoon garlic salt
½ teaspoon dried whole oregano
¼ teaspoon pepper

Place lettuce, spinach, peas, onions, cucumber, and celery in a large bowl; toss. Combine remaining ingredients in a jar; cover tightly, and shake vigorously. Pour over salad; toss lightly. Yield: 8 servings (about 77 calories per serving).

ARTICHOKE-TOMATO SALAD

1 (14-ounce) can artichoke hearts, drained and coarsely chopped
¼ cup finely chopped celery
¼ cup chopped green onions
¼ cup reduced-calorie mayonnaise
¼ teaspoon dried whole marjoram
⅛ teaspoon freshly ground pepper
4 medium tomatoes, sliced
Leaf lettuce
1 tablespoon chopped fresh parsley

Combine first 6 ingredients and toss; chill until serving time.

Arrange tomato slices on lettuce leaves; spoon artichoke mixture evenly over tomatoes. Sprinkle with chopped parsley. Yield: 8 servings (about 52 calories per serving).

TARRAGON ASPARAGUS SALAD

1 pound fresh asparagus
⅓ cup Italian reduced-calorie salad dressing
⅓ cup tarragon vinegar
½ teaspoon dried whole tarragon
½ teaspoon freshly ground pepper
¼ teaspoon garlic powder
Shredded lettuce

Snap off tough ends of asparagus. Remove the scales with a knife or a vegetable peeler, if desired. Cook asparagus, covered, in small amount of boiling water 6 to 8 minutes or until crisp-tender; drain.

Layer asparagus in a shallow dish. Combine next 5 ingredients in a glass jar; cover tightly, and shake vigorously. Pour marinade over asparagus; cover and chill 6 hours or overnight.

Drain and arrange on shredded lettuce. Yield: 4 servings (about 31 calories per serving).

Note: 1 (15-ounce) can asparagus spears, drained, may be substituted for fresh asparagus.

LIGHT ASPARAGUS VINAIGRETTE

2 (10-ounce) packages frozen asparagus spears
½ cup vinegar
½ cup water
2 tablespoons chopped fresh parsley
2 tablespoons chopped fresh chives
2 tablespoons Dijon mustard
½ teaspoon dried whole tarragon
½ pound fresh spinach leaves
2 medium tomatoes, cut into wedges

Cook asparagus according to package directions; drain and place in a shallow container.

Combine next 6 ingredients; pour over asparagus. Chill for 3 to 5 hours.

Place asparagus on spinach leaves; spoon remaining dressing over salad. Garnish with tomato wedges. Yield: 6 servings (about 51 calories per serving).

ASPARAGUS-YOGURT SALAD

1 pound fresh asparagus
½ cup plain low-fat yogurt
1 tablespoon chopped fresh parsley
1 small clove garlic, crushed
¼ teaspoon Worcestershire sauce
1 small head Boston or Bibb lettuce
1 hard-cooked egg yolk, sieved

Snap off tough ends of asparagus. Remove the scales from stalks with a knife or vegetable peeler, if desired.

Cook asparagus, covered, in a small amount of boiling water 6 to 8 minutes or until crisp-tender; drain. Chill asparagus.

Combine yogurt, parsley, garlic, and Worcestershire sauce; cover and chill at least 1 hour.

To serve, arrange asparagus on lettuce leaves; top with yogurt mixture, and sprinkle with egg yolk. Yield: 6 servings (about 38 calories per serving).

3-BEAN SALAD

1 (16-ounce) can green beans, drained
1 (16-ounce) can wax beans, drained
1 (15-ounce) can kidney beans, rinsed and drained
1 medium-size green pepper, sliced
4 green onions, chopped
⅔ cup unsweetened apple juice
⅓ cup cider vinegar
½ teaspoon pepper
¼ teaspoon dry mustard
¼ teaspoon paprika
⅛ teaspoon dried whole oregano

Combine beans, green pepper, and green onions in a large bowl, stirring gently.

Combine apple juice, vinegar, and seasonings in a jar; cover tightly, and shake vigorously. Pour over vegetables, stirring gently. Cover and chill overnight. Yield: 10 servings (about 71 calories per ½-cup serving).

BEAN SPROUT SALAD

6 ounces fresh bean sprouts, washed and drained
½ cup diagonally sliced celery
⅓ cup sliced green onions
1 small green pepper, cut into thin strips
2 tablespoons water
2 tablespoons cider vinegar
1 tablespoon soy sauce
⅛ teaspoon pepper
3 medium tomatoes, coarsely chopped
Lettuce leaves

Combine first 4 ingredients in a medium bowl. Combine water, vinegar, soy sauce, and pepper; pour over vegetables in bowl, and toss lightly. Cover and chill at least 3 hours, stirring occasionally.

Just before serving, add tomatoes; toss. Spoon onto lettuce leaves to serve. Yield: 6 servings (about 41 calories per serving).

GARBANZO BEAN SALAD

½ pound dried garbanzo beans
½ cup chopped celery
½ cup chopped green pepper
¼ cup chopped fresh parsley
½ cup sliced green onions
1 (2-ounce) jar diced pimiento, drained
½ cup Italian reduced-calorie salad dressing
¼ teaspoon freshly ground pepper
Lettuce leaves

Sort and wash beans; place in a Dutch oven. Cover with water 2 inches above beans; let soak overnight. Drain beans; cover with water. Bring to a boil; cover, reduce heat, and simmer 1 hour or until beans are tender. Drain; let cool.

Combine beans and remaining ingredients except lettuce; cover and chill several hours or overnight, stirring occasionally. To serve, spoon onto lettuce leaves using a slotted spoon. Yield: 8 servings (about 120 calories per serving).

FRESH BROCCOLI SALAD

1 (1¼-pound) bunch fresh broccoli
4 green onions, sliced
3 hard-cooked eggs, chopped
2 medium carrots, grated
½ cup reduced-calorie mayonnaise
¼ cup grated Parmesan cheese
1 tablespoon Dijon mustard
1 tablespoon lemon juice
½ teaspoon salad seasoning
½ teaspoon pepper

Trim off large leaves of broccoli. Remove tough ends of lower stalks, and wash broccoli thoroughly; chop coarsely. Add onions, eggs, and carrots to broccoli; toss.

Combine remaining ingredients in a small bowl; pour over broccoli mixture, and toss gently. Cover and refrigerate overnight. Yield: 12 servings (about 75 calories per ⅔-cup serving).

Note: This salad will keep well in refrigerator 3 to 4 days.

COMPANY COLESLAW

1 small cabbage (about 1¾ pounds), coarsely chopped
1 (20-ounce) can unsweetened crushed pineapple, undrained
2 medium apples, diced
1½ cups grated carrot
1 cup chopped celery
¼ cup raisins
¼ cup reduced-calorie mayonnaise

Combine all ingredients in a large bowl; toss. Cover and refrigerate overnight. Toss again before serving. Yield: 11 servings (about 87 calories per 1-cup serving).

ZESTY COLESLAW

5 cups shredded cabbage
½ cup chopped green pepper
½ cup shredded carrot
¼ cup minced dill pickle
¼ cup minced onion
¼ cup reduced-calorie mayonnaise
2 tablespoons Italian reduced-calorie salad dressing
½ teaspoon prepared mustard
Dash of paprika

Combine first 5 ingredients in a large bowl. Combine mayonnaise, salad dressing, mustard, and paprika in a small bowl; add to cabbage mixture, and toss until well mixed. Cover and chill at least 1 hour. Yield: 6 servings (about 56 calories per serving).

HOT CABBAGE SLAW

1 small cabbage, shredded (about 8 cups)
¼ cup cider vinegar
1 teaspoon sugar
½ teaspoon dried whole tarragon
¼ teaspoon salt
⅛ teaspoon dry mustard
2 medium apples, unpeeled and coarsely chopped

Place cabbage in a Dutch oven. Combine next 5 ingredients; pour over cabbage, and toss.

Cover and cook over medium heat, stirring occasionally, 12 to 15 minutes or until cabbage is tender. Remove from heat, and stir in apples. Yield: 8 servings (about 36 calories per serving).

CUCUMBER-YOGURT SALAD

½ cup plain low-fat yogurt
2 tablespoons tarragon vinegar
¼ teaspoon dried whole dillweed
¼ teaspoon ground cardamom
2 medium cucumbers, peeled and diced (about 2 cups)
5 radishes, sliced
Lettuce leaves

Combine first 4 ingredients in a medium bowl, stirring until well blended. Cover and chill at least 1 hour.

Just before serving, add cucumber and radishes to yogurt mixture; toss. Serve on lettuce leaves. Yield: 4 servings (about 35 calories per serving).

DILLED CUCUMBER SALAD

2 medium cucumbers, thinly sliced
1 medium onion, sliced
⅓ cup vinegar
½ teaspoon dried whole dillweed
⅛ teaspoon pepper

Combine cucumbers and onion in a shallow serving dish. Combine remaining ingredients, and pour over cucumbers. Cover and refrigerate at least 1 hour. Yield: 4 servings (about 25 calories per serving).

CUCUMBER-ZUCCHINI CRUNCH

2 large cucumbers, sliced
1 medium zucchini, thinly sliced
1 medium-size green pepper, seeded and sliced into rings
½ cup sliced green onions
½ cup Italian reduced-calorie salad dressing
¼ cup reduced-calorie catsup
2 tablespoons vinegar
Romaine lettuce
2 tablespoons chopped cashews

Combine first 4 ingredients in a shallow dish. Combine salad dressing, catsup, and vinegar; pour over vegetables, and toss. Cover and refrigerate overnight.

To serve, arrange marinated vegetables on lettuce leaves; pour any remaining dressing over salad. Top with cashews. Yield: 6 servings (about 55 calories per serving).

MUSHROOM-ZUCCHINI SALAD

½ pound fresh mushrooms, sliced
1 medium zucchini, thinly sliced
1 medium tomato, chopped
¼ cup sliced green onions
2 tablespoons grated Parmesan cheese
2 tablespoons Italian reduced-calorie salad dressing
2 tablespoons wine vinegar
1 teaspoon dried whole marjoram
½ teaspoon freshly ground pepper

Combine vegetables in a shallow dish. Combine remaining ingredients in a small bowl; stir well. Pour over vegetables, and toss. Cover and chill 4 hours. Yield: 6 servings (about 35 calories per serving).

POTATO SALAD SURPRISE

3 pounds new potatoes
2 hard-cooked eggs, chopped
2 large dill pickles, finely chopped
4 green onions, thinly sliced
½ cup reduced-calorie mayonnaise
½ cup plain low-fat yogurt
¼ cup minced fresh parsley
2 tablespoons prepared mustard
2 teaspoons dill pickle liquid or vinegar
¼ teaspoon freshly ground pepper
Paprika

Cook potatoes in boiling water about 30 minutes or until tender. Drain well, and cool. Peel potatoes, and cut into ½-inch cubes.

Combine potatoes, eggs, pickles, and onions in a large bowl; toss lightly.

Combine mayonnaise, yogurt, parsley, mustard, vinegar, and pepper, blending well; stir into potato mixture. Sprinkle salad with paprika; cover and chill thoroughly. Yield: 12 servings (about 123 calories per ¾-cup serving).

CITRUS SPINACH SALAD

¾ pound fresh spinach leaves, torn
1 cup shredded iceburg lettuce
1 medium orange, sectioned
1 medium grapefruit, sectioned
¼ cup French reduced-calorie salad dressing, chilled
½ teaspoon ground ginger

Combine first 4 ingredients in a salad bowl. Combine salad dressing and ginger. Pour over spinach mixture, and toss. Yield: 6 servings (about 58 calories per serving).

ORIENTAL SPINACH SALAD

1 pound fresh spinach leaves, torn
2 cups shredded Chinese cabbage
½ pound fresh mushrooms, sliced
3 green onions, sliced
2 tablespoons toasted sesame seeds
2 tablespoons vinegar
2 tablespoons vegetable oil
1 tablespoon soy sauce
¼ teaspoon ground ginger

Combine first 5 ingredients in a large salad bowl, and toss lightly. Combine vinegar, oil, soy sauce, and ginger in a jar; cover tightly, and shake vigorously. Pour over salad, and toss; serve immediately. Yield: 8 servings (about 72 calories per serving).

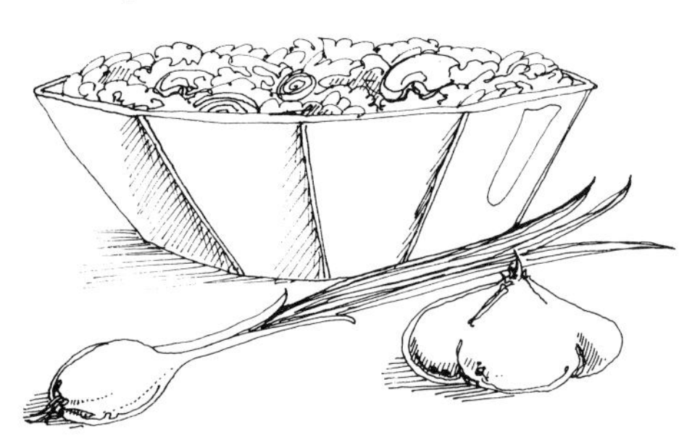

SPINACH-MUSHROOM SALAD

1 pound fresh spinach leaves, torn into bite-size pieces
½ pound fresh mushrooms, sliced
¼ cup red wine vinegar
1 tablespoon soy sauce
2 teaspoons vegetable oil
1 clove garlic, crushed
¼ teaspoon freshly ground pepper

Combine spinach and mushrooms in a salad bowl; set aside.

Combine remaining ingredients in a small saucepan; bring to a boil. Remove from heat, and let cool.

Pour dressing over spinach and mushrooms; toss. Serve immediately. Yield: 6 servings (about 46 calories per serving).

MARINATED TOMATO SLICES

2 large tomatoes, cut into ¼-inch slices
1 tablespoon instant minced onion
2 tablespoons lemon juice
1 tablespoon red wine vinegar
¼ teaspoon dried whole basil
⅛ teaspoon garlic powder
⅛ teaspoon pepper
Lettuce leaves

Arrange tomato slices in a shallow glass baking dish. Combine next 6 ingredients in a small bowl. Spoon marinade evenly over tomatoes. Cover and chill 1 hour or until serving time.

Arrange tomato slices on a bed of lettuce; pour marinade over tomatoes. Yield: 4 servings (about 28 calories per serving).

GAZPACHO SALAD MOLD

1½ tablespoons unflavored gelatin
⅓ cup water
1½ cups tomato juice
4 large tomatoes, peeled, seeded, and finely chopped
1 medium cucumber, peeled, seeded, and finely chopped
1 medium-size green pepper, finely chopped
½ cup finely chopped celery
⅓ cup thinly sliced radishes
2 tablespoons finely chopped green onions
1½ tablespoons red wine vinegar
1 tablespoon lemon juice
⅛ teaspoon hot sauce
Vegetable cooking spray
Lettuce leaves
Parsley Dressing

Soften gelatin in ⅓ cup water, and set aside.

Heat tomato juice in a saucepan to boiling; add gelatin, stirring until dissolved. Stir in next 9 ingredients. Chill 30 to 45 minutes or until the consistency of unbeaten egg white.

Stir vegetable mixture gently, and pour into 8

(10-ounce) custard cups or molds coated with cooking spray. Chill until firm. Unmold onto lettuce leaves, and serve with Parsley Dressing. Yield: 8 servings (about 42 calories per serving plus 22 calories per tablespoon dressing).

PARSLEY DRESSING:

½ cup reduced-calorie mayonnaise
¾ cup plain low-fat yogurt
¾ cup minced fresh parsley

Combine all ingredients, stirring until blended. Chill thoroughly. Yield: 1¼ cups.

TOMATO-VEGETABLE ASPIC

1 envelope unflavored gelatin
2 cups tomato juice, divided
1 tablespoon Worcestershire sauce
½ cup minced celery
¼ cup minced onion
¼ cup minced green pepper
Vegetable cooking spray
Lettuce leaves

Soften gelatin in ½ cup tomato juice. Bring remaining tomato juice to a boil. Remove from heat; add gelatin mixture and Worcestershire sauce, stirring until gelatin dissolves. Chill until consistency of unbeaten egg white.

Fold next 3 ingredients into gelatin mixture. Spoon into 6 individual salad molds coated with cooking spray. Refrigerate until firm. Unmold onto lettuce leaves. Yield: 6 servings (about 26 calories per serving).

PERFECTION SALAD

2 envelopes unflavored gelatin
2⅓ cups apple juice
¼ cup vinegar
½ teaspoon celery seeds
1½ cups finely grated cabbage
2 tablespoons shredded carrot
2 tablespoons finely chopped green pepper
Lettuce leaves

Combine gelatin and apple juice in a small saucepan; let stand 1 minute. Cook over medium heat about 1 minute or until gelatin is completely dissolved. Stir in vinegar and celery seeds. Chill until the consistency of unbeaten egg white. Stir in cabbage, carrot, and green pepper. Pour into 6 individual salad molds. Chill until firm. Unmold onto lettuce leaves to serve. Yield: 6 servings (about 62 calories per serving).

GARDEN FRESH VEGETABLE SALAD

2 large zucchini
2 large yellow squash
1 large cucumber, peeled
2 medium carrots, grated (about 1½ cups)
1 medium-size green pepper, chopped
¼ cup finely chopped onion
1 (2-ounce) jar diced pimiento, drained
½ cup vinegar
¼ cup water
2 tablespoons oil
1 tablespoon Dijon mustard
¼ teaspoon garlic powder
⅛ teaspoon onion powder
⅛ teaspoon red pepper

Cut squash and cucumber in half lengthwise; scoop out seeds. Cut squash and cucumber crosswise into thin slices. Combine squash, cucumber, and next 4 ingredients in a large bowl.

Combine vinegar, water, oil, mustard, and seasonings in a glass jar; cover tightly, and shake vigorously. Pour over vegetables; toss well. Cover and refrigerate overnight, tossing occasionally.

Serve with a slotted spoon. Yield: 10 servings (about 63 calories per ⅔-cup serving).

If you eat at fast-food restaurants for lunch, choose one that has a salad bar. Eat fresh vegetables instead of the higher calorie burgers and fries.

MARINATED VEGETABLE SALAD

4 small yellow squash, sliced
2 small zucchini, sliced
¾ cup water
½ cup white wine vinegar
1½ teaspoons mustard seeds
1 teaspoon celery salt
¼ teaspoon black pepper
Dash of red pepper
1 (6-ounce) package frozen Chinese pea pods, thawed and drained
1 head Bibb lettuce
6 cherry tomatoes

Place sliced squash in a shallow baking dish, and set aside.

Combine water, vinegar, and seasonings in a small saucepan. Bring to a boil; cook 1 minute, stirring constantly. Pour vinegar mixture over squash, tossing gently. Cover and chill.

Just before serving, add snowpeas; toss. Spoon onto lettuce leaves, using a slotted spoon, and garnish with cherry tomatoes. Yield: 6 servings (about 39 calories per serving).

ITALIAN VEGETABLE SALAD

6 medium-size ripe tomatoes, cut into wedges
1 green pepper, cut into thin strips
1 medium onion, sliced and separated into rings
1 cucumber, cut into ¼-inch slices
¾ cup white wine vinegar
¼ cup water
1½ teaspoons mustard seeds
1½ teaspoons celery salt
¼ teaspoon black pepper
Dash of red pepper
Lettuce leaves

Combine vegetables, and set aside.

Combine vinegar, water, and seasonings in a saucepan. Bring to a boil; cook 1 minute, stirring constantly. Pour hot mixture over vegetables, tossing gently.

Cover salad, and chill thoroughly. Serve on lettuce leaves. Yield: 8 servings (about 35 calories per serving).

BROWN RICE AND VEGETABLE SALAD

1 (10-ounce) package frozen English peas
½ cup uncooked brown rice
1 medium zucchini, unpeeled and shredded
2 tablespoons chopped pimiento
¼ teaspoon dried whole basil
1 (1.3 ounce) package Italian reduced-calorie salad dressing mix
Lettuce leaves

Cook peas according to package directions, omitting salt. Drain and set aside.

Cook rice according to package directions, omitting salt. Combine peas, rice, zucchini, pimiento, and basil in a large bowl.

Prepare salad dressing mix according to package directions; pour over rice mixture, and stir gently to combine. Cover and chill thoroughly. To serve, spoon salad onto lettuce leaves using a slotted spoon. Yield: 7 servings (about 92 calories per serving).

TABBOULEH

1 cup bulgur wheat
2 cups boiling water
1 large tomato, unpeeled and chopped
½ cup minced fresh parsley
¼ cup chopped green onions
1 tablespoon minced fresh mint leaves
¼ cup lemon juice
1 tablespoon olive oil
¼ teaspoon salt
¼ teaspoon pepper
Lettuce leaves

Combine bulgur and water; let stand 1 hour. Drain bulgur; add next 4 ingredients, and toss.

Combine lemon juice, oil, salt, and pepper; pour over bulgur mixture, and toss well. Cover and refrigerate overnight. Spoon onto lettuce leaves to serve. Yield: 8 servings (about 101 calories per serving).

CURRIED WILD RICE SALAD

2 cups cooked wild rice
½ cup grated carrot
⅓ cup finely chopped green pepper
¼ cup sliced green onions
6 pitted large black olives, sliced
2 tablespoons raisins
2 tablespoons chopped cashews or peanuts
½ cup reduced-calorie mayonnaise
¼ cup unsweetened crushed pineapple, undrained
1 tablespoon lemon juice
1 teaspoon curry powder
Lettuce leaves (optional)

Combine first 7 ingredients in a bowl. Combine mayonnaise, pineapple, lemon juice, and curry powder; stir into rice mixture. Chill. Spoon onto lettuce leaves, if desired. Yield: 6 servings (about 147 calories per serving).

DELIGHTFUL CHICKEN SALAD

3 cups diced cooked chicken breast
1 cup diced celery
¼ cup minced onion
2 tablespoons lemon juice
½ teaspoon ground coriander
¼ teaspoon salt
⅛ teaspoon pepper
1 (8-ounce) can unsweetened pineapple chunks, drained
1 cup seedless green grapes
⅓ cup reduced-calorie mayonnaise
3 tablespoons slivered almonds, toasted
Lettuce leaves

Combine first 7 ingredients; chill thoroughly. Add pineapple, grapes, mayonnaise, and almonds; toss well. Serve on lettuce leaves. Yield: 6 servings (about 223 calories per serving).

CHICKEN-FRUIT SALAD

6 chicken breast halves, skinned
1½ cups water
1 (15¼-ounce) can unsweetened pineapple chunks, undrained
1 medium apple, unpeeled
1 cup seedless grapes, halved
1¼ cups reduced-calorie mayonnaise
Lettuce leaves

Place chicken and water in a Dutch oven; cover and cook 15 to 20 minutes or until tender. Drain and remove chicken from bone; coarsely chop, and set aside.

Drain pineapple, and reserve juice. Coarsely chop apple; dip in pineapple juice to prevent browning. Combine chicken, pineapple, apple, grapes, and mayonnaise; mix well. Cover and chill 2 hours. Serve on lettuce leaves. Yield: 6 servings (about 237 calories per serving).

CRAB AND RICE SALAD

1 (6-ounce) package frozen crabmeat, thawed, drained, and flaked
2 cups cooked brown rice, chilled
1 medium tomato, chopped
¼ cup chopped green pepper
3 tablespoons chopped fresh parsley
2 tablespoons minced onion
⅓ cup plain low-fat yogurt
1½ tablespoons lemon juice
¼ teaspoon salt
¼ teaspoon pepper
Lettuce leaves
1 medium tomato, cut into wedges

Combine all ingredients except lettuce and tomato wedges. Cover and chill. Serve salad on lettuce leaves; garnish with tomato wedges. Yield: 4 servings (about 177 calories per serving).

TASTY SALMON SALAD

1 (15½-ounce) can red salmon
1 cup diced celery
2 tablespoons chopped dill pickle
1 tablespoon chopped green pepper
1 teaspoon chopped chives
⅓ cup reduced-calorie mayonnaise
2 tablespoons lemon juice
Lettuce leaves
1 medium tomato, cut into wedges

Drain salmon, and remove skin and bones; flake salmon with a fork. Add celery, pickle, green pepper, and chives; mix well. Combine mayonnaise and lemon juice; add to salmon, stirring well. Chill 2 to 3 hours. Serve salad on lettuce leaves; garnish with tomato wedges. Yield: 4 servings (about 262 calories per serving).

TUNA CHEF SALAD

Lettuce leaves
1 (14½-ounce) can asparagus spears, drained and chilled
2 (6½-ounce) cans water-packed tuna, drained and chilled
Curry Dressing
3 hard-cooked eggs, sliced
Paprika

Place lettuce leaves on a serving platter. Arrange asparagus spears on lettuce; top with tuna. Spoon Curry Dressing over tuna. Arrange egg slices on top, and sprinkle lightly with paprika. Yield: 4 servings (about 240 calories per serving).

CURRY DRESSING:

1 (8-ounce) carton plain low-fat yogurt
½ teaspoon curry powder
¼ teaspoon salt
⅛ teaspoon ground ginger
Dash of red pepper

Combine all ingredients; mix well. Chill. Yield: about 1 cup.

TUNA-MACARONI SALAD

½ cup uncooked elbow macaroni
1 (6½-ounce) can water-packed tuna, drained and flaked
1 hard-cooked egg, chopped
¼ cup reduced-calorie mayonnaise
2 tablespoons finely chopped onion
2 tablespoons finely chopped celery
2 tablespoons finely chopped dill pickle
2 tablespoons chopped green pepper
1 tablespoon diced pimiento
2 teaspoons prepared mustard
Lettuce leaves

Cook macaroni according to package directions, omitting salt; drain. Rinse with cold water, and drain well.

Combine macaroni and remaining ingredients except lettuce; cover and refrigerate at least 3 hours. Spoon onto lettuce leaves to serve. Yield: 4 servings (about 181 calories per serving).

BLUE CHEESE DRESSING

1 cup low-fat cottage cheese
½ cup buttermilk
¼ cup crumbled blue cheese
2 tablespoons white wine vinegar
¼ teaspoon salt
⅛ teaspoon pepper

Combine all ingredients in container of an electric blender; process until smooth. Chill thoroughly. Serve over salad greens. Yield: 2 cups (about 14 calories per tablespoon).

SEASONED BUTTERMILK DRESSING

2 cups buttermilk
2 cups reduced-calorie mayonnaise
2½ tablespoons minced fresh parsley
1 teaspoon onion powder
½ teaspoon garlic powder
½ teaspoon white pepper

Combine all ingredients in a medium bowl, stirring until well blended. Cover and refrigerate at least 4 hours. Serve over salad greens. Yield: 4 cups (about 23 calories per tablespoon).

CELERY SEED DRESSING

1 (1¾-ounce) package powdered fruit pectin
1 teaspoon celery seeds
⅛ teaspoon salt
1 cup unsweetened pineapple juice
2 tablespoons lemon juice
2 tablespoons honey

Combine first 3 ingredients in a small bowl. Stir in pineapple juice, lemon juice, and honey, blending well. Cover and refrigerate 2 hours. Serve over fresh fruit salads. Yield: 1⅓ cups (about 16 calories per tablespoon).

CREAMY CUCUMBER SALAD DRESSING

1 medium cucumber, peeled and sliced
1 (12-ounce) carton low-fat cottage cheese
2 tablespoons prepared horseradish
½ teaspoon dried whole dillweed

Combine all ingredients in container of electric blender; process until smooth. Store in an airtight container in refrigerator. Yield: about 2 cups (about 8 calories per tablespoon).

DIET SALAD DRESSING

1 tablespoon all-purpose flour
2 teaspoons sugar
1 teaspoon dry mustard
½ teaspoon salt
Dash of red pepper
¾ cup skim milk
2 egg yolks, beaten
3 tablespoons vinegar

Combine first 5 ingredients in a small saucepan; gradually stir in milk until smooth. Cook over low heat, stirring constantly, until mixture is thickened and bubbly.

Gradually stir about one-fourth of the hot mixture into egg yolks. Stir yolk mixture into remaining hot mixture; cook, stirring constantly, 2 minutes. Place a piece of waxed paper over surface; let cool to room temperature. Stir in vinegar. Transfer mixture to a jar; close tightly, and chill. Serve over salad greens. Yield: 1 cup (about 18 calories per tablespoon).

MIRACLE FRENCH DRESSING

½ teaspoon unflavored gelatin
1 tablespoon cold water
¼ cup boiling water
½ cup tomato juice
3 to 4 tablespoons vinegar
1 tablespoon sugar
1 tablespoon Worcestershire sauce
½ teaspoon salt
¼ teaspoon dry mustard
⅛ teasoon garlic powder
Dash of pepper

Dissolve gelatin in cold water, stirring well. Add boiling water; stir gelatin well, and set aside.

Combine remaining ingredients in container of electric blender; process on low speed. Add gelatin mixture; process until smooth (about 1 minute). Chill thoroughly. Stir well before serving. Serve over salad greens or fresh fruit. Yield: 1 cup (about 5 calories per tablespoon).

TANGY FRUIT DRESSING

1 tablespoon all-purpose flour
¼ cup sugar
1 egg, beaten
2 tablespoons vinegar
¾ cup unsweetened orange juice

Combine flour and sugar in a saucepan; mix well. Stir in egg. Add vinegar and juice; stir until smooth. Cook over low heat, stirring constantly, until thickened. Chill. Serve over fruit. Yield: ¾ cup (about 31 calories per tablespoon).

CREAMY HERB DRESSING

½ cup plain low-fat yogurt
1½ teaspoons lemon juice
1 cup low-fat cottage cheese
1 medium carrot, scraped and finely grated
2 teaspoons grated onion
¼ teaspoon dried whole thyme
¼ teaspoon dried whole basil
¼ teaspoon dried whole oregano
¼ teaspoon dried whole marjoram
¼ teaspoon salt

Combine first 3 ingredients in the container of an electric blender; process until smooth. Stir in remaining ingredients. Cover and chill thoroughly. Serve over salad greens. Yield: 2 cups (about 8 calories per tablespoon).

ZESTY ITALIAN DRESSING

1½ teaspoons unflavored gelatin
1⅓ cups water, divided
½ cup tarragon vinegar
6 cloves garlic, finely chopped
4 green onions, coarsely chopped
⅓ cup chopped pimiento-stuffed olives
¼ cup grated Parmesan cheese
3 tablespoons chopped fresh parsley
1 tablespoon plus 1 teaspoon lemon juice
1 tablespoon plus 1 teaspoon anchovy paste
1 tablespoon capers
2 teaspoons sugar
2 teaspoons freshly ground pepper
1 teaspoon dried whole basil
1 teaspoon dried whole oregano

Combine gelatin and ⅔ cup water in a small saucepan; let stand 1 minute. Cook over low heat, stirring constantly, until gelatin is dissolved. Remove from heat, and stir in remaining ⅔ cup water.

Combine gelatin mixture and remaining ingredients in container of an electric blender; process 30 seconds. Refrigerate 3 hours or until thoroughly chilled. Serve over salad greens. Yield: 2 cups (about 13 calories per tablespoon).

THOUSAND ISLAND DRESSING

1 (8-ounce) carton plain low-fat yogurt
3 tablespoons dill pickle relish
3 tablespoons reduced-calorie chili sauce
2 tablespoons reduced-calorie mayonnaise
1 tablespoon minced onion
1 teaspoon vinegar
1 teaspoon prepared mustard

Combine all ingredients in a small bowl. Cover and refrigerate at least 1 hour. Serve over salad greens. Yield: 1½ cups (about 11 calories per tablespoon).

YOGURT-DILL SALAD DRESSING

½ cup plain low-fat yogurt
½ cup skim milk
1 tablespoon lemon juice
2 teaspoons grated onion
1 teaspoon dried whole dillweed
½ teaspoon garlic salt
⅛ teaspoon dried whole oregano
⅛ teaspoon freshly ground pepper

Combine all ingredients in container of an electric blender; process until smooth. Cover; refrigerate 1 hour. Serve over salad greens. Yield: 1 cup (about 8 calories per tablespoon).

YOGURT-HONEY POPPYSEED DRESSING

1 (8-ounce) carton plain low-fat yogurt
¼ cup honey
1 tablespoon plus 1 teaspoon lemon juice
1 teaspoon poppyseeds

Combine all ingredients, mixing well; chill. Serve dressing over fresh fruit. Yield: 1⅓ cups (about 18 calories per tablespoon).

SAUCES AND MARINADES

Who would think that a dieter could indulge in Remoulade Sauce, Swiss Cheese Sauce, or Cherry Sauce and enjoy it with a clear conscience? The special light sauces and marinades included in the following recipes will help you to liven up your meals while keeping calories to a minimum. The fat or oil and sugar content which is usually high in sauces and marinades has been limited in our recipes, thus decreasing the number of calories.

Several of the sauce recipes start with a mixture of melted margarine and flour. When shopping for margarine, look for a tub margarine that lists one of the following oils as the first ingredient on the package label: safflower, soybean, corn, cottonseed, or sesame. Although the calories are the same as in other margarines, the concentration of saturated fats is lower.

Make low-calorie gravy by thickening fat-free broth with cornstarch. Cornstarch has twice the thickening power of flour. Therefore, you should use half as much cornstarch as flour to thicken the gravy. Mix cornstarch with a little cold water before stirring it into the hot broth. Add some herbs for seasoning, and cook gently until the mixture thickens. The result — a tasty gravy minus the usual fat and calories.

Our light fruit dessert sauces can turn a simple scoop of ice milk or slice of angel food cake into a gourmet delight. The secret to keeping the sauces light lies in limiting the amount of sugar and in utilizing the natural sweetness of fruit.

When a recipe calls for fresh fruit, make sure that it is very ripe, since riper fruit usually has a sweeter flavor. Enhance the natural taste of fruit by adding spices such as cinnamon, ginger, or nutmeg.

TART CHERRY SAUCE

2 cups fresh or frozen unsweetened tart cherries
⅓ cup unsweetened white grape juice
1 tablespoon sugar
2 tablespoons cornstarch
2 tablespoons water
½ teaspoon almond extract

Combine cherries, grape juice, and sugar in a medium saucepan. Bring to a boil; cover, reduce heat, and simmer 4 minutes. Dissolve cornstarch in water; add to cherry mixture. Cook over low heat, stirring constantly, 5 to 10 minutes or until thickened.

Remove sauce from heat, and stir in almond extract. Serve warm over ice milk, pancakes, or waffles. Yield: 2 cups (about 11 calories per tablespoon).

CHERRY SAUCE

1 pound fresh sweet cherries, pitted
½ cup water
¼ cup sugar
1 tablespoon brandy

Combine cherries and water in a medium saucepan; bring to a boil. Cover, reduce heat, and simmer 4 minutes; stir in sugar, and cook 1 minute. Remove from heat, and stir in brandy; cool. Serve over ice milk. Yield: 2 cups (about 62 calories per ¼ cup sauce).

CREAMY LIGHT COCONUT SAUCE

2 eggs, beaten
2 tablespoons sugar
1⅓ cups skim milk
1 teaspoon vanilla extract
¼ cup plus 2 tablespoons flaked coconut, toasted

Combine eggs and sugar in a small, heavy saucepan; mix well. Gradually stir in milk with a wire whisk. Cook over low heat, stirring constantly, 15 to 20 minutes or until thickened. Remove from heat, and stir in vanilla. Cover and refrigerate.

Just before serving, stir in ¼ cup coconut; garnish with remaining coconut. Serve with assorted fresh fruit or over ice milk. Yield: 1¾ cups (about 19 calories per tablespoon).

MANDARIN SAUCE

1 (11-ounce) can mandarin oranges, undrained
¼ cup reduced-calorie strawberry jam
1 tablespoon lemon juice
2 teaspoons cornstarch
⅛ teaspoon ground nutmeg

Drain oranges, reserving ¼ cup liquid. Set oranges aside.

Combine reserved ¼ cup liquid, strawberry jam, lemon juice, cornstarch, and nutmeg in a small saucepan; cook over medium heat, stirring constantly, until thickened and bubbly. Stir in orange sections; reduce heat, and simmer 5 minutes, stirring occasionally. Serve warm over ice milk, sherbet, or angel food cake. Yield: 1¼ cups (about 46 calories per ¼ cup sauce).

FRESH PLUM SAUCE

1 pound fresh plums, peeled, pitted, and sliced
1 (3-inch) stick cinnamon
½ cup unsweetened apple juice
1 tablespoon cornstarch
2 tablespoons lemon juice

Combine plums, cinnamon, and apple juice in a small saucepan. Bring to a boil; cover, reduce heat, and simmer 5 minutes or until plums are tender. Discard cinnamon.

Combine cornstarch and lemon juice, stirring

until blended; stir into plum mixture. Cook, stirring constantly, until thickened and bubbly. Cool. Serve over fresh fruit, ice milk, or angel food cake. Yield: 2¼ cups (about 40 calories per ¼ cup sauce).

MANGO SAUCE

1 cup cubed mango
2 tablespoons Cointreau or other orange-flavored liqueur
3 tablespoons unsweetened orange juice

Combine all the ingredients in container of an electric blender; process until smooth. Serve over lemon sherbet or ice milk. Yield: 1¼ cups (about 42 calories per ¼ cup sauce).

SUMMER FRUIT SAUCE

¼ cup reduced-calorie strawberry jam
1½ tablespoons cornstarch
1 cup unsweetened orange juice
1 cup sliced fresh nectarines
1 cup fresh sweet cherries, pitted
½ cup fresh blueberries

Melt strawberry jam in a medium saucepan over low heat.

Combine cornstarch and orange juice, stirring until smooth; add to jam, mixing well.

Bring jam mixture to a boil; cook 1 minute, stirring constantly. Remove from heat, and stir in nectarines, cherries, and blueberries. Serve warm over ice milk or angel food cake. Yield: 2½ cups (about 47 calories per ¼ cup sauce).

SPICY APPLESAUCE

10 large cooking apples (about 4 pounds)
1 cup unsweetened apple juice
¼ teaspoon ground cloves
1½ teaspoons ground cinnamon
¼ teaspoon ground nutmeg

Peel, core, and quarter apples; combine with remaining ingredients in a large Dutch oven. Cook mixture over medium-low heat 25 to 30 minutes or until apples are tender, stirring frequently. Mash the apple mixture to desired consistency with a potato masher.

Quickly spoon applesauce into hot sterilized jars, leaving ¼-inch headspace. Cover at once with metal lids, and screw bands tight. Process jars in boiling-water bath for 25 minutes. Yield: 3 pints (about 11 calories per tablespoon).

BANANA JAM

2 tablespoons cornstarch
1 (6-ounce) can frozen apple juice concentrate, thawed and undiluted
3 cups sliced ripe bananas
3 tablespoons lemon juice
2 whole cloves
1 (2-inch) stick cinnamon

Combine cornstarch and apple juice concentrate in a heavy saucepan; stir until smooth. Add remaining ingredients, stirring well. Cook over medium heat, stirring constantly, until thickened and bubbly. Cook an additional 3 to 5 minutes. Remove cloves and cinnamon stick; discard.

Quickly spoon banana mixture into hot sterilized jars, leaving ¼-inch headspace. Cover at once with metal lids, and screw bands tight. Cool. Store jam in the refrigerator. Yield: 2 half pints (about 23 calories per tablespoon).

FREEZER PEACH JAM

4 cups peeled, coarsely chopped peaches
1 (1¾-ounce) package powdered fruit pectin
1 tablespoon sugar
1 tablespoon lemon juice
½ teaspoon ascorbic acid

Crush peaches in a medium saucepan; stir in remaining ingredients. Bring to a boil; boil 1 minute, stirring constantly. Remove from heat; stir 3 minutes. Spoon jam into freezer containers, leaving ½-inch headspace. Cover at once with lids. Let stand at room temperature 24 hours; freeze. To serve, thaw jam. Yield: 2½ half pints (about 11 calories per tablespoon).

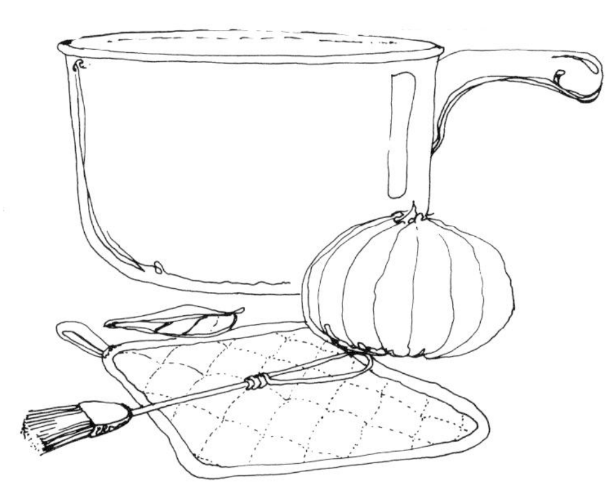

EASY BARBECUE SAUCE

1 tablespoon margarine
1 medium onion, chopped
1¼ cups tomato sauce
1 tablespoon vinegar
1 small bay leaf
¼ teaspoon salt
¼ teaspoon dry mustard
¼ teaspoon curry powder
¼ teaspoon hot sauce
⅛ teaspoon pepper

Melt margarine in a medium saucepan; add onion, and sauté until tender. Stir in remaining ingredients, and simmer 15 minutes. Remove bay leaf; discard. Use sauce to baste chicken when baking or grilling. Yield: 1½ cups (about 11 calories per tablespoon).

SPECIAL BARBECUE SAUCE

½ cup water
¼ cup vinegar
2 tablespoons lemon juice
1 tablespoon prepared mustard
½ teaspoon salt
½ teaspoon pepper
¼ teaspoon red pepper
1 medium onion, chopped
½ cup catsup
2 tablespoons Worcestershire sauce
1½ teaspoons liquid smoke

Combine first 8 ingredients in a large saucepan. Bring to a boil; reduce heat to medium. Cook, uncovered, 20 minutes, stirring occasionally; stir in the remaining ingredients. Use to baste chicken or other meats. Yield: 1½ cups (about 10 calories per tablespoon).

TANGY LIGHT MARINADE

1 cup unsweetened pineapple juice
⅓ cup soy sauce
1 teaspoon ground ginger
1 small clove garlic, crushed
⅓ cup Italian reduced-calorie
salad dressing

Combine all ingredients, stirring well. Use to marinate flank steak or pork chops before grilling. Baste meat with remaining marinade during grilling. Yield: 1⅔ cups (about 9 calories per tablespoon).

FLANK STEAK MARINADE

⅔ cup dry red wine
1 tablespoon soy sauce
¼ teaspoon dried whole marjoram
¼ teaspoon dried whole oregano
¼ teaspoon pepper

Combine all ingredients in a glass jar; cover tightly, and shake vigorously. Pour over flank steak; cover and marinate in refrigerator overnight. Brush on remaining marinade during grilling. Yield: ⅔ cup (about 14 calories per tablespoon).

BASIC CHEESE SAUCE

2 tablespoons reduced-calorie margarine
2 tablespoons all-purpose flour
1 cup skim milk
2 slices low-fat process American cheese, torn into small pieces
¼ teaspoon salt
⅛ teaspoon white pepper

Melt margarine in a heavy saucepan over low heat; add flour, stirring until smooth (mixture will be dry). Cook 1 minute, stirring constantly. Gradually add milk; cook over medium heat, stirring constantly with a wire whisk, until thickened and bubbly. Add cheese, salt, and pepper; stir until cheese melts. Serve sauce over broccoli or other vegetables. Yield: 1 cup (about 20 calories per tablespoon).

Note: One tablespoon regular margarine may be substituted for 2 tablespoons reduced-calorie margarine. The flour-and-margarine mixture will be dry.

SWISS CHEESE SAUCE

3 tablespoons reduced-calorie margarine
2 tablespoons grated onion
2 tablespoons all-purpose flour
¼ teaspoon salt
¼ teaspoon white pepper
1¾ cups skim milk
1 tablespoon minced fresh parsley
1 bay leaf
½ cup (2 ounces) shredded Swiss cheese

Melt margarine in a heavy saucepan over low heat; add onion, and sauté 3 to 4 minutes. Stir in flour, salt, and pepper; cook 1 minute, stirring constantly (mixture will be dry).

Gradually add milk, parsley, and bay leaf, stirring with a wire whisk until smooth. Cook over medium heat, stirring constantly, until thickened and bubbly. Remove bay leaf and discard. Add cheese, stirring until melted. Serve sauce over steamed asparagus, poached eggs, or seafood. Yield: 1¾ cups (about 20 calories per tablespoon).

MOCK SOUR CREAM

1 cup low-fat cottage cheese
2 tablespoons skim milk
1 tablespoon lemon juice
¼ teaspoon salt (optional)

Combine all ingredients in container of an electric blender; process at medium-high speed until smooth and creamy. Cover and chill thoroughly. Serve as a topping for baked potatoes. Yield: 1¼ cups (about 9 calories per tablespoon).

YOGURT-HERB SAUCE

1 (8-ounce) carton plain low-fat yogurt
½ cup low-fat cottage cheese
2 tablespoons tarragon vinegar
1 hard-cooked egg, coarsely chopped
4 green onions, sliced
½ cup packed fresh parsley sprigs
1 teaspoon dried whole thyme
1 teaspoon dry mustard
½ teaspoon dried whole marjoram
½ teaspoon dried whole oregano
½ teaspoon dried whole savory
½ teaspoon garlic salt
¼ teaspoon hot sauce

Combine all ingredients in container of an electric blender; process at medium speed until smooth, scraping sides of container often. Serve over asparagus. Yield: 2 cups (about 11 calories per tablespoon).

TANGY CHIVE SAUCE

2 tablespoons all-purpose flour
⅛ teaspoon salt
Dash of white pepper
⅔ cup chicken broth
⅓ cup skim milk
2 teaspoons chopped chives
1 teaspoon prepared mustard
1 teaspoon lemon juice

Combine flour, salt, and pepper in a saucepan; gradually add chicken broth and milk, stirring with a wire whisk until smooth. Place over medium heat and cook, stirring constantly, until thickened. Add remaining ingredients; mix well. Cook 2 minutes, stirring constantly. Spoon sauce over steamed broccoli to serve. Yield: ¾ cup (about 10 calories per tablespoon).

CUCUMBER-DILL SAUCE

1 large cucumber, peeled, seeded, and minced
¼ teaspoon salt
1 (8-ounce) carton plain low-fat yogurt
2 tablespoons grated onion
1 teaspoon dried whole dillweed
½ teaspoon lemon juice
¼ teaspoon white pepper

Combine cucumber and salt; let stand 15 minutes. Drain well. Combine cucumber and remaining ingredients in a small bowl; cover and refrigerate at least 2 hours. Serve with fish or hamburgers. Yield: 2 cups (about 6 calories per tablespoon).

LIGHT MUSTARD SAUCE

¼ cup sugar
2 tablespoons dry mustard
½ teaspoon salt
2 egg yolks, beaten
1 (13-ounce) can evaporated skim milk
½ cup vinegar

Combine first 4 ingredients in top of a double boiler; gradually add evaporated milk, and stir until smooth. Bring water to a boil; reduce heat to low. Cook mixture until smooth and thickened, stirring constantly.

Stir in vinegar; cook until creamy and slightly thickened. Serve hot over ham slices. Yield: 2 cups (about 20 calories per tablespoon).

HORSERADISH-APPLE SAUCE

¼ small onion, cubed
½ stalk celery, cut into 1-inch pieces
1½ pounds tart apples, pared, cored, and cubed
2 tablespoons unsweetened orange juice
1 tablespoon freshly grated horseradish
¼ teaspoon fennel seeds, crushed

Position knife blade in food processor bowl; add onion and celery. Process until vegetables are finely chopped. Add apple, orange juice, and horseradish to bowl; process at high speed until mixture is almost smooth (scrape bowl during chopping if necessary). Stir in fennel seeds. Refrigerate several hours. Serve sauce with poultry or pork. Yield: 2 cups (about 12 calories per tablespoon).

RAISIN-PINEAPPLE SAUCE

¾ cup unsweetened pineapple juice
½ cup raisins
1 tablespoon vinegar
Dash of Worcestershire sauce
⅛ teaspoon ground cloves
2 teaspoons cornstarch
2 tablespoons water

Combine first 5 ingredients, and bring to a boil; cook until raisins are plump. Dissolve cornstarch in water, and gradually add to hot mixture; cook until clear, stirring constantly. Serve hot over ham slices. Yield: ⅔ cup (about 33 calories per tablespoon).

REMOULADE SAUCE

1 cup reduced-calorie mayonnaise
1 hard-cooked egg, chopped
2 tablespoons minced fresh parsley
1 tablespoon red wine vinegar
2 teaspoons capers
½ to 1 teaspoon dry mustard
1 teaspoon dried whole tarragon
1 teaspoon minced garlic
1 teaspoon chopped chives
1 teaspoon anchovy paste
Dash of onion powder

Combine all ingredients, stirring well. Chill several hours. Serve sauce over broiled fish or other seafood. Yield: 1⅓ cups (about 35 calories per tablespoon).

TARRAGON SAUCE

½ cup reduced-calorie mayonnaise
3 tablespoons water
2 to 3 teaspoons lemon juice
1 teaspoon prepared mustard
¼ teaspon dried whole tarragon
⅛ teaspoon white pepper

Combine all ingredients in a saucepan; stir until smooth. Cook mixture over low heat, stirring constantly, 3 to 4 minutes or until thoroughly heated. Serve over broccoli, poached eggs, or fish. Yield: ¾ cup (about 27 calories per tablespoon).

MARINARA SAUCE

1 (46-ounce) can tomato juice
½ pound fresh mushrooms, sliced
2 medium-size green peppers, chopped
1 red sweet pepper, chopped
2 teaspoons minced onion
½ teaspoon dried whole basil
½ teaspoon dried whole oregano
Dash of garlic powder

Combine all ingredients in a large Dutch oven; simmer, uncovered, 45 minutes. Serve over cooked spaghetti, rice, or noodles. Yield: 5 cups (about 32 calories per ½ cup sauce).

SPICY HOT RELISH

1 cup minced onion
½ cup chopped green pepper
2 cloves garlic, minced
1 (16-ounce) can whole tomatoes, drained and chopped
1 (7-ounce) can whole kernel corn, drained
1 (4-ounce) can chopped green chiles, undrained
½ cup green chili salsa
1 tablespoon chili powder
1 teaspoon pepper

Combine all ingredients in a bowl. Cover and refrigerate mixture at least 12 hours. Serve as a sauce on hamburgers. Yield: 3½ cups (about 7 calories per tablespoon).

> Go easy on catsup, sweet pickles, steak sauce, chili sauce, and other condiments which are high in calories and salt.

SOUPS AND STEWS

Choosing low-fat ingredients and following low-calorie cooking methods is the secret to making light soups and stews. For instance, a cream soup can be just as good, but lower in calories, when made with skim milk rather than half-and-half. In some of our recipes, such as Peppery Carrot Soup and Creamy Potato Soup, the thickness comes from pureed vegetables instead of from the usual cream.

You'll need broth or stock for many soup recipes. Canned broth is fine, but you'll save money by making your own. Start by boiling meat or poultry bones in water to extract the tasty meat flavor. If you are in a hurry, let the broth stand for a few minutes to allow any fat to rise to the top. Use a bulb-type baster to remove the layer of liquid fat, or skim the fat off with a spoon. If time allows, refrigerate the broth so that the fat will harden. The solid fat can then be lifted off the broth and discarded. What's left is a flavorful fat-free broth that can be used in making soups and stews or as a seasoning for almost any vegetable.

When making a light chili or stew, it's essential to remove as much fat as possible from the ground beef or other meat. After browning the meat, take the time to drain the meat well. Use a colander to drain the excess fat from browned ground beef and pat the meat with a paper towel to absorb any remaining fat.

Many soup and stew recipes yield several servings — maybe more than you would want to use over a two or three day period. Freeze any remaining servings in small containers so that several weeks later you can enjoy an easy-to-reheat soup.

For a change of pace, try Fresh Blueberry Soup or one of our other refreshing fruit soups as an appetizer or dessert. The addition of unsweetened fruit juices and spices keeps the flavor high and the calories low.

FRESH BLUEBERRY SOUP

1½ cups fresh blueberries
1¼ cups unsweetened grape juice
1 cup water
1 (3-inch) stick cinnamon
2 teaspoons sugar
1 tablespoon cornstarch
¼ cup water
¼ teaspoon ground cardamom

Combine blueberries, grape juice, 1 cup water, cinnamon, and sugar in a medium saucepan. Bring to a boil; cover, reduce heat, and simmer 5 minutes.

Combine cornstarch and ¼ cup water, stirring until blended; stir cornstarch mixture and cardamom into soup. Cook, stirring constantly, until mixture is thickened.

Remove soup from heat, and let cool. Cover and refrigerate until thoroughly chilled. Remove stick cinnamon before serving. Yield: 3¼ cups (about 126 calories per 1-cup serving).

CANTALOUPE SOUP

1 large cantaloupe (about 3 pounds)
4½ cups unsweetened orange juice, divided
3 tablespoons lemon juice
¼ teaspoon ground ginger
¼ teaspoon ground allspice
Fresh mint leaves (optional)

Cut cantaloupe in half, and remove seeds. Peel each half, and cut fruit into 1-inch cubes. Combine half of cantaloupe and ½ cup orange juice in container of an electric blender; process until mixture is smooth. Repeat processing with remaining cantaloupe cubes and an additional ½ cup orange juice.

Combine cantaloupe mixture, remaining 3½ cups orange juice, and next 3 ingredients, blending well; cover and chill thoroughly. Garnish with mint leaves, if desired. Yield: 6 cups (about 112 calories per 1-cup serving).

PEACH SOUP

3½ cups peeled, diced peaches
½ cup Chablis or other dry white wine
1½ cups unsweetened white grape juice
1 cup water
1 (3-inch) stick cinnamon
½ teaspoon ground cardamom
½ teaspoon vanilla extract

Combine peaches, wine, grape juice, water, and cinnamon in a medium saucepan. Bring to a boil; cover, reduce heat, and simmer 30 minutes. Remove from heat, and stir in cardamom and vanilla; discard cinnamon. Pour half the mixture into container of an electric blender; process until smooth. Repeat with remaining mixture. Chill thoroughly. Yield: 6 cups (about 104 calories per 1-cup serving).

RUBY RED BORSCHT

5 large beets (about 1¾ pounds), peeled and grated
2 medium onions, finely chopped
6 cups chicken broth
1 tablespoon lemon juice
¼ teaspoon sugar
¼ teaspoon pepper
2 eggs, slightly beaten
Fresh dill (optional)

Combine beets, onion, and broth in a Dutch oven. Cover and bring to a boil. Reduce heat; simmer 45 minutes. Add lemon juice, sugar, and pepper; simmer an additional 15 minutes.

Remove Dutch oven from heat. Gradually stir about one-fourth of hot mixture into beaten eggs; add to the remaining hot mixture, stirring constantly. Chill thoroughly. Garnish soup with dill, if desired. Yield: 8 cups (about 75 calories per 1-cup serving).

Note: Soup may also be served hot.

CHILLED CUCUMBER SOUP

1 tablespoon reduced-calorie margarine
1 medium cucumber, peeled, seeded, and chopped
2 tablespoons sliced green onions
2 teaspoons cornstarch
1¼ cups skim milk, divided
1 teaspoon chicken-flavored bouillon granules
¼ teaspoon dried whole dillweed
½ cup plain low-fat yogurt
Thin cucumber slices (optional)
Fresh parsley sprigs (optional)

Melt margarine in a small saucepan; add cucumber and onions, and sauté until vegetables are tender.

Combine cornstarch and ¼ cup milk, stirring until blended; add cornstarch mixture, remaining 1 cup milk, bouillon granules, and dillweed to saucepan. Cook, stirring constantly, over medium heat until thickened. Pour mixture into container of an electric blender; process until smooth. Let cool slightly.

Stir yogurt into cucumber mixture; cover and chill 2 hours. Garnish with cucumber slices and parsley, if desired. Yield: 2 cups (about 146 calories per 1-cup serving).

COOL TOMATO SOUP

2 (10¾-ounce) cans chicken broth, undiluted
1½ cups water
1 (28-ounce) can whole tomatoes, undrained and coarsely chopped
1 large onion, coarsely chopped
1 large baking potato, peeled and cubed
4 bay leaves
½ teaspoon dried whole basil
⅛ teaspoon pepper
½ cup plain low-fat yogurt

Combine all ingredients except yogurt in a small Dutch oven. Bring to a boil; cover, reduce heat, and simmer 20 minutes or until vegetables are tender. Remove and discard bay leaves.

Pour soup mixture, one-third at a time, into container of an electric blender; process until smooth. Chill soup thoroughly; ladle into individual bowls to serve. Top each serving with 1 tablespoon yogurt. Yield: 8 cups (about 77 calories per 1-cup serving).

FRESH BROCCOLI SOUP

2 (1-pound) bunches fresh broccoli
2 cups water
1 (14½-ounce) can chicken broth
1 teaspoon dried whole marjoram
¼ teaspoon salt
⅛ teaspoon pepper
2 large carrots, scraped and sliced
1 medium onion, quartered
½ cup skim milk

Trim leaves and touch ends of lower stalks from broccoli. Cut into 1-inch pieces; set aside.

Combine broccoli and remaining ingredients except milk in a Dutch oven; cover and simmer 15 to 20 minutes or until vegetables are tender.

Remove 2 cups broccoli flowerets from soup mixture with a slotted spoon; set aside. Spoon half of soup mixture into container of an electric blender; process until smooth. Repeat with remaining soup mixture. Return soup mixture to Dutch oven; stir in milk and reserved flowerets.

Cook soup over low heat, stirring constantly, until thoroughly heated. Yield: 6¾ cups (about 56 calories per 1-cup serving).

PEPPERY CARROT SOUP

Vegetable cooking spray
4 cups sliced carrots
1 cup sliced celery
1 cup coarsely chopped onion
5 cups chicken broth
½ cup uncooked regular rice
¼ teaspoon white pepper
¼ teaspoon dried whole thyme
2 cups water
¼ to ½ teaspoon salt (optional)

Coat a Dutch oven with cooking spray. Add carrots, celery, and onion. Cover and cook over medium heat 15 to 20 minutes or until carrots are tender.

Add next 4 ingredients; cover and simmer 30 to 40 minutes. Pour half of carrot mixture into container of an electric blender; process until smooth. Repeat with remaining mixture. Return blended mixture to Dutch oven; add water and salt, if desired, stirring well. Place over low heat until thoroughly heated. Serve warm. Yield: 7 cups (about 115 calories per 1-cup serving).

EGG DROP SOUP

1½ tablespoons cornstarch
2 tablespoons water
4 cups chicken broth
1 tablespoon soy sauce
4 eggs, slightly beaten
⅓ cup minced green onions

Combine cornstarch and water, stirring until blended; set aside.

Combine broth and soy sauce in a medium saucepan; bring to a boil. Slowly pour eggs (1 at a time) into rapidly boiling broth, stirring constantly. (The egg forms lacy strands as it cooks.)

Stir cornstarch mixture into soup; cook, stirring constantly, until thickened. Remove from heat; stir in onions. Serve immediately. Yield: 4 cups (about 136 calories per 1-cup serving).

CHINESE CHICKEN SOUP

2 chicken breast halves (about ¾ pound), skinned and boned
Vegetable cooking spray
1 teaspoon vegetable oil
8 large fresh mushrooms, sliced
4 cups chicken broth
1 tablespoon cornstarch
2 tablespoons water
1 tablespoon soy sauce
2 tablespoons lemon juice
Lemon slices

Cut chicken into 2- x ½-inch strips. Coat a medium saucepan with cooking spray; add oil, and place over medium-high heat until hot. Add chicken and mushrooms to saucepan; sauté, stirring occasionally, until chicken is no longer pink and mushrooms are tender.

Add chicken broth to saucepan; bring to a boil. Combine cornstarch, water, and soy sauce, stirring until blended; stir into saucepan. Reduce heat, and simmer 5 minutes.

Remove from heat, and stir in lemon juice. To serve, ladle soup into bowls, and garnish each serving with a lemon slice. Yield: 4½ cups (about 128 calories per 1-cup serving).

CARAWAY-MUSHROOM SOUP

Vegetable cooking spray
1 pound fresh mushrooms, sliced
1 medium onion, sliced
1 clove garlic, minced
1 (10½-ounce) can beef broth, undiluted
2 cups water
⅓ cup Chablis or other dry white wine
1 teaspoon caraway seeds, crushed
¼ teaspoon pepper
¼ cup grated Parmesan cheese

Coat a small Dutch oven with cooking spray; place over medium heat until hot. Add mushrooms, onion, and garlic to Dutch oven; cover and cook 5 minutes, stirring frequently.

Stir in next 5 ingredients; cover, reduce heat, and simmer 30 minutes. Uncover and simmer an additional 30 minutes. Stir in cheese, and simmer 5 minutes. Serve immediately. Yield: 6 cups (about 61 calories per 1-cup serving).

FRENCH ONION SOUP

5 medium onions (about 2 pounds), thinly sliced and separated into rings
6 cups beef broth
2 bay leaves
¼ teaspoon pepper
¼ cup brandy
4 (1-inch-thick) slices French bread, halved and toasted
2 tablespoons plus 2 teaspoons grated Parmesan cheese

Combine onion, broth, bay leaves, and pepper in a Dutch oven. Bring to a boil; cover. Reduce heat; simmer 35 minutes. Add brandy; simmer, uncovered, 2 minutes. Discard bay leaves.

Ladle soup into bowls, and float 1 toasted bread half in each serving of soup. Sprinkle each with 1 teaspoon Parmesan cheese. Yield: 8 cups (about 106 calories per 1-cup serving).

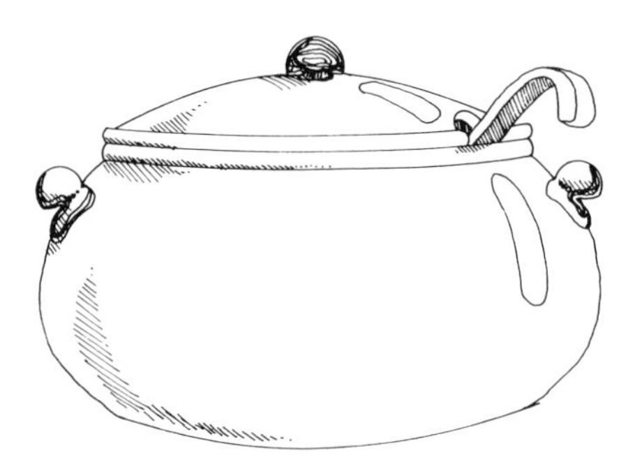

PEPPERY PEA SOUP

1 quart water
4 chicken-flavored bouillon cubes
2 (16-ounce) packages frozen peas and carrots
¼ cup minced onion
½ teaspoon celery seeds
½ teaspoon pepper
Green onion strips
Thin carrot strips

Bring water to a boil; add bouillon cubes, stirring to dissolve. Add next 4 ingredients; cover, reduce heat, and simmer 8 to 10 minutes.

Pour soup mixture into container of an electric blender, and process until smooth. Serve immediately. Garnish with green onion strips and thin carrot strips. Yield: 7 cups (about 78 calories per 1-cup serving).

SPLIT PEA SOUP

½ pound dried split peas
4 cups water
¾ cup chopped onion
½ cup chopped carrots
½ cup chopped lean ham
½ teaspoon ground celery seeds
¼ teaspoon salt
¼ teaspoon freshly ground pepper
¼ teaspoon dried whole marjoram, crushed
⅛ teaspoon dried whole thyme

Sort and wash peas; place in a Dutch oven. Add remaining ingredients, and bring to a boil; cover, reduce heat, and simmer 1 hour or until peas are tender.

Pour half of mixture into container of an electric blender; process until smooth. Repeat with remaining mixture. Serve hot. Yield: 5½ cups (about 198 calories per 1-cup serving).

POTATO SOUP

5 medium potatoes, peeled and cubed
1 medium onion, chopped
⅓ cup chopped celery
3 cups water
1 cup skim milk
1 teaspoon salt
1 teaspoon chicken-flavored bouillon granules
2 teaspoons chopped chives
⅛ teaspoon pepper
Additional chopped chives (optional)

Combine potatoes, onion, celery, and water in a 3-quart Dutch oven. Bring to a boil; cover, reduce heat, and simmer 20 minutes or until potatoes are tender. Drain, setting vegetables aside and reserving 1½ cups cooking liquid in Dutch oven.

Mash vegetable mixture with a potato masher or electric mixer; add to reserved cooking liquid, along with milk, salt, bouillon granules, 2 teaspoons chives, and pepper. Cook, stirring constantly, until soup is thoroughly heated. Garnish with chopped chives, if desired. Yield: 6 cups (about 116 calories per 1-cup serving).

CREAMY POTATO SOUP

3 medium potatoes (about 1 pound), peeled and thinly sliced
1 medium onion, thinly sliced
1 large stalk celery, thinly sliced
1 (10¾-ounce) can chicken broth
1¼ cups water
¼ teaspoon white pepper
Minced chives

Combine all ingredients except chives in a small Dutch oven. Bring to a boil; cover, reduce heat, and simmer 30 minutes or until potatoes are tender.

Process mixture, 1½ cups at a time, in container of an electric blender until smooth. Return to saucepan, and cook until thoroughly heated. Garnish with minced chives. Yield: 9 cups (about 48 calories per 1-cup serving).

SQUASH SOUP

Vegetable cooking spray
1 tablespoon margarine
1 medium onion, chopped
2 tablespoons chopped fresh parsley
½ teaspoon dried whole basil
6 medium-size yellow squash, cut into ¼-inch slices
1 medium zucchini, cut into ¼-inch slices
1 cup chicken broth
¼ teaspoon salt
¼ teaspoon white pepper
1 cup skim milk
Thin carrot strips (optional)
Chopped chives (optional)

Coat a large saucepan with cooking spray; add margarine, and place over medium heat until margarine is melted. Add onion, parsley, and basil; sauté until tender.

Add next 5 ingredients to saucepan; cover and bring to a boil. Reduce heat, and simmer 15 minutes. Remove from heat, and stir in milk. Pour broth mixture into container of an electric blender, and process until smooth. Serve soup hot or cold. Garnish with carrot strips and chives, if desired. Yield: 6½ cups (about 61 calories per 1-cup serving).

SPICY TOMATO SOUP

Vegetable cooking spray
2 large onions, thinly sliced
1 (28-ounce) can Italian-style tomatoes
3 tablespoons tomato paste
1 teaspoon dried whole thyme
1 teaspoon dried whole basil
¼ teaspoon pepper
½ cup all-purpose flour
1 (10¾-ounce) can chicken broth, undiluted
4¾ cups water
Celery leaves (optional)

Coat a large Dutch oven with cooking spray; place over medium heat until hot. Add onion, and sauté over low heat until tender. Stir in next 5 ingredients.

Combine flour and broth in a small bowl, stirring until well blended; add to vegetable mixture, stirring well. Stir in water. Bring to a boil, stirring constantly; cover, reduce heat, and simmer 30 minutes, stirring often.

Pour soup, one-fourth at a time, into container of an electric blender; process until smooth. Return mixture to Dutch oven; cook until thoroughly heated. Garnish with celery leaves, if desired. Yield: 10 cups (about 58 calories per 1-cup serving).

Cooking the light way does not have to be boring. Add variety to your meals by selecting recipes that have a foreign flavor.

CHILI SURPRISE

1 cup dried kidney beans
1 cup dried pinto beans
½ cup dried black beans
5 stalks celery and leaves, chopped
1 large carrot, shredded
3 large tomatoes, peeled and cubed
1 large green pepper, chopped
1 medium onion, chopped
½ cup raisins
2 cloves garlic, minced
2 bay leaves
2 tablespoons chili powder
¼ cup plus 2 tablespoons minced fresh parsley
1 teaspoon dried whole dillweed
1 teaspoon dried whole basil
1 teaspoon dried whole oregano
1 teaspoon ground cumin
1 teaspoon ground allspice
¼ teaspoon freshly ground pepper
¼ teaspoon hot sauce
½ cup unsalted dry roasted cashews
¼ cup unsalted sunflower kernels
Bean sprouts (optional)

Sort and wash beans; place in a large Dutch oven. Cover with water 2 inches above beans; let soak overnight. Drain beans; cover with water. Cover and bring to a boil; reduce heat, and simmer for 1 hour.

Add remaining ingredients except cashews, sunflower kernels, and bean sprouts; simmer 30 minutes or until beans are tender and chili is thickened. (Add more water if necessary.) Remove and discard bay leaves. Stir in cashews and sunflower kernels. Serve topped with bean sprouts, if desired. Yield: 10 servings (about 259 calories per 1-cup serving).

> You can decrease your fat intake by using more vegetarian sources of protein (dried beans and peas) in place of protein from animal sources.

TURKEY CHILI

Vegetable cooking spray
2 pounds uncooked ground turkey
1 medium onion, chopped
1 medium-size green pepper, chopped
2 cloves garlic, minced
1 (16-ounce) can whole tomatoes, undrained
1 (10-ounce) can tomatoes and green chiles, undrained
2 cups tomato juice
1 to 2 tablespoons chili powder
1 tablespoon prepared mustard
1 teaspoon paprika
½ teaspoon salt
¼ teaspoon pepper
1 (15½-ounce) can kidney beans, drained

Coat a Dutch oven with cooking spray; add turkey, onion, green pepper, and garlic. Sauté mixture over medium-high heat until turkey loses its pink color.

Stir in remaining ingredients except beans. Bring to a boil; cover, reduce heat, and simmer 1 hour. Stir in beans; cover and simmer an additional 15 minutes. Yield: 8 cups (about 223 calories per 1-cup serving).

DELICIOUS CORN CHOWDER

2 cups water
2 cups diced potatoes
½ cup chopped onion
½ cup diced celery
½ teaspoon dried whole basil
1 large bay leaf
1 (16½-ounce) can cream-style corn
2 cups skim milk
1 cup drained canned tomatoes, chopped
½ teaspoon salt
⅛ teaspoon pepper
½ cup (2 ounces) shredded Cheddar cheese
Fresh parsley sprigs

Combine first 6 ingredients in a large Dutch oven, and bring to a boil. Reduce heat, and simmer about 10 minutes or until potatoes are tender. Discard bay leaf. Stir in corn, milk, tomatoes, salt, and pepper; cook until thoroughly heated (do not allow to boil).

Add cheese; cook over low heat, stirring constantly, until cheese is melted and mixture thickens. Garnish with fresh parsley sprigs before serving. Yield: 8 cups (about 130 calories per 1-cup serving).

OKRA CHOWDER

Vegetable cooking spray
1 medium onion, minced
1 medium-size green pepper, cut into strips
4 cups sliced okra
4 medium tomatoes, peeled and chopped
1 cup fresh shelled lima beans
1 cup fresh cut corn from cob
½ cup diced cooked ham
1 teaspoon chopped fresh parsley
½ teaspoon salt
¼ teaspoon pepper
2 cups water

Coat a large Dutch oven with cooking spray; place over medium heat until hot. Add onion and green pepper; cook over low heat, stirring constantly, until tender.

Stir in remaining ingredients, and bring to a boil. Cover, reduce heat, and simmer 30 minutes, stirring occasionally. Yield: 10 cups (about 79 calories per 1-cup serving).

CREOLE SEAFOOD GUMBO

1 pound unpeeled fresh shrimp
Vegetable cooking spray
1 teaspoon margarine
1 cup chopped onion
1 clove garlic, minced
7 cups water
1 (10-ounce) package frozen sliced okra
1 cup sliced celery
¾ cup chopped green pepper
½ cup uncooked regular rice
1 (16-ounce) can whole tomatoes, undrained and chopped
1 (8-ounce) bottle clam juice
3 tablespoons all-purpose flour
1 teaspoon Worcestershire sauce
¾ teaspoon salt
1 teaspoon gumbo filé or ½ teaspoon dried whole thyme
¼ teaspoon pepper
⅛ teaspoon hot sauce
1 pound fresh crabmeat
1 (4-ounce) jar diced pimiento, drained

Peel and devein shrimp; set aside.

Coat a 5-quart Dutch oven with cooking spray; add margarine, and place over medium heat until melted. Add onion and garlic; sauté until tender. Add shrimp, okra, celery, green pepper, rice, and tomatoes; bring to a boil. Reduce heat; simmer, uncovered, 30 to 35 minutes. Stir in tomatoes.

Combine clam juice, flour, Worcestershire sauce, salt, gumbo filé, pepper, and hot sauce; add to gumbo mixture, stirring well. Cook over medium heat until mixture begins to thicken. Stir in crabmeat and pimiento. Yield: 17 cups (about 91 calories per 1-cup serving).

BEEF STEW

1½ pounds lean round steak (½-inch-thick)
4 medium carrots, scraped and cut into 1-inch pieces
1 large potato (about ½ pound), peeled and cut into 1-inch cubes
1 medium onion, chopped
¼ cup chopped celery
¼ cup chopped green pepper
1 slice whole wheat bread, crumbled
2 tablespoons quick-cooking tapioca
½ teaspoon dried whole thyme
¼ teaspoon dried whole rosemary, crushed
¼ teaspoon salt
¼ teaspoon pepper
1 (16-ounce) can whole tomatoes, drained and chopped
1 cup water
¾ cup dry red wine

Trim excess fat from steak; cut meat into 1-inch squares.

Combine meat and remaining ingredients in a Dutch oven; bring to a boil. Cover, reduce heat, and simmer 1 to 1¼ hours or until meat is tender, stirring occasionally. Yield: 9 cups (about 170 calories per 1-cup serving).

POLYNESIAN BEEF STEW

2 pounds lean round steak
2 cups tomato juice
½ cup unsweetened orange juice
½ cup unsweetened crushed pineapple
½ cup cider vinegar
1 tablespoon instant minced onion
1 tablespoon Worcestershire sauce
½ teaspoon garlic powder
½ teaspoon dry mustard
½ teaspoon ground cinnamon
⅛ teaspoon ground ginger
4 cups hot cooked rice

Trim excess fat from meat. Partially freeze steak; cut into 1-inch squares.

Place meat on a broiling rack; broil 6 inches from heat until browned on all sides, turning as needed. Drain meat on paper towels.

Combine meat and remaining ingredients except rice in a small Dutch oven. Bring to a boil; cover, reduce heat, and simmer 1½ hours or until meat is tender. Uncover and simmer an additional 20 minutes or until sauce is thickened. Serve over rice. Yield: 8 servings (about 183 calories per serving plus 90 calories per ½ cup cooked rice).

ZUCCHINI-BEEF STEW

1½ pounds ground chuck
1½ cups sliced celery
3 medium zucchini (about 1½ pounds), cut into ½-inch slices
¾ cup chopped onion
2 (16-ounce) cans whole tomatoes, undrained and cut into quarters
¾ teaspoon dried Italian seasoning
¾ teaspoon dried whole oregano
½ teaspoon dried whole basil
½ teaspoon salt
½ teaspoon pepper
2 green peppers, cut into ½-inch squares
¼ cup plus 1 tablespoon grated Parmesan cheese

Cook beef in a large Dutch oven over medium heat until browned, stirring to crumble; drain meat in a colander, and pat dry with a paper towel. Wipe pan drippings from Dutch oven with a paper towel.

Return meat to Dutch oven; add celery, and cook over medium heat 10 minutes. Stir in next 8 ingredients; bring to a boil. Cover, reduce heat, and simmer 30 minutes.

Add green peppers; cover and simmer an additional 10 minutes. Spoon stew into bowls; sprinkle each serving with ½ tablespoon Parmesan cheese. Yield: 10 cups (about 169 calories per 1-cup serving).

LIGHT BEER STEW

1 pound lean round steak
Vegetable cooking spray
1 teaspoon vegetable oil
1 cup chopped onion
1 (12-ounce) can light beer
2 bay leaves
½ teaspoon dried whole thyme
½ teaspoon freshly ground pepper
¼ teaspoon salt
5 medium carrots, scraped and cut into ½-inch slices
½ pound fresh mushrooms
2 teaspoons cornstarch
2 tablespoons water
3 (¼-inch) slices whole wheat bread, toasted
1 tablespoon Dijon mustard

Trim excess fat from steak. Partially freeze steak; slice across grain into thin strips. Coat a small, heavy Dutch oven with cooking spray; add oil, and place over medium-high heat until hot. Add meat to Dutch oven, and cook until meat is browned.

Reduce heat to medium low; add onion, and cook 10 minutes or until onion is tender and lightly browned. Stir in next 7 ingredients. Bring to a boil; cover, reduce heat, and simmer 1 to 1½ hours or until meat is tender.

Combine cornstarch and water, stirring until blended; stir into meat mixture, and cook, uncovered, an additional 10 minutes, stirring occasionally. Remove and discard bay leaves.

Cut each slice toasted bread into 2 triangles; spread evenly with mustard. Spoon stew into bowls; float toast triangles on top of stew. Yield: 4 servings (about 277 calories per serving).

WHITE WINE STEW

2¼ pounds lean round steak, trimmed and cut into 1-inch cubes
Vegetable cooking spray
2 large onions, diced
1 large green pepper, cut into 1-inch pieces
1 pound carrots, scraped and cut into 1-inch pieces
3 stalks celery, cut into 1-inch pieces
2 cups light Chablis
2 cups water
1 teaspoon dried whole rosemary
1 teaspoon dried whole basil
1 teaspoon dried whole thyme
Freshly ground pepper to taste
2 tablespoons cornstarch
¼ cup water
Minced fresh parsley (optional)

Sauté steak in a Dutch oven coated with cooking spray. Add onion and pepper; cook, stirring often, until vegetables are tender. Add next 8 ingredients; bring to a boil. Cover and simmer stew 1 hour and 15 minutes.

Combine cornstarch and ¼ cup cold water, mixing well; stir into stew. Cook over medium-high heat, stirring constantly, until thickened and bubbly. Garnish with parsley, if desired. Yield: 8 servings (about 295 calories per 1-cup serving).

Refrigerate soups, stews, and broth before serving so the dispersed fat will rise to the top. Each tablespoon of hardened fat you remove contains about 100 calories. Plan ahead so that you can chill the soup, and then reheat it before serving time.

OYSTER STEW

2 large baking potatoes (about 1¼ pounds)
1 cup chopped onion
1 cup thinly sliced celery
2⅔ cups chicken broth
½ cup Chablis or other dry white wine
2 to 3 teaspoons Worcestershire sauce
½ teaspoon celery salt
¼ to ½ teaspoon white pepper
1 cup instant nonfat dry milk powder
2 tablespoons all-purpose flour
¼ cup cold water
1 pint oysters, undrained

Peel potatoes, and cut into ¼-inch cubes. Combine potatoes and next 7 ingredients in a large saucepan. Bring to a boil; cover, reduce heat, and simmer 25 to 30 minutes or until vegetables are tender. Stir in milk powder; cook, stirring constantly, until powder is dissolved.

Combine flour and ¼ cup water, blending until smooth. Stir into stew; cook, stirring constantly, until thickened. Stir in oysters; cook about 5 minutes or until edges of oysters curl (do not boil). Yield: 8 cups (about 149 calories per 1-cup serving).

LENTIL STEW

2 large onions, chopped
2 medium carrots, scraped and chopped
1 cup dry lentils
½ cup chopped fresh parsley
1 (16-ounce) can whole tomatoes, undrained and coarsely chopped
3 cups chicken broth
¼ cup dry sherry
½ teaspoon dried whole thyme
½ teaspoon dried whole marjoram
½ teaspoon pepper

Combine all ingredients in a Dutch oven. Bring to a boil; cover, reduce heat, and simmer 45 minutes or until lentils are tender. Yield: 8½ cups (about 116 calories per 1-cup serving).

By avoiding extras like butter, bacon drippings, and heavy cream, calories in these soups are minimized. Clockwise from top: Chilled Cucumber Soup (page 208), Spicy Tomato Soup (page 211), and Squash Soup (page 211).

VEGETABLES

Nutrition experts tell us that we would be better off eating more foods containing complex carbohydrates and starch. What foods fit into this recommended category? Vegetables. From artichokes to zucchini, fiber-rich vegetables are relatively low in calories, especially when prepared the *Cooking Light* way.

In general, vegetables provide more nutrients and fiber when eaten raw. Overcooking can destroy important nutrients. When boiling vegetables use as little water as possible and cook for as short a time as possible in order to preserve the water-soluble vitamins and minerals. Cook vegetables whole when possible to save additional nutrients. Try scrubbing potatoes and carrots instead of peeling them before cooking. A large proportion of the nutrients in vegetables are found just beneath the skin and are more likely to be lost if the skin is removed.

Steaming is an especially nutritious cooking method since vegetables cook above, not in, the boiling water. Place herbs or spices in the water before steaming so that the vegetables will absorb the herb flavor during cooking.

Stir-frying and sautéing are nutritious and light ways to cook vegetables. Use vegetable cooking spray or a small amount of oil for stir-frying and sautéing.

Keep calories low in vegetables by cutting back on the usual fattening seasonings such as ham hock, bacon grease, salt pork, butter, and margarine. Use low-calorie and low-sodium herbs and spices to open up a whole new world of flavors for your vegetables. As you experiment with the different seasonings, you will begin to enjoy the natural taste of vegetables.

Some of the lowest calorie and most nutritious foods are vegetables. Be sure to choose seasonings and sauces that keep the calories down. From top: Bean-Stuffed Tomatoes (page 235), Chinese Vegetable Medley (page 236), Celery-Parmesan Toss (page 225), and Tropical Carrots (page 225).

CRUSTLESS ARTICHOKE QUICHE

1 (14-ounce) can artichoke hearts
Vegetable cooking spray
¼ pound fresh mushrooms, sliced
1 tablespoon reduced-calorie margarine, melted
2 cups (8 ounces) shredded Muenster cheese
4 eggs, beaten
1 cup skim milk
⅛ teaspoon pepper
¼ teaspoon dried whole basil
Paprika

Drain artichokes. Chop artichokes, and place on paper towels; squeeze until barely moist. Coat a 9-inch quiche dish with cooking spray. Place artichokes in quiche dish.

Sauté mushrooms in margarine until tender; drain and place in quiche dish. Sprinkle with cheese. Combine next 4 ingredients; pour over cheese. Sprinkle with paprika. Bake at 350° for 30 to 40 minutes or until firm in center. Yield: 8 servings (about 154 calories per serving).

PARMESAN ARTICHOKES

¼ cup fine, dry breadcrumbs
2 tablespoons grated Parmesan cheese
3 tablespoons Italian reduced-calorie salad dressing
1 (9-ounce) package frozen artichoke hearts, thawed and drained
1 tablespoon Italian reduced-calorie salad dressing
2 medium tomatoes, peeled and quartered

Combine breadcrumbs, cheese, and 3 tablespoons salad dressing; set aside.

Toss artichoke hearts in 1 tablespoon salad dressing; arrange artichokes and tomatoes in a 1-quart casserole. Sprinkle breadcrumb mixture over vegetables. Bake at 350° for 35 to 40 minutes or until topping is lightly browned. Yield: 4 servings (about 80 calories per serving).

ASPARAGUS SUPREME

2 (10-ounce) packages frozen asparagus spears
2 tablespoons reduced-calorie margarine
2 tablespoons all-purpose flour
¾ cup skim milk
¼ teaspoon salt
¼ teaspoon dry mustard
Dash of white pepper
½ cup low-fat cottage cheese
1 hard-cooked egg, finely chopped

Cook asparagus according to package directions, omitting salt; drain well. Place in a shallow serving dish, and keep warm.

Melt margarine in a heavy saucepan over low heat; add flour, stirring until smooth (mixture will be dry). Cook 1 minute, stirring constantly. Gradually add milk; cook over medium heat, stirring constantly with a wire whisk, until thickened and bubbly. Stir in salt, dry mustard, and pepper. Gently stir in cottage cheese; cook over low heat 1 minute.

Spoon sauce over asparagus, and sprinkle egg over sauce. Yield: 8 servings (about 54 calories per serving).

PUFFED ASPARAGUS BAKE

1 (10-ounce) package frozen asparagus spears
3 tablespoons reduced-calorie margarine
3 tablespoons all-purpose flour
1 cup skim milk
2 eggs, separated
½ teaspoon dried whole basil
¼ teaspoon salt
¼ teaspoon pepper
Dash of ground nutmeg
2 tablespoons grated Parmesan cheese
Vegetable cooking spray

Cook asparagus according to package directions, omitting salt. Drain; thinly slice spears, and set aside.

Melt margarine in a small heavy saucepan over low heat; add flour, stirring until smooth (mixture will be dry). Cook 1 minute, stirring constantly. Gradually add milk; cook, stirring constantly with a wire whisk, until mixture is thickened and smooth.

Beat egg yolks until thick and lemon colored. Gradually stir about one-fourth of the hot mixture into egg yolks. Stir yolk mixture into remaining white sauce. Stir in asparagus, seasonings, and Parmesan cheese.

Beat egg whites (at room temperature) until stiff peaks form; fold into asparagus mixture. Spoon into a 1½-quart soufflé dish or casserole coated with cooking spray; bake at 375° for 40 minutes. Serve immediately. Yield: 6 servings (about 102 calories per serving).

RED BEANS AND RICE

¾ pound ham hocks
1 quart water
1 pound dried red beans
1½ cups chopped onion
1 cup chopped fresh parsley
1 cup chopped green pepper
½ cup chopped green onions
2 cloves garlic, pressed
1 (8-ounce) can tomato sauce
1 tablespoon Worcestershire sauce
1 teaspoon pepper
½ teaspoon red pepper
¼ teaspoon dried whole oregano
¼ teaspoon dried whole thyme
3 dashes of hot sauce
5 cups hot cooked rice

Wash ham hocks, and place in a large saucepan. Add 1 quart water, and bring to a boil. Cover, reduce heat, and simmer 30 minutes or until meat is tender. Remove ham hocks, and discard. Strain broth, and chill overnight or until fat rises to the surface and hardens. Remove the fat, and discard; set broth aside.

Sort and wash beans; place in a Dutch oven. Cover with water, and soak overnight.

Drain beans; combine beans and broth in Dutch oven. Cover and cook over low heat 45 minutes. Add remaining ingredients except rice; cover and cook over low heat 2 to 2½ hours, stirring occasionally and adding additional water, if desired. Serve over rice. Yield: 10 servings (about 192 calories per 1-cup serving plus 90 calories per ½ cup cooked rice).

DILLED GREEN BEANS

1 pound fresh green beans
Vegetable cooking spray
1 tablespoon reduced-calorie margarine
1 medium-size green pepper, chopped
3 medium tomatoes, peeled, seeded, and chopped
½ cup water
1 teaspoon dried whole dill seeds
¼ teaspoon salt
⅛ teaspoon freshly ground pepper

Remove strings from beans; wash and cut into 2-inch pieces. Set aside.

Coat a medium saucepan with cooking spray. Place margarine in saucepan; place over medium heat until margarine is melted. Add green pepper; sauté 4 minutes or until just tender.

Add next 5 ingredients to saucepan. Bring to a boil; cover, reduce heat, and simmer 10 minutes. Stir in green beans; cover and simmer 10 to 12 minutes or until beans are tender. Yield: 8 servings (about 36 calories per serving).

SAVORY GREEN BEANS

Vegetable cooking spray
½ cup chopped onion
2 cups fresh cut green beans, cut into 2-inch pieces
2 large tomatoes, peeled and chopped
3 tablespoons diced pimiento
¼ teaspoon dried whole savory, crushed
¼ teaspoon salt
⅛ teaspoon freshly ground pepper

Coat a large nonstick skillet with cooking spray; place over medium heat until hot. Add onion, and sauté until tender.

Add remaining ingredients to skillet; cover and simmer 15 minutes or until beans are just tender. Yield: 6 servings (about 36 calories per serving).

ORANGE GLAZED BEETS

¾ cup unsweetened orange juice
1 tablespoon cornstarch
½ teaspoon grated orange rind
¼ teaspoon ground ginger
⅛ teaspoon salt
1 (16-ounce) can sliced beets, drained

Combine first 5 ingredients in a medium skillet; stir until blended. Add beets to skillet. Bring to a boil over medium heat; cook 1 minute or until sauce thickens, stirring constantly. Yield: 4 servings (about 66 calories per serving).

BROCCOLI SUPREME

2 (1-pound) bunches fresh broccoli
2 tablespoons reduced-calorie margarine
2 tablespoons all-purpose flour
1 cup chicken broth
½ teaspoon Worcestershire sauce
⅛ teaspoon salt
Dash of pepper
2 hard-cooked eggs, sliced
¼ cup sliced pimiento-stuffed olives

Trim off large leaves of broccoli, and remove tough ends of lower stalks. Wash broccoli thoroughly, and separate into spears. Cook broccoli, covered, in a small amount of boiling water 10 minutes or until crisp-tender. Arrange in a serving dish, and keep warm.

Melt margarine in a heavy saucepan over low heat; add flour, stirring until smooth (mixture will be dry). Cook 1 minute, stirring constantly. Gradually add broth; cook over medium heat, stirring constantly with a wire whisk, until thickened and bubbly.

Stir in Worcestershire sauce, salt, and pepper. Pour sauce over broccoli, and garnish with egg slices and olives. Yield: 8 servings (about 76 calories per serving).

BROCCOLI WITH CITRUS SAUCE

1 (1½ pound) bunch fresh broccoli
1½ tablespoons reduced-calorie margarine
1½ tablespoons all-purpose flour
½ teaspoon grated orange rind
½ cup unsweetened orange juice
½ cup fresh orange sections
¼ teaspoon dried whole tarragon

Trim off large leaves of broccoli, and remove tough ends of lower stalks. Wash broccoli thoroughly, and separate into spears. Make lengthwise slits in thick stalks. Arrange broccoli in steaming rack with stalks to center of rack. Place over boiling water; cover and steam 10 to 15 minutes or until crisp-tender. Arrange on a serving platter; keep warm.

Melt margarine in a heavy saucepan over low heat; add flour, and cook 1 minute, stirring constantly (mixture will be dry). Gradually add orange rind and juice, stirring with a wire whisk until smooth.

Add orange sections and tarragon to sauce; cook over medium heat, stirring constantly, until thickened and bubbly. Spoon sauce over steamed broccoli. Yield: 6 servings (about 58 calories per serving).

COLORFUL BROCCOLI

2 (1-pound) bunches fresh broccoli
Vegetable cooking spray
½ cup sliced green onions
1 (2-ounce) jar diced pimiento, undrained
1 teaspoon grated lemon rind
2 tablespoons lemon juice
½ teaspoon chicken-flavored bouillon granules
⅛ teaspoon pepper

Trim off large leaves of broccoli, and remove tough ends of lower stalks. Wash broccoli thoroughly. Make lengthwise slits in thick stalks. Arrange broccoli on steaming rack with stalks to center of rack. Place over boiling water; cover and steam 10 to 15 minutes or until crisp-tender. Place in serving dish, and keep warm.

Coat a small saucepan with cooking spray. Place over medium heat until hot. Add onions, and sauté until tender. Remove from heat, and stir in remaining ingredients. Divide broccoli into 6 portions, and spoon about 1 tablespoon onion mixture over each portion of broccoli. Yield: 6 servings (about 36 calories per serving).

ORIENTAL BROCCOLI

¼ cup boiling water
2 tablespoons soy sauce
1 tablespoon dry sherry
1 teaspoon sugar
1 (1-pound) bunch fresh broccoli
Vegetable cooking spray
1 teaspoon vegetable oil
1 small onion, chopped

Combine first 4 ingredients; set aside.

Trim off large outer leaves of broccoli, and remove tough ends of stalks. Wash broccoli thoroughly. Cut stalks diagonally into 1-inch-thick slices; if stalks are more than 1 inch in diameter, cut in half lengthwise. Cut broccoli flowerets into 1-inch pieces.

Coat a wok or skillet with cooking spray; allow to heat at medium high (325°) for 2 minutes. Add oil and broccoli, and stir-fry 2 minutes; add onion, and stir-fry an additional 3 minutes. Add soy sauce mixture; cover and reduce heat to low (225°). Simmer 5 minutes or until broccoli is crisp-tender. Yield: 4 servings (about 50 calories per serving).

SESAME BROCCOLI STIR-FRY

1 (1½-pound) bunch fresh broccoli
Vegetable cooking spray
1 tablespoon sesame seeds
1 teaspoon vegetable oil
3 to 4 cloves garlic, crushed
½ cup sliced water chestnuts
⅓ cup Chablis or other dry white wine
2 tablespoons soy sauce
½ teaspoon sugar

Trim off large leaves of broccoli. Remove tough ends of lower stalks, and wash broccoli thoroughly. Cut away tops, separating into flowerets; set aside. Cut stems into ¼-inch slices; set aside.

Coat a wok or skillet with cooking spray; allow to heat at medium high (325°) for 1 to 2 minutes. Toast sesame seeds in wok; remove and set aside. Add oil and garlic to wok; stir-fry briefly.

Add broccoli slices; stir-fry 5 minutes. Add broccoli flowerets and remaining ingredients. Reduce heat to low (225°); cover and cook 4 to 5 minutes or until broccoli is crisp-tender. Sprinkle sesame seeds over broccoli to serve. Yield: 6 servings (about 48 calories per serving).

SHERRIED BROCCOLI STIR-FRY

1 tablespoon cornstarch
2 tablespoons soy sauce
½ cup chicken broth
1 (1¼-pound) bunch fresh broccoli
Vegetable cooking spray
2 teaspoons vegetable oil
1 clove garlic, minced
2 tablespoons sherry

Combine cornstarch, soy sauce, and chicken broth, stirring until blended; set aside.

Trim off large leaves of broccoli. Remove tough ends of lower stalks; wash broccoli thoroughly. Cut away tops, separating into flowerets; cut stems into ¼-inch slices, and set aside.

Coat a wok or skillet with cooking spray; allow to heat at medium high (325°) for 3 minutes. Pour oil around top of wok, coating sides. Add garlic, and stir-fry briefly. Add broccoli tops and slices; stir-fry 2 minutes. Add sherry; cover and cook 2 minutes. Stir in cornstarch mixture; cook, stirring constantly, until sauce is thickened. Yield: 4 servings (about 62 calories per serving).

HERBED BRUSSELS SPROUTS AND CARROTS

¾ pound fresh brussels sprouts
2 cups chicken broth
½ pound baby carrots, scraped
1 tablespoon lemon juice
2 teaspoons reduced-calorie margarine
½ teaspoon dried whole tarragon, crushed
Dash of ground nutmeg

Wash brussels sprouts thoroughly, and remove any wilted outer leaves. Cut a cross in the root end of each brussels sprout. Bring chicken broth to a boil in a 2-quart saucepan; add brussels sprouts and carrots. Return to a boil; cover, reduce heat, and simmer 6 to 8 minutes or until vegetables are tender.

Drain vegetables; toss with lemon juice, margarine, tarragon, and nutmeg. Yield: 6 servings (about 52 calories per serving).

Note: 4 large carrots, scraped and sliced, may be substituted for baby carrots.

CARAWAY CABBAGE

1 (2-pound) cabbage, coarsely shredded
1 (16-ounce) can stewed tomatoes, undrained
1 to 2 teaspoons caraway seeds
2 bay leaves
2 teaspoons lemon juice
¼ teaspoon salt
¼ teaspoon pepper
2 tablespoons grated Parmesan cheese

Combine all ingredients except cheese in a Dutch oven. Bring to a boil; cover, reduce heat, and simmer 15 minutes or until cabbage is tender. Transfer to a serving bowl; remove bay leaves. Sprinkle with cheese before serving. Yield: 8 servings (about 43 calories per serving).

CARDAMOM CARROTS

¾ pound carrots, scraped and sliced into thin strips (about 3 cups)
½ cup water
2 teaspoons reduced-calorie margarine
1 teaspoon brown sugar
½ teaspoon ground cardamom

Combine carrots and water in a medium saucepan; cover and cook until carrots are crisp-tender. Drain carrots, and set aside.

Melt margarine in saucepan; stir in sugar and cardamom. Cook over low heat, stirring constantly, until sugar is dissolved. Add carrots; continue to cook over low heat, stirring gently until well coated and thoroughly heated. Yield: 4 servings (about 43 calories per serving).

CARROTS MARSALA

1½ pounds carrots, scraped and diagonally sliced
¼ cup plus 2 tablespoons Marsala wine
¼ cup plus 2 tablespoons water
1½ tablespoons reduced-calorie margarine
½ teaspoon salt
⅛ teaspoon pepper
1½ tablespoons chopped fresh parsley

Combine first 6 ingredients in a large saucepan. Bring to a boil; cover, reduce heat, and simmer 10 minutes or until most of liquid evaporates, tossing carrots occasionally. Before serving, sprinkle with parsley. Yield: 6 servings (about 54 calories per serving).

TROPICAL CARROTS

4 medium carrots, cut into 3- x ¼-inch strips (about 2 cups)
½ cup water
¾ cup unsweetened pineapple tidbits, undrained
2 teaspoons cornstarch
¼ teaspoon ground ginger

Combine carrots and water in a small saucepan; cover and cook until carrots are crisp-tender.

Combine pineapple, cornstarch, and ginger in a small bowl; mix well. Add pineapple mixture to carrots; cook over low heat, stirring constantly, until thickened. Yield: 4 servings (about 59 calories per serving).

CELERY-PARMESAN TOSS

3 cups diagonally sliced celery
1 tablespoon reduced-calorie margarine
⅓ cup minced fresh parsley
¼ cup grated Parmesan cheese
Chopped pimiento (optional)

Cook celery in a small amount of boiling water 8 minutes or until crisp-tender; drain. Return to saucepan, and stir in margarine; cover and cook over low heat 2 minutes.

Remove from heat, and toss with parsley and cheese. Sprinkle with chopped pimiento, if desired. Serve immediately. Yield: 6 servings (about 40 calories per serving).

SOUTHERN-STYLE COLLARDS

About ¾ pound ham hocks
1 quart water
1 bunch (about 5 pounds) collard greens
1 teaspoon salt

Wash ham hocks, and place in a Dutch oven. Add water, and bring to a boil. Reduce heat; simmer, uncovered, 30 to 45 minutes or until meat is tender. Remove ham hocks and discard, or reserve any meat for use in other recipes. Strain the broth, and chill until fat rises to the surface and hardens. Remove fat and discard.

Check leaves of collards carefully; remove pulpy stems and discolored spots on leaves. Wash leaves thoroughly; drain well and chop. Place collards, broth, and salt in a large Dutch oven; bring to a boil. Cover, reduce heat, and simmer about 30 to 45 minutes or until collards are tender. Yield: 10 servings (about 60 calories per 1-cup serving).

> You can eliminate salt from any recipe (except breads containing yeast and pickles) without affecting the quality of the product. (Salt is added to yeast breads for a smooth texture and to pickles for prevention of bacterial growth.)

MEXI-CORN MEDLEY

Vegetable cooking spray
2 tablespoons reduced-calorie margarine
2 cups fresh corn cut from cob (about 4 ears)
1 cup sliced onion, separated into rings
⅓ cup chopped green pepper
⅓ cup chopped red pepper
¼ teaspoon dried whole oregano
⅛ teaspoon garlic powder
Dash of red pepper
1 medium tomato, peeled and diced

Coat a large skillet with cooking spray; add margarine, and place over medium heat until margarine is melted. Add remaining ingredients except tomato; cover and cook over medium heat 7 to 8 minutes or until corn is tender, stirring occasionally.

Stir in tomato; cook, uncovered, 2 minutes or until thoroughly heated. Yield: 6 servings (about 79 calories per serving).

SAVORY STUFFED EGGPLANT

2 large eggplants (about 1½ pounds each)
2 tablespoons Italian reduced-calorie salad dressing
Vegetable cooking spray
2 medium onions, finely chopped
1 medium-size green pepper, finely chopped
1 clove garlic, minced
1 large tomato, peeled and chopped
¼ cup chopped fresh parsley
½ teaspoon dried whole basil
¼ teaspoon salt
⅛ teaspoon pepper
1 (8-ounce) can tomato sauce

Cut eggplants lengthwise into quarters; brush cut sides with salad dressing. Place quarters, cut side up, in a shallow baking pan; cover and bake at 450° for 25 minutes or just until tender.

Coat a large nonstick skillet with cooking spray; place over medium-high heat until hot. Add onion, green pepper, and garlic to skillet; sauté until vegetables are tender. Remove from heat; stir in next 5 ingredients.

Cut a lengthwise slit down center of each eggplant quarter, cutting to within ½-inch of peel; spoon vegetable mixture into slits. Return stuffed eggplant quarters to baking pan; spoon tomato sauce over eggplant. Bake at 375° for 30 minutes. Serve warm. Yield: 8 servings (about 64 calories per serving).

CREOLE EGGPLANT

1 medium eggplant, peeled and cubed
1 medium-size green pepper, chopped
1 medium onion, chopped
2 cloves garlic, minced
1 (8-ounce) can tomato sauce
½ teaspoon dried whole dillweed
¼ teaspoon dried whole rosemary, crushed
¼ teaspoon dried whole thyme

Combine all ingredients in a skillet. Cover and cook over low heat 15 to 20 minutes or until tender, stirring occasionally. Yield: 6 servings (about 38 calories per serving).

TANGY PARMESAN EGGPLANT

1 medium eggplant (about 1¼ pound)
3 tablespoons Italian reduced-calorie salad dressing
⅓ cup fine, dry breadcrumbs
2 tablespoons grated Parmesan cheese
1 tablespoon minced fresh parsley
¼ teaspoon ground oregano
¼ teaspoon pepper
Vegetable cooking spray
2 teaspoons margarine

Peel eggplant, and cut into ½-inch thick slices; brush all sides with salad dressing. Combine next

5 ingredients; dredge eggplant slices in breadcrumb mixture.

Coat a large skillet with cooking spray; add margarine. Place skillet over medium heat until margarine is melted. Add eggplant to skillet; cook 5 to 7 minutes on each side or until lightly browned and tender. Yield: 4 servings (about 100 calories per serving).

CRAB-STUFFED MUSHROOMS

12 large fresh mushrooms (about 1 pound)
Vegetable cooking spray
1 (6½-ounce) can lump crabmeat, rinsed, drained, and flaked
¼ cup grated Parmesan cheese
¼ cup thinly sliced green onions
2 tablespoons reduced-calorie mayonnaise
1 teaspoon Worcestershire sauce
1 teaspoon Dijon mustard
¼ teaspoon white pepper

Clean mushrooms with damp paper towels. Remove mushroom stems, and chop enough to measure 1 cup; set mushroom caps aside.

Coat a small skillet with cooking spray; place over medium heat until hot. Add 1 cup chopped mushroom stems to skillet; cover and cook 5 minutes or until tender, stirring occasionally.

Combine cooked mushroom stems and remaining ingredients except mushroom caps in a small bowl, mixing well. Spoon mixture into mushroom caps; arrange in a baking pan coated with cooking spray. Bake at 350° for 15 minutes or until lightly browned. Yield: 6 servings (about 92 calories per serving).

OKRA-RICE MEDLEY

Vegetable cooking spray
1 medium onion, chopped
½ cup chopped green pepper
2 medium tomatoes, peeled, seeded, and chopped
1 cup thinly sliced okra
1 cup cooked rice (cooked without salt)
¼ cup water
½ teaspoon chicken-flavored bouillon granules
⅛ teaspoon pepper

Coat a large skillet with cooking spray. Place over medium heat until hot; add onion and green pepper, and sauté until tender. Add tomatoes and okra; cover and cook an additional 10 minutes.

Stir in remaining ingredients; simmer, uncovered, 8 to 10 minutes or until liquid is evaporated, stirring frequently. Yield: 6 servings (about 57 calories per serving).

SUMMERTIME OKRA

3 cups sliced fresh okra
2 cups fresh corn cut from cob
4 medium tomatoes, peeled and chopped
2 bay leaves
3 tablespoons chopped fresh parsley
½ teaspoon salt
¼ to ½ teaspoon freshly ground pepper
½ teaspoon gumbo filé
⅛ teaspoon hot sauce

Thoroughly rinse okra under running water; drain well.

Combine okra and next 6 ingredients in a large skillet. Cover and simmer 10 minutes; uncover and simmer an additional 20 minutes.

Stir in gumbo filé and hot sauce; cook, stirring constantly, 1 minute. Remove bay leaves before serving. Yield: 10 servings (about 52 calories per ½-cup serving).

OVEN-FRIED OKRA

1¼ cups cornmeal
½ teaspoon salt
Pepper to taste
1¾ pounds fresh okra
Vegetable cooking spray

Combine first three ingredients; set aside.

Wash okra; drain. Cut off tip and stem ends; cut okra into ½-inch slices. Dredge in cornmeal mixture. (Okra must be moist for cornmeal mixture to coat well. Rinse again before dredging, if necessary.)

Lightly coat a 15- x 10- x 1-inch jellyroll pan with cooking spray. Spread okra in a single layer in pan. Bake at 450° for 30 to 40 minutes or until crisp, stirring occasionally. Yield: 6 servings (about 111 calories per serving).

GOURMET ONIONS

24 small boiling onions (about 1¾ pounds)
½ teaspoon salt
2 tablespoons reduced-calorie margarine
2 tablespoons all-purpose flour
1½ cups skim milk
¼ cup (1 ounce) extra-sharp Cheddar cheese
1½ tablespoons dry sherry

Peel onions; place in a large saucepan. Add water to cover; sprinkle with salt, and bring to a boil. Cover, reduce heat, and cook 10 to 15 minutes or until tender. Drain well, and place onions in an 8-inch square baking dish.

Melt margarine in a heavy saucepan over low heat; add flour, stirring until smooth. Cook 1 minute, stirring constantly (mixture will be dry). Gradually add milk, stirring with a wire whisk until smooth; cook over medium heat, stirring constantly, until thickened and bubbly.

Add cheese to sauce, stirring until cheese is melted and sauce is smooth. Stir in sherry, and pour sauce over onions. Bake at 350° for 20 minutes or until thoroughly heated. Yield: 8 servings (about 85 calories per serving).

FANCY GREEN PEAS

2 (10-ounce) packages frozen English peas
Vegetable cooking spray
2 tablespoons reduced-calorie margarine
¾ cup finely chopped onion
¼ cup finely chopped green pepper
1 (2-ounce) jar diced pimiento, drained
2 tablespoons minced fresh parsley
1 bay leaf
½ teaspoon vinegar
¼ teaspoon salt
⅛ teaspoon ground nutmeg

Cook peas according to package directions, omitting salt; drain and set aside.

Coat a large skillet with cooking spray; add margarine. Place skillet over medium heat until margarine is melted.

Add next 5 ingredients to skillet; sauté 5 minutes or until vegetables are tender. Stir in peas, vinegar, salt, and nutmeg; cook until thoroughly heated. Remove bay leaf before serving. Yield: 8 servings (about 70 calories per serving).

SHERRIED PEAS AND MUSHROOMS

2 pounds fresh English peas
Vegetable cooking spray
1 (4½-ounce) jar sliced mushrooms, undrained
¼ cup minced onion
1 tablespoon reduced-calorie margarine
2 tablespoons dry sherry
½ teaspoon salt
⅛ teaspoon dried whole marjoram
Dash of pepper

Shell and wash peas. Place in a medium saucepan, and add just enough water to cover peas. Bring to a boil; cover, reduce heat, and simmer 8 to 12 minutes or until tender. Drain.

Coat a large skillet with cooking spray; place over medium-high heat until hot. Add mushrooms and onion, and sauté until onions are tender. Stir in peas and remaining ingredients; cook 1 minute. Yield: 4 servings (about 95 calories per serving).

ORIENTAL SNOW PEA STIR-FRY

1 teaspoon cornstarch
¼ cup chicken broth
Vegetable cooking spray
1 to 2 cloves garlic, minced
1 teaspoon soy sauce
2 cups fresh snow peas
1 (8-ounce) can sliced bamboo shoots, drained
1 (8-ounce) can sliced water chestnuts, drained

Combine cornstarch and chicken broth, mixing well; set aside.

Coat a nonstick skillet with cooking spray; place over low heat until hot. Add garlic to skillet; sauté until garlic is lightly browned. Add soy sauce, snow peas, bamboo shoots, and chestnuts to skillet; stir-fry over high heat 1 minute.

Reduce heat to medium; add chicken broth mixture, stirring well. Bring to a boil, and cook, stirring constantly, about 1 minute or until sauce is thickened. Yield: 4 servings (about 61 calories per serving).

SHERRIED PEPPERS AND BEAN SPROUTS

2 medium-size green peppers, cut into thin strips
2 cups fresh bean sprouts
2 teaspoons soy sauce
1 tablespoon dry sherry
1 teaspoon vinegar

Combine first 4 ingredients in a skillet; cover and cook 5 minutes over medium heat or until vegetables are crisp-tender. Stir in vinegar just before serving. Yield: 4 servings (about 28 calories per serving).

CHIVE-POTATO BAKE

3 medium-size baking potatoes (about 1 pound), thinly sliced
Vegetable cooking spray
3 tablespoons minced chives
2 to 3 tablespoons minced fresh parsley
½ teaspoon freshly ground pepper
¼ teaspoon paprika

Layer one-third of potatoes in a 13- x 9- x 2-inch baking pan coated with cooking spray. Sprinkle with one-third of chives, parsley, pepper, and paprika. Repeat layers until remaining ingredients are used. Cover with foil, bake at 400° for 45 minutes or until done. Yield: 6 servings (about 46 calories per serving).

GRILLED POTATOES

4 large baking potatoes (about 2 pounds)
1 tablespoon plus 1 teaspoon reduced-calorie margarine
1 tablespoon plus 1 teaspoon grated Parmesan cheese
1 teaspoon chopped chives
¼ to ½ teaspoon pepper
⅛ teaspoon garlic powder
1 medium onion, thinly sliced

Scrub potatoes. Cut potatoes in half crosswise. Cut slits crosswise into potatoes, ¾-inch apart, leaving bottom edge intact; set aside.

Combine next 5 ingredients; mix well. Divide mixture evenly and place into slit potatoes. Place onion slices into slits.

Wrap potatoes in aluminum foil. Bake at 400° for 45 to 55 minutes or until done. Yield: 8 servings (about 88 calories per serving).

> You can still enjoy mashed potatoes when you're eating light if you remember to make them with skim milk and little, if any, margarine.

COTTAGE POTATO CASSEROLE

4 cups peeled, cubed potatoes
1 (8-ounce) carton plain low-fat yogurt
1 cup low-fat cottage cheese
¼ cup chopped chives
½ teaspoon salt
Dash of garlic powder
Vegetable cooking spray

Cook potatoes in boiling water to cover 15 minutes or until tender; drain. Combine potatoes and next 5 ingredients; spoon into a 9-inch square baking pan coated with cooking spray. Bake at 350° for 30 minutes. Yield: 8 servings (about 90 calories per serving).

CREAMED NEW POTATOES AND PEAS

12 small new potatoes (1¼ pounds)
1 (10-ounce) package frozen English peas
1 tablespoon reduced-calorie margarine
1 tablespoon all-purpose flour
1 cup skim milk
¼ teaspoon salt
⅛ teaspoon white pepper
Dash of ground nutmeg

Cook potatoes in boiling water 15 to 20 minutes or until tender. Drain well; place in a serving dish, and keep warm.

Cook peas according to package directions, omitting salt. Drain and set aside.

Melt margarine in a small heavy saucepan over low heat; add flour, stirring until smooth (mixture will be dry). Cook 1 minute, stirring constantly. Gradually add milk, stirring with a wire whisk until smooth; cook over medium heat, stirring constantly, until thickened and bubbly. Stir in seasonings and peas; cook until thoroughly heated.

Pour creamed peas over potatoes. Yield: 6 servings (about 117 calories per serving).

OVEN-FRIED POTATOES

3 medium baking potatoes (about 1¼ pounds)
1 tablespoon water
1 tablespoon vegetable oil
Vegetable cooking spray

Scrub potatoes, and cut into lengthwise strips, ½-inch wide. Combine water and oil in a medium bowl; toss potato strips in oil mixture until well coated. Pour off excess oil mixture.

Coat a 15- x 10- x 1-inch jellyroll pan with cooking spray; place potatoes strips in a single layer in pan. Bake at 475° for 30 minutes or until done, turning slices after 15 minutes. Yield: 4 servings (about 119 calories per serving).

SPECIAL HASH BROWNS

½ cup frozen English peas
2 large baking potatoes (about 1¼ pounds)
Vegetable cooking spray
¼ pound fresh mushrooms, thinly sliced
3 tablespoons reduced-calorie margarine
¼ teaspoon salt
⅛ teaspoon pepper
1 tablespoon chopped fresh parsley
1 small clove garlic, pressed

Cook peas according to package directions, omitting salt; drain and set aside.

Peel potatoes, and cut into ½-inch cubes. Cook in boiling water to cover about 4 minutes. Drain and set aside.

Coat a large skillet with cooking spray; place over medium-high heat until hot. Add mushrooms, and sauté until tender. Remove mushrooms from skillet, and set aside.

Wipe skillet clean with paper towels; coat again with cooking spray. Add margarine, and place over medium-high heat until margarine is melted. Add potatoes; sauté until tender and golden brown. Add next 4 ingredients; reduce heat to low, and cook until thoroughly heated. Add parsley and garlic; toss gently. Yield: 6 servings (about 99 calories per serving).

CARDAMOM SWEET POTATOES

2 medium-size sweet potatoes (¾ pound)
1 tablespoon reduced-calorie margarine
1 teaspoon brown sugar
¼ teaspoon ground cardamom

Peel and dice sweet potatoes. Arrange sweet potatoes in a steaming rack. Place over boiling water; cover and steam until tender.

Combine remaining ingredients; blend well, and toss with hot sweet potatoes. Yield: 4 servings (about 93 calories per serving).

PINEAPPLE-STUFFED SWEET POTATOES

6 small sweet potatoes (2¼ pounds)
1 (8-ounce) can unsweetened crushed pineapple, undrained
2 tablespoons reduced-calorie margarine
¼ teaspoon salt
¼ teaspoon ground ginger
⅛ teaspoon ground nutmeg
Orange rind curls (optional)

Scrub sweet potatoes thoroughly; pierce with a fork. Bake at 375° for 45 minutes or until done.

Allow potatoes to cool to touch. Cut a small lengthwise strip from top of each potato; carefully scoop out potato pulp, leaving ¼-inch of potato shell intact.

Drain pineapple, reserving juice. Combine potato pulp, pineapple juice, margarine, salt, and spices in a small bowl; beat at medium speed of electric mixer until fluffy. Stir in pineapple. Stuff shells with potato mixture. Place in a shallow baking dish; bake at 375° for 15 minutes or until thoroughly heated. Garnish with orange rind curls, if desired. Yield: 6 servings (about 194 calories per serving).

SWEET POTATOES IN ORANGE CUPS

4 small oranges
2 cups cooked, mashed sweet potatoes
1 teaspoon grated orange rind
¼ cup plus 2 tablespoons unsweetened orange juice
1 teaspoon butter flavoring
¾ teaspoon ground cinnamon
¼ teaspoon salt
Orange rind curls (optional)

Cut oranges in half crosswise. Clip membranes, and carefully remove pulp (do not puncture bottom). Reserve orange pulp for other uses.

Combine next 6 ingredients; stuff each orange cup with ¼ cup potato mixture. Place orange cups in a 13- x 9- x 2-inch baking pan; cover and bake at 350° for 20 minutes. Top each with an orange rind curl, if desired. Yield: 8 servings (about 79 calories per serving).

SPINACH QUICHE

1 (10-ounce) package frozen chopped spinach
½ pound Swiss cheese, diced
2 tablespoons all-purpose flour
3 eggs, beaten
1 cup skim milk
½ teaspoon salt
⅛ teaspoon pepper
Dash of ground nutmeg
Vegetable cooking spray

Cook spinach according to package directions, omitting salt; place on paper towels, and squeeze until barely moist. Set aside. Combine cheese and flour; set aside.

Combine eggs, milk, salt, pepper, and nutmeg; stir in spinach and cheese until well blended. Pour mixture into a 9-inch deep-dish pieplate coated with cooking spray; bake at 350° for 55 to 60 minutes or until set. Let stand 5 to 10 minutes before serving. Yield: 8 servings (about 165 calories per serving).

BAKED SPINACH CUPS

1 (10-ounce) package frozen chopped spinach
½ cup skim milk
2 eggs
½ teaspoon onion powder
¼ teaspoon salt
⅛ teaspoon pepper
Dash of ground nutmeg
Vegetable cooking spray

Cook spinach according to package directions, omitting salt; place on paper towels, and squeeze until barely moist. Combine spinach, milk, eggs, onion powder, salt, pepper, and nutmeg in container of a food processor or electric blender; process until mixture is pureed.

Coat 4 (6-ounce) custard cups or ramekins with cooking spray; divide spinach mixture evenly into custard cups. Place cups in a baking pan; pour boiling water into pan to come halfway up sides of custard cups. Bake at 350° for 35 to 40 minutes or until knife inserted between center and edge of custard cup comes out clean.

To unmold, loosen edge of mold with tip of a sharp knife; turn upright to serve. Yield: 4 servings (about 66 calories per serving).

STIR-FRY SPINACH AND MUSHROOMS

1 pound fresh spinach
1 tablespoon lemon juice
1 teaspoon sugar
¼ teaspoon salt
Dash of ground nutmeg
Vegetable cooking spray
2 teaspoons peanut or vegetable oil
1 cup sliced fresh mushrooms
1 onion, chopped
1 clove garlic, minced

Remove stems from spinach. Wash leaves thoroughly in lukewarm water; set aside.

Combine lemon juice, sugar, salt, and nutmeg; mix and set aside.

Coat a wok or large skillet with cooking spray; add oil, and allow to heat at medium high (325°) for 2 minutes. Add mushrooms, onion, and garlic; stir-fry 3 minutes. Add spinach and lemon juice mixture; stir-fry an additional 3 minutes or until spinach is wilted. Yield: 4 servings (about 62 calories per serving).

SQUASH JULIENNE

1 pound yellow squash (3 medium)
1 pound zucchini (3 medium)
1½ tablespoons grated onion
½ teaspoon dried whole chervil
¼ teaspoon salt
¼ teaspoon dried whole thyme
¼ teaspoon freshly ground pepper
Pimiento strips (optional)

Wash squash, and cut into 3- x ¼- inch strips. Arrange squash on steaming rack, and place over boiling water; cover and steam 5 to 7 minutes or until crisp-tender.

Combine steamed squash, grated onion, chervil, salt, thyme, and pepper in a serving dish; toss gently. Garnish with pimiento strips, if desired. Yield: 8 servings (about 21 calories per serving).

SUMMER SQUASH CASSEROLE

1 pound yellow squash, cut into ½-inch slices
1 pound zucchini, cut into ½-inch slices
Vegetable cooking spray
1 medium onion, finely chopped
1 clove garlic, minced
1 (8-ounce) can tomato sauce
1 (4-ounce) can chopped green chiles, drained
¼ cup (1 ounce) shredded Cheddar cheese
2 tablespoons seasoned, dry breadcrumbs

Cook yellow squash and zucchini separately in a small amount of boiling water 5 minutes; drain well, and set aside.

Coat a nonstick skillet with cooking spray; place over medium-high heat until hot. Add onion and garlic to skillet; sauté until tender. Remove from heat, and stir in tomato sauce and green chiles.

Place yellow squash in a deep 1½-quart casserole. Spread half of sauce mixture evenly over yellow squash; arrange zucchini over sauce. Pour remaining sauce over top. Sprinkle with cheese, and top with breadcrumbs. Bake at 350° for 30 minutes or until bubbly. Yield: 6 servings (about 80 calories per serving).

STUFFED SQUASH

6 small yellow squash
¾ cup frozen small English peas
3 slices whole wheat bread, toasted and crumbled
3 tablespoons chopped pimiento
3 tablespoons minced onion
¼ to ½ teaspoon dried whole marjoram
¼ teaspoon pepper

Cook squash in boiling water to cover 6 to 8 minutes or until tender but still firm. Drain and cool slightly. Trim off stems. Cut squash in half lengthwise; remove and reserve pulp, leaving firm shells.

Cook peas in a small amount of boiling water until tender; drain and set aside.

Mash reserved pulp in a medium bowl; mix with cooked peas and remaining ingredients. Place squash shells in a 13- x 9- x 2-inch baking dish. Spoon pulp mixture into shells. Bake at 350° for 30 minutes or until lightly browned. Yield: 6 servings (about 73 calories per serving).

SPINACH-STUFFED SQUASH

8 medium-size yellow squash
1 chicken-flavored bouillon cube
1 (10-ounce) package frozen chopped spinach
¼ cup low-fat cottage cheese
1 tablespoon Parmesan cheese
1 large egg, beaten
¼ teaspoon seasoned salt
¼ teaspoon onion salt
¼ teaspoon coarsely ground black pepper
3 tablespoons dry breadcrumbs
Paprika
Vegetable cooking spray

Wash squash thoroughly. Drop in boiling water with bouillon cube; cover and simmer 8 to 10 minutes or until tender but still firm. Drain and cool slightly; trim off stems. Cut squash in half lengthwise. Scoop out pulp, leaving firm shells; mash the pulp.

Cook spinach according to package directions; drain well, and add to squash pulp. Add cottage cheese, and mix well. Stir in next 5 ingredients; spoon into squash shells.

Sprinkle squash shells with breadcrumbs and paprika. Place on a baking sheet coated with cooking spray; cover with foil, and bake at 325° for 30 minutes. Yield: 8 servings (about 55 calories per serving).

> Since many vegetables are low in calories and high in fiber, they may be eaten in larger quantities than other foods. High fiber vegetables are a plus for dieters because they fill you up without adding many extra calories.

SQUASH BAKE

2 small yellow squash, sliced
1 medium zucchini, sliced
1 large tomato, peeled and cut into wedges
1 small onion, sliced and separated into rings
1 teaspoon dried whole basil
Vegetable cooking spray
2 tablespoons grated Parmesan cheese

Combine vegetables and basil in a 1¾-quart casserole coated with cooking spray; toss lightly. Sprinkle with cheese. Cover and bake at 350° for 25 to 30 minutes or until done. Yield: 6 servings (about 35 calories per serving).

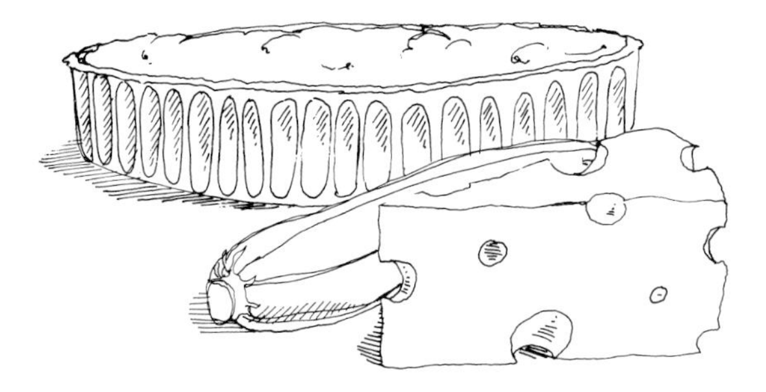

SWISS-ZUCCHINI QUICHE

1½ cups (⅛-inch-thick slices) zucchini
Vegetable cooking spray
¼ pound fresh mushrooms, sliced
1 small onion, chopped
3 eggs, beaten
½ cup evaporated skim milk
¼ cup water
½ teaspoon salt
¼ teaspoon pepper
¾ cup (3 ounces) shredded Swiss cheese, divided
Rice-Cheese Shell

Cook zucchini in a small amount of unsalted boiling water 3 minutes; drain and press gently to remove excess water.

Coat a small skillet with cooking spray. Sauté mushrooms and onion in skillet over low heat until tender but not brown; set aside.

Combine eggs, milk, water, salt, and pepper; mix well. Add zucchini, mushroom mixture, and ½ cup cheese; stir well. Pour zucchini mixture into Rice-Cheese Shell; top with remaining ¼ cup cheese. Bake at 375° for 40 minutes or until set. Let stand 5 minutes before serving. Yield: 6 servings (about 197 calories per serving).

RICE-CHEESE SHELL:

Vegetable cooking spray
1½ cups cooked rice
1 egg, beaten
¼ cup (1 ounce) shredded Swiss cheese

Coat a 10-inch pieplate with vegetable spray.

Combine remaining ingredients; stir well. Press mixture into pieplate; bake at 350° for 5 minutes. Press rice mixture back up sides of pieplate, if necessary. Yield: one 10-inch shell.

HERBED ZUCCHINI AND TOMATOES

3 medium zucchini, sliced
3 medium tomatoes, peeled and diced
1 tablespoon finely chopped onion
½ teaspoon dried whole oregano
½ teaspoon garlic powder
Dash of pepper

Combine all ingredients in a large skillet; cook, uncovered, over medium heat 20 to 25 minutes, stirring frequently. Yield: 6 servings (about 31 calories per serving).

FRUIT-STUFFED ACORN SQUASH

2 medium acorn squash (about ¾ pound each)
1 (8-ounce) can unsweetened crushed pineapple, drained
1 medium apple, chopped
¼ teaspoon ground cinnamon
1 tablespoon plus 1 teaspoon reduced-calorie margarine

Cut each squash in half lengthwise, and remove seeds. Place squash halves, cut side down, in a shallow baking dish. Bake at 350° for 45 minutes. Cut each squash half again lengthwise, and set aside.

Combine pineapple, apple, and cinnamon; spoon into each squash quarter. Dot each with ½ teaspoon margarine. Bake, uncovered, at 350° for 30 minutes or until squash is tender. Yield: 8 servings (about 54 calories per serving).

BEAN-STUFFED TOMATOES

2 (9-ounce) packages frozen French-style green beans
1 (4-ounce) can sliced mushrooms, drained
⅓ cup Italian reduced-calorie salad dressing
¼ cup sliced green onions
⅛ teaspoon dried whole basil
⅛ teaspoon pepper
6 medium tomatoes

Cook green beans according to package directions, omitting salt; drain well. Combine beans and remaining ingredients except tomatoes in a medium bowl. Cover and chill 3 to 4 hours.

Cut off top of each tomato; scoop out pulp, leaving shells intact (reserve pulp for other uses). Invert tomato shells on paper towels to drain. To serve, fill tomato shells with bean mixture. Yield: 6 servings (about 74 calories per serving).

HERBED TOMATOES

6 medium tomatoes
Salt
¼ cup plus 2 tablespoons fine, dry breadcrumbs
1 clove garlic, minced
3 tablespoons chopped onion
1½ teaspoons chopped fresh parsley
¾ teaspoon celery seeds
⅛ teaspoon dried whole basil
⅛ to ¼ teaspoon pepper
Chopped fresh parsley

Wash tomatoes thoroughly. Cut tops from tomatoes; scoop out pulp, leaving shells intact. Chop pulp, and set aside. Sprinkle inside of tomato shells lightly with salt; invert to drain.

Combine tomato pulp and next 7 ingredients; stir well. Fill tomato shells with breadcrumb mixture; sprinkle with additional parsley. Bake at 350° for 10 to 15 minutes. Yield: 6 servings (about 57 calories per serving).

STEWED TOMATO CASSEROLE

2 (16-ounce) cans stewed tomatoes, undrained
1 tablespoon cornstarch
½ teaspoon dried whole basil
¼ teaspoon dried whole marjoram
¼ teaspoon pepper
10 saltine crackers, crushed
2 tablespoons grated Parmesan cheese
1 tablespoon butter-flavored granules (optional)

Drain tomatoes, reserving juice. Combine ¼ cup reserved tomato juice and cornstarch, blending until smooth; add remaining tomato juice, and stir well. Pour into in an 8-inch square baking dish; add drained tomatoes, basil, marjoram, and pepper. Bake at 450° for 15 minutes; remove from oven, and stir.

Combine cracker crumbs, cheese, and butter-flavored granules, if desired; sprinkle evenly over tomatoes. Bake an additional 5 to 10 minutes or until lightly browned. Yield: 6 servings (about 56 calories per serving).

Keep plenty of fresh, low-calorie vegetables, such as radishes, celery, and carrots, washed and sliced in the refrigerator for a quick snack. Make them more available than higher calorie crackers and chips.

STEWED TOMATOES

4 quarts peeled, chopped tomatoes
1½ cups chopped celery
1 cup chopped onion
¾ cup chopped green pepper
1 tablespoon dried whole basil
1 tablespoon dried whole oregano
2 bay leaves

Combine all ingredients in large Dutch oven. Bring to a boil. Reduce heat and simmer, uncovered, 1 hour, stirring occasionally. Remove bay leaves. Spoon hot mixture into hot sterilized jars, leaving ½-inch headspace. Cover at once with metal lids, and screw bands tight. Process in pressure canner at 10 pounds pressure (240°) for 15 minutes. Yield: 7 pints (about 41 calories per ½-cup serving).

PARSLEYED TURNIPS AND CARROTS

3 cups peeled, diced turnips
3 cups coarsely chopped carrots
2 tablespoons reduced-calorie margarine
2 tablespoons minced fresh parsley
¼ teaspoon salt
Dash of pepper

Cook turnips and carrots, covered, in a small amount of boiling water 7 to 10 minutes or just until tender; drain. Add margarine, parsley, salt, and pepper; toss well. Yield: 8 servings (about 48 calories per serving).

SEASONED HASH BROWN TURNIPS

3 cups peeled, diced turnips
Vegetable cooking spray
½ cup chopped onion
¼ teaspoon salt
⅛ teaspoon pepper
⅛ teaspoon poultry seasoning

Cook turnips, covered, in a small amount of boiling water 15 minutes or until tender; drain.

Coat a medium nonstick skillet with cooking spray; place over medium-high heat until hot. Add turnips, onion, salt, pepper, and poultry seasoning; cook, stirring occasionally, until turnips are lightly browned. Yield: 4 servings (about 38 calories per serving).

CHINESE VEGETABLE MEDLEY

Vegetable cooking spray
1 teaspoon vegetable oil
1 (6-ounce) package frozen Chinese pea pods, thawed and drained
6 water chestnuts, sliced
½ cup diagonally sliced carrots
¼ cup sliced bamboo shoots
1 teaspoon sugar
1 teaspoon soy sauce
½ teaspoon cornstarch
¼ cup chicken broth

Coat a nonstick wok or skillet with cooking spray; add oil, and heat at medium high (325°) until hot. Add vegetables, and stir-fry 2 to 3 minutes or until vegetables are crisp-tender.

Combine sugar, soy sauce, cornstarch, and chicken broth; add to vegetables. Cook, stirring constantly, until thickened. Yield: 4 servings (about 60 calories per serving).

FRESH VEGETABLE SAUTÉ

Vegetable cooking spray
1 teaspoon vegetable oil
1 medium onion, thinly sliced and separated into rings
1 large green pepper, cut into ½-inch strips
12 fresh mushrooms, sliced
½ teaspoon garlic powder
½ teaspoon seasoned salt
½ teaspoon dried whole oregano
½ teaspoon dried whole basil

Coat a large skillet with cooking spray; add oil, and place over medium high heat until hot. Add onion; sauté 1 minute, stirring constantly.

Add remaining ingredients to skillet; reduce heat to medium, and sauté 2 to 3 minutes, or until peppers are crisp-tender. Cover; remove from heat, and let stand 2 minutes. Yield: 2 servings (about 59 calories per serving).

RATATOUILLE

Vegetable cooking spray
1 medium onion, sliced and separated into rings
1 clove garlic, minced
1 (1 pound) eggplant, peeled and cut into ¾-inch cubes
2 medium tomatoes, coarsely chopped
1 medium zucchini, sliced
1 medium-size green pepper, sliced
½ teaspoon dried whole thyme
¼ teaspoon dried whole basil
¼ teaspoon dried whole oregano
¼ teaspoon pepper

Coat a large skillet with cooking spray; place over medium heat until hot. Sauté onion and garlic in skillet 5 minutes. Add eggplant; cover and cook 5 minutes, stirring occasionally.

Stir in remaining ingredients; cover and reduce heat to medium-low. Cook an additional 10 minutes or until vegetables are tender, stirring occasionally. Yield: 6 servings (about 38 calories per serving).

SAUTÉED VEGETABLE MEDLEY

Vegetable cooking spray
1 large clove garlic, minced
1 small onion, sliced and separated into rings
1 small green pepper, chopped
2 medium-size yellow squash, sliced
2 medium zucchini, sliced
2 small tomatoes, peeled and chopped
¼ teaspoon dried whole basil
⅛ teaspoon pepper

Coat a large skillet with cooking spray; place over medium heat until hot. Add garlic and onion; cook until onion is transparent, stirring constantly. Add green pepper; cook 5 minutes, stirring constantly. Add yellow squash and zucchini; cover and cook 5 minutes.

Stir in tomatoes, basil, and pepper; cover and cook about 10 to 15 minutes. Yield: 4 servings (about 55 calories per serving).

STIR-FRIED VEGETABLE MEDLEY

Vegetable cooking spray
10 large fresh mushrooms, sliced
1 medium onion, thinly sliced and separated into rings
1 medium zucchini, thinly sliced
1 tablespoon soy sauce
⅛ teaspoon salt
⅛ to ¼ teaspoon pepper

Coat a large skillet with cooking spray, and place over medium-high heat until hot. Add remaining ingredients; stir-fry about 5 minutes or until zucchini is crisp-tender. Yield: 4 servings (about 38 calories per serving).

> Stir-frying is a quick, nutritious way of preparing meats and vegetables. If you don't have a wok, use a large skillet coated with vegetable cooking spray.

HERB AND SPICE CHART

HERB OR SPICE	BREADS & CEREALS	DESSERTS	EGGS & CHEESE	FISH & SHELLFISH
ALLSPICE		Most fruit		Boiled shellfish Poached fish
BASIL	Noodles Pasta Rice		Cheese dishes Omelets Scrambled eggs	Crab Shrimp Tuna Other fish
BAY LEAF	Rice			Poached fish Shellfish
CARAWAY SEEDS	Breadsticks Pumpernickel bread Rye bread		Cottage cheese Mild cheese	Tuna casserole
CARDAMOM	Yeast bread	Custards Fruit desserts Rice pudding		
CELERY SEED	Fish stuffing Meat stuffing Poultry stuffing Rolls		Cheese dishes	Baked or broiled fish
CINNAMON	Hot cereals	Apples Bananas Oranges Peaches Pears Puddings	Cottage cheese French toast	
CLOVES		Apples Oranges Peaches Pears Gingerbread		Baked or broiled fish
DILL	Pumpernickel bread Rye bread		Cottage cheese Deviled eggs	Halibut Mackerel Salmon Shellfish

HERB AND SPICE CHART

MEATS	POULTRY	SALADS & SALAD DRESSING	SAUCES & MARINADES	SOUPS & STEWS	VEGETABLES
Baked ham Meat loaf Pot roast		Fruit salads	Barbecue sauce Beef marinades Cranberry sauce Tomato sauce	Asparagus soup Pea soup Vegetable soup Beef stew Chicken stew	Beets Carrots Sweet potatoes Turnips Winter squash
Beef Lamb Meat loaf Pork	Chicken	Green salad Vegetable salad dressings	Spaghetti sauce Tomato sauce	Bean soup Potato soup Vegetable soup Beef stew	Broccoli Eggplant Green beans Summer squash Tomatoes
Beef Lamb Pot roast		Tomato aspic	Meat gravy Meat marinades	Chowder Chicken soup Pea soup Vegetable soup Most stews	Beets Carrots Green beans Onions Summer squash Tomatoes
Pork roast		Coleslaw Potato salad	Cheese sauce Meat marinades	Beef stew Seafood stew	Asparagus Cabbage Mushrooms Sauerkraut Turnips
Beef roast Pork roast				Fruit soup Pea soup	Carrots Sweet potatoes Winter squash
Meat loaf	Chicken Turkey	Coleslaw Egg salad Potato salad Tuna salad	Cream sauces	Chicken soup Vegetable soup Most stews	Cabbage Mushrooms Onions Tomatoes
Lamb chops Pork chops	Chicken		Applesauce Fruit dessert sauces	Fruit soup Beef stew Lamb stew	Beets Carrots Sweet potatoes Winter squash
Baked ham Roast pork			Meat marinades Tomato sauce	Bean soup Borscht Fruit soup Potato soup Split pea soup	Beets Carrots Sweet potatoes Winter squash
Lamb chops Veal		Coleslaw Cucumber salad Potato salad	Cocktail sauce Sauces for fish	Beef stew Lamb stew	Cabbage Cauliflower Green beans Potatoes

HERB OR SPICE	BREADS & CEREALS	DESSERTS	EGGS & CHEESE	FISH & SHELLFISH
GINGER		Cookies Honeydew Fresh fruit Puddings		Oriental stir-fries
MARJORAM	Biscuits Fish stuffing Poultry stuffing		Cheese dishes Omelets Scrambled eggs	Baked or broiled fish
MUSTARD			Cheese dishes Deviled eggs	Deviled crab Fish Shellfish
NUTMEG	Rice	Custard Fresh fruit Rice pudding Stewed prunes	Scrambled eggs	Fish casseroles
OREGANO	Pasta Meat stuffing Poultry stuffing		Cheese dishes Omelets Scrambled eggs	Shellfish
ROSEMARY	Cornbread Poultry stuffing		Cheese dishes Omelets Scrambled eggs	Baked or broiled fish
SAGE	Pork stuffing Poultry stuffing		Cottage cheese	Baked or broiled fish
SAVORY	Poultry stuffing		Deviled eggs Scrambled eggs	Baked or broiled fish
TARRAGON	Poultry stuffing		Egg dishes	Baked or broiled fish
THYME	Dumplings Fish stuffings Poultry stuffings		Cheese dishes Omelets Scrambled eggs	Baked or broiled fish Shellfish

MEATS	POULTRY	SALADS & SALAD DRESSING	SAUCES & MARINADES	SOUPS & STEWS	VEGETABLES
Hawaiian dishes Oriental stir-fries Pot roast Veal	Oriental stir-fries Roasted chicken	Pear salad		Bean soup Onion soup Potato soup Most stews	Beets Carrots Sweet potatoes Winter squash
Lamb Pork Roast beef Veal	Chicken Turkey	Chicken salad Green salad Meat salad		Chicken soup Vegetable soup Most stews	Carrots Eggplant English peas Lima beans Spinach Tomatoes
Hamburger Hash Lamb Meat loaf	Chicken	Coleslaw Potato salad Vegetable salad dressings	Barbecue sauce Meat marinades Sauces for vegetables	Bean soup Cream soup Lentil soup	Beets Cabbage Sauerkraut
Beef Meat loaf	Creamed chicken	Fruit salad dressing	Cream sauces	Chicken soup Cream soup	Carrots Green beans Spinach Squash Sweet potatoes
Beef Lamb Lasagna Meat loaf Meatballs Pizza Pork Pot roast	Chicken	Vegetable salad dressing Potato salad Seafood salad	Meat gravy Spaghetti sauce	Tomato soup Vegetable soup Beef stew Chili	Dry beans Eggplant Green beans Potatoes Spinach Tomatoes Zucchini
Beef Lamb Pork Veal	Chicken Turkey	Chicken salad Potato salad		Chicken soup Pea soup Spinach soup	Cauliflower Peas Potatoes Summer squash Turnips
Pork	Chicken Turkey			Chicken soup Chowder Cream soup Vegetable soup	Eggplant Lima beans Onions
Meatballs Meat loaf Pot roast	Chicken Turkey	Green salads	Sauces for meat	Bean soup Lentil soup Pea soup Potato soup Beef stew	Cabbage English peas Green beans Lima beans Sauerkraut
Lamb	Chicken Turkey	Green salads Seafood salads			Tomatoes
Beef Lamb Pork	Chicken Turkey	Fresh tomato salad	Sauces for fish	Clam chowder Beef stew Chicken stew Lamb stew Veal stew	Dry beans Carrots Eggplant English peas Green beans Mushrooms Spinach Tomatoes Zucchini

CALORIE/NUTRIENT CHART

FOOD	APPROXIMATE MEASURE	FOOD ENERGY (CALORIES)	PROTEIN (GRAMS)	FAT (GRAMS)	CARBOHYDRATES (GRAMS)	SODIUM (MILLIGRAMS)
Apple						
Fresh	1 medium	96	.3	1.0	24.0	2
Fresh	1 small	61	.2	.6	15.3	1
Dried rings, uncooked	½ cup	117	.5	.7	30.5	2
Juice, unsweetened	1 cup	117	.2	Tr	29.5	2
Applesauce, unsweetened	½ cup	50	.3	.3	13.2	3
Apricot						
Fresh	3 medium	55	1.1	.2	13.7	1
Canned, unsweetened	½ cup	47	.9	.1	11.8	1
Canned, in syrup	½ cup	111	.8	.2	28.4	2
Dried, uncooked	5 medium halves	46	.9	.1	11.6	5
Artichokes, fresh, boiled	1 medium	51	2.8	.2	9.9	30
Asparagus						
Fresh, cooked	4 medium spears	12	1.3	.1	2.2	1
Canned, regular pack	½ cup	22	2.3	.4	3.6	288
Avocado	1 medium	378	4.8	37.1	14.3	9
Bacon, fried and drained						
Cured, sliced	1 medium slice	43	1.9	3.9	.3	77
Canadian-style	1 (⅔-ounce) slice	58	5.7	3.7	.1	537
Bamboo shoots, raw	1 cup	41	3.9	.5	7.9	-
Banana						
Whole	1 medium	101	1.3	.2	26.4	1
Mashed	1 cup	191	2.5	.5	50.0	2
Beans						
Baked, canned with pork and tomato sauce	½ cup	156	7.8	3.3	24.3	591
Great Northern, dry, cooked	½ cup	106	7.0	.6	19.1	7
Green, fresh, cooked	½ cup	16	1.0	.2	3.4	3
Green, canned, regular pack	½ cup	22	1.2	.1	5.0	282
Kidney, dry, cooked	½ cup	109	7.2	.5	19.8	3
Lima, canned, regular pack	½ cup	88	5.1	.4	16.6	293
Lima, immature seeds, cooked	½ cup	95	6.5	.5	16.8	1
Lima, mature seeds, cooked	½ cup	131	7.8	.6	24.3	2
Yellow or wax, fresh, cooked	½ cup	14	.9	.2	2.9	2
Yellow or wax, canned, regular pack	½ cup	23	1.2	.3	5.0	282
Bean sprouts, mung, raw	1 cup	37	4.0	.2	6.9	5

Tr = Trace amount of nutrient   Dash (-) indicates insufficient data available

FOOD	APPROXIMATE MEASURE	FOOD ENERGY (CALORIES)	PROTEIN (GRAMS)	FAT (GRAMS)	CARBOHYDRATES (GRAMS)	SODIUM (MILLIGRAMS)
Beef, trimmed of excess fat						
Chuck roast (arm and round bone cuts), braised and drained	3 ounces	164	25.9	6.0	0	45
Flank steak, braised and drained	3 ounces	167	25.9	6.2	0	45
Round steak, braised and drained	3 ounces	161	26.6	5.2	0	65
Rump roast, roasted	3 ounces	177	24.7	7.9	0	61
Sirloin, broiled	3 ounces	176	27.4	6.5	0	67
Beef, corned, canned	3 ounces	198	23.2	11.0	0	-
Beef, dried	1 ounce	58	9.7	1.8	0	1,219
Beef, ground						
10% fat, broiled	3 ounces	186	23.3	9.6	0	57
21% fat, broiled	3 ounces	235	19.8	16.6	0	49
Beet greens, cooked	½ cup	13	1.3	.2	2.4	55
Beets						
Fresh, diced, cooked	½ cup	27	1.0	.1	6.1	37
Canned, regular pack	½ cup	42	1.1	.1	9.7	291
Beverages, alcoholic						
Beer	1 ounce	13	.1	0	1.1	2
Gin, rum, vodka, whiskey (90-proof)	1 ounce	74	-	-	Tr	Tr
Wine, dessert	1 ounce	41	Tr	0	2.3	1
Wine, table	1 ounce	25	Tr	0	1.2	1
Beverages, non-alcoholic						
Carbonated, artificially sweetened dietary drinks	1 ounce	-	0	0	-	-
Carbonated, cola-type, sweetened	1 ounce	12	0	0	3.1	-
Carbonated, ginger ale	1 ounce	9	0	0	2.4	-
Carbonated, unsweetened (club soda)	1 ounce	0	0	0	0	-
Biscuit, 2-inch diameter	1 biscuit	103	2.1	4.8	12.8	175
Blackberries, fresh	½ cup	42	.9	.7	9.3	Tr
Blueberries, fresh	½ cup	45	.5	.4	11.1	Tr
Bouillon, instant	1 cube	5	.8	.1	.2	960
Bread, cut into approximately 1-ounce slices						
French or Vienna	1 slice	88	2.8	1.0	16.6	174
Italian	1 slice	83	2.7	.2	16.9	176
Pumpernickel	1 slice	69	2.5	.4	14.8	158
Raisin	1 slice	74	1.9	.8	15.0	102
Rye	1 slice	68	2.6	.3	14.6	156
White	1 slice	76	2.4	.9	14.1	142
Whole wheat	1 slice	68	2.9	.8	13.3	148

FOOD	APPROXIMATE MEASURE	FOOD ENERGY (CALORIES)	PROTEIN (GRAMS)	FAT (GRAMS)	CARBOHYDRATES (GRAMS)	SODIUM (MILLIGRAMS)
Breadcrumbs, dry	1 cup	392	12.6	4.6	73.4	736
Broccoli, fresh, cooked, chopped	½ cup	20	2.4	.3	3.5	8
Brussels sprouts, fresh, cooked	½ cup	28	3.3	.3	4.9	8
Bulgur, dry	1 cup	628	15.2	2.5	139.1	-
Butter						
Regular type	1 tablespoon	102	.1	11.5	.1	140
Whipped type	1 tablespoon	67	.1	7.6	Tr	93
Cabbage, common varieties						
Raw, shredded	1 cup	17	.9	.1	3.8	14
Cooked	½ cup	15	.8	.2	3.1	10
Cake						
Angel food, tube cake, cut into 12 slices	1 (2-ounce) slice	161	4.3	.1	36.1	170
Chocolate (2 layers) with chocolate icing, cut into 12 slices	1 slice	365	4.5	16.2	55.2	233
Pound, cut into 3½- x 3- x ½-inch slices	1 (1-ounce) slice	142	1.7	8.9	14.1	33
Sponge, tube cake, cut into 12 slices	1 slice	131	3.3	2.5	23.8	73
Candy						
Caramels	1 ounce	113	1.1	2.9	21.7	64
Chocolate, milk	1 ounce	147	2.2	9.2	16.1	27
Fudge, chocolate	1 (1-inch) cube	84	.6	2.6	15.8	40
Gum drops	1 ounce	98	Tr	.2	24.8	10
Hard	1 ounce	109	0	.3	27.6	9
Jellybeans	1 ounce	104	Tr	.1	26.4	3
Marshmallows, regular-size	1 marshmallow	23	.1	Tr	5.8	3
Cantaloupe, diced	1 cup	48	1.1	.2	12.0	19
Carrot						
Raw	1 medium	30	.8	.1	7.0	34
Fresh, sliced, cooked	½ cup	24	.7	.2	5.5	26
Canned, regular pack	½ cup	35	.8	.3	8.0	291
Catsup	1 tablespoon	16	.3	.1	3.8	156
Cauliflower						
Raw, sliced	1 cup	23	2.3	.2	4.4	11
Fresh, sliced, cooked	½ cup	14	1.5	.2	2.6	6
Celery, raw, diced	½ cup	10	.6	Tr	2.4	76

Tr = Trace amount of nutrient   Dash (-) indicates insufficient data available

FOOD	APPROXIMATE MEASURE	FOOD ENERGY (CALORIES)	PROTEIN (GRAMS)	FAT (GRAMS)	CARBOHYDRATES (GRAMS)	SODIUM (MILLIGRAMS)
Cereal						
Bran, whole	1 cup	129	6.2	1.1	40.0	567
Bran flakes	1 cup	106	3.6	.6	28.2	207
Corn flakes	1 cup	84	1.5	0	19.1	216
Granola	½ cup	240	6.0	8.0	38.0	80
Shredded wheat	1 biscuit	89	2.5	.5	20.0	1
Wheat, puffed	1 cup	53	2.2	.2	10.7	1
Chard, Swiss, cooked	½ cup	13	1.3	.2	2.4	63
Cheese, natural						
Blue or Roquefort	1 ounce	104	6.1	8.6	.6	-
Camembert	1 ounce	85	5.0	7.0	.5	-
Cheddar	1 ounce	113	7.1	9.1	.6	198
Cottage (4% milk fat)	½ cup	120	15.3	4.8	3.3	258
Cottage (0.3% milk fat)	½ cup	63	12.4	.2	2.0	211
Cream	1 ounce	106	2.3	10.7	.6	71
Mozzarella, part-skim	1 ounce	72	6.9	4.5	.8	132
Neufchatel	1 ounce	73	2.8	6.6	.8	112
Parmesan, grated	1 tablespoon	23	2.1	1.5	.2	44
Swiss	1 ounce	105	7.8	7.9	.5	201
Cheese, process American	1 ounce	105	6.6	8.5	.5	322
Cherries, pitted						
Fresh, sour	½ cup	45	1.0	.3	11.1	2
Fresh, sweet	½ cup	51	1.0	.2	12.6	2
Sweet, canned, unsweetened	½ cup	60	1.1	.2	14.8	1
Sweet, canned in syrup	½ cup	104	1.2	.2	26.3	1
Candied	10 cherries	119	.2	.1	30.3	-
Chicken, skinned and roasted						
Dark meat	3 ounces	147	23.5	5.3	0	71
Light meat	3 ounces	140	26.6	2.9	0	53
Chili, with beans	1 cup	339	19.1	15.6	31.1	1,354
Chocolate, unsweetened	1 (1-ounce) square	143	3.0	15.0	8.2	1
Chocolate syrup	1 tablespoon	62	1.0	2.6	10.2	17
Clams						
Raw, hard-shelled	5 large	80	11.1	.9	5.9	205
Raw, soft-shelled	4 large	82	14.0	1.9	1.3	36
Canned, drained	½ cup	98	15.8	2.5	1.9	-
Cocoa, dry	1 tablespoon	14	.9	1.0	2.8	Tr
Coconut, fresh, grated	1 cup, packed	450	4.6	45.9	12.2	30
Coffee, prepared as beverage	1 cup	2	Tr	Tr	Tr	2
Collards, fresh, cooked	½ cup	32	3.4	.7	4.9	-
Cookies						
Chocolate chip	1 (2¼-inch diameter)	50	.6	2.2	7.3	42
Oatmeal	1 (2½-inch diameter)	60	.8	2.0	9.5	21

FOOD	APPROXIMATE MEASURE	FOOD ENERGY (CALORIES)	PROTEIN (GRAMS)	FAT (GRAMS)	CARBOHYDRATES (GRAMS)	SODIUM (MILLIGRAMS)
Cookies (*continued*)						
Sandwich type	1 (1¾-inch diameter)	50	.5	2.2	6.9	48
Vanilla wafers	1 cookie	14	.2	.5	2.2	8
Corn						
Fresh, kernels, cooked	½ cup	68	2.7	.9	15.5	Tr
Canned, cream-style, regular pack	½ cup	105	2.7	.8	25.6	302
Cornmeal						
Enriched, dry	1 cup	502	10.9	1.7	108.2	1
Self-rising, dry	1 cup	491	10.9	1.6	105.9	1,946
Cornstarch	1 tablespoon	29	Tr	Tr	7.0	Tr
Crab						
Fresh, steamed	3 ounces	78	14.5	1.6	.4	-
Canned, drained, flaked	½ cup	86	14.8	2.1	.9	850
Crackers						
Animal	1 cracker	11	.2	.2	2.1	8
Butter (1⅞-inch rounds)	1 cracker	15	.2	.6	2.2	36
Graham (2½-inch squares)	1 square	28	.6	.7	5.2	48
Saltines	1 cracker	12	.3	.3	2.0	31
Cranberries, fresh	½ cup	22	.2	.4	5.2	1
Cranberry sauce, canned	¼ cup	101	.1	.2	25.9	1
Cream						
Half-and-half	1 cup	324	7.7	28.3	11.1	111
Sour	1 tablespoon	26	.4	2.5	.5	6
Whipping	1 cup	838	5.2	89.5	7.4	76
Cucumber, raw						
Whole	1 large	45	2.7	.3	10.2	18
Sliced	1 cup	16	.9	.1	3.6	6
Dates, pitted	5 medium	110	.9	.2	29.2	Tr
Doughnut, plain	1 doughnut	176	2.7	11.3	16.0	99
Egg						
Whole	1 large	82	6.5	5.8	.5	61
White	1 white	17	3.6	Tr	.3	48
Yolk	1 yolk	59	2.7	5.2	.1	9
Eggplant, cooked without salt	½ cup	19	1.0	.2	4.1	1
Farina, enriched, cooked without salt	1 cup	103	3.2	.2	21.3	Tr
Fig, raw	1 medium	40	.6	.2	10.2	1

Tr = Trace amount of nutrient   Dash (-) indicates insufficient data available

FOOD	APPROXIMATE MEASURE	FOOD ENERGY (CALORIES)	PROTEIN (GRAMS)	FAT (GRAMS)	CARBOHYDRATES (GRAMS)	SODIUM (MILLIGRAMS)
Fish						
Bass, broiled	3 ounces	191	17.0	10.8	6.8	50
Cod, broiled	3 ounces	143	23.0	4.4	0.0	92
Flounder, baked	3 ounces	170	25.2	6.9	0	199
Haddock, broiled	3 ounces	118	16.9	5.5	.3	60
Halibut, broiled	3 ounces	143	21.1	5.9	0	113
Mackerel, broiled	3 ounces	200	18.9	13.7	0	-
Salmon, broiled	3 ounces	153	22.7	6.2	0	97
Salmon, canned	1 (7¾-ounce) can	376	44.7	20.5	0	1,148
Sardines, canned in oil	1 (½-ounce) fish	24	2.9	1.3	-	99
Trout, cooked	3 ounces	165	19.7	9.4	.3	-
Tuna, canned in oil	1 (7-ounce) can	570	47.9	40.6	0	1,584
Tuna, canned in water	1 (6½ ounce) can	234	51.5	1.5	0	1,610
Flour						
All-purpose, sifted	1 cup	419	12.1	1.2	87.5	2
Rye, sifted	1 cup	314	8.3	.9	68.6	1
Whole wheat, stirred	1 cup	400	16.0	2.4	85.2	4
Frankfurter	1 frankfurter	170	6.9	15.2	.9	-
Fruit cocktail						
Canned, unsweetened	½ cup	46	.5	.1	11.9	6
Canned, in syrup	½ cup	97	.5	.2	25.1	7
Garlic	1 clove	4	.2	Tr	.9	1
Gelatin						
Unflavored, dry	1 envelope	23	6.0	Tr	0	-
Flavored, prepared with water	½ cup	71	1.8	0	16.9	61
Grapefruit						
Fresh	½ grapefruit	40	.5	.1	10.3	1
Juice, unsweetened	1 cup	96	1.2	.2	22.6	.2
Grapes						
Green	10 grapes	34	.3	.2	8.7	2
Juice, unsweetened	1 cup	167	.5	Tr	42.0	5
Grits, cooked without salt	½ cup	63	1.5	.1	13.5	Tr
Honey	1 tablespoon	64	.1	0	17.3	1
Honeydew, diced	1 cup	56	1.4	.5	13.1	20
Horseradish, prepared	1 tablespoon	6	.2	Tr	1.4	14
Ice cream, vanilla, 10% fat	½ cup	128	3.0	7.1	13.9	42
Ice milk, vanilla	½ cup	100	3.2	3.4	14.7	45

FOOD	APPROXIMATE MEASURE	FOOD ENERGY (CALORIES)	PROTEIN (GRAMS)	FAT (GRAMS)	CARBOHYDRATES (GRAMS)	SODIUM (MILLIGRAMS)
Jams and Jellies	1 tablespoon	54	.1	Tr	14.0	2
Kale, cooked	½ cup	22	2.5	.4	3.4	24
Kohlrabi, raw, diced	1 cup	41	2.8	.1	9.2	11
Lamb, trimmed of excess fat						
Leg, roasted	3 ounces	158	24.4	6.0	0	60
Loin chops, broiled and drained	2.3 ounces	122	18.3	4.9	0	45
Lard	1 tablespoon	117	0	13.0	0	0
Lemon						
Fresh	1 medium	20	.8	.2	6.0	1
Juice	1 tablespoon	4	.1	Tr	1.2	Tr
Lemonade, frozen, sweetened, reconstituted	1 cup	107	.1	Tr	28.3	1
Lentils, cooked	½ cup	106	7.8	Tr	19.3	-
Lettuce						
Boston or Bibb, chopped	1 cup	8	.7	.1	1.4	5
Iceberg, chopped	1 cup	10	.7	.1	2.2	.7
Romaine, chopped	1 cup	10	.7	.2	1.9	5
Lime	1 medium	19	.5	.1	6.4	1
Liver						
Beef, fried	3 ounces	195	22.4	9.0	4.5	156
Chicken, simmered	3 ounces	137	22.2	3.7	2.7	50
Lobster, cooked, meat only	3 ounces	81	15.3	1.2	.3	172
Luncheon meats						
Bologna	1 ounce	86	3.4	7.8	.3	369
Deviled ham	¼ cup	184	7.2	16.8	0	-
Salami	1 ounce	128	6.7	10.8	.3	-
Macaroni, cooked tender without salt	½ cup	78	2.4	.3	16.1	Tr
Mango, raw, diced	½ cup	55	.6	.4	13.9	6
Margarine						
Regular type	1 tablespoon	102	.1	11.5	.1	140
Mayonnaise	1 tablespoon	101	.2	11.2	.3	84
Milk						
Buttermilk	1 cup	88	8.8	.2	12.5	319
Skim	1 cup	88	8.8	.2	12.5	127
Low-fat	1 cup	145	10.3	4.9	14.8	150

Tr = Trace amount of nutrient   Dash (-) indicates insufficient data available

FOOD	APPROXIMATE MEASURE	FOOD ENERGY (CALORIES)	PROTEIN (GRAMS)	FAT (GRAMS)	CARBOHYDRATES (GRAMS)	SODIUM (MILLIGRAMS)
Milk (*continued*)						
Whole	1 cup	159	8.5	8.5	12.0	122
Evaporated	1 cup	345	17.6	19.9	24.4	297
Evaporated skim	1 cup	184	18.4	Tr	27.2	280
Sweetened condensed	1 cup	982	24.8	26.6	166.2	343
Instant nonfat dry milk	1 cup powder	244	24.3	.5	35.1	358
Molasses, cane	1 tablespoon	50	0	0	13.0	3
Mushrooms, fresh	1 cup	20	1.9	.2	3.1	11
Mustard, prepared	1 teaspoon	4	.2	.2	.3	63
Mustard greens, cooked	½ cup	16	1.6	.3	2.8	13
Nectarine, fresh	1 medium	88	.8	Tr	23.6	8
Noodles, cooked without salt	½ cup	100	3.3	1.2	18.7	2
Noodles, chow mein	½ cup	110	2.9	5.3	13.1	-
Oatmeal, cooked without salt	1 cup	132	4.8	2.4	23.3	1
Oil, vegetable	1 tablespoon	120	0	13.6	0	0
Okra, cooked	½ cup	23	1.6	.3	4.8	2
Olives						
Green	10 small	33	.4	3.6	.4	686
Ripe	10 small	61	.5	6.5	1.2	385
Onions						
Mature, raw, chopped	½ cup	33	1.3	.1	7.4	9
Mature, cooked	½ cup	31	1.3	.1	6.9	8
Green, chopped	1 tablespoon	2	.1	Tr	.5	Tr
Orange						
Fresh	1 medium	64	1.3	.3	16.0	1
Juice, unsweetened	1 cup	112	1.7	.5	25.8	2
Oysters, raw	1 cup	158	20.2	4.3	8.2	175
Papaya, fresh, cubed	½ cup	28	.4	Tr	7.0	2
Parsley, fresh, chopped	1 tablespoon	2	.1	Tr	.3	2
Parsnip, diced, cooked	½ cup	51	1.2	.4	11.6	6
Peach						
Fresh	1 medium	58	.9	.2	14.8	2
Canned, unsweetened	½ cup	38	.5	.1	9.9	3
Canned, in syrup	½ cup	100	.5	.2	25.8	3
Dried	5 halves	171	2.0	.5	44.4	11
Peanuts, chopped, unsalted	1 tablespoon	52	2.4	4.4	1.9	Tr
Peanut butter	1 tablespoon	94	4.0	8.1	3.0	97
Pear						
Fresh	1 medium	100	1.1	.7	25.1	3
Canned, unsweetened	½ cup	39	.3	.3	10.2	1
Canned, in syrup	½ cup	97	.3	.3	25.0	2
Dried	5 halves	235	2.7	1.6	58.9	6

FOOD	APPROXIMATE MEASURE	FOOD ENERGY (CALORIES)	PROTEIN (GRAMS)	FAT (GRAMS)	CARBOHYDRATES (GRAMS)	SODIUM (MILLIGRAMS)
Peas						
Black-eyed, fresh, cooked	½ cup	89	6.7	.7	15	1
Black-eyed, canned, regular pack	½ cup	90	6.4	.4	15.8	301
English, fresh, cooked	½ cup	57	4.3	.3	9.7	1
English, canned, regular pack	½ cup	82	4.4	.4	15.6	294
Split, dry, cooked	½ cup	115	8.0	.3	20.8	13
Pecans, chopped	1 tablespoon	52	.7	5.3	1.1	Tr
Pepper, green	1 medium	16	.9	.1	3.5	10
Pickle						
Dill, whole	1 pickle (4 inches long)	15	.9	.3	3.0	1,928
Dill, sliced	¼ cup	4	.3	.1	.9	553
Sweet, whole	1 pickle (3 inches long)	51	.2	.1	12.8	-
Sweet, chopped	¼ cup	59	.3	.1	14.6	-
Pie, baked, 9-inch diameter, cut into 8 slices						
Apple	1 slice	302	2.6	13.1	45.0	355
Chocolate meringue	1 slice	287	5.5	13.7	38.2	292
Pecan	1 slice	431	5.3	23.6	52.8	228
Pumpkin	1 slice	241	4.6	12.8	27.9	244
Pimiento	1 (4-ounce) jar	31	1.0	.6	6.6	-
Pineapple						
Fresh, diced	½ cup	41	.3	.2	10.6	1
Canned, unsweetened	½ cup	48	.4	.1	12.6	1
Canned, in syrup	½ cup	95	.4	.2	24.8	2
Juice, unsweetened	1 cup	138	1.0	.3	33.8	3
Plum, fresh	1 medium	32	.3	.1	8.1	1
Popcorn						
Unpopped	1 cup	742	24.4	9.6	147.8	6
Popped, plain without fat or salt	1 cup	23	.8	.3	4.6	Tr
Pork, trimmed of excess fat						
Ham, baked	3 ounces	184	25.2	8.5	0	62
Loin chops, broiled and drained	2 ounces	151	17.1	8.6	0	42
Picnic, simmered	3 ounces	180	24.7	8.3	0	3
Spareribs, braised	3 ounces	377	18.0	33.6	0	31
Potato						
Whole (about 3 per pound), baked	1 potato	103	2.8	.1	23.1	4

Tr = Trace amount of nutrient   Dash (-) indicates insufficient data available

FOOD	APPROXIMATE MEASURE	FOOD ENERGY (CALORIES)	PROTEIN (GRAMS)	FAT (GRAMS)	CARBOHYDRATES (GRAMS)	SODIUM (MILLIGRAMS)
Potato (*continued*)						
Diced, boiled	½ cup	59	1.7	.1	13.3	3
Potato chips	10 chips	114	1.1	8.0	10.0	-
Pretzels, thin sticks	10 pretzels	23	.6	.3	4.6	101
Prunes						
Dried, pitted	5 medium	130	1.1	.3	34.4	4
Juice	1 cup	197	1.0	.3	48.6	5
Pumpkin	½ cup	41	1.3	.4	9.7	3
Radishes, raw, sliced	½ cup	10	.6	Tr	2.1	11
Raisins, seedless	1 tablespoon	26	.2	Tr	7.0	2
Raspberries, fresh						
Black	½ cup	49	1.0	1.0	10.5	Tr
Red	½ cup	35	.8	.3	8.4	Tr
Rhubarb, raw, diced	½ cup	10	.4	Tr	2.3	1
Rice						
Brown, cooked without salt	½ cup	116	2.5	.6	24.9	2
White, parboiled, cooked without salt	½ cup	90	1.9	.1	20.4	2
Roll						
Bun, frankfurter or hamburger	1 bun	120	3.3	2.2	21.2	202
Hard	1 (1-ounce) roll	78	2.5	.8	14.9	156
Plain, brown-and-serve	1 (1-ounce) roll	84	2.2	1.9	14.2	136
Rutabaga, cubed, cooked	½ cup	30	.8	.1	6.9	4
Salad dressing, commercial						
Blue cheese	1 tablespoon	76	.7	7.8	1.1	164
French	1 tablespoon	66	.1	6.2	2.8	219
Italian	1 tablespoon	83	Tr	9.0	1.0	314
Russian	1 tablespoon	74	.2	7.6	1.6	130
Thousand Island	1 tablespoon	80	.1	8.0	2.5	112
Salt	1 teaspoon	.2	0	0	0	2,132
Sauerkraut	½ cup	21	1.2	.3	4.7	878
Sausage, pork, cooked						
Links	1 ounce	144	5.6	12.8	1.0	-
Patty	1 ounce	146	5.7	13.0	.9	-
Scallops, steamed	3 ounces	95	20.0	1.2	-	228
Sesame seeds	1 tablespoon	47	1.5	4.3	1.4	-
Sherbet, orange	½ cup	129	.9	1.2	29.7	10
Shortening	1 tablespoon	111	0	12.5	0	0
Shrimp, fresh, raw	½ pound	207	42.8	1.8	3.5	319
Shrimp, canned, drained	½ cup	74	15.5	.7	.5	-

FOOD	APPROXIMATE MEASURE	FOOD ENERGY (CALORIES)	PROTEIN (GRAMS)	FAT (GRAMS)	CARBOHYDRATES (GRAMS)	SODIUM (MILLIGRAMS)
Soups, condensed, prepared with equal amount of water						
Beef broth or boullion	1 cup	31	5.0	0	2.6	782
Chicken, cream of	1 cup	94	2.9	5.8	7.9	970
Chicken Noodle	1 cup	62	3.4	1.9	7.9	979
Mushroom, cream of	1 cup	134	2.4	9.6	10.1	955
Tomato	1 cup	88	2.0	2.5	15.7	970
Vegetable	1 cup	78	2.7	1.7	13.5	845
Soy sauce	1 tablespoon	12	1.0	.2	1.7	1,319
Soybeans, cooked	½ cup	117	9.9	5.2	9.7	2
Spaghetti, cooked without salt	½ cup	90	3.0	.3	18.3	Tr
Spinach						
Raw, chopped	1 cup	14	1.8	.2	2.4	39
Fresh, cooked	½ cup	21	2.7	.3	3.3	45
Canned, regular pack	½ cup	22	2.3	.5	3.5	274
Squash						
Yellow, sliced, cooked	½ cup	14	.9	.2	2.8	1
Winter, cooked, mashed	½ cup	65	1.9	.4	15.8	1
Zucchini, sliced, cooked	½ cup	11	.9	.1	2.3	1
Strawberries, fresh, whole	1 cup	55	1.0	.7	12.5	1
Sugar						
Brown, packed	1 tablespoon	51	0	0	13	4
Granulated	1 tablespoon	46	0	0	11.9	Tr
Powdered	1 tablespoon	31	0	0	8.0	Tr
Sunflower kernels, unsalted	¼ cup	203	8.7	17.2	7.2	11
Sweet potato						
Whole (about 2½ per pound), baked	1 potato	148	2.2	.5	34.1	13
Boiled, mashed	½ cup	146	2.2	.5	33.6	13
Syrup, maple	1 tablespoon	50	0	0	12.8	2
Tangerine, fresh	1 medium	39	.7	.2	10.0	2
Tapioca, dry	1 tablespoon	30	.1	Tr	7.3	Tr
Tofu	4 ounces	80	8.7	4.7	2.7	8
Tomato						
Juice	1 cup	46	2.2	.2	10.4	486

Tr = Trace amount of nutrient   Dash (-) indicates insufficient data available

FOOD	APPROXIMATE MEASURE	FOOD ENERGY (CALORIES)	PROTEIN (GRAMS)	FAT (GRAMS)	CARBOHYDRATES (GRAMS)	SODIUM (MILLIGRAMS)
Tomato (*continued*)						
Fresh, raw	1 medium	27	1.4	.2	5.8	4
Fresh, cooked	½ cup	32	1.6	.3	6.7	5
Canned, regular pack	½ cup	26	1.2	.3	5.2	157
Paste, regular pack	1 (6-ounce) can	139	5.8	.7	31.6	65
Puree, regular pack	1 (29-ounce) can	321	14.0	1.6	73.2	3,280
Turkey, roasted						
Dark meat, without skin	3 ounces	173	25.5	7.1	0	84
Light meat, without skin	3 ounces	150	28.0	3.3	0	70
Turnip, cubed, cooked	½ cup	18	.6	.2	3.8	27
Turnip greens						
Fresh, cooked	½ cup	15	1.6	.2	2.6	-
Canned, regular pack	½ cup	21	1.8	.4	3.7	274
Veal, trimmed of excess fat						
Loin cut, broiled	3 ounces	199	22.4	11.4	0	55
Round, broiled	3 ounces	184	23.0	9.4	0	56
Vegetable juice cocktail	1 cup	41	2.2	.2	8.7	484
Vinegar	1 tablespoon	2	Tr	0	.9	Tr
Water chestnuts, Chinese	4	20	.4	.1	4.8	-
Watermelon, fresh, diced	1 cup	42	.8	.3	10.2	2
Yeast, dry	1 package	20	2.6	0.1	2.7	4
Yogurt, plain						
Low-fat	1 cup	123	8.3	4.2	12.7	125
Made from whole milk	1 cup	152	7.4	8.3	12.0	115

Sources of Data:

Adams, Catherine F. *NUTRITIVE VALUE OF AMERICAN FOODS*. Washington: U. S. Government Printing Office, 1975.

Church, Helen Nichols, and Jean A. T. Pennington. *BOWES AND CHURCH'S FOOD VALUES OF PORTIONS COMMONLY USED*. Philadelphia: J. B. Lippincott Company, 1980.

RECIPE INDEX

SUBJECT INDEX

RECIPE CONTRIBUTORS

Iris Allen, Kathy Amiss, Frances C. Andrews, Patricia Hamby Andrews, Mrs. W. Antalek, Mrs. Walter Arehart, Lisa Ash, Mrs. Robert Bailey, Sheri Beaver, Paula Beckham, Anna Beyer, Kathryn Bibelhauser, Mary Boden, Susan Boren, Mary Boydston, Susan Bradbury, Mrs. Joseph T. Brown, Sally M. Brown, Susan Buckmaster, Becky Burnett, M. B. Burnham, Kay Caspersen, Mae Certain, Edna Chadsey, Joy Clinton, Helen Cohrs, Pamela Copenhaver, Ann Criswell, Ruth Crowe, Mrs. David Culp, Ruth E. Cunliffe, Mrs. Blair Cunnyngham, Mrs. J. R. Currie, Diana Curtis, Kathleen M. Davie-Hoge, Mary C. Davis, Frances C. DeLoach, Helen Dill, Betty J. Dompnier, Mary Frances Donnelley, Mrs. E. Donohue, Mrs. H. G. Drawdy, Kay Eaddy, Belinda B. Early, Mrs. J. Edward Ebel, Cheryl Edmond, Louise E. Ellis, Mrs. T.D. Ennis, Mrs. Charles R. Field, Margot Foster, Candy Gardner, Doris Garton, Katherine Gillespie, Josephine Grainger, Mrs. John E. Graudin, Dolly D. Green, Nettie Hackley, Bettina Hambrick, Deborah Hammond, Leslie Haynes, Pat Helms, Susan Hester, Shirley W. Hodge, Nell H. Hodges, Joan Hoffman, Melinda Hoffman, Jan Hughes, Linda Jones, Susan Kamer-Shinaberry, Betty Keisling, Mrs. John H. Kolek, Mrs. James E. Krachey, Dollye Leathers, Evelyn M. Lemcke, Gwen Louer, Janet MacHardy, Gay McClelland, Eleanor N. McDowell, Linda McIntosh, Noel Todd McLaughlin, Alice McNamara, Deborah McPherson, Lynda L. Medaugh, Diana Mick, Betty Minick, Abby Moore, Linda Morgan, Mrs. William J. Morgan, Johanna Morrell, Betty Jane Morrison, Ethel Murray, Mary Lou Natto, Carol Neff, Mrs. Robert M. Neumann, Mrs. Roy Nieman, Thelma Olson, Vicki L. Owens, Debi Palmer, Mabel Pellettirer, Mrs. N. Pleimann, Elizabeth A. Pothoven, Sarah S. Ramsey, Kay Rankin, Mrs. Paul A. Raper, Deann J. Reed, Debra Rich, Sherrie Rizer, B. Lynne Schifreen, Mrs. W. B. Shepard, Jr., Cindy Shipman, Doris S. Shortt, Amy Shuman, Mrs. William A.L. Sibley, Harry Douglas Smith, Wilmina R. Smith, Mrs. Delbert R. Snyder, Maryanne Southard, Mrs. Richard L. Sparling, Clarine Spetzler, Mrs. R. J. Spitzer, Mrs. James S. Stanton, Jean Sternberger, Ella Stivers, Mrs. Harlan J. Stone, Kathleen Stone, Debra Stroud, Kay Stubbs, Mrs. J. E. Sutphin, Syble M. Tackett, Ruth Taylor, Dana Thomas, Evelyn D. Thompson, Donna Tindall, Mrs. James A. Tuthill, Mitze Waddle, Mrs. W. J. Wallace, Judy Warren, Mrs. Rudolph F. Watts, Eunice Webb, Lynn Weeks, Eileen Wehling, Mrs. A. M. Welsh, Margie Wesinger, Marcella R. White, Ginny Whitt, Jerry Williams, Fran Williamson, Jeanne R. Wood, Mrs. Paul Wood, Nancy E. Wright.